Artificial Intellig

Rosario Girasa

# Artificial Intelligence as a Disruptive Technology

## Economic Transformation and Government Regulation

Rosario Girasa
Goldstein Academic Center 203
Pace University
Pleasantville, NY, USA

ISBN 978-3-030-35977-5          ISBN 978-3-030-35975-1    (eBook)
https://doi.org/10.1007/978-3-030-35975-1

This Palgrave Macmillan imprint is published by the registered company Springer Nature Switzerland AG.
The registered company address is: Gewerbestrasse 11, 6330 Cham, Switzerland

*To*
*Susanne Marolda and Kenneth Marolda*
*(Mother and Son)*
*Former Students Who Taught the Instructor*

# Other Publications by Author Under Name of Roy J. Girasa or Rosario Girasa

Cyberlaw: National and International Perspectives (Prentice-Hall, 2002)
Corporate Governance and Finance Law (Palgrave Macmillan, 2013)
Laws and Regulations of Global Financial Markets (Palgrave Macmillan, 2013)
Shadow Banking: Rise, Risks, and Rewards of Non-Bank Financial Services (Palgrave Macmillan, 2018)
Regulation of Cryptocurrencies and Blockchain Technologies (Palgrave Macmillan, 2018)

# Preface

I had written a book entitled "Regulation of Cryptocurrencies and Blockchain Technologies," which was published in July, 2018. A former student came to my university office who told me about her position at a "big-4" accounting firm which had called in all of the employed accountants and announced the firm's new priorities, namely, blockchain and artificial intelligence. Both are transformative developments that will occur exponentially in the coming years. Although there are thousands of articles and many books on artificial intelligence (AI), this text is aimed at fulfilling a perceived need for the regulatory aspect of AI. The goal of this text is that it will assist in that regard.

It is almost without precedent that a subject matter encompasses the broadest spectrum of human knowledge. At first blush, AI is the emanation of the immense research, testing, and expansion of the scientific frontiers encompassing the pure sciences of physics, chemistry, and biology, utilizing the language of mathematics based in great part to the creation and exponential growth of computers. The rise of robotics brings to the forefront the social sciences which include sociological issues especially that of job losses or substitutions; economics which is profoundly affected by the effects of AI creations both nationally and globally; political science which is concerned with how governments respond to the challengers wrought by the new technologies including military uses; psychology concerning AI's effect on the many changes in jobs and social norms that new generations will experience; arts, literature, movies, and the entertainment industry in general with the many fantasies and possibilities of AI which have featured numerous works of fiction and movies of robots and other AI advances as they interrelate to human persons; philosophy, especially concerning the concept of consciousness in robots should they attain the level of superintelligence; and other areas of human knowledge.

Having attained more than eight decades of life, no other subject matter has ever intrigued this author as AI, having made research and writing totaling, engrossing, and endlessly fascinating. I truly wish upon the reader a desire to explore this area of knowledge which will profoundly affect all of our future lives.

Special thanks to Professor Victor Lopez of Hofstra University, Dr. Sharlene A. McEvoy of Fairfield University, and John Hardiman, who is an engineer and past editor of Delmar for their interest and opinions. Also special thanks to Rachael Ballard, Head of Science and Society for Palgrave Macmillan for her review, support, and furthering the production of this text; Joanna O'Neill, Assistant Editor at Palgrave Macmillan for walking me through the editorial process; G. NirmalKumar for his excellent editorial assistance; and my very special program advisers at Pace University, Patricia Saviano and Suzanne DeRosa for all their invaluable assistance.

Please note. This author researched all of the material and wrote all of the words except for quotes stated in the text and, thus, all errors are those of the author. The text is not intended to offer legal advice but rather is the author's analysis and opinions based on the numerous articles, commentaries, speeches, regulations, and other materials read and downloaded in an attempt to understand the new technologies and provide a text in readable format for students, professors, and all other interested persons in the subject matter. For all personal, legal, and related questions, refer to competent counsel for up-to-date advice and suggestions.

Pleasantville, NY        Rosario Girasa

# Contents

# Acronyms and Abbreviations

| | |
|---|---|
| ACLU | American Civil Liberties Union |
| AGI | Artificial general intelligence |
| AI | Artificial intelligence |
| AIE | Artificial Intelligence Exploration |
| AIRA | Artificial Intelligence Research Associate |
| ANI | Artificial narrow intelligence |
| ANN | Artificial neural network |
| API | Application programming interface |
| ASI | Artificial superintelligence |
| ASPEN | Automated Scheduling and Planning Environment System |
| ATEAC | Advanced Technology External Advisory Council |
| ATM | Automated teller machine |
| CBP | Customs and Border Protection |
| CCW | Convention on Certain Conventional Weapons |
| CDS | Credit default swaps |
| CDT | Center for Democracy & Technology |
| CIA | Central Intelligence Agency |
| COiN | Contract Intelligence |
| COPPA | Children's Online Privacy Protection Act |
| DARPA | Defense Advanced Research Projects Agency |
| DESA | Department of Economic and Social Affairs |
| DHS | Department of Homeland Security |
| DoD | Department of Defense |

| | |
|---|---|
| DoE | Department of Energy |
| DoT | Department of Transportation |
| E.U. | European Union |
| ECOSOC | Economic and Social Council |
| EEA | Economic Espionage Act |
| EPO | European Patent Office |
| ERF | European Robotics Forum |
| FAA | Federal Aviation Administration |
| FCC | Federal Communications Commission |
| FDA | Food and Drug Administration |
| FICO | Fair, Isaac and Company (original company name) |
| FIPPs | Fair Information Practice Principles |
| FLI | Future of Life Institute |
| FMCSA | Federal Motor Carrier Safety Administration |
| FMVSS | Federal Motor Vehicle Safety Standards |
| FTC | Federal Trade Commission |
| GDP | Gross domestic product |
| GDPR | General Data Protection Regulation |
| GGE | Group of Governmental Experts |
| GPS | Global positioning system |
| GVA | Gross value added |
| HIPAA | Health Insurance Portability and Accountability Act |
| HR | Human Resources |
| HTML | Hypertext markup language |
| HVAC | Heating, ventilation, and air conditioning |
| IBM | International Business Machines |
| ICRAC | International Committee for Robot Arms Control |
| ICT | Information and communications technology |
| IoT | Internet of Things |
| IPE | Intellectual Property Enforcement |
| IPR | Intellectual property rights |
| IRS | Internal Revenue Service |
| ITS | Intelligent Transportation Systems |
| JAIC | Joint Artificial Intelligence Center |
| JPO | Joint Program Office |
| KAIROS | Knowledge-directed Artificial Intelligence Reasoning Over Schemas |
| LGBT | Lesbian, gay, bisexual, transgender |
| MAARS | Modular Advanced Armed Robotic System |

| | |
|---|---|
| MAD | Mutual Assured Destruction |
| MOD | Mobility on Demand |
| MRI | Magnetic resonance imaging |
| NGO | Non-governmental organizations |
| NHTSA | National Highway Traffic Safety Administration |
| NIST | National Institute of Standards and Technology |
| NLP | Natural language progressing |
| NSA | National Security Agency |
| NSF | National Science Foundation |
| NSPM | National Security Presidential Memorandum |
| NSTC | National Science Technology Council |
| NTIA | National Telecommunications and Information Administration |
| NTM | Neural Touring Machine |
| OECD | Organization for Economic Cooperation and Development |
| OIG | Office of Inspector General |
| OSTP | Office of Science and Technology Policy |
| QIS | Quantum information science |
| R&D | Research and development |
| RAS | Robotic and Autonomous Systems |
| RPI | Rensselaer Polytechnic Institute |
| SEC | Securities and Exchange Commission |
| SIPRI | Stockholm International Peace Research Institute |
| SNAP | Supplemental Nutrition Assistance Program |
| SPARC | Scholarly Publishing and Academic Resources Coalition |
| SPOT | Screening of Passengers by Observation Techniques |
| SRA | Sentencing Reform Act |
| STEM | Science, Technology, Engineering and Mathematics |
| TANF | Temporary Assistance for Needy Families |
| TRIPS | Trade-Related Aspects of Intellectual-Property Rights |
| U.K. | United Kingdom |
| U.N. | United Nations |
| UAE | United Arab Emirates |
| UAS | Unmanned aircraft systems |
| UNESCO | United Nations Economic and Social Council |
| UNU | United Nations University |
| USPTO | United States Patent and Trademark Office |
| WIPO | World Intellectual Property Organization |
| WTO | World Trade Organization |

# List of Figures

# Table of Cases

# Part I

## Artificial Intelligence: Disruption, Application, and U.S. Policies

# 1

# AI as a Disruptive Technology

The world currently and will in the future experience economic and social changes which will alter society in nearly all of its manifestations so as to make it almost unrecognizable as it exists today. This occurrence is unique because of the rapidity in which it is taking place, all due to technological advances that have spread even to the poorest segments of society. Consider the effect of miniaturization on cell phones, computers, and other devices in addition to innumerable other innovations. These advances are incredibly exhilarating and also frightening to those persons who lack knowledge or capabilities to keep pace with the immense transformations. Not many decades ago an individual could pursue a course of studies which would permit a lifetime of work and comfort. Today, no assurance can be made to anyone that his or her knowledge or skill base will be sufficient to last more than a few years.

## The Four Industrial Revolutions

We are in the midst of a Fourth Industrial Revolution. The First Industrial Revolution, which took place in the eighteenth century and continued onto the nineteenth century, witnessed the change from an agrarian

© The Author(s) 2020
R. Girasa, *Artificial Intelligence as a Disruptive Technology*,
https://doi.org/10.1007/978-3-030-35975-1_1

society (consider that 97% of individuals in early America were farmers) to an industrial society promoted by steam and water. The Second Industrial Revolution, generally attributed to the years between 1870–1914, was characterized by newly discovered forms of energy such as electricity, oil, and steel that became the bases from which evolved the inventions of the telephone, light bulbs, and internal combustion engine. The Third Revolution refers to the modern-day advances in technology, e.g., miniaturization which was the foundation of the use of computers by any individual; the Internet that gave access to the world of knowledge without the need to leave one's desk; and advances in communication such as cell phones, Facebook, Instagram, Twitter, and other comparable devices and social media. This text discusses the transformative changes that are taking place today and which have been described as the "Fourth Industrial Revolution."[1]

## Disruptive Technologies

The advances of technology, i.e., the practical applications of knowledge over the past several decades, have escalated exponentially with the creation of micro-computer chips coupled with the Internet all of which has transformed how we think, act, learn, and go about our daily personal and business-related activities. The current so-called "hot area" resulting therefrom that has encouraged enormous investments of time and money and which has become "disruptive" in daily living is the proliferation of cryptocurrencies with their bases in *blockchain* technology (the *first disruptive technological development*). A *second disruptive technological development* is that of *artificial intelligence* ("AI" hereafter). Both developments have the potential of creating vast changes in the way we behave and go about our daily activities. Disruption is a fact of life that continually occurs whenever new inventions and processes enter the marketplace.

---

[1] Jacob Morgan, *What is the Fourth Industrial Revolution?* FORBES (Feb. 19, 2016) https://www.forbes.com/sites/jacobmorgan/2016/02/19/what-is-the-4th-industrial-revolution/#3a92fc57f392.

This author wrote about the first major prong of the disruptive technologies that characterize the Fourth Industrial Revolution in his book, REGULATION OF CRYPTOCURRENCIES AND BLOCKCHAIN TECHNOLOGIES (Palgrave Macmillan, 2018).

The naysayers' fear, with some justification, that numerous jobs will be lost as a result of innovation; but changes also bring about a transformation evidenced by new jobs, directly or indirectly, brought about by the new technologies.

*Stages of Disruptive Technologies.* Scholars who have commented on the stages of disruption of existing modes of doing business generally assert a three-stage process, while other scholars emphasize as many as five stages. For example, one scholar contended that the three stages consist of an initial *paralysis stage* whereby the disruption is unanticipated and thus not planned, e.g., Amazon's entry into the book sales marketplace; then proceeds to a *reaction stage* whereby the affected company comes to the realization of the threat to its existence or market share and advances in a number of ways to thwart the onslaught, e.g., by political lobbying for protection, making small improvements, and other reactive efforts; and finally, the *third transformation stage* whereby the affected company institutes major changes within the firm. This last stage occurs with the firm, e.g., adding new technological tools, building customer relations, merging with other companies similarly affected, expanding its ability to offer additional services or product lines, establishing a center for excellence, additional advertising, and other efforts.[2] Another commentator suggested a five-stage process of *confusion* (not sure what is occurring), *repudiation* (claiming lack of importance), *shaming* (saying, e.g., it is just a fad), *acceptance* (realization that the new entrant is for real), and *forgetting* (minimizing past behavior and adaptation to new circumstances).[3]

The creators of blockchain technology sought a mechanism by which persons could transact their daily business and personal happenings by bypassing third parties while also preserving personal safety, and by permanent recordation of transactions. AI likewise will be as transformative to our daily lives. There are, of course, other disruptive technologies; however, this author believes the two technologies cited have the greatest futuristic impact. Some authors exhibit a listing of a dozen or so

---

[2] Mike Bainbridge, *3 Phases of Disruption*, DISRUPTION HUB (May 4, 2017), https://distruptionhub.com/3-phases-distruption/.

[3] Grant McCracken, *The Five Stages of Disruption Denial*, HBR (April, 2013), https://hbr.org/2013/04/distruption-denail.

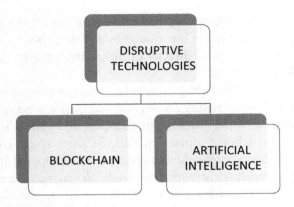

**Fig. 1.1** Major disruptive technologies

disruptive technologies but most are based on AI technology.[4] This text will examine the meaning of AI, its rapid developments and uses, the benefits and risks, and whether and to what extent should regulatory agencies become concerned about protection against harmful misuse thereof (Fig. 1.1).[5]

# Artificial Intelligence (AI)

*AI Antecedents.* Historically, the words "Artificial Intelligence" were first coined by John McCarthy in 1955 in a proposal for a conference to be held at Dartmouth College. He was a computer scientist who taught mathematics therein and later founded AI laboratories both at MIT and Stanford. The six-week Dartmouth Conference of 1956 became a seminal event in which artificial intelligence or thinking machines was first enunciated in an organized manner and in which additional topics were

---

[4] Examples include: mobile internet, Internet of Things (discussed in Chap. 5), automation of knowledge work, advanced robotics, cloud, autonomous or semi-autonomous vehicles, next generation genomics, next generation storage, 3D printing, advanced materials, advanced oil and gas exploration and recovery, and renewable energy. Maria Fonseca, *Guide to 12 Technology Examples*, Intelligent HQ (March 2, 2014), https://www.intelligenthq.com/technology/12-disruptive-technologies/.

[5] For a lengthy itemized history of AI from which this discussion relied on, see *A Brief History of AI*, AI TOPICS, https://aitopics.org/misc/brief-history.

discussed such as neural networks, natural language progressing, and other topics now commonplace in today's depictions of the numerous subsets of AI. McCarthy believed that "every aspect of learning or any other feature of intelligence can in principle be so precisely described that a machine can be made to simulate it."[6] AI has a long history in a broad sense extending back as early as the fourth century B.C. to Aristotle who invented syllogistic logic, the first formal deductive reasoning system. Thereafter, AI is traceable successively to 1206 A.D. whereby Al-Jasari invented the first programmable humanoid robot; the invention of the printing press in the fifteenth century; the first mechanical digital calculating machine by Pascal in 1642; and the numerous mathematical advances of the first half of the 20th particularly by Bertrand Russell and Alfred North Whitehead in their treatise on formal logic in *Principia Mathematica*. The more recent history has witnessed greatly increased understanding of AI with technology companies coming into existence, advances in computer technology that explored its uses, and numerous other programs that enabled highly significant revolutionary advances in technological development.

Preceding McCarthy's coining of AI was the remarkable effort of Alan Turing, famed for his effort in decrypting the German enciphering machine, Enigma, which was a major factor in aiding Allied efforts to end World War II victoriously. He was particularly known for his "Turing machine" which strived to imitate the human mind by the use of a precise mathematical formulation of computability. He sought to create a machine which could play chess, i.e., with thought processes emulating the human brain. He conceived of an apparent contradictory expression "machine intelligence" whereby a machine was thought of by its very nature to be incapable of intelligence. He expressed the hope and desire to create robotic machines that could eventually compete with human intelligence. The concept had broad philosophical and societal implications as well as a scientific mathematical basis which became increasingly

---

[6] Martin Childs, *John McCarthy: Computer scientist known as the father of AI*, INDEPENDENT (Nov. 1, 2011), https://www.independent.co.uk/news/obituaries/john-mccarthy-computer-scientist-known-as-the-father-of-ai-6255307.html.

relevant in later decades.[7] We will discuss Turing's contributions further in Chap. 8.

The chess victory by the IBM Deep Blue known as "Watson" in 1997 over two of the world's best chess players, with its ability to analyze some 200 million possible chess positions in front of an international audience, gave credence to Turing's formulation.[8] The latest emanation of non-human triumph over human intelligence was Alphabet's U.K.-based AI DeepMind's AI bot, "AlphaStar," which defeated a champion professional player in the complex real-time strategy videogame, StarCraft II.[9] By such enhancement of credibility, creators of the innumerable formulations of AI began to take note of the possibilities previously not feasible to consider. Thus, the said AI development has given credence to the said fears of job losses and other possible negative consequences while also simultaneously bringing about vast improvements in productive capacities of workers at all levels of corporate governance and production, expanded life expectancies, and, ultimately, attain interplanetary or even inter-stellar occupation.

## Definitions of AI

There are numerous definitions of "AI" dependent upon the particular profession or activity. A sampling of definitions is as follows:

- AI is "the ability of a digital computer or computer-controlled robot to perform tasks commonly associated with intelligent beings."[10]

---

[7] *Alan Turing*, STANFORD ENCYCLOPEDIA OF PHILOSOPHY, rev. Sept. 30, 2013, https://plato.stanford.edu/entries/turing/.

[8] *Deep Blue*, IBM 100, https://www.ibm.com/ibm/history/ibm100/us/en/icons/deepblue/.

[9] Tom Simonite, *DeepMind Beats Pros at Starcraft in Another Triumph for Bots*, WIRED (Jan. 25, 2019), https://technewstube.com/wired/1074075/deepmind-beats-pros-at-starcraft-in-another-triumph-for-bots/.

[10] *Artificial Intelligence*, ENCYCLOPAEDIA BRITANNICA, https://www.britannica.com/technology/artificial-intelligence.

- AI is "the study and design of intelligent agents" where an intelligent agent is a system that perceives its environment and takes actions which maximizes its chances of success.[11]
- AI is "[T]he theory and development of computer systems able to perform tasks normally requiring human intelligence, such as visual perception, speech recognition, decision-making, and translation between languages."[12]
- "Artificial intelligence (AI), sometimes called machine intelligence, is intelligence demonstrated by machines, in contrast to natural intelligence displayed by humans and other animals."[13]
- Artificial Intelligence is defined, in current U.S. legislation, as "(A) Any artificial system that performs tasks under varying and unpredictable circumstances without significant human oversight, or that can learn from experience and improve performance when exposed to data sets. (B) An artificial system developed in computer software, physical hardware, or other context that solves tasks requiring human-like perception, cognition, planning, learning, communication, or physical action. (C) An artificial system designed to think or act like a human, including cognitive architectures and neural networks. (D) A set of techniques, including machine learning, that is designed to approximate a cognitive task. (E) An artificial system designed to act rationally, including an intelligent software agent or embodied robot that achieves goals using perception, planning, reasoning, learning, communicating, decision-making, and acting."[14]

---

[11] *Artificial Intelligence*, SCIENCE DAILY, https://www.sciencedaily.com/terms/artificial_intelligence.htm.

[12] *Artificial Intelligence*, OXFORD LIVING DICTIONARY, https://en.oxforddictionaries.com/definition/artificial_intelligence.

[13] *Artificial Intelligence*, WIKIPEDIA, https://en.wikipedia.org/wiki/Artificial_intelligence.

[14] NATIONAL SECURITY COMMISSION ON ARTIFICIAL INTELLIGENCE ACT OF 2018, S. 2806, 115th Cong. (2018), https://www.congress.gov/115/bills/s2806/BILLS-115s2806is.pdf.

# Types of AI Intelligence

AI may be characterized as *Artificial Narrow Intelligence* (ANI), *Artificial General Intelligence* (AGI), and *Artificial Superintelligence* (ASI). ANI is depicted as "weak" intelligence because it concerns the performance of a singular task which it generally accomplishes very well as, e.g., playing chess against human experts, making sales predictions, autonomously driving automobiles, and may, at this juncture, include speech and image recognition. "Weak" is used in the sense of its limitation to the one task rather than having a broader usage.[15] AGI, also known as "Strong AI" or "Human-Level AI," is the next higher level of AI progression in that it seeks to imitate the human brain, albeit its development continues to lack the reasoning and other attributes of the brain. ASI is a futuristic characterization which will disputably occur when AI has surpassed the capacity of the human brain in creativity, social skills, and wisdom.[16] This last development poses unique challenges that potentially are extraordinarily beneficial or detrimental to society. Whether a particular robot is either an ANI or AGI depends on whether it meets the *Turing test* standard, i.e., whether its behavior resembles that of human and other measures. The more it resembles a human person, e.g., one working on an assembly plant, the more likely it would be characterized as an AGI.[17]

ASI is the focus of innumerable sci-fi books, articles, movies, and the like about robots becoming so intelligent as to make humans subject to their control. A noted book which explores intellectually the options and possibilities of ASI is MIT scientist, Max Tegmark's, *Life 3.0*, which examines the expansion of AI from its earlier promulgations to the possibility of ASI. He stated that to arrive at the ASI stage, three logical steps are required: Step 1: Build human-level AGI; Step 2: Use this AGI to create superintelligence; and Step 3: Use or unleash this superintelligence

[15] Ben Dickson, *What is Narrow, General, and Super Artificial Intelligence?*, TECHTALKS (May 12, 2017), https://bdtechtalks.com/2017/05/12/what-is-narrow-general-and-super-artificial-intelligence/.
[16] *Id.*
[17] Tetiana Shevchenko, *3 Types of Artificial Intelligence Everyone Knows About*, LETZGRO (Aug. 10, 2016), http://letzgro.net/blog/3-types-of-artificial-intelligence/.

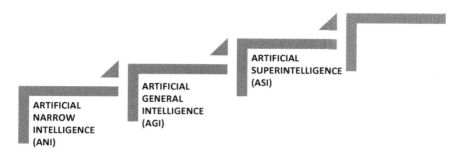

**Fig. 1.2**  Types of artificial intelligence

to take over the world.[18] He surmises that it is unclear whether ASI will lead to totalitarian control, especially if in the control of dictators as evidenced in the twentieth century by a Hitler or Stalin, or a more individual empowerment. The AI scenario offers a very wide range of possibilities from a libertarian utopia, wherein humans, "cyborgs," uploads, and superintelligences co-exist peacefully, to the 1984 superintelligence led by an Orwellian surveillance state, or to self-destruction by humans (Fig. 1.2).[19]

Another classification of the kinds of AI intelligence states that there are four types, namely: (1) *reactive machines*, i.e., those that do not form memories or benefit from past experiences—the IBM that beat chess masters (equivalent to ANI above); (2) *limited memory*—able to benefit from past experience, e.g., autonomous automobiles (equivalent to AGI); (3) *theory of the mind*—form representations of the world, possess self-awareness and also construct representations about other agents in the world; and (4) *self-awareness*—able to form representations about themselves and possess consciousness—futuristic capability (equivalent to ASI).[20]

---

[18] MAX TEGMARK, LIFE 3.0: BEING HUMAN IN THE AGE OF ARTIFICIAL INTELLIGENCE, at 134 (Vintage Books, 2017).

[19] *Id.* at 162.

[20] Aaron Hintze, *Understanding the Four Types of Artificial Intelligence*, GOVERNMENT INTELLIGENCE (Nov. 14, 2016), http://www.govtech.com/computing/Understanding-the-Four-Types-of-Artificial-Intelligence.html.

Yet again, AI could be thought of, as stated in Fortune Magazine by Kai-Fu Lee, a venture capitalist and former head of Google China and CEO of Sinovation Ventures, as possessing four waves that are occurring simultaneously which characterized AI's ascendance to prominence: *First Stage: Internet A.I.* whereby users, examining the vast amount of data derived from the Internet, label the data as buying or not, clicking or not, and so on and which reflects individual preferences, demands, habits, and desires seeking particular platforms to maximize profit; *Second Stage: Business A.I.* whereby, through the use of algorithms trained on proprietary data sets, managers can improve their decision-making by the analysis of customer purchases, machine maintenance, and complex business processes. Examples given are the use of deep-learning algorithms, which, the author stated, were game changers for AI, to the study of thousands of bank loans and repayment rates to reflect risks of default, and to medical researchers—to learn of optimum health outcomes from data on patient profiles and types of therapies used.[21]

Kai-Fu Lee's *Third Stage: Perception A.I.* is illustrated by the collection and analyses of data not previously accomplished such as that found in smart devices, smart interfaces, face recognition, and computer-vision applications; and, finally, the *Fourth Stage: Autonomous A.I.* whereby the previous three stages are integrated so that machines are able to perceive and react to the world from which the data flows, move instinctively, manipulate objects as a human person is enabled, "see" the environment around them, recognize patterns, determine how to correlate the data, make decisions such as in automated assembly lines and warehouses, implement commercial tasks, and perform consumer chores. The author minimizes fears that computers and robots are at the ASI stage stating that, at best, AI has attained only ANI progression, limited to a single domain standing, albeit the future may witness further advancement that should cause us to reflect on its monumental impact and benefits but also challenges therefrom.[22]

---

[21] Kai-Fu Lee, *The Four Waves of A.I.*, FORTUNE (Nov. 1, 2018) at 91–94, fortune.com/2018/10/22/artificial-intelligence-ai-deep-learning-kai-fu-lee/.

[22] *Id.* at 94.

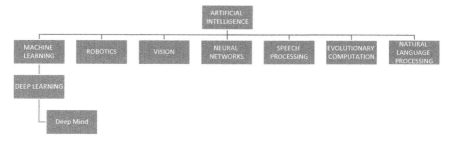

**Fig. 1.3**  AI partial subfields

# Subfields of AI

The subfields of AI are as extensive as scientists, technologists, and other researchers can devise. One student-researcher recited 87 subfields albeit observing that some of them overlap.[23] Nevertheless, for purposes of this text and based on review of numerous citations, we note the following major subsets (Fig. 1.3).

## Machine Learning

AI is the umbrella or generic expression which includes both machine learning and its subset of deep learning. All machine learning is AI but not the reverse. It is the science of training devices or software to perform a task and improve its capabilities by feeding it data and information so that it can "learn" over time without being explicitly programmed. The programs or algorithms therein enable machines to improve with added data. It may be sub-classified, using the categorization stated above, as *applied AI*, i.e., a narrower or weak version of AI and most commonly used whereby it is applied to machines to manage specific tasks, or *generalized AI* when applied can encompass any technology that can evolve and improve any task. Machine learning is expected to become more prominent in the forthcoming years. Sixty percent of all moneys invested

---

[23] Yasir Arfat, QUORA (April 17, 2016), https://www.quora.com/What-are-the-subfields-of-AI.

in AI was expended for machine learning.[24] In a 2016 McKinsey Global Institute Study, it noted that the total annual external investment in AI was between $8-to-12 billion and confirmed the said 60 percent machine learning expenditure noting that robotics and speech recognition garnered much of the said percentage.[25]

*Deep Learning.* Deep learning is a subset of machine learning which, in turn, is a subset of AI. It is usually referred to as *deep artificial neural networks*, or *deep reinforcement learning*.[26] It is concerned with algorithms[27] analogous to the human brain cells called neurons.[28] It is an artificial neural network modeled by use of layers of artificial neurons or computational units to receive input and apply an activation function along with the threshold.[29] As each massive layer of data is added, the machine undergoes a training process. The *deep* in *deep learning* describes all the layers and their interconnections in the neural network. If there is only one layer, then it is called a *hidden layer.* Applications include use in autonomous automobiles; recoloring of black and white images to restore colors that humans could recognize; prediction of the outcome of legal proceedings; prescription of medicines for the patient's particular genome; and assistance in breakthroughs in speech recognition, natural language processing, and robotics.[30]

[24] *The Difference Between AI, Machine Learning & Robots*, DELL TECHNOLOGIES, https://www.delltechnologies.com/en-us/perspectives/the-difference-between-ai-machine-learning-and-robotics/.

[25] Louis Columbus, *McKinsey's State of Machine Learning and AI, 2017*, FORBES (July 9, 2017), https://www.forbes.com/sites/louiscolumbus/2017/07/09/mckinseys-state-of-machine-learning-and-ai-2017/#291e5bd175b6.

[26] *Artificial Intelligence (AI) vs. Machine Learning vs. Deep Learning*, SKYMIND, https://skymind.ai/wiki/ai-vs-machine-learning-vs-deep-learning.

[27] *Algorithm* is a set of instructions or procedure for performing a calculation or solving a mathematical problem generally by use of a computer.

[28] *Neurons* are electrically excitable cells in the nervous system that function to process and transmit information, SCIENCEDAILY, https://www.sciencedaily.com/terms/neuron.htm.

[29] Seema Singh, *Cousins of Artificial Intelligence*, TOWARDS DATA SCIENCE (May 26, 2018), https://towardsdatascience.com/cousins-of-artificial-intelligence-dda4edc27b55.

[30] Raja Mitra, *Understanding AI and the Shades of Difference among its Subsets*, MEDIUM.COM (May 6, 2017), https://medium.com/@montouche/understanding-ai-and-the-shades-of-difference-among-its-subsets-4c84b106d0c1.

*DeepMind.* DeepMind was created by British researchers Dennis Hassabis, Shane Legg, and Mustifa Suleyman in 2010 who sought to construct a neural network equivalent to AGI. Their research is based on generating a single program for application to games and which program is able to teach itself how to play and win at 49 completely different 2600 Atari games, as well as beat the player at Go, a very complex game.[31] Unlike ANI, it is not preprogrammed but learns from experience and thus is an AGI. It is currently applying its technology for environmental causes and for improvement of health care.[32] Among the environmental initiatives is the enabling of machine learning, through the use of a neural network that was inculcated on available weather forecasts and historical turbine data, to predict wind power output 36 hours before its actual generation. In so doing, the use of wind power became more feasible and enabled recommendations of how to make hourly delivery commitments to the power grid a day in advance. It transformed an unpredictable source into one with much more reliability (about 20 percent greater efficiency) and of great benefit to the environment.[33] *DeepMind Health*, through its Streams, is a secure mobile phone app that is able to pick up signs of medical conditions, such as sepsis and acute kidney injury, well before clinicians are enable to do so. It has purportedly saved numerous patients from injury and death.[34] It was acquired by Google in 2014 for $400 million which created its artificial neural network to play games as a human person and also as a Neural Turing Machine (NTM) to enable access to external memory (Fig. 1.4).[35] It is currently owned by Alphabet Inc.

---

[31] *AlphaGo*, https://deepmind.com/research/alphago/.

[32] *Solve Intelligence. Use it to make the world a better place*, DEEPMIND, https://deepmind.com/about/.

[33] *Machine learning can boost the value of wind energy*, DEEPMIND, https://deepmind.com/blog/machine-learning-can-boost-value-wind-energy/.

[34] *How we're helping today*, DEEPMIND, https://deepmind.com/applied/deepmind-health/working-partners/how-were-helping-today/.

[35] For a discussion how the NTM seeks to mimic the human brain's short-term memory, see *Google's Secretive DeepMind Startup Unveils a "Neural Turing Machine,"* MIT TECHNOLOGY REVIEW (Oct. 29, 2014), https://www.technologyreview.com/s/532156/googles-secretive-deepmind-startup-unveils-a-neural-turing-machine/.

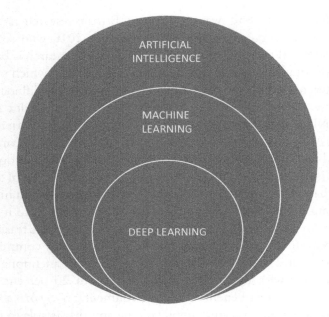

Fig. 1.4   Machine learning and deep learning. (Source: *Artificial Intelligence: The Road Ahead in Low and Middle-Income Countries*, WORLD WIDE WEB FOUNDATION (June, 2017) at 5, http://webfoundation.org/docs/2017/07/AI_Report_WF.pdf)

# Robotics

Robotics is the science or study of technology associated with the design, fabrication, theory, and application of robots.[36] It is an interdisciplinary branch of science which comprises a number of types of engineering disciplines such as mechanical, electronic, and information engineering and computer systems.[37] In this text, we are particularly concerned with how AI-based robots are utilized. There are many types of robots whose applications are virtually numberless (discussed in Chap. 2).

---

[36] *Robotics*, THE AMERICAN HERITAGE DICTIONARY OF THE ENGLISH LANGUAGE, https://www.ahdictionary.com/word/search.html?q=robotics/.

[37] *Robotics*, WIKIPEDIA, https://en.wikipedia.org/wiki/Robotics.

## Vision (Computer Vision)

*Vision* is a subfield of AI and is defined as the science and technology whereby AI systems are able to extract information, build models, and apply multi-dimensional data in a broad range of computer-generated activities.[38] There are a number of subfields of computer vision including computational vision (computer vision) and machine vision. *Computational vision* is the process of recording, analyzing, and comprehending visual images which are then utilized in machine vision for a variety of social and scientific purposes including the use of feature engineering to make machine learning algorithms operate efficiently.[39] Examples of uses of computational vision in AI are the Robocup tournament, i.e., tournament of robot dogs playing soccer by reacting to images received by the robots, and ASIMO, which is a Honda created robot that can analyze its environment, walk, talk, climb stairs, maneuver around objects, act as a companion to humans, and other features.[40] *Machine vision* is comprised of a number of technologies including systems engineering and, generally, is the application of computational vision in an industrial or practical application or process.[41]

*Facial recognition* is a sub-domain of computer vision which is able to extract data that can assist in identifying and/or verifying a particular individual from a digital image or video frame.[42] Heretofore, the most common mode of identification, particularly for police objectives, was the use of fingerprints, voice, eyes, and lineups. AI's facial recognition system, also known as a Biometric Artificial Intelligence, in conjunction

---

[38] Taniya Arya, *What is computer vision in artificial intelligence?*, QUORA, https://www.quora.com/What-is-computer-vision-in-artificial-intelligence.

[39] *Vision and AI*, VISION RECOGNITION, MBHA, https://mbhs.edu/~lpiper/computer_vision03/visionai.html.

[40] *Honda*, ASIMO, http://asimo.honda.com/downloads/pdf/asimo-technical-information.pdf.

[41] *Computer Vision vs. Machine Vision*, AIA VISION ONLINE, https://www.visiononline.org/vision-resources-details.cfm/vision-resources/Computer-Vision-vs-Machine-Vision/content_id/4585.

[42] Other sub-domains of computer vision are: scene reconstruction, event detection, video tracking, object recognition, 3D pose estimation, learning, indexing, motion estimation, and image restoration. *Computer vision*, WIKIPEDIA, https://en.wikipedia.org/wiki/Computer_vision.

with other biometrics such as eye (iris) recognition systems, has been used for a wide variety of additional purposes.[43] At sporting events, the system has been used to identify players, recognize visitors, celebrities, known criminals, and other possible troublemakers. It has been employed for advertising and for the identification of individuals, especially well-known persons at events, albeit it may run afoul of their privacy rights. Law enforcement has used it at police stops, sporting events, and other locations. Its application has expanded exponentially such as at international airports and it is estimated that the facial recognition market for it will reach $9.6 billion by 2022.[44] (Legal and ethical issues of facial recognition are discussed in Chap. 4.)

## Artificial Neural Network

An artificial neural network (ANN) is a computational model based on the structure and functions of biological neural networks. Information that flows through the network affects the structure of the network because a neural network changes, or learns in a sense, grounded on that input and output.[45] It is based on observational analogical reasoning of the biological process of the human brain which is able to accomplish the connections of axons among its 86 billion nerve cells (neurons) from external stimuli. It was defined by the inventor of the first neurocomputers, Dr. Robert Hecht-Nielsen, as "…a computing system made up of a number of simple, highly interconnected processing elements, which process information by their dynamic state response to external inputs."[46] ANN seeks to imitate the process by learning from examples fed from complex data inputs. It is a framework for algorithms to work together.

---

[43] *Facial recognition system*, WIKIPEDIA, https://en.wikipedia.org/wiki/Facial_recognition_system.

[44] *Facial Recognition Market Worldwide Expected to Reach $9.6 Billion by 2022*, HT HOSPITAL TECHNOLOGY (July 1, 2016), https://hospitalitytech.com/facial-recognition-market-expected-reach-96-billion-worldwide-2022.

[45] *Artificial neural network*, TECHOPEDIA, https://www.techopedia.com/definition/5967/artificial-neural-network-ann.

[46] *A Basic Introduction to Neural Networks*, http://pages.cs.wisc.edu/~bolo/shipyard/neural/local.html.

ANNs have been used to perform a variety of tasks such as computer vision, speech recognition machine translation, social network, medical diagnosis, video games, and other uses.[47]

## Speech Processing

Speech processing has been defined as "the study of speech signals and processing methods … and is at the intersection of speech signals and natural language processing."[48] The signals are in digital format and includes the acquisition, manipulation, storage, transfer, and output of speech signals without use of hands or eyes. Speech processing poses many problems due to the vast number of forms of speech such as loudness or softness, accents, particular mode of speaking, use of language, and other characteristics. A viewer watching translations or recitations of discussions on television will note how often the speech download contains numerous inaccuracies. Thus, AI has been instrumental in creating greater reliability of setting forth accurately what has been stated by speakers. Individuals using speech processing software, particularly by disabled persons unable to type on computers persons, have specific needs for accuracy of statements made. Speech recognition software may be, as one scholarly paper defined, either *Speaker-Dependent*, whereby the computer software adapts to the particular mode of speech by an individual, or *Speaker-Independent* that is able with greater inaccuracies to transforms speech behavior by many persons with varying modes of speech.[49]

---

[47] *Artificial neural network*, WIKIPEDIA, https://en.wikipedia.org/wiki/Artificial_neural_network; https://www.sciencedirect.com/topics/neuroscience/speech-processing.

[48] *Speech Processing*, SCIENCEDIRECT, https://www.sciencedirect.com/topics/neuroscience/speech-processing.

[49] G. Harsha Vardham and G. Hari Charan, *Artificial Intelligence and its Applications for Speech Recognition*, 3 INTERNATIONAL J. OF SCIENCE & RESEARCH, Issue 8 (Aug. 12, 2014), https://www.ijsr.net/archive/v3i8/MDUwODE0MDU=.pdf.

## Evolutionary Computation

Evolutionary computation is a subfield of AI that is composed of algorithms that relate to the use of evolutionary systems as computational processes for solving complex problems. It is a tool used by scientists and engineers who commence a set of candidate solutions which is updated periodically through a process of trial and error. Each generation is produced stochastically (randomly determined), removing fewer desirable solutions coupled with random changes. In this manner, optimal solutions are periodically presented and altered to achieve maximum optimization.[50]

## Natural Language Processing (NLP)

NLP is a subfield of AI that focuses on the interactions between computers and human language. It is at the intersection of computer science, AI, and computational linguistics and is concerned with how computers process and analyze large amounts of natural language data. Natural language is the way we humans communicate with each other through speech and text. NLP is the process of building computational tools that respect language by use of machine translation, summarization, questions and answers which draw upon a variety of scientific disciplines.[51]

In Chap. 2, we will explore some of the innumerable ways in which AI has and will continue to transform almost every aspect of society to a degree previously relegated to the realm of science fiction but now, in many ways, exceeds the creative imagination of earlier authors. This progression has come about with the expansion of computer technology that has enabled researchers to engage in the exploration of deep learning

---

[50] Kenneth A. DeJong, *Evolutionary Computation: A Unified Approach*, AMAZON CO UK, https://www.amazon.com/Evolutionary-Computation-Approach-Kenneth-Jong/dp/0262529602 and *Evolutionary Computation*, WIKIPEDIA, https://en.wikipedia.org/wiki/Evolutionary_computation.

[51] Jason Brownlee, *What is Natural Language Processing?*, MACHINE LEARNING MASTERY (Sept. 22, 2017), https://machinelearningmastery.com/natural-language-processing/; and Matt Kiser, *Introduction Language Processing*, ALGORITHMIA (Aug. 11, 2016), https://blog.algorithmia.com/introduction-natural-language-processing-nlp/.

neural networks. Human past history evolved rather slowly whereby major thinkers could predict events that will occur in the several decades to follow. In as brief a time as a decade from now, with the addition of quantum computing and other advances in computational technologies, the attempt to render an informed opinion will tax the predictive capabilities of the greatest of our futurists, the most prescient of our seers.

# 2

# Applications of AI and Projections of AI Impact

In Chap. 1, we noted how AI is at the forefront of societal changes that have exhibited substantial impact in almost all endeavors. There have been numerous movies, commentaries, science fiction novels, and other media pronouncements and projections concerning what the future will be like with the scientific and technological advances that have taken place, currently are happening, and will occur in the future. The applications and projected ways in which AI will affect the ways they are utilized are almost incalculable. This chapter discusses some of the major applications that have already been adapted or are currently under research and development that will affect the manner in which business is conducted; how we live our daily lives; the uncertainties of future advancements; and a panoply of numerous other issues that tax the minds and energies of pioneers who bring about pronouncements (almost daily) of innovative technologies. We then examine some of the issues which leading researchers in the field are contemplating and how humankind may respond. We begin with an overview of how AI has transformed some of the major areas that affect our lives.

© The Author(s) 2020
R. Girasa, *Artificial Intelligence as a Disruptive Technology*,
https://doi.org/10.1007/978-3-030-35975-1_2

# Applications of AI

## Health Care

There have been numerous studies concerning diagnostic errors which have caused substantial harm to patients. It has been estimated that diagnostic errors accounted for 17 percent of preventable errors in hospitalized patients. Approximately 9 percent of patients studied in a systematic review of autopsy studies disclosed that they had experienced major diagnostic errors which may have contributed to their demise.[1] More than 12 million serious diagnostic errors occur each year and a third of the $3.6 trillion dollars spent each year on medical care resulted in waste.[2] The application of AI to healthcare has raised questions about whether physicians or particular specialties of the profession will be replaced by robots and other AI technologies. All physicians today use computers in their practice but AI has become and will increasingly be used as a tool for diagnostic purposes which heretofore often lacked proper identification and treatment of diseases. It has been estimated that AI can identify most of over 700 diseases, which often are not discovered or discoverable by radiologists and pathologists. Neural networks have been utilized to examine retinal images to locate cardiovascular risk factors. The Mayo clinic, together with an Israeli startup company, Beyond Verbal, have analyzed acoustic features in voices to uncover distinct features in patients to detect coronary artery disease.[3]

Persons with neurological diseases and trauma can now interact with physicians and their loved ones through use of AI brain-computer interfaces. Radiologists benefit from AI tools that greatly enhance diagnostic imaging by reading radiology scans and which can enable visualization of

---

[1] *Diagnostic Errors*, PSNET (Jan. 2019), U.S. DEPARTMENT OF HUMAN SERVICES, https://psnet.ahrq.gov/primers/primer/12/diagnostic-errors.

[2] Eric Topol, *Making Health Care Human Again*, FORTUNE (Oct. 22, 2018), http://fortune.com/2018/10/22/artificial-intelligence-ai-healthcare/.

[3] *Top Healthcare AI Trends To Watch*, CB INSIGHTS, https://www.cbinsights.com/reports/CB-Insights_AI-Trends-In-Healthcare.pdf?utm_campaign=ai-healthcare-trends_2018-09&utm_source=hs_automation&utm_medium=email&utm_content=65885394&_hsenc=p2ANqtz-8-MebChVT0AOP0XM7vhQB2EfRZvAmnzLEuZyLwkBnnua70fhND0OwjPzKXPSPO2C9tIwhfQ0Dellt95S5jGjkHO2SWnA&_hsmi=65885394.

virtual biopsies rather than by invasive tissue sampling. Other AI uses include new technologies of 3D printers and procedures in operating rooms; employment of robots for performing surgeries; application of analytics in the identification of diseases by pathologists which have greatly enhanced identification abnormalities from greater imaging of tissue samples; machine learning algorithms to synthesize highly complex data sets[4]; IBM Watson for oncology, i.e., to assist in the diagnosis of cancer; use of an AI system to restore the movement of patients with quadriplegia[5]; retinal imaging by use of Google's DeepMind; and many other benefits.

The changes in a positive mode that AI brings to the health professions was graphically set forth in an article which imagines a pathologist rendering an opinion based on a small tissue sample of a patient who coughed up blood. Currently, the sample may be erroneously classified, target cells missed entirely, or other possible errors resulting in inappropriate treatment that can cost the patient's life. With AI, the pathologist would be enabled to render a more accurate diagnosis that recognizes subtle features which even well-trained eyes would miss. AI will aid in much better diagnosis, e.g., for wrist fractures, diabetic eye disease, signs of stroke, and other medical issues. A company which enabled the advancements is Boston-based PathAI whose software maps the types of tissue that shows in a red color the cells that may lead to a cancer's progression. The information is used by drug companies to determine particular drugs' responses to particular cancer cells. Presently, the company is working on developing algorithms to identify metastases in lymph nodes, the grading of the cancer which heretofore was somewhat subjective; and the development of biomarker detection tools for use by pharmaceutical companies for validation of drugs for effective treatment.[6]

---

[4] Jennifer Bresnick, *Top 12 Ways Artificial Intelligence Will Impact Healthcare*, HEALTH IT ANALYTICS (April 30, 2018), https://healthitanalytics.com/news/top-12-ways-artificial-intelligence-will-impact-healthcare.

[5] Fei Jiang, Yong Jiang, Hui Zhi, Yi Dong, Hao Lim Sufeng Ma, Yilong Wang, Qiang Dong, Haipeng Shen, and Yongiun Wang, *Artificial Intelligence in healthcare: past, present and future*, 2 BMJ JOURNALS, Issue 4 (June, 2017), https://svn.bmj.com/content/2/4/230.

[6] Eile Dolgin, *This is how a pathologist could save your life*, SPECTRUM.IEEE.ORG (Dec. 2018) at 24–29.

The problem is the slowness of hospitals and surgeons to adapt to digitized imaging due, in part, to the costs for scanners, the training of physicians to use a whole new methodology of diagnosis and treatments, and the early stages of the development of algorithms appropriate for diagnostic use. Google, IBM, and medical-device manufacturers, such as Philips, Leica Biosystems, and many startups, are working to develop pattern-recognition algorithms to assist pathologists to identify cancer cells by use of digitized imagery of tissue on glass slides. Tau AI is at the forefront of a revolution in medicine whereby the physician is better enabled to perform life-saving diagnosis and treatment.[7] AI-based computer vision algorithm has been used to aid patients with prolonged, high-intensity care who often suffer greatly from long-term cognitive and physical impairment with accompanying decline in functional status. The algorithm is exploited to shorten the time they are subject to mechanical ventilation thereby reducing delirium and preventing muscle wasting and dysfunction.[8]

As in other areas, the possible uses of AI, machine learning, and natural language progressing (NLP) for medical and psychological purposes are almost endless. A mental health app, Ginger, was developed to assist persons who need an on-demand health system that consist of trained emotional health coaches, therapists, and psychiatrists who help persons in need of immediate assistance, e.g., contemplating suicide.[9] There are numerous other sites based on AI such as "VeryWellMind,"[10] which is a virtual counselor or chatbot for mental health; IntelliCare, a free app

---

[7] *Id.*, at 26.

[8] Serena Yeung, Francesca Rinaldo, Jeffrey Jopling, Bingbin Liu, Rishab Mehra, Nance Downing, Michelle Guo, Gabriel M. Bianconi, Alexandre Alahi, Julia Lee, Brandi Campbell, Kayla Deru, William Beninati, Li Fei-Fei & Arnold Milstein, *A computer vision system for deep learning-based detection of patient mobilization activities in the ICU*, 2 NPJ DIGITAL MEDICINE No. 11 (2019), https://www.nature.com/articles/s41746-019-0087-z?utm_campaign=the_algorithm.unpaid. engagement&utm_source=hs_email&utm_medium=email&utm_content=71042128&_ hsenc=p2ANqtz-_rUDmLuHQXLr0ezrVuHmrF5c8Br9J2aII_lDqdeZjIumkd5OlRI8gPRnzkM-RXBf85j8Wv7tesh4tad02nUGkVltkzfrQ&_hsmi=71042130.

[9] Ginger, https://www.ginger.io/. For a discussion, see Molly Fosco, *Can Artificial Intelligence Save Us from Depression?*, OZY (Jan. 25, 2019), https://www.ozy.com/fast-forward/can-artificial-intelligence-save-us-from-depression/91451.

[10] Michael Rucker, *Using Artificial Intelligence for Mental Health*, VERYWELL MIND (Nov. 19, 2018), https://www.verywellmind.com/using-artificial-intelligence-for-mental-health-4144239.

suite for android users which assists people with depression, anxiety, sleep disorders and the like and which is a method developed through machine learning; and many other AI-based applications.[11] Amazon's Web Services, as well as Google, are investing heavily in testing how AI can simplify medical care. Through the use of machine learning, the Harvard Medical School is experimenting with AI-based ways to cut costs in the health industry that has excessive inefficiencies by assuring that the hospital's data is immediately accessible in the event of a disaster that would cut off its back-up servers. By analysis of surgeries tracing back into the 1980s, a new scheduling system was developed that increased operating capacity by 30 percent by allowing doctors to reserve operating time much more easily.[12]

Women who require in vitro fertilization had to undergo extensive procedures that necessitated well-trained embryologists to collect eggs, fertilize them and then implant the embryos into the uterus. The procedure was extensively time consuming and required some guess work especially when grading embryos and assigning a quality score. Cornell University scientists have been able to apply Google's deep learning algorithm to rate the embryo in question as good, fair, or poor with reference to the likelihood that such implantation would be successful. The prior subjectivity of embryologists in this regard is now made more objectively accurate in rendering the said ratings, thereby increasing the chances for a successful outcome.[13]

*Drug Companies and AI. Drug* companies are using their large cache of data derived from clinical trials to underlie AI for better and effective treatment of illnesses. AI companies are partnering with drug companies

---

[11] *Can These Artificial Intelligence Apps Improve Mental Health?*, COLUMBIA U. (Jan. 10, 2017) https://www.mailman.columbia.edu/public-health-now/news/can-these-artificial-intelligence-apps-improve-mental-health.

[12] John Tozzi, *Amazon Gives AI to Harvard Hospital in Tech's Latest Health Push*, BLOOMBERG (March 4, 2019), https://www.bloomberg.com/news/articles/2019-03-04/amazon-gives-ai-to-harvard-hospital-in-tech-s-latest-health-push.

[13] Megan Molteni, *AI Could Scan IVF Embryos to Help Make Babies More Quickly*, WIRED (April 4, 2019), https://www.wired.com/story/ai-could-scan-ivf-embryos-to-help-make-babies-more-quickly/?CNDID=39532555&CNDID=39532555&bxid=MzI1OTUzNjAzMjkxS0&hasha=d8eee 610920ee24961d98d5f1e658eb8&hashb=c852d7725efa76448f0f20caa3d8cbf5706677a4&mbi d=nl_040619_daily_list1_p2&source=DAILY_NEWSLETTER&utm_brand=wired&utm_ mailing=WIRED%20NL%20040619%20(1)&utm_medium=email&utm_source=nl.

through algorithms to identify better treatments and provide an enhanced understanding as to why certain drugs do well or not well with particular patients. Uses of AI will offer more effective treatment at a significant saving of money and human effort. Examples are: Berg and Rolvent Sciences, and Exscientis with Berg partnering with the pharmaceutical firms of AstraZeneca and Sanofi Pasteur[14]; Johnson & Johnson with IBM's Watson Health; sedation in the operating room using SEDASYS, which is the first computer-assisted personalized sedation system; Pfizer's use of the IBM Watson for Drug Discovery cloud-based platform; and other drug companies such as Bayer and Roche which are also partnering with the IBM Watson Health services.[15] It has been projected that half of all drug companies and health care services have used AI.[16]

## Robots and Robotics

*Robot* is defined as a machine that can behave independently like a human person to perform specific mechanical chores automatically, either autonomously or semi-autonomously. Robots interact with the physical world through sensors[17] and actuators.[18] *Robotics* is a branch of technology

---

[14] Sy Mukherjee, *Reinventing Drug R&D*, FORTUNE (Oct. 22, 2018), http://fortune.com/2018/10/22/artificial-intelligence-ai-healthcare/.

[15] Kumba Sennaar, *AI in Pharma and Biomedicine: Analysis of the Top 5 Global Drug Companies*, EMERJ (Jan. 9, 2019), https://emerj.com/ai-sector-overviews/ai-in-pharma-and-biomedicine/.

[16] Daniel Faggella, *Machine Learning in Healthcare: Expert Consensus from 50+ Executives*, EMERJ (Nov. 29, 2018), https://emerj.com/ai-market-research/machine-learning-in-healthcare-executive-consensus/.

[17] *Sensors*, e.g., video camera, temperature and humidity, force torque for touch and many other sensors. *Sensors*, ROBOTICS BIBLE, http://www.roboticsbible.com/sensors-used-in-robotics.html. A cautionary note regarding IBM Watson was raised in a recent article which said that AI has yet to be able to "make sense of complex medical information" and to encode the expertise of physicians. Eliza Strickland, *How IBM Watson Overpromised and Undelivered on AI Health Care*, IEEE SPECTRUM (April 2, 2019), https://spectrum.ieee.org/biomedical/diagnostics/how-ibm-watson-overpromised-and-underdelivered-on-ai-health-care.

[18] An *actuator* is an electromechanical device which converts energy into mechanical work (or motion). For robots, actuators are like muscles that perform work, ROBOT PLATFORM, http://www.robotplatform.com/knowledge/actuators/actuators.html. For a discussion of the types of robots see Alex Owen-Hill, *What's the Difference Between Robotics and Artificial Intelligence*, BLOG (July 19, 2017), https://blog.robotiq.com/whats-the-difference-between-robotics-and-artificial-intelligence.

which deals with the design, construction, and operation of robots in automation.[19] AI and robotics initially had a common root with the latter thought of as intelligent machines. The connection underwent a separation in the 1970s with Robotics employed for industrial purposes such as that used in automobile assembly plants. The word "robot" was first used in a 1921 play by Karel Capek which even then contained the ultimate fear that the subjugated robots ultimately made humans their slaves. Later emanations included the creation of a 2-ton robotic arm made by the company Unimation that could perform heavy lifting of objects which was used by General Motors in 1961. Eight years later, Victor Scheinmann developed the Stanford Arm which was electrically powered and was much more flexible. Honda's ASIMO robot was displayed in the year 2000 that could walk on two legs. The 2003 KIVA Systems, which could move pallets and goods within a warehouse, opened the field for greatly expanded uses of robots. Within a few years thereafter, robots have been applied broadly for specified purposes and now encompass 1.6 million robots globally.[20]

*Types and Uses of Robots.* Elderly readers will recall the advice given decades ago when purchasing an automobile. They were cautioned not to purchase an automobile assembled by human workers on a Monday because some workers were allegedly recovering from hangovers from excessive alcoholic binges or a Friday because of excessive speed and/or lack of attention from overwork to end the week. Robots never tire, engage in excessive drinking, drugs, or other errant pursuits, and may work 24/7. Other problems that may arise are the risks of moving heavy equipment and other dangerous and costly work-related activities that are better resolved by the use of robots. Thus, the replacement of workers by robots at automobile assembly plants has greatly increased the reliability and life management of vehicles.

Depending on usage and purpose, there are many types of robots. They may be characterized by application such as industrial, consumer

---

[19] *Definition of Robotics*, MERRIAN WEBSTER DICTIONARY, https://www.merriam-webster.com/dictionary/robotics#other-words.

[20] Benedict Dellot and Fabian Wallace-Stephens, *What is the difference between AI & robotics?*, MEDIUM.COM (Sept. 17, 2017), https://medium.com/@thersa/what-is-the-difference-between-ai-robotics-d93715b4ba7f.

(household or personal), military, medical, service, entertainment, space, hobby, and other purposes.[21] Within each category of usage are subcategories. The most widely utilized robots are for industrial purposes. Within this category are the types of arms managed which include handling, welding, painting, and other uses. Thus, the common types of industrial robots, that work by locomotion, are: *articulated* (rotary joints with a range of motion), *Cartesian* (3 linear joints deliver linear motion along the axis), *cylindrical* (rotational motion along the joint axis), *spherical* or *polar* (2 rotary and 1 linear joint axes to create a spherical-shaped work envelope), *scara* (used for assembly applications, has a compliant arm), *delta* (spider-like robots applied in food, pharmaceutical, and electric industries), and others.[22] Robots may be stationary, wheeled, legged, swimming, flying, mobile, spherical, and swarm.[23] In China, wherein workers are plentiful, nevertheless, due to U.S. tariff restrictions and other internal and external pressures, the garment industry has adapted AI to sub-processes such as stitching sleeves and cuffs. Industrial robots within the country has risen by 59 percent in 2017 to 138,000. Workers who feared displacement by these robots at one time, later on, took to assisting and benefiting in the design of the machines that removes much of the grunge work they are happy to relinquish.[24]

*AI Robotics*, in essence, evolved from a singular task machine (without AI) to one that operates within an environment whereby it is able to perceive, plan, and execute in accordance with the massive data incorporated within it and continuously added thereto. Thus, the exploitation of robots is limited only by the imagination of the scientists and engineers creating them. They are applied in industry as: *Industrial Robotics* for safety and control within the workplace; *Robot Vision* in connection with Computer Vision acting in real-time to locate its information sources and maximize the visual information; *Cognitive Robotics* that can accomplish complex tasks, which approximates reasoning by incorporating a

[21] *Types of Robots*, ALL ON ROBOTS, http://www.allonrobots.com/types-of-robots.html.

[22] *What Are The Main Types of Robots?*, ROBOTWORX, https://www.robots.com/faq/what-are-the-main-types-of-robots.

[23] There are numerous websites that illustrate the many types of robots, e.g., *images*, BING, https://www.bing.com/images/search?q=types+of+ai+robots&qpvt=types+of+ai+robots&FORM=IGRE.

[24] Shumpeter (Adrian Wooldridge), *Shirt Tales*, THE ECONOMIST (Jan. 5, 2019).

description of the world and expressing tasks to be performed; *Human Robot Interface*, which analyzes information flowing between the user and the robot; *Rescue Robotics* for the design and systems to search and rescue for large scale disasters; *Space Robotics* for planetary exploration missions; *RoboCare* for services for the elderly and disabled; and many other connections and applications.[25]

Notwithstanding all of the discussions of the wonders of robots and robotics, Bill Gates cautions that robots have not attained the dexterity that is required by industry noting that, while they can operate 24/7 on repeated pick up and assembly of a particular component, if one were to move the object an inch away, it cannot adjust to the movement. He further observed that robots are now able to learn how to maneuver objects through the process of trial and error. For example, in a project conducted by Open AI named Dactyl, the robot was able to teach itself to be more dexterous through reinforcement learning, neural-network software.[26] Boston Dynamics apparently disagrees with Gates by the claim that its humanoid Atlas robot can do backflips; another is able to pen doors; and a Segway-on-mescaline named Handle can go around picking up and stacking boxes with a vacuum arm. It has a camera to localize its space, another camera to avoid obstacles, and yet another for more general purposes.[27]

Additional utilizations are almost endless. Consumers may use robots at home as vacuum cleaners, pool cleaners, and other household chores; *medical robots* are currently applied for surgery and other related purposes; *service robots* for gathering data, research, and the like; *military robots* for bomb disposal, transportation, recognizance, search and rescue; *entertainment robots* especially as toys; *space robots* including employment

---

[25] Antonio Chella, Luca Iocchi, Irene Macaluso, and Daniele Nardi, *Artificial Intelligence and Robotics*, RESEARCH GATE (Jan. 2006), https://www.researchgate.net/publication/220672741_Artificial_Intelligence_and_Robotics.

[26] Bill Gates, *How we'll invent the future: Robot dexterity*, MIT TECHNOLOGY REVIEW (Feb. 27, 2019), https://www.technologyreview.com/lists/technologies/2019/.

[27] Matt Simon, *What Boston Dynamics' Rolling 'Handle' Robot really Means*, WIRED (April 2, 2019), https://www.wired.com/story/what-boston-dynamics-rolling-handle-robot-really-means/.

by the International Space Station for exploration of planets; and *hobby robots* for enthusiasts, which are as numerous as inventors can create.[28]

It was unusual that robots, in the form of drones, were used in the eradication of a rat invasion that threatened to destroy the delicate ecosystem of the Galapagos Islands, off the coast of Ecuador, by their consumption of insects that are pollinators on the island. Rats had caused the decimation of birds, which were not accustomed to predators, and other destructive activities. Drones were used to carry 44-pound payloads of blue-covered rodenticide (birds apparently do not consume blue-colored pellets) to rid the Islands of these pests.[29] A current innovative application of drones, which initially was sanctioned by the Federal Aviation Administration (FAA), was its encouragement of the United Parcel Service's (UPS) use of autonomous drones created by the technology firm, Matternet, to transport blood samples for immediate analyses. The drones are 2-feet square and can deliver payloads of 5 pounds for 12.5 miles. They are currently being utilized by a hospital in Raleigh N.C. It was initially tested and used in Rwanda in 2016 and further employed on some 3000 flights in Switzerland.[30]

*Military Robots.* Robots for military operations are engendering much comment and there have been a number of demands for international regulation. In an analysis of 154 existing weapons systems with automated-target capabilities, 49 are able to detect possible military targets without human intervention. Among the systems having such capabilities is the Harop drone system that is currently sold by the Israeli Aerospace Industries, which can be exploited either by operators or autonomously against any perceived target. It searches, finds, identifies,

---

[28] *See* Columbia, *supra*, note 63.

[29] Matt Simon, *Drones Drop Poison Bombs to Fight One Island's Rat Invasion*, WIRED (Jan. 24, 2019), https://technewstube.com/wired/1073598/drones-drop-poison-bombs-to-fight-one-islands-rat-invasion/.

[30] Eric Adams, *UPS Drone Are Now Moving Blood Samples Over North Carolina*, WIRED (April 1, 2019), https://www.wired.com/story/ups-matternet-drone-delivery-north-carolina/?CNDID=395 32555&CNDID=39532555&bxid=MzI1OTUzNjAzMjkxS0&hasha=d8eee610920ee24961d98 d5f1e658eb8&hashb=c852d7725efa76448f0f20caa3d8cbf5706677a4&mbid=nl_040119_daily_ list1_p2&source=DAILY_NEWSLETTER&utm_brand=wired&utm_mailing=WIRED%20 NL%20040119%20(1)&utm_medium=email&utm_source=nl.

attacks, and destroys targets independent of real-time intelligence.[31] The rise of autonomous weapons has been attributed to the great enhancement of computers coupled with machine learning that has changed the thinking of military planners seeking to find systems which do not require human intervention. DARPA has U.S. defense industries employed to work on autonomous *attack swarms* (a series of drones unleashed to attack particular targets and which can regroup if one or more are destroyed or fail) that can affect the outcome of perceived military battles.[32] The rise of such weapons has led to a call by the Stockholm International Peace Research Institute (SIPRI) for an investigation whether they should come within the governance of Lethal Autonomous Weapons Systems pursuant to the 1980 U.N. Convention on Certain Conventional Weapons.[33]

## Autonomous Vehicles

Perhaps the most publicized use of AI known to the public is the driverless automobile. Having a value of some $783 million in 2017, it is anticipated that by 2025 its value will approximate $11 billion. The vehicle autonomy is based on five levels: Level 0—human driver performs all driving task and is in complete control of the vehicle; Level 1—the driver is in control but some functions such as steering and accelerating can be performed by the vehicle; Level 2—the human driver controls but has at least one driver assistance system of both steering and acceleration using information about the driving environment, e.g., automated acceleration such as cruise control and lane centering; Level 3—the driver is still required if necessary to intervene but there has been a shift of safety-critical functions to the vehicle; Level 4—the vehicle is

---

[31] IAI, Israel Aerospace Industries, HAROP, http://www.iai.co.il/2013/36694-46079-en/Business_Areas_Land.aspx. For a discussion of the weapon, see *trying to restrain the robots*, THE ECONOMIST (Jan. 19, 2019) at 22–23, https://www.economist.com/briefing/2019/01/19/autonomous-weapons-and-the-new-laws-of-war.

[32] *Id.* at 23.

[33] *Autonomy in weapon systems*, STOCKHOLM INTERNATIONAL PEACE INSTITUTE, https://www.sipri.org/research/armament-and-disarmament/emerging-military-and-security-technologies/autonomy-weapon-systems. (A discussion of the ethical dimensions of the topic is discussed in Chap. 4.)

fully autonomous, able to perform all safety-critical driving functions, monitor roadway conditions, but is limited to the "operational design domain" of the vehicle (not all possible driving conditions are covered); and Level 5—the vehicle is fully autonomous, able to act as any human person in every driving scenario including extreme environments such as dirt roads and other comparable situations.[34]

Currently, manufacturers are developing vehicles at levels 4 and 5 based on deep learning (learning based on extensive data inputs), with the accumulation of a massive degree of data derived from the use of cameras, sensors, and communications systems that illustrate almost all of the actions on the road that emulate human-driver experiences, so that AI is or will be able to allow driverless automobiles and trucks. Major investments are currently being made by Ford, Nvidia Drive PX, Drive AI, and other startup companies, which will cause human drivers of transportation vehicles to gradually adapt to not driving vehicles that will result in loss of jobs for commercial drivers. For example, some 3.5 million truck drivers are at the forefront of job losses as a result of the disruptive technology.[35] Additionally, possible comparable usage will include shared electronic scooters and bikes which will be able to ride themselves using micromobility robotics.[36]

## Worker Safety

AI has increased worker safety and health as employed by companies such as SAP Connected Worker Safety, which offers products consistent with Internet of Things that are designed to provide real-time visibility of a company's workers' environment and safety conditions. It utilizes cloud deployment, provides immediate remediation of hazardous situations,

[34] Hope Reese, *Updated: Autonomous driving levels 0–5: Understanding the differences*, TECHREPUBLIC (Jan. 20, 2016), https://www.techrepublic.com/article/autonomous-driving-levels-0-to-5-understanding-the-differences/.
[35] Suhasini Gadam, *Artificial Intelligence and Autonomous Vehicles*, MEDIUM (April 19, 2018); and Colin Pawsey, *How Artificial Intelligence Is Key to Autonomous Vehicles*, TRUCKS, https://www.trucks.com/2017/11/29/artificial-intelligence-key-autonomous-vehicle-development/.
[36] Alex Davies and Aarian Marshall, *So Uber Wants Self-Driving Bikes and Scooters. Why? And How?*, WIRED (Jan. 24, 2019), https://www.wired.com/story/uber-self-driving-scooters/.

monitors risk-inducing behavior, and assures consistent compliance of workplace safety rules. It employs comprehensive analytics to combine and visualize data streams from various devices and workers; links information flowing from the worker to enterprise data for better insight; and applies analytical tools to gain deep insight to derive preventive and corrective action.[37] Microsoft has developed software that operates a system of cameras, software, and networked devices such as smart phones to track people, ascertain how they interact with machines and other devices, as well as monitor their activities in real-time to ensure worker training, performance, and safety. It accomplishes the tasks by means of some 27 million recognitions per second of people which oversees their activities.[38]

## Energy and Energy Management

AI is transforming the energy industry, which currently is reliant upon aged equipment that is subject to major breakdowns, is environmentally inefficient, is experiencing difficulty in a transformation by many customers who have installed solar panels and other electrical saving devices, and is open to possible future hacking. Accordingly, the U.S. Department of Energy has invested extensive monetary resources to upgrade the power grid ("smart grid") to meet much greater energy demands having at its basis AI as the brain of the future smart grid. It will do so by gathering massive quanta of data from smart sensors and make advances from deep learning algorithms by ascertaining patterns and anomalies in the system.[39] In addition to the smart grid, AI is the basis for *smart buildings* whose global market is estimated to be $31.74 billion by 2022 inasmuch as it is revolutionizing energy management particularly in commercial buildings. An example of AI's contribution is "Sam" which acts as a

---

[37] *Ensure industrial safety with real-time hazard and exposure monitoring*, SAP, https://www.sap.com/products/connected-worker-safety.html.

[38] Avi Meyerstein, *Microsoft AI getting into workplace safety?*, HUSCH BLACKWELL (June 8, 2017), https://www.safetylawmatters.com/2017/06/microsoft-ai-getting-workplace-safety/.

[39] Franklin Wolfe, *How Artificial Intelligence Will Revolutionize the Energy Industry*, HARVARD U. SCIENCE in the NEWS (Aug. 28, 2017), http://sitn.hms.harvard.edu/flash/2017/artificial-intelligence-will-revolutionize-energy-industry/.

virtual assistant for providing a comprehensive utility bill management and payment services by gathering data of external conditions impacting cost and usage, competitive alternatives, existing conditions of installed technology, and which can alert and respond to queries of customers.[40] Siemens, through its Energy Management Division, offers the Siemens Smart Grid Suite that provides customized solutions for smarter infrastructure grids and new business models which, among other advantages, reduces power outages from hours and days to minutes.[41]

## Banking

Banks have expressed interest in computerizing their operations since computers entered into the mainstream of business transactions. For example, automated teller machines (ATMs) have replaced human tellers for decades. With AI and machine learning, there has been an enhanced interest in the transformation of routine operations. Heightened interest in AI has occurred because of both, capabilities and business needs. As with other areas of business and social pursuits, there are similar advantages and disadvantages to the adoption of AI. The advantages need little explanation which include error resistance, operating 24/7 without fatigue that is experienced by humans, cost efficiency, speed of transactions, risk management, customer satisfaction, regulatory compliance, and many other advantages. The general problem is the lack of personnel able to adapt to the new technologies.[42]

Nevertheless, U.S. banking institutions are readily adapting to the use of AI in their operations. The seven leading U.S. banks[43] have all invested

---

[40] Emily Holbrook, *The Impact of Artificial Intelligence on Energy Management*, ENERGY MANAGER TODAY (Jan. 9, 2018), https://www.energymanagertoday.com/impact-artificial-intelligence-energy-management-0174116/.

[41] *Energy Management*, SIEMENS, https://www.siemens.com/businesses/us/en/energy-management.htm.

[42] Jim Marous, *The Use of AI in Banking is Set to Explode*, THE FINANCIAL BRAND, https://thefinancialbrand.com/63322/artificial-intelligence-ai-banking-big-data-analytics/.

[43] The 7 leading US banks, according to the Federal Reserve, are J.P. Morgan Chase, Bank of America, Wells Fargo, Citibank, US Bank of North America, PNC Bank of North America, and TD Bank of North America. *Large Commercial Banks*, FEDERAL RESERVE, https://www.federalreserve.gov/releases/lbr/current/default.htm.

in AI technology for their operations. JPMorgan Chase Bank has inaugurated a Contract Intelligence (COiN) platform to interpret approximately 12,000 annual commercial loan agreements in seconds which had taken attorneys and loan offices 360,000 hours annually. Moreover, it does not make errors and operates 24/7 without complaint.[44] It is heavily engaged in data analytics having AI as its basis.[45] Wells Fargo inaugurated a new Artificial Intelligence Enterprise Solutions team to focus on emerging technologies that will affect its operations. The team formed a Payments, Virtual Solutions, and Innovation Group to make banking and managing finances convenient and easy.[46] The Bank of America launched "Erica" in 2016, which is a chatbot,[47] a voice AI banking system that, although robotic in nature, is able to match conversations that otherwise would be rendered by a human person in response to almost all inquiries from the many millions of customers of the Bank. It leverages predictive analytics and cognitive messaging.[48]

Citibank launched a number of initiatives having AI as its underlying technology. Among them are Citi's automated processing of cross-border payments via a link between the CitiConnect for Blockchain connectivity platform and the Linq Platform powered by the Nasdaq Financial Network[49]; D10X, whereby bank employees identify critical problems of customers which are then engaged in hypothesis testing and validated and then launched to better serve the bank's customers[50]; and Citi Global

---

[44] Hugh Son, *JPMorgan Software Does in Seconds What Took Lawyers 360,000 Hours*, BLOOMBERG (Feb. 27, 2017), https://www.bloomberg.com/news/articles/2017-02-28/jpmorgan-marshals-an-army-of-developers-to-automate-high-finance. This overall segment for discussion on banking is based upon Kumba Senaar, *AI in Banking – An Analysis of America's Top 7 Banks*, EMERJ (Jan. 19, 2019), https://emerj.com/ai-sector-overviews/ai-in-banking-analysis/.

[45] *AI*, J.P. MORGAN, https://www.jpmorgan.com/global/jpmorgan-AI.

[46] Grace Noto, *Wells Fargo Gets New Focus on Innovation, AI*, BANK INNOVATION (Feb. 17, 2017), https://bankinnovation.net/2017/02/wells-fargo-gets-new-focus-on-innovation-ai/.

[47] A "chatbot," a/k/a chatterbot, talkbot, smartbot, Bot, IM bot, and other comparable expressions, is a computer program that engages in a conversation textually or by auditory means that simulates the conversation of a human person. *Chatbot*, https://en.wikipedia.org/wiki/Chatbot.

[48] Robert Barba, *Bank of America launches Erica chatbot*, BANKRATE (March 19, 2018), https://www.bankrate.com/banking/bank-of-america-boa-launches-erica-digital-assistant-chatbot/.

[49] *Nasdaq and Citi Announce Pioneering Blockchain and Global Banking Integration*, CITIGROUP (May 22, 2017), https://www.citigroup.com/citi/news/2017/170522a.htm.

[50] *D10X*, CITI VENTURES, http://citi.com/ventures/d10x.html.

Innovation Labs has spread globally including London and Singapore, and coordinates with Feedzai, a data science company that engages in fraud detection.[51]

US Bank inaugurated its Salesforce AI-powered Einstein features to convert retail banking customers to its wealth management program.[52] The bank has been a leader in AI-based programs for more than a decade and has centered its attention on Salesforce with a user base of 15,000 staff members. It has embraced machine learning features in the Salesforce's Einstein brand to understand and coordinate the large volume of data accumulated throughout its banking operations. The bank was adept through AI to understand its customers in a manner not previously capable such as the discovery that customers between 35 and 44 years of age were more prone to increase assets under management by opening credit card accounts. It also enabled the bank to use predictive factors, such as meeting minimum levels of asset management and mortgages,[53] and was able to ascertain, e.g., which callers are military veterans who thereby receive messages of thanks for their services.[54]

PNC has been at the forefront in integrating AI into its operations. It invited companies leading in AI and machine learning to its Pittsburgh headquarters to incorporate both technologies into its operations. Among the perceived uses from its immense data sets are the reconciliation of ledger book or the input of data from invoices for accounts payable.[55] Chris Ward, PNC's executive vice president and head of product management for Treasury Management, has promoted the bank's adoption of AI and machine learning. He predicted that 90 percent of global financial

---

[51] *Citi Ventures Makes Strategic Investment in Feedzai*, FEEDZAI (Oct. 19, 2016), https://feedzai.com/press-releases/citi-ventures-makes-strategic-investment-feedzai/.

[52] For a discussion of the Salesforce program, see *Salesforce*, https://www.salesforce.com/form/sem/salesforce.jsp?nc=70130000002Duio&d=7010M000002MHWl&DCMP=KNC-Bing&s_kwcid=AL!4604!10!14687661958!25686226907&ef_id=W36r6wAACaKanxGW:20190121130200:s.

[53] Nadia Cameron, *U.S. Bank's head of CRM outlines keys to AI success*, CMO (Nov. 8, 2017), https://www.cmo.com.au/article/print/629704/us-bank-head-crm-outlines-keys-ai-success/.

[54] Penny Crossman, *U.S. Bank bets AI can finally deliver 360-degree view*, AMERICAN BANKER (July 20, 2017), https://www.americanbanker.com/news/us-bank-bets-ai-can-finally-deliver-360-degree-view.

[55] Aaron Aupperlee, *PNC hosts AI experts to explore its roles for banking*, TRIBLIVE (Aug. 30, 2017), https://triblive.com/business/technology/12677369-74/pnc-hosts-ai-experts-to-explore-its-roles-in-banking.

institutions will have adopted the technology by 2024 and that Global FIs (financial institutions) will have adopted the technology in some capacity by 2024. There are hurdles to be overcome: from internal challenges of adaptation of employees to the new technologies to customers who may be initially resistant. Nevertheless, the technology will enhance the speed of operations and decision-making.[56]

The Bank of NY Mellon Corp. became one of the first banks to deploy more than AI-based 220 bots (automated computer programs)[57] in its everyday operations in order to create a more efficient operation and lower its costs. By use of robotics or software, it has dealt with repetitive operations that previously were performed by human persons but now are able to respond 24/7 to data requests from external auditors, requests for dollar funds transfers, and enable systems to correct formatting and data mistakes.[58] With its robotics operations team in coordination with other bank' executives, it created eight pilot programs, four of which resulted in production. Among them are trade settlements, as custodian to settle trades, that use the robotic process automation software derived from Blue Prism.[59] The software facilitates the bank to program bots with rules that enable research on orders, resolve discrepancies, and clear trades.[60]

## Speech (Voice) Recognition

*Speech Translation.* Individuals, either domestically or when traveling abroad, have faced numerous situations of awkwardness in attempting to

---

[56] *How PNC Is Adapting To The Rise Of AI*, PYMNTS (2018), https://www.pymnts.com/news/digital-banking/2018/pnc-artificial-intelligence-mobile-banking/.

[57] A "bot" is software using natural language processing to respond back to user inputs based on input keywords. *Bots and Artificial Intelligence*, DZONE, https://dzone.com/articles/bots-and-artificial-intelligence.

[58] Anna Irrera, *BankNY Mellon advances artificial intelligence tech across operations*, REUTERS (May 10, 2017), https://www.reuters.com/article/us-bony-mellon-technology-ai/bny-mellon-advances-artificial-intelligence-tech-across-operations-idUSKBN186253.

[59] Blue Prism pioneered robotic process automation which is software with the ability to learn and perform repetitive tasks, *Who We Are*, BLUEPRISM, https://www.blueprism.com/who-we-are.

[60] Penny Crosman, *How BankNY Mellon Became a Pioneer in Bots*, AMERICAN BANKER (Aug. 25, 2016), https://www.americanbanker.com/news/how-bny-mellon-became-a-pioneer-in-bots.

communicate with a person who speaks an unfamiliar language. Fortunately, companies, like Google, have made it much easier by use of AI to automatically translate conversations and written texts into readable formats. Among the latest devices that enhance such communication are Google's Pixel Buds which incorporates Google Assistant, a smart voice assistant that supports Google Translate. They enable the user's earbuds to translate conversations in 40 different languages.[61] The device reads text into over 60 languages in real-time.[62] Indirectly competitive and also AI-based are Apple's Airpods, which are wireless Bluetooth earbuds, that play music, and relay telephone calls through its supporting digital assistant.[63] The battle among the giants, Amazon, Microsoft, Google, Facebook, and Apple, for the projected $49 billion market, has intensified with all vying to expand the voice market. For example, Google has entered into the health care and travel markets, as well as search and conversational AI; Amazon, through Amazon Choice "Beyond Alexa" is promoting intersecting voice and e-commerce and auto integration; Apple's HomePod especially excels in privacy and security; Microsoft with Cortana is coordinating with Amazon to integrate Windows 10 and Alexa; and Facebook with its entry of Portal, a video communication device. The major competitors of U.S. companies in facial recognition are Chinese companies such as Alibaba and Xiaomi. The fear is alleged misuse of the new technology by the Chinese government.[64]

*AI Chatbots.* Most customers have experienced speaking with frustration to a voice on the other end that is not responsive to the particular question asked or problem to be solved. After attempting for what appears to be an inordinate amount of time, a "live" person finally addresses your particular question or issue. AI chatbots are becoming far better in rendering the customer an appropriate response as greater and greater data and experience become part of the particular responsive program. Although AI and bots are two completely different mechanisms (a *bot* is a script that does precisely what it has been programmed to do while AI

---

[61] *Google Pixel Buds*, WIKIPEDIA, https://en.wikipedia.org/wiki/Google_Pixel_Buds.

[62] *Skype Translator*, MICROSOFT, https://www.skype.com/en/features/skype-translator/.

[63] *Airpods*, APPLE, https://www.apple.com/airpods/.

[64] *How Big Tech Is Battling To Own The $49B Voice Market*, CBINSIGHTS (Feb. 13, 2019), https://www.cbinsights.com/research/facebook-amazon-microsoft-google-apple-voice/.

is a system that makes decisions based on conscious or semi-conscious reasoning[65]), nevertheless, AI chatbots technology will bridge the gap between businesses and customers.

The most popular AI-based voice computing platforms are Amazon's Alexa, Microsoft's Cortana, and Google Assistant, which are voice-activated smart speakers that answer questions addressed to them. Almost everyone using smartphones today knows the drill of "OK Google, tell me (question)...." The ability to ask a question in simple language and immediately receive an educated response was the aspiration of a British academician in the late 1990s, William Turnstall-Pedoe, who thereafter sought to make it a reality.[66] Although initially beset by occasional answers to queries that were in error, nevertheless, each of the firms constantly is improving the data base to improve its performance. For example, Alexa automatically analyzes, on a monthly basis, the numerous requests for particular questions posed.[67] It is now being trained to recognize the voices of persons making inquiries which will extend to all of Amazon's Echo devices.[68]

Chatbots still are deficient by their generation of inappropriate responses, their interpretation of user requests, and by their errors in retrieval of the requested information. It has been suggested that chatbots should utilize *human computation* (human-aided bots) which would provide more flexibility and robustness when compared to rule-based algorithms and machine learning. They are already used extensively by many thousands of persons, e.g., Facebook M in California. The merger of human input with machines appears to be a growing trend as evidenced by the significant growth of *cobot* (cooperative robots working with humans) in China.[69] A fear that some authors have expressed is: "Who controls the narrative?" In the case of a one-party state such as China or where the company in democratic countries is in possession and control

---

[65] Roman Trusov, *What is the best AI bot?*, QUORA, https://www.quora.com/What-is-the-best-AI-bot.

[66] James Vlahos, *Alexa, I Want Answers*, WIRED (March 2019), at 58–67.

[67] Ruhi Sarikaya, *How Alexa Learns*, SCIENTIFIC AMERICAN (March 6, 2019), https://blogs.scientificamerican.com/observations/how-alexa-learns/.

[68] Ry Crist, *Amazon's Alexa can now recognize your voice*, CNET (Oct. 11, 2017), https://www.cnet.com/news/amazons-alexa-can-now-recognize-your-voice/.

[69] Pavel Kucherbaev, Alessandro Bozzon, and Geert-Jan Houben, *Human-Aided Bots*, IEEE COMPUTING EDGE (March, 2019), at 33–39.

of the information, the question arises to what extent they may manipulate facts to the detriment of the populace.[70]

## Employment: Impact of AI Automation

The effect of AI on employment unquestionably will be profound both positively and negatively. McKinsey Global Institute estimates that one-half of all activities humans are engaged in could be automated with technologies already in existence, albeit less than 5 percent can be fully automated. A third of the activities in 60 percent of occupations may be automated. Whether or not automation will take place on a massive scale is subject to a number of factors such as the costs in the substitution of AI for human-based work, quality and quantity of labor and wages affected thereto, benefits of automation, regulatory factors, and social acceptance.[71] Up to 370 million people worldwide in advanced economies, whose jobs are expected to disappear, may bring about major disruptions, albeit job losses will vary country by country. The workers most affected are the less educated. More time will be spent on activities whereby machines have less capability than human persons such as the management of people, application of expertise programs, and communication with other persons. Conversely, jobs requiring physical labor will likely be accomplished by machines.[72]

In the U.S., the Washington-based Brookings Institution, in its January 2019 Report,[73] found that middle-wage jobs have diminished with changes in employment, in part due to AI replacing jobs with repetitive task content. Both high-end and low-end jobs experienced wage increases

[70] Vlahos, *supra* at note 118 at 67.

[71] James Manyika, Susan Lund, Michael Chui, Jacques Bughin, Jonathan Woetzel, Parul Batra, Ryan Ko, Saurabh Sanghvi, *Jobs Lost, Jobs Gained: Workforce Transitions in a Time of Automation*, MCKINSEY GLOBAL INSTITUTE (Dec. 2017), at 2. https://www.mckinsey.com/~/media/mckinsey/featured%20insights/future%20of%20organizations/what%20the%20future%20of%20work%20will%20mean%20for%20jobs%20skills%20and%20wages/mgi%20jobs%20lost-jobs%20gained_report_december%202017.ashx.

[72] *Id.* at 6–16.

[73] Mark Muro, Robert Maxim, and Jacob Whiton, *Automation and Artificial Intelligence: How machines are affecting people and places*, BROOKINGS (Jan. 2019), https://www.brookings.edu/research/automation-and-artificial-intelligence-how-machines-affect-people-and-places/.

and mid-level positions having stagnated or diminished. The Report found that while automation will affect almost all occupational groups, nevertheless, the overall impact on total employment will be muted. The impact of automation in future decades will vary across occupations but will have the most effect on the lower wage, lower-educated workforce. It will also vary among the states with states having higher educated workforce faring much better than the "Heartland" (American Midwest) states which are characterized by the greatest percentage of routine work positions that are readily replaceable by automation.[74] Examples from the above sources illustrate the division that will take place in the next two decades. It is expected that 91 percent of food preparation will be fully automated by robotic food processing but only 8 percent for those employed in software development. Half of all jobs presently accomplished by young persons between the ages of 16–24 can be automated in the said time frame while a lesser percentage (40 percent) of tasks by older workers will suffer the same fate. Hispanic, Native American, and African-American workers will be more affected by automation than Caucasian workers (about 45 percent vs. 40 percent).[75] In Chap. 6 we will explore the issue of substitution of workers by automation in greater depth.

## Workplace Environment and Human Resources

As stated above, new inventions create winners and losers in the workplace. Advances in technology, which are inevitable, cause major changes in the workplace leading to layoffs of numerous employees but on the other hand also create equal or often even greater positions for those employees willing and able to adapt to the new environments. AI has and will profoundly affect the workplace with respect to hiring and retention of new employees. Issues arise concerning evident biases, errors, or skewed questionnaires by human resources (HR) interviewers, relations among

---

[74] *Id.*, at 29–37.

[75] Tom Simonite, *Robots Will Take Jobs From Men, the Young, and Minorities*, WIRED (Jan. 24, 2019), https://hawaiidigest.science.blog/2019/01/24/wired-magazine-latest-technology-news-24-25-jan-2019/.

employees and with their supervisors, conformity to governmental regulations, and other issues. In play are a variety of programs to assist HR personnel and managers to properly and effectively perform their duties.

HR can benefit from using AI in a number of ways. According to one author, HR can take advantage from the new technology in candidate screening, candidate engagement, candidate re-engagement, post-offer acceptance, new hire onboarding, career development, employee relations, HR compliance and case management, and scheduling.[76] Some of the numerous AI programs and formats are discussed hereafter.

According to statistics compiled by Pymetrics, HR hiring personnel perform poorly in evaluating prospective employees for positions within a company. In general, hiring practices are 70 percent ineffective, biased half of the time, and 83 percent of candidates interviewed rate their experiences as poor. Almost half of all candidates never received a response to their request for positions within the company. Accordingly, the said firm has received noteworthy praise from the New York Times, The Economist, the Financial Times, and the Wall Street Journal. It has been prominent in assisting HR managers and senior managers to engage in bias-free hiring. It does so using AI by having existing employees play pymetrics neuroscience games, analyze trait data and trends, build customized algorithms representing success audits for bias, and has candidates for positions play other pertinent games to match their opportunities. The neuroscience games are based on collective objective behavioral data which uses exercises proven to be the gold standard of neuroscience research. The games maximize prediction and increase efficiency through customized but automated machine learning algorithms, removal of bias from algorithms by iterative algorithm auditing process, and possibly matching rejected candidates to other firms for their services.[77]

---

[76] A summary of the ways may be found in a number of websites. Some of the categories stated herein are from Jessica Miller-Merrell, *9 Ways to Use Artificial Intelligence in Recruiting and HR*, WORKOLOGY (Oct. 27, 2016), https://workology.com/artificial-intelligence-recruiting-human-resources/.

[77] *Pymetrics*, https://www.pymetrics.com/employers/. For a discussion, see Josh Constine, *Pymetrics attacks discrimination in hiring with AI and recruiting games*, TECHCRUNCH (Sept. 20, 2017), https://techcrunch.com/2017/09/20/unbiased-hiring/.

There are many search firms that have arisen which are utilizing AI programs, particularly deep learning analyses such as ZipRecuiter and Eightfold. Eightfold claims it has experienced an 80 percent decrease in cost, low costs and turnover.[78] Nevertheless, a number of problems may cause the selection process to be skewed. There is the possibility of "gaming" by prospective employees who are aware that certain key words are looked for by AI algorithms while the opposite result occurs for otherwise excellent potential candidates who fail to insert relevant wording. There is also the problem of lower wages for prospective employees because the employer has a greater selection of candidates to choose from for the particular talent needed. AI programs may include many millions of data to suggest potential candidates, particularly as candidates' performances are fed back to the referral companies, giving hiring personnel even greater analytic capability. The programs are less effective for non-traditional jobs where data is less abundant.[79]

Humanyze employs analytics and breakthroughs in behavioral science, organizational network analysis, and advanced computing power to improve the performance of employees, e.g., by experimenting with ID badges to track how employees interact with each other and how work is performed. Its analysis is based on a decade of MIT Media Lab Research to assist on digital performance, the impact of decisions on the firm's business, and their impact of the interventions in real-time.[80] Textio is a firm that specializes in augmented writing, aids companies in creating ads based on massive amounts of data from companies in diverse industries globally, and uses its predictive engine based on AI to uncover meaningful patterns in language. It thereby assists companies to engage in better communication and better business outcomes. Companies that apply augmented AI programs create a learning loop that delivers insights of the world at one's desktop which are utilized, e.g., in attracting more diverse candidates for employee and managerial positions.[81] Intel employs

---

[78] *Talent Intelligence Platform*, EIGHTFOLD, https://eightfold.ai/.

[79] Noam Scheiber, *A.I as Talent Scout: Unorthodox Hires, and Maybe Lower Pay*, NEW YORK TIMES (Dec. 6, 2016), https://www.nytimes.com/2018/12/06/business/economy/artificial-intelligence-hiring.html?utm_source=outbrain&utm_medium=paid&utm_campaign=nyt.

[80] *Humanyse*, https://www.humanyze.com/.

[81] *Textio*, https://textio.com/.

AI for many purposes—for HR, it expands its power to match employees to a variety of alternate positions so as to have better retention of the employees.[82]

The "big-4" accounting firm of Deloitte has a number of divisions devoted to the workplace environment including consulting and human capital services. It claims that it matches humans with machines to make output much more efficient thereby resulting in substantial lessening of time for performance and costs thereof. Among the AI-based programs are contract reviews in coordination with machine-learning developer Kira systems. The program enables the scanning of thousands of pages of complex documents for analysis of particular sought data such as risks, suppliers dealt with, counter-parties, and the like.[83] The Kira system imports documents in any of 60 formats, processes them into machine-ready format, and employs machine-ready models to identify the concepts and clauses identified by the user. It searches and reviews, edits the documents for the client in real-time, provides analysis including risk assessments, and then creates and exports custom summary charts and summaries of data points.[84]

## Marketing

AI has been especially useful in marketing. A number of websites illustrate the many ways in which AI is utilized in marketing products and services to consumers.[85] Discussed hereafter are some of the cited ways in which AI formulates a major aspect of a firm's marketing strategy.

[82] *Intel*, https://www.intel.ai/#gs.mNytqPJs. This segment is based upon the discussion in Fortune Magazine, *supra* at note 54 at 99.

[83] Dom Nicastro, *8 Examples of Artificial Intelligence (AI) in the Workplace*, CMS WIRE (Dec. 7, 2017), https://www.cmswire.com/digital-workplace/8-examples-of-artificial-intelligence-ai-in-the-workplace/. A number of examples given in this segment were taken in part from the article.

[84] *How Kira Works*, KIRA, https://kirasystems.com/how-it-works/.

[85] See, e.g., Robert Allen, *15 Applications of Artificial Intelligence in Marketing*, SMART INSIGHTS (May 2, 2017), https://www.smartinsights.com/managing-digital-marketing/marketing-innovation/15-applications-artificial-intelligence-marketing/; and Ben Davis, *15 examples of artificial intelligence in marketing*, ECONSULTANCY (April 14, 2016), https://econsultancy.com/15-examples-of-artificial-intelligence-in-marketing/.

*Advertising. Advertising* is making known to potential and current customers a particular product or service through various forms of media while *marketing* of a product or service is more generic and encompasses a wide range of activities that includes advertising, promotions, and public relations.[86] AI has altered the face of advertising through developments in natural language progressing, logo recognition, and other technologies that permit vast quanta of data to be organized, segmented, and made ready instantaneously. GoogleAdWords is AI-based that permits anyone to create its own ads by specifying in three short sentences: (1) What is best about the advertiser's business? (2) Set budget caps; and (3) To whom the product or service is to given? The questions and responses then appear on Google Search and Maps, which later can be altered for improved marketing.[87] Advertisers' targeting ad messages have been enhanced by deep learning which enables significant cost savings and greater results by understanding particular users' behavior. Thus, rather than a scattered approach often seen on televisions and magazine advertisements, AI enables the advertiser to promote ads directed at more likely users of the products or services.[88]

*Website Design*[89] Whereas designing a website ordinarily could cost several or many thousands of dollars depending on their complexity, new startups, such as Grid,[90] Responsive Grid, and Wix, have used AI algorithms to initiate designs in minutes by responding to questions regarding the nature of the business and type of website desired. Based on the responses, a website can be generated in as little as two minutes and is ideally suited to new firms that have little financial backing.[91] For example, Responsive Grid enables the customer to determine the number of

---

[86] Carter McNamara, *Definitions*, FREE MANAGEMENT LIBRARY, https://managementhelp.org/marketing/advertising/defined.htm.

[87] *Google Ads*, https://www.wordstream.com/articles/what-is-google-adwords.

[88] Ben Davis, *supra* at note 137.

[89] The topical headings and guidance were taken in part by the above cited applications and, particularly, Sophia Bernazzani, *AI in Marketing: 10 Early Use Cases*, HUBSPOT (July 28, 2017), https://blog.hubspot.com/marketing/ai-marketing-use-cases.

[90] *Grid*, https://thegrid.io/.

[91] For a discussion, see, Harold Stark, *Worlds Collide: Artificial Intelligence Meets Web Design*, HUFFPOST (Dec. 6, 2017), https://www.huffingtonpost.com/harold-stark/worlds-collide-artificial_b_11664470.html.

columns and width desired, insert content to automatically fit the grid, and connect with existing HTML (Hypertext Markup File) and CSS (Cascading Style Sheets) without any mathematical background possessed by the owner of the site.[92]

*Content Creation. Content* is information derived from oral, written, performance, or other medium. *Content creation* is the transmission of the said information in a variety of formats to end users such as by websites, blogging, digitally, photography, and other such means.[93] Tools for developing content creation include Wordsmith and Quill. According to its website, Wordsmith is a natural language generation platform that transforms data into a narrative speedily and scale. Examples of use are client communications, video game narratives, football recapitulation, and other applications. It enables users such as the Associated Press and Forbes to create clickable news content that appears to have been human generated.[94] Quill likewise provides content visually or in written format in 40 languages including updating and refining content.[95]

*Content Curation. Content curation* is defined as a process of selection by individuals or firms (curators) by means of a particular form of communication relating to a particular topic. We have all experienced, often with the wonder of understanding by external forces, our preferences whether it be the selection of movies, travel, or the many other favorite areas. For example, when viewing a movie selection on Netflix or seeking information on the Internet of a travel destination or mode of transportation, we note the suggestions of other comparable movies to be viewed or travel to the particular location previously downloaded. It is by means of AI-based IBM Watson that enables sponsors of the sites to offer suggestions to consumers or other persons. The methodology used to enable content curation is by *collaborative filtering* (predictions based on prior selection—used by Amazon and You Tube), *semantic analysis* (based on

---

[92] *Responsive Grid System*, http://www.responsivegridsystem.com/.
[93] *Content Creation*, WIKIPEDIA, https://en.wikipedia.org/wiki/Content_creation.
[94] *Wordsmith*, https://automatedinsights.com/wordsmith/. Discussion in part is taken from Sophia Bernazzani, *supra* at note 141.
[95] *Quill*, https://www.quillcontent.com/services.

words or sources of information), or *social rating* (based on ratings or recommendations of prior users, e.g., Facebook).[96] Firms, such as Affectiva, employ computer vision, speech analytics, learning, decoding facial expressions of millions of persons, and large quanta of data to gain emotional insight for business firms concerning potential customers' preferences.[97]

## Search Engines

When writing this volume this author made innumerable requests for information from Google by inserting a particular word, expression, or concept to which many possible sites were then offered for download- ing. One could misspell, insert inexact wording and the like, and yet, surprisingly, most often receive the information or sources sought. This is accomplished by Google's use of the AI system, beginning in April 2015, called RankBrain, an algorithmic learning system which uses machine learning that embeds vast amounts of words and expressions. It then responds to search inquiries containing the said or similar words by guessing what information the inquirer is seeking. For example, if one were to type "artificial intelligence" RankBrain offers numerous suggestions ranging from Wikipedia to PDF articles and other offerings which discuss the topic. It also responds in many languages globally.[98] Additional comparable search engines include Amazon Echo, Google Home, Apple's Siri, and Microsoft's Cortana, which enable the user to download information required by a voice command or by pressing the "Enter" key on a computer.[99]

---

[96] *Content Curation*, WIKIPEDIA, https://en.wikipedia.org/wiki/Content_curation.

[97] *Affectiva*, https://www.affectiva.com/.

[98] For a discussion, see, Kristine Schachinger, *A Complete Guide to the Google RankBrain Algorithm*, SEARCH ENGINE JOURNAL (SEJ) (Dec. 14, 2017, https://www.searchenginejournal.com/google-algorithm-history/rankbrain/.

[99] Bernazzani, *supra* at note 141.

# Image Recognition

Mostly everyone has viewed or heard of Snapchat which permits the sharing of photos, short videos, as well as enables the user to filter, alter, limit use, and even send and receive money through the use of neural networks that recognizes and identifies shapes and faces. Other firms, which perform similar or comparable services, include Facebook, Google Photos, and DuLight. Baidu offers high quality lighting and also uses technologies in deep learning, image recognition, and speech recognition to help visually impaired people to identify people and objects in their lives.[100] Instagram also offers taking, sharing, and editing of photos.[101]

# Entertainment and Consumer Usages

The possibilities for home and external entertainment by use of algorithms are almost endless. For example, in Hamburg, Germany, a new $843 million concert hall has a central auditorium which consists of a *parametric design*, i.e., "a process by which designers use algorithms to develop an object's form" in order to create a unique shape for the 10,000 gypsum panels that constitutes the ceiling, walls, and balustrades of the auditorium.[102] On a more practical home use of AI, machine learning has created new spices and altered other spices to make them more tasteful. For example, basil plants were created in hydroponic[103] units in modified shipping containers in Massachusetts based on MIT's machine learning algorithms that incorporated ideal growing conditions for basil plants. The tests are undertaken to optimize plant yield and properties especially when plants are grown in greenhouses.[104]

---

[100] *Baidu, DuLight*, www.dulights.com.

[101] *Instagram*, https://www.instagram.com/.

[102] Elizabeth Stinson, *What Happens When Algorithms Design a Concert Hall? The Stunning Elbphilharmonie*, WIRED (Jan. 12, 2017), https://www.wired.com/2017/01/happens-algorithms-design-concert-hall-stunning-elbphilharmonie/.

[103] Hydroponics is a method of growing plants in water without soil using mineral nutrient solutions. *Hydroponics*, WIKIPEDIA, https://en.wikipedia.org/wiki/Hydroponics.

[104] Will Knight, *Machine learning is making pesto even more delicious*, MIT TECHNOLOGY REVIEW (April 3, 2019), https://www.technologyreview.com/s/613262/machine-learning-is-making-pesto-even-more-delicious/.

## Law Firms

AI will affect law firms as other professional endeavors. Among the applications are the review of documents wherein thousands of documents could readily be examined in a short time frame, e.g., when performing due diligence and other endeavors especially for mergers and acquisitions, thereby eliminating the need for hundreds of hours of examination by a considerable number of attorneys. The cost savings to the business entities involved would be quite extensive. AI could be used to look for evidence of employment discrimination; search for anomalies in corporate documents; predict outcome of cases based on comparing key details to many thousands of other cases; increase competition among firms; and other uses.[105] For example, ROSS intelligence, which consists of AI specialists and attorneys, is able to enhance substantially the speed in conducting research of new and old cases, unique factual situations, and other issues that law firms typically handle but allegedly with much greater rapidity and accuracy thereby saving clients and law firms time and money.[106] Other purposes, which AI may offer law firms and their clients substantial advantages, include automation of divorce cases; risk assessment; freedom for attorneys to perform higher end services and analyses; engagement with clients more attentively; be creative; and permit more social interactions rather than being compelled to perform mundane, time-consuming low-end work.[107]

---

[105] James Watkins, *Why Artificial Intelligence Might Replace Your Lawyer*, OZY (Feb. 10, 2017), https://www.ozy.com/fast-forward/why-artificial-intelligence-might-replace-your-lawyer/75435.

[106] *Exceed Expectations*, ROSS INTELLIGENCE, http://rossintelligence.com/. For a listing of some of the advantages and uses of AI for law firms, see Bernard Marr, *How AI and Machine Learning are Transforming Law Firms and the Legal Sector*, FORBES (May 23, 2018), https://www.forbes.com/sites/bernardmarr/2018/05/23/how-ai-and-machine-learning-are-transforming-law-firms-and-the-legal-sector/.

[107] Avaneesh Marwaha, *Seven Benefits of Artificial Intelligence for Law Firms*, LAW TECHNOLOGY TODAY (July 13, 2017), https://www.lawtechnologytoday.org/2017/07/seven-benefits-artificial-intelligence-law-firms/.

## Accounting

The "big 4"[108] accounting firms have all incorporated or are pursuing the addition of AI, as well as blockchain, to their practices. They are using AI to analyze large volumes of data, particularly for large corporate clients, at much greater speed with far less need for accountants to do "grunt" work. Deloitte auditors are accessing AI tools with natural language capabilities to comprehend and interpret for its clients, numerous contracts, deeds, leases, and other data effectively, all at a lower cost. The firm is enabled to speedily conduct accurate assessments of large real estate holdings and contracts and render risk assessments thereto.[109] Additional uses include discovery of fraud, e.g., concerning invoices, emails, instant messaging, and voicemail, and for regulatory compliance. The barriers affecting widespread use include lack of talent in AI to assist auditors, immaturity of existing platforms, bias, and possible overregulation.[110]

The technologies being utilized are NLP and robotic process automation that enable auditors to decrease the time required for tax preparation, auditing, and consultation to hours rather than weeks using human capital. The firms are devoting significant resources in developing additional tools to better serve their clients' worldwide. AI permits the incorporation of regulatory changes to existing leases that are much more efficient, speedier, and consistent than by non-AI methods. AI is especially useful for mergers and acquisitions that involve hundreds of millions of data concerning non-standardized accounts payable, for uncovering anomalies in corporate payments of credit card charges and other forms of payments, and for detection of questionable payments in

---

[108] The four largest accounting firms are: Deloitte Touche Tohmatsu Limited (Deloitte), PricewaterhouseCoopers (PwC), Ernst & Young (E&Y), and Klynveld Peat Marwick Goerdeler (KPMG).

[109] Sarah Ovaska-Few, *How artificial intelligence is changing accounting*, AICPA (Oct. 10, 2017), https://www.journalofaccountancy.com/newsletters/2017/oct/artificial-intelligence-changing-accounting.html.

[110] *What are the barriers top organizations adopting AI technology more quickly?* and *What risks should businesses consider when looking to implement AI?*, ERNST & YOUNG, https://www.ey.com/gl/en/issues/business-environment/ey-innovation-matters-putting-artificial-intelligence-to-work/.

violation of the Foreign Corrupt Practices Act.[111] IBM's Watson, which relies on NLP to comprehend data submitted to it, is being used by H&R Block to assist tax professionals for tax preparation. Cloud-based accounting software, grounded on machine learning systems, assist in assuring that clients' incorrectly coded entries are properly entered. The machine learning process is premised upon prior invoice coding behavior, errors and mistakes therein, and the significant amount of data entered from the many clients of the firm.[112]

It appears beyond question that AI will be a dominant factor in the manner in which the accounting profession will perform its services. AI will assist accountants to perform their services more accurately, efficiently, and at a lower cost to their clients. It is thus incumbent upon the profession and, more particularly, the colleges and universities preparing students for the accounting and finance professions, to be open and adaptable to the major changes taking place within the profession, understand that AI is a tool that will enhance the accuracy and efficiency of their services, and to modify existing old standards for professional recognition to the new realities.[113]

A downside to AI is the cost for its implementation by smaller accounting firms. The problem of AI generally is the lack of AI skills demanded of accountants generally thereby necessitating the services of AI savvy persons to assist. The problem is the near total lack of persons having the said skills, which currently are scarce commodities. An additional issue that arises is whether accountants will be totally replaced by AI. For the foreseeable future, accountants will be compelled to conduct in depth analyses of their clients' business and tax issues which AI is not able to accomplish. As in other types of uses, it appears, at the present time, that AI is a tool for accountants rather than an overall replacement for their services. Nevertheless, even though only larger accounting firms are able

---

[111] Adelyn Zhou, *Artificial Intelligence For Tax and Accounting*, FORBES (Nov. 14, 2017), https://www.forbes.com/sites/adelynzhou/2017/11/14/ey-deloitte-and-pwc-embrace-artificial-intelligence-for-tax-and-accounting/#48d321013498.

[112] Ryan Watson, *Accounting for AI*, INSIGHT (Summer, 2017) https://www.icpas.org/information/copy-desk/insight/article/summer-2017/accounting-for-ai.

[113] *Artificial intelligence and the future of accountancy*, ICAEW, https://www.icaew.com/-/media/corporate/files/technical/information-technology/technology/artificial-intelligence-report.ashx?la=en.

cost-wise to utilize AI, there are services that have arisen to serve the needs of smaller firms. A German firm, Smacc, utilizes AI to assist these firms to automate their accounting systems and financial reporting whereby clients submit their receipts which are converted into machine readable form. Its software uses 60 data points to review the receipts and invoices, and further applies the value added tax (VAT—applicable to businesses doing business in Europe) to the appropriate invoices.[114]

## Military and National Security

In a major study commenced on behalf of DARPA by the Belfer Center for Science and International Affairs of the Harvard Kennedy School[115] concerning advances in machine learning and AI, the authors noted that the goals of the technology are: "preserving U.S. technological leadership, supporting peaceful and commercial use, and mitigating catastrophic risk."[116] The findings concluded: AI has advanced much further than anticipated which will accelerate rapidly; the private sector has funded research much more than the government; and machine learning could greatly enhance the degrees of automation in labor-intensive activities such as satellite imagery analysis and cyber defense which has the potential to be a transformative national security technology that is as crucial as nuclear weapons, aircraft, and computers. Accordingly, AI will deeply affect national security by changes in the three areas of: (1) military superiority, (2) information superiority, and (3) economic superiority. The fear that deeply concerns national security is that "weak" (underdeveloped or lacking in governmental oversight) states and non-state actors may acquire access to long-range strike capability and the ability to engage in forgery and truth concealment.[117]

---

[114] Dennis Najjar, *Is Artificial Intelligence (AI) the Future of Accounting?*, THE BALANCE SMALL BUSINESS (July 15, 2018), https://www.thebalancesmb.com/is-artificial-intelligence-the-future-of-accounting-4083182.

[115] Greg Allen and Taniel Chan, *Artificial Intelligence and National Security*, HARVARD U. BELFER CENTER FOR SCIENCE AND INT'L AFFAIRS (July, 2017), https://www.belfercenter.org/sites/default/files/files/publication/AI%20NatSec%20-%20final.pdf.

[116] *Id.*, Project Overview (unpaged).

[117] *Id.* at 2–3.

The authors of the study suggest three goals for the protection of national security, namely, (1) *preserve* U.S. technological leadership by conducting AI-focused war games to identify potential disruptive innovations; fund diverse long-term strategic analyses of AI technology; prioritize AI R&D spending; and invest heavily in counter-AI defenses; (2) *support* peaceful use of the technology by increased funding of certain U.S. agencies engaged in AI and promote collaboration with industry; and (3) *manage* catastrophic risks by restrictions of AI applications via treaties with other countries; establish AI-safety organizations; fund fail-safe and safety-for-performance technology for AI systems; and explore technological options for countering AI-enabled forgery.[118]

An example of AI as the basis of military use is Project Maven that has captivated the attention of the U.S. Department of Defense (DoD). At a Defense One Tech Summit in Washington D.C. in April, 2017, the discussion focused on how to deploy the Mayhem Cyber

Reasoning System. DoD is integrating *field advanced computer algorithms*, defined as a set of rules to be followed during problem-solving operations onto government platforms to decode objects from the massive amount of moving or still imagery data. Project Maven, which is overseen by an Algorithmic Warfare Functional Team, integrates AI and machine learning to counteract the increased military capabilities of adversaries and competitors. The work to be accomplished includes triaging and labeling data so that algorithms could be trained, cleaned up, and labeled to prepare it for machine learning.[119] The Project marks the first use by the DoD to deploy deep learning and neural networks for use in combat.[120]

There are numerous other military uses projected by DARPA for current and future use. Among them are: a Universal Reading System that can read any natural text and apply the knowledge; combine natural

---

[118] *Id.* at 5–6.

[119] Cheryl Pellerin, *Project Maven to Deploy Computer Algorithms to War Zone by Year's End*, U.S. DEPT. OF DEFENSE (July 21, 2017), https://dod.defense.gov/News/Article/Article/1254719/project-maven-to-deploy-computer-algorithms-to-war-zone-by-years-end/.

[120] Gregory C. Allen, *Project Maven brings AI to the fight against ISIS*, BULLETIN OF THE ATOMIC SCIENTISTS (Dec. 21, 2017), https://thebulletin.org/2017/12/project-maven-brings-ai-to-the-fight-against-isis/.

language and AI; insert radar Apache Longbow on helicopters that can determine whether an attack is taking place; autopilot planes that can act offensively and defensively without human crew being placed in danger; implement the Automated Scheduling and Planning Environment System (ASPEN) that enables scientists to engage in data mining; an AI data synchronization software package, ScoutWare, that connects terminals from one location to ongoing naval vessels; a *snakebot* (snakelike robot) to penetrate inaccessible areas; and numerous other AI uses.[121]

A much more likely beneficial use of AI for the military is military intelligence. By use of NLP and machine learning, AI enables a better warning system; gathers intelligence regarding possible cyber threats and other forms of cyber warfare; monitors machine and human activities; determines effectiveness of military operations; greatly assists in intelligence gathering; provides in-depth training in AI systems; and other uses.[122] An interesting DARPA research project is the study of how insects use intelligence for survival. It posted a research project opportunity by "inviting submissions of innovative basic research concepts exploring new computational frameworks and strategies drawn from the impressive computational capabilities of very small flying insects.... Nature has forced on these small insects' drastic miniaturization and energy efficiency, some having only a few hundred neurons in a compact form-factor, while maintaining basic functionality.... Furthermore, these organisms are possibly able to display increased subjectivity of experience, which extends simple look-up table responses to potentially AI-relevant problem solving." It added. "This research could lead to capability of inference, prediction, generalization and abstraction of problems in systematic or entirely new ways in order to find solutions to compelling problems."[123]

[121] Zarnigar Altaf, *AI Application in Military*, SCRIBD, https://www.scribd.com/doc/109329863/AI-application-in-Military.

[122] Mary Beth Ainsworth, *13 Ways to Use AI in Military Intelligence*, SAS BLOGS (Feb. 1, 2018), https://blogs.sas.com/content/sascom/2018/02/01/13-ways-use-ai-military-intelligence/.

[123] Tom O'Connor, *U.S. Military is Building Smarter Robots and Thinks Insects Might Be Key to New Artificial Intelligence*, NEWSWEEK (Jan. 20, 2019), https://www.newsweek.com/us-military-robots-insects-artificial-intelligence-micro-brain-1290804.

Future use of AI-based weaponry appears to be inevitable with persuasive arguments rendered that the U.S. must keep up with AI advances made by alleged possible enemies, albeit there is much opposition to the development by national and international organizations. Proponents of AI-based robotic machines, whether in the form of drones, soldiers, and the like, argue that such use may substantially limit casualties due to "collateral damage," i.e., to civilians caught in the throes of military combat, as well as human combat troops. Opponents, which includes persons cited previously such as Elon Musk, Stephen Hawking, and others, object to the use of fully autonomous weapons such as "killer robots" which enable destruction of targets without human intervention. Human Rights Watch has called for a pre-emptive ban on the development, production, and use of fully autonomous weapons.[124] The problem is that advancements in AI-related military use are inevitable and are being developed by China, Israel, South Korea, Russia, the U.K, and likely other nations and terrorist organizations. The fear always is that failure to take the lead in the creation of such weaponry could subject the U.S. to the mercy of countries that are its potential enemies. We will discuss further the ethical aspects AI for military usage in Chap. 4.

## Government

The ascendance of AI will necessarily impact governmental services which accumulate data far more extensively than any private concern. Thus, the need for digital government arises which necessitates training of senior and middle-level executives to respond more efficiently to the burgeoning regulatory requirements for its increasing populations. The U.S. government has already begun the process especially where security of data is vitally necessary from the prying eyes of unfriendly foreign entities and governments. It is incorporating blockchain which is, in essence, not subject to hacking and which is cost effective and quick responding. Examples are DHS' award of a contract to "Prove Integrity of Captured Data From Border Devices" and the FDA's use for real-time application for portable

---

[124] *Killer Robots*, HUMAN RIGHTS WATCH, https://www.hrw.org/topic/armas/killer-robots.

interactive devices.[125] The Defense Department is also incorporating the technology for disaster relief and, presumably, for secret military use.[126]

AI is the second digital means of providing essential government services. The Internal Revenue Service (IRS), the U.S. Customs and Border Protection, and other federal and also state agencies have already in part digitized their operations. Nevertheless, there is a call for governments to further digitize in order to meet the needs of citizens by the provision of autonomous services that ordinarily cannot be performed by the limited number of personnel in their attempt to respond to almost innumerable demands. Recommendations by Gartner include the promotion of inter-governmental interoperability solutions and platforms to deliver digital value at scale; establishment of a data-driven government transformation strategy by coupling IT and digital KPIs (key performance indicators); the need to build the organizations' knowledge and skills with respect to IoT, analytics, robotic process automation; and other current and future technologies.[127]

## Sports

AI has also entered the sports arena by providing a large quanta of data for analysis reminiscent of the famed movie *Moneyball*,[128] which related the expert use of statistics and analysis of which ballplayers to retain, how to pitch to certain opposing ballplayers, and how to build a champion major baseball team (Oakland Athletics). Today, sports teams and owners are similarly using AI to automate the industry for ticket sales, training of athletes, data analysis for decision-making, officiating by use

---

[125] Steve Delahunty, *Developments and Adoption of Blockchain in the U.S. Federal Government*, FORBES (Jan 15, 2018), https://www.forbes.com/sites/forbestechcouncil/2018/01/25/developments-and-adoption-of-blockchain-in-the-u-s-federal-government/#310bda4e3d99.

[126] Yogita Khatri, *US Defense Department Says Blockchain Can Help In Disaster Relief*, COINDESK (Dec. 27, 2018), https://www.coindesk.com/us-defense-department-says-blockchain-can-help-disaster-relief.

[127] Dean Lacheca, Rick Howard, and Rick Holgate, *Digital government 2030: Predictive Government Anticipates Citizen needs With Autonomous Services*, GARTNER (Ja. 31, 2018), https://www.gartner.com/doc/3850280/digital-government%2D%2Dpredictive-government.

[128] Moneyball, 2011 movie was based on MICHAEL LEWIS, MONEYBALL: THE ART OF WINNING AN UNFAIR GAME, W.W. Norton (2003).

of technology and cameras, determining racing infractions, health care for athletes, and as a caddy for golfers.[129] Other uses include *chatbots* (computer program conducting conversations by auditory or textual means) as virtual assistants to respond to inquiries by fans; computer vision especially in auto racing; AI-driven automation by media outlets; and wearable AI tech devices to gather data.[130]

## Prediction by Businesses

AI apps coupled with Predictive Analysis and ML algorithms can assist businesses to predict market trends; gather user data through Point-of-Sale machines; collect information such as traffic; reduce app security concerns; enhance searching and product recommendations; analyze consumer behavior; and alert customers to possible fraudulent use and threats.[131]

# Sampling of Companies Engaged in AI Use[132]

*Tesla.* Tesla is engaged in many AI-related technologies. Its Autopilot is an advanced driver-assistance program that sends directly to the cloud, is able to automatically make repairs to its software, crowdsources its data from all of its vehicles to enable it to refine its systems, educates its entire fleet of vehicles through machine learning in the cloud, shares information with other Tesla vehicles, has lane centering, self-parking, and is a pioneer in autonomous vehicles which are anticipated to become

---

[129] *Artificial Intelligence in Sports*, SPORTTECCHIE (Sept. 19, 2017), https://www.sporttechie.com/artificial-intelligence-sports/.

[130] Kumba Sennaar, *Artificial Intelligence in Sports – Current and Future Applications*, EMERG (Dec. 12, 2018), https://emerj.com/ai-sector-overviews/artificial-intelligence-in-sports/.

[131] Nitish Singh, *The Future of Artificial Intelligence: 2018 and Beyond*, DZONE (July 2, 2018), https://dzone.com/articles/future-of-artificial-intelligence-2018-and-beyond.

[132] The list used herein is from R.L. Adams, *10 Powerful Examples of Artificial Intelligence in Use Today*, FORBES (Jan. 10, 2017). https://www.forbes.com/sites/robertadams/2017/01/10/10-powerful-examples-of-artificial-intelligence-in-use-today/#7e1c2d97420d.

widespread in use in the near future.[133] Other developments that are AI-based are SpaceX, the introduction of Autopilot @.0 and its Vision system that has gathered billions of real-world driving data to create a detained 3D map of the world to enable safety and widespread use of autonomous vehicles.[134]

*Amazon.com.* Anyone who has ever made a purchase through Amazon is aware of the company's ability to gauge what would appeal to the customer. Thus, if one is selecting a particular book, Amazon then illustrates a series of books related to the purchase that may induce the customer to purchase additional items. The ability of Amazon to do so is by use of AI whereby its computers analyze a vast amount of data, then makes decisions and perform tasks that formerly was made by human intelligence. Through AI, it is able to select the requested item and have it on its way to the customer for arrival as soon as in two days with Amazon Prime Now. AI is at the heart of Amazon's operations for extraordinarily fast delivery through its "anticipatory shipping." Its Kiva robots, which move racks of merchandise to the workers for processing orders, are powered by AI. AI-powered stores have eliminated the need for cashiers by use of advanced cameras.[135]

*Alexa.* Owned and distributed by Amazon, Alexa with AI at its root is a voice-control system that permits an individual to speak to an Echo smart speaker to make a wide variety of requests from dimming lights, playing music, place orders, call for an Uber vehicle, purchase food, trivia, games, and some 25,000 other skill sets that essentially eliminates need for a phone device. A rival to Alexa is Google Home which is comparable especially for the depth of its information base.[136] Siri is Apple's

[133] Bernard Marr, *The Amazing Ways Tesla is Using Artificial Intelligence and Big Data*, FORBES (Jan. 8, 2018), https://www.forbes.com/sites/bernardmarr/2018/01/08/the-amazing-ways-tesla-is-using-artificial-intelligence-and-big-data/#6d5ef1ea4270.

[134] Charlotte Hu, *Tesla Autopilot and artificial intelligence: The unfair advantage*, TESLARATI (July 6, 2017), https://www.teslarati.com/tesla-autopilot-ai-artificial-intelligence-unfair-advantage/.

[135] Alina Selyukh, *Optimized Prime: How AI And Anticipation Power Amazon's 1-Hour Delivery*, NATIONAL PUBLIC RADIO (Nov. 21, 2018), https://www.npr.org/2018/11/21/660168325/optimized-prime-how-ai-and-anticipation-power-amazons-1-hour-deliveries.

[136] *What is Alexa? What is the Amazon echo? And should you get one?* WIRECUTTER, https://thewirecutter.com/reviews/what-is-alexa-what-is-the-amazon-echo-and-should-you-get-one/#what-can-alexa-skills-do.

version of personal assistant based on machine learning technology and is a voice-activated computer that responds to a very broad variety of questions asked.[137]

*Netflix.* A viewer downloading a movie from the numerous categories and selections therein is automatically recorded and added to billions of data gathered by the company. Through AI, suggestions are made for comparable movies to watch giving percentages of how closely the suggested movies are to the one viewed. As the database grows, its predictive capability becomes more and more accurate affording the viewer ease in making the determination whether to watch the suggested movie. Netflix uses AI algorithms, called the Dynamic Optimizer, to review each frame of a video and compress it without lessening the image quality to make it available to 190 countries worldwide wherein bandwidth issues pose problems for streaming.[138]

*Pandora.* Pandora uses the AI engine known as the Music Genome Project to customize recommendations by analyzing hundreds of attributes of songs to match the tastes of its listeners. If one selects songs by a particular artist, Pandora will suggest recommendations of comparable artists. The more feedback data Pandora receives, the better it is able to make recommendations suitable to the viewing audience. A rival alternative source of music is Spotify which also uses AI to examine 2 billion user playlists to determine those who are listening to particular playlists. It launched Discover Weekly that personalizes playlists to the listening habits of individual audience members.[139]

*Nest.* According to its website, the Nest Learning Thermostat is the first thermostat to get ENERGY STAR certified. It learns what temperature you like and builds a schedule around yours. Since 2011, the Nest Thermostat has saved billions of kWh (kilowatt) of energy in millions of homes worldwide.[140] Purchased by Google in 2014 for over $3 billion, it

---

[137] *Siri*, APPLE, https://www.apple.com/siri/.

[138] Danny Vena, *Netflix Is Using AI to Conquer the World … and Bandwidth Issues*, THE MOTLEY FOOL (March 21, 2017), https://www.fool.com/investing/2017/03/21/netflix-is-using-ai-to-conquer-the-worldand-bandwi.aspx.

[139] David Deal, *Artificial Intelligence is the Future of Music and Here's Why*, HYPEBOT, https://www.hypebot.com/hypebot/2017/04/ai-is-the-future-of-music-heres-why.html.

[140] NEST, https://nest.com/thermostats/nest-learning-thermostat/overview/.

uses AI algorithms to predict usage by the individual homeowners for day/night temperatures as they customarily use. It is voice-activated by Alexa and also has other functions and products such as Nest cameras.[141]

*Cogito.* Cogito is a company founded in 2007 that uses AI to detect and interpret social signals in human communication. Funded in part by DARPA, its technology is used in health care management by major health and insurance companies. It alleges that it delivers in-call behavioral guidance to agents and a real-time measure of customer perception for every phone conversation. The purpose is for agents to develop a better understanding and relationship with the companies' agents with their millions of customers.[142]

*Boxever.* Boxever, a company founded in 2011, uses machine learning which, according to its website, brings the most inaccessible data together to create a complete picture of a company's customers especially in the travel industry. It uses analytics to understand what they like and do not like. It makes decisions about which personalized messages to exhibit to customers, when they should be rendered, and which channels to use.[143]

# Projections of Impact of AI

## Projected Risks of AI

We discussed above the applications of AI which, in essence, state only a few of the almost innumerable applications and, thus, rewards of AI. As with any technological development and inventions, there are negative

---

[141] *Learn all about Nest Learning Thermostat,* ELPROCUS, https://www.elprocus.com/nest-thermostat-features/.

[142] *Cogito's Story,* COGITO, https://www.cogitocorp.com/company/.

[143] BOXEVER, https://www.boxever.com/.

aspects dependent on the uses made thereto. The focus is on some of the naysayers of AI.

*Negative Comments Concerning AI.* There are numerous commentators alleging positive and negative views concerning the impact of AI and whether and to what extent should AI be regulated. Some of the naysayers may come as a surprise to the reader given their contributions to the advancement of AI. For example, Elon Musk, who became extremely wealthy as an engineer and technology entrepreneur and co-founder of PayPal and as the founder and CEO of the Tesla automobile and SpaceX, warned, at a meeting of the National Governors Association in Rhode Island in July, 2017, in a response to a question about the displacement of jobs by robots, that AI will definitely do better than humans but added that "AI is a fundamental existential risk for human civilization, and I don't think people fully appreciate that" and that is "the scariest problem."[144] "I think we should be very careful about artificial intelligence. If I had to guess at what our biggest existential threat is, it's probably that…. I'm increasingly inclined to think there should be some regulatory oversight, maybe at the national and international level, just to make sure that we don't do something very foolish."[145] "The least scary future I can think of is one where we have at least democratized AI because if one company or small group of people manages to develop godlike digital superintelligence, they could take over the world…. At least when there's an evil dictator, that human is going to die. But for AI superintelligence machines, there would be no death. It would live forever and then you'd have an immortal dictator from which we can never escape."[146]

Microsoft's' Bill Gates gave both positive and negative views concerning AI's impact on society. On the one hand, he indicated that AI is the

---

[144] Camila Domonoske, *Elon Musk Warns Governors: Artificial Intelligence Poses 'Existential Risk'*, NATIONAL PUBLIC RADIO INC. (July 17, 2017), https://www.npr.org/sections/thetwo-way/2017/07/17/537686649/elon-musk-warns-governors-artificial-intelligence-poses-existential-risk.

[145] Aileen Graef, *Elon Musk: We Are "Summoning a Demon" with Artificial Intelligence*, UPI (Oct. 27, 2014, 7:50 AM), http://www.upi.com/Business_News/2014/10/27.

[146] Ryan Browne, *Elon Musk warns AI could create an 'immortal dictator from which we could never escape*, CNBC (April 6, 2018), https://www.cnbc.com/2018/04/06/elon-musk-warns-ai-could-create-immortal-dictator-in-documentary.html.

latest technology that allows us to produce a lot more goods with less labor thereby benefiting society albeit displacing workers who then can fill vacancies in other necessary services.[147] Nevertheless, he warned at a later date: "I am in the camp that is concerned about super intelligence," Gates wrote. "First the machines will do a lot of jobs for us and not be super intelligent. That should be positive if we manage it well. A few decades after that though the intelligence is strong enough to be a concern. I agree with Elon Musk and some others on this and don't understand why some people are not concerned."[148]

The famed physicist, Stephen Hawking, commented "Success in creating effective AI, could be the biggest event in the history of our civilization. Or the worst. We just don't know. So, we cannot know if we will be infinitely helped by AI, or ignored by it and side-lined, or conceivably destroyed by it....Unless we learn how to prepare for, and avoid, the potential risks, AI could be the worst event in the history of our civilization. It brings dangers, like powerful autonomous weapons, or new ways for the few to oppress the many. It could bring great disruption to our economy."[149]

Commenting on Elon Musk remarks, Oren Etzioni, an entrepreneur, professor of computer science and CEO of the Allen Institute for Artificial Intelligence, stated (1) "an A.I. system must be subject to the full gamut of laws that apply to its human operator"; (2) "an A.I. system must clearly disclose that it is not human"; and (3) "an A.I. system cannot retain or disclose confidential information with explicit approval from the source of that information."[150]

---

[147] Catherine Clifford, Bill Gates: 'AI can be our friend', CNBC Feb. 16, 2018), https://www.cnbc.com/2018/02/16/bill-gates-artificial-intelligence-is-good-for-society.html.

[148] Peter Holley, "Bill Gates on dangers of artificial intelligence: 'I don't understand why people are not concerned'," WASHINGTON POST (Jan. 29, 2015), https://www.washingtonpost.com/news/the-switch/wp/2015/01/28/bill-gates-on-dangers-of-artificial-intelligence-dont-understand-why-some-people-are-not-concerned/?utm_term=.9a9bb2de4a42.

[149] Arjun Kharpal, Stephen Hawking says AI could be 'worst event in the history of our civilization', CNBS (Nov. 6, 2017), https://www.cnbc.com/2017/11/06/stephen-hawking-ai-could-be-worst-event-in-civilization.html.

[150] Oren Etzioni, How to Regulate Artificial Intelligence, NEW YORK TIMES (Sept. 1, 2017), https://www.nytimes.com/2017/09/01/opinion/artificial-intelligence-regulations-rules.html.

Other commentators espouse the view that AI will be exceptionally difficult to regulate. One scholar, John Danaher,[151] who also noted the negative views of Elon Musk and Bill Gates, observed that there are three main arguments illustrating the difficulty of regulating AI, namely, (1) *The Definitional Argument* which holds that a regulatory regime cannot be effective absent a clear definition of the meaning of AI; (2) *The Ex Post Facto Argument: Liability Gaps and Control Problems* which discusses the foreseeability problem that AI poses for traditional standards of legal liability given that AI systems act autonomously and creatively; and (3) *The Ex Ante Argument: Discreetness, Diffuseness, and Discreteness and Opacity* whereby AI R&D operates outside visible structures available to regulators; the researchers are located in many jurisdictions; and the hardware may run afoul of intellectual property rights.

In Matthew Scherer's article, "Regulating Artificial Intelligence Systems,"[152] he cites a leading introductory textbook on AI, Stuart Russell and Peter Norvig's *Artificial Intelligence: A Modern Approach*,[153] which posits eight different definitions of AI organized into four categories: (1) thinking humanly, (2) acting humanly, (3) thinking rationally, and (4) acting rationally. The first two categories, thinking and acting humanly, were commonly posed by commentators, including Alan Turing, because they mimic human capabilities albeit may also surpass them as illustrated by the IBM chess victory over two famed chess players. Currently, the views have tended toward thinking and acting rationally inasmuch as machines are goal oriented.[154]

Although the quotes of Elon Musk, Stephen Hawking, and Bill Gates appear ominous, nevertheless, a founder of the Asilomar Conference, Max Tegmark, which took place in January, 2017, stated some of the

---

[151] John Danaher, *Is effective regulation of AI possible? Eight potential regulatory problems*, INSTITUTE FOR ETHICS AND EMERGING TECHNOLOGIES (Sept. 27, 2018), https//ieet.org/index. php/IEET2/more/Danaher20180927.

[152] Matthew U. Scherer, Regulating Artificial Intelligence Systems: Risks, Challenges, Competencies, and Strategies, 29 HARVARD J. of LAW & TECHNOLOGY No. 2 (Spring, 2016), https:// papers.ssrn.com/sol3/papers.cfm?abstract_id=2609777.

[153] Stuart J. Russell and Peter Norvig, ARTIFICIAL INTELLIGENCE: A MODERN APPROACH 1034 (3rd ed. 2010).

[154] Danaher, *supra*, note 204.

comments were made out of context, particularly those of Elon Musk.[155] The Conference was sponsored by the Future of Life Institute in which almost all of the leading AI researchers, including Elon Musk, are members who took part in discussions concerning ethics and related issues to assure that AI technological developments create the future as beneficial as possible. At the conclusion of the Conference, the Asilomar Principles were agreed upon which set forth guidelines to "help and empower people [concerning AI] in the decades and centuries ahead." The Principles are set forth in Appendix B.

A control problem, as highlighted by Bill Gates and Elon Musk, is whether AI can be regulated by humans particularly on a global basis. The ex-ante (before the fact) argument is AI research and development may occur without regulators having an awareness and may be so diffuse as to pose jurisdictional problems concerning which governmental entities may regulate and enforce. There are issues of proprietary ownership and AI systems that tend to be much more opaque (muddy) than other intellectual advancements.[156]

The attempt to predict the future is most often a fool's errand particularly in the present era when technological progression is occurring at an exponential pace. Various commentators have delved into the mire. It is safer to conceive of the technologies that will dominate AI within the year. One commentator listed AI technologies to dominate 2019 and shortly thereafter. They are: (1) face detection, (2) AI chatbots, and (3) image and voice recognition. With respect to *face detection*, AI coupled with deep learning features will enable recognition of faces within 98 percent accuracy. Companies have commenced using Image Recognition technology for security-based and tracking apps to verify faces, which technology may soon be used for credit card payments without the need to swipe cards in the store mechanism. The discussion is elaborated upon in Chap. 4.

---

[155] MAX TEGMARK, *Life 3.0: Being Human in the Age of Artificial Intelligence*, VINTAGE BOOKS, 2017 at 322.

[156] Danaher, *supra*, note 204.

We began our text by examining AI as a disruptive technology. We then proceeded to discuss the types of AI and its subfields. In this chapter we examined some of the almost infinite number of applications of AI and discussed the risks and some of the companies engaged in AI development and application. We now turn to U.S. government policies, especially the initiatives of the past two presidents and their executive departments.

# 3

# AI U.S. Policies and Regulations

The U.S. is especially aware of the incredible possibilities, the impending transformation of society, and the dangers that may arise as a result of AI, particularly from the perceived risks and threats from its major competitive nation-states such as China and Russia. The People's Republic of China (China), in particular, has taken enormous strides in its attempt to overcome its deficit AI standing in relation to the U.S. as stated hereafter in Chap. 8. The last two presidents, from President Barack Obama and continuing under President Donald Trump, in coordination with Congress, have expressed major concerns that future wars would consist of technological and economic challenges rather than the historical mode of sending soldiers into the battlefield. In this chapter we will discuss U.S. policy goals affecting AI and recommendations made by government agencies particularly those goals emanating from the executive branch.

© The Author(s) 2020
R. Girasa, *Artificial Intelligence as a Disruptive Technology*,
https://doi.org/10.1007/978-3-030-35975-1_3

# U.S. Government AI Policy Goals

The U.S. government has taken a number of initiatives to address the going concern of AI's relationship to national security. Among them is the creation of the Defense Innovation Board launched in 2016 with a renewable 2-year mandate whose mission, in part, is to provide the Secretary of Defense and other related government officials with advice and recommendations to address future challenges in technology and capabilities.[1] Its initial recommendations, some of which directly apply to AI, were as follows.

## Defense Innovation Board Recommendations

- Appoint a DoD (Department of Defense) chief innovation officer to coordinate, oversee and synchronize innovation activities across the department.
- Establish a career track for computer science and a digital Reserve Officer's Training Corps program.
- Build a culture of evidence-based, outcome-driven policies and experimentation by, among other things, offering bonuses, recognition, awards and other incentives for managers who promote innovation, give employees greater voice and encourage creativity and divergent views.
- Direct Cybercom, working in coordination with the National Security Agency, to conduct a security review of every DoD system.
- Establish an institute for studying artificial intelligence and machine learning.
- Increase the speed and timeliness of acquisition processes by increasing the use of mechanisms for waivers and exemptions and offering incentives for quickly resolving concerns.
- Increase investment in DARPA, the Strategic Capabilities Office, the Defense Innovation Unit Experimental, rapid equipping units and other small, agile, innovative organizations and create more connections among them.

---

[1] *About*, DEFENSE INNOVATION BOARD, https://innovation.defense.gov/.

- Establish a computer science resource—a "human cloud" of computer programmers and software developers who are available on demand to swiftly solve software problems.[2]

The Board, in 2018, issued, what it termed the *Ten Commandments of Software* as follows:

1. Make computing, storage, and bandwidth abundant to DoD developers and users.
2. All software procurement programs should start small, be iterative, and build on success—or be terminated quickly.
3. Budgets should be constructed to support the full, iterative life cycle of the software being procured with amount proportional to the criticality and utility of the software.
4. Adopt a DevOps [development and operations] culture for software systems.
5. Automate testing of software to enable critical updates to be deployed in days to weeks, not months or years.
6. Every purpose-built DoD software system should include source code as a deliverable.
7. Every DoD system that includes software should have a local team of DoD software experts who are capable of modifying or extending the software through source code or API (application programming interface) access.
8. Only run operating systems that are receiving (and utilizing) regular security updates for newly discovered security vulnerabilities.
9. Data should always be encrypted unless it is part of an active computation.
10. All data generated by DoD systems—in development and deployment—should be stored, mined, and made available for machine learning.[3]

---

[2] Cheryl Pellerin, *Defense Innovation Board Makes Interim Recommendations*, DEPARTMENT OF DEFENSE NEWS (Oct. 5, 2016), https://dod.defense.gov/News/Article/Article/965196/defense-innovation-board-makes-interim-recommendations/.

[3] *Ten Commandments of Software*, DEFENSE INNOVATION BOARD (April 20, 2018), https://media.defense.gov/2018/Apr/22/2001906836/-1/-1/0/DEFENSEINNOVATIONBOARD_TEN_COMMANDMENTS_OF_SOFTWARE_2018.04.20.PDF.

*The National Security Commission on Artificial Intelligence (NSCAI).*
NSCAI, created under a statute of a comparable name,[4] is an independent agency in the executive branch composed of 15 members appointed by congressional leaders and the Secretaries of Defense and Commerce. Its mission is to review advances in AI, related machine learning developments, and associated technologies.[5] Among the duties of the Commission to be rendered in a report to Congress are the assessment of U.S. competitiveness in the following areas: the means to maintain a technological advantage; review of trends and developments on international cooperation and competitiveness; national security risks; educational and workforce efforts; lawful use by law enforcement officers to address technological barriers in criminal investigations and apprehension of criminals; and ethical concerns especially relating to privacy and security.[6] With initial funding of $10 million, additional funding will include a reprogramming of $70 million to set up a joint center to oversee AI efforts at the Department of Defense (DoD). Its Joint Artificial Intelligence Center is expected to receive some $1.75 billion in funding through 2026.[7] Among the members appointed to advise the Commission is Eric Schmidt, Executive Chairman of Google and Chairman of NSCAI, and Eric Horvitz of Microsoft Research Labs.[8] Schmidt stated that "This is the beginning of a very, very large program that will affect everyone."[9]

In a commentary in the Foreign Policy magazine,[10] the fear of China's massive entry into AI has caused considerable anguish among policy

---

[4] NATIONAL SECURITY COMMISSION ARTIFICIAL INTELLIGENCE ACT OF 2018, H.R. 5356 — 115th (2019), GovTrack.us. (2018), https://www.govtrack.us/congress/bills/115/hr5356.

[5] §2(2)(1) of the Act.

[6] §2(c) of the Act.

[7] June Edwards, *FY 2019 NDAA to Authorize $10M for AI National Security Commission*, EXECUTIVEGOV (Aug. 21, 2018), https://www.executivegov.com/2018/08/fy-2019-ndaa-to-authorize-10m-for-ai-national-security-commission/.

[8] *Alphabet, Microsoft leaders named to the National Security Commission on Artificial Intelligence*, FEDSCOOP (Jan. 26, 2019), https://www.fedscoop.com/alphabet-microsoft-leaders-named-national-security-commission-artificial-intelligence/.

[9] Tajha Chappellet-Lanier, *Pentagon's Joint AI Center is 'established,' but there's much more to figure out*, FEDSCOOP (July 20, 2018), https://www.fedscoop.com/dod-joint-ai-center-established/.

[10] Yuval Noah Harari, *The race to develop artificial intelligence (AI) is gathering*, FOREIGN POLICY (Winter, 2019), https://foreignpolicy.com/the-magazine/.

makers. The author, a distinguished Oxford University historian, called for a national plan for AI having noted that half of the top 10 AI startups are Chinese—among them are Alibaba, Baidu, Tencent, and SenseTime, as well as numerous other startups commencing almost daily. It appears that many of the reforms suggested have or are being adopted by the current U.S. Administration (as of October, 2019) in order to maintain AI-competitive advantage. It noted that the U.S. must educate, recruit, and retain the best researchers in STEM; end its anti-immigrant stance as evidenced by the fact that fully one-fourth of startups in the U.S. are by immigrants; enact a federal data privacy legislation to secure data sets for creation of machine-learning algorithms; expand the Pentagon's new Joint Artificial Intelligence Center; increase funding for AI research; expand programs such as facial recognition; and other related suggestions.[11]

*DOD's Joint Artificial Intelligence Center (JAIC): Third Offset Strategy.* In a memorandum of June 27, 2016, Deputy Defense Secretary, Patrick Shanahan formally established the JAIC whose goal in part is to remove layers of bureaucratic decision-making to speed the then 600 existing projects that implicate AI in order to better compete with the advances being made by the U.S.' perceived, as possibly its future, antagonistic competitors such as China and Russia.[12] The main goals of the JAIC are "accelerating delivery of AI-enabled capabilities, scaling the impact of AI, and synchronizing DoD AI activities to expand Joint Force advantages."[13] The goals are part of the DoD's Third Offset Strategy[14] aimed at maintaining an advantage in critical areas at the operational level of war in

---

[11] Paul Scharre and Michael C. Horowitz, *Congress Can Help in the United States Lead in Artificial Intelligence*, FOREIGN AFFAIRS (Dec. 10, 2018), https://foreignpolicy.com/2018/12/10/congress-can-help-the-united-states-lead-in-artificial-intelligence/.

[12] Paul McCleary, *Pentagon-Run AI Center Coming, Hypersonics Work in Progress*, BREAKING DEFENSE (April 25, 2018), https://breakingdefense.com/2018/04/pentagon-run-ai-center-coming-hypersonics-work-in-progress/.

[13] *Establishment of the Joint Artificial Intelligence Center*, DEPARTMENT OF DEFENSE (June 27, 2018), https://admin.govexec.com/media/establishment_of_the_joint_artificial_intelligence_center_osd008412-18_r....pdf.

[14] The First Offset Strategy occurred during the 1950s Cold War with the Soviet Union by increasing superiority in nuclear weapons and miniaturizing them. The Second Offset Strategy occurred in the 1970s and 1980s with advances in precision-guided weapons, information technologies, and digital microprocessors. Katie Lange, *3rd Offset Strategy 101: What It Is, What the Tech Focuses Are*, DODLIVE (March 30, 2016), http://www.dodlive.mil/2016/03/30/3rd-offset-strategy-101-what-it-is-what-the-tech-focuses-are/.

order to deter possible aggressive actions against the U.S. According to the Deputy Defense Secretary, Bob Work, the offset "is to exploit all the advances of artificial intelligence and autonomy and insert them into DoD's battle networks to achieve a step increase in performance that the department believes will strengthen conventional deterrence. The offset includes technological leaps ... [and is an] institutional strategy ... to compete in this new dynamic environment."[15]

The five technological-operational components of the Third Offset Strategy are: (1) *deep-learning autonomous systems* used for analyzing bid data speedily, warnings in cyber defense, electronic warfare, and large-density missile raids; (2) *human-machine collaboration* as exemplified in drone strikes whereby a computer operator selects targets for destruction and the naval Aegis weapon system that acts in a similar way—emphasis is the ultimate human control over AI-based weaponry; (3) *human-machine combat teaming*, especially with humans working with unmanned systems to perform operations more effectively, which includes the U.S. Apache helicopter and Gray Eagle Unmanned Aerial Vehicle, and the swarming unmanned aircraft like the Perdix mini-drone; (4) *assisted human operations* whereby electronic devices are worn by individuals enabling much greater ability to understand data, or are combat applications, and heads-up displays; (5) *network-enabled, cyber-hardened semi-autonomous weapons* to ward off cyberattacks as e.g., modifying existing systems to operate without Global Positioning System (GPSD) if enemy is able to instigate a denial-of-service attack.[16] We discuss the five components in greater detail in Chap. 4.

*Controversy Regarding Military Use of AI.* Cooperation in AI between the U.S. government and private technology companies is not without controversy. Many scientists and tech innovators are opposed to the use of AI for military purposes. In a Bulletin of the Atomic Scientists, a "clash of cultures" between Silicon Valley and the military establishment in Washington is taking place reminiscent of an alleged comparable concept as stated in "The Clash of Civilizations" by Professor Samuel P. Huntington

---

[15] Cheryl Pellerin, *Deputy Secretary: Third Offset Strategy Bolsters America's Military Deterrence,* DEPARTMENT OF DEFENSE (Oct. 31, 2016), https://dod.defense.gov/News/Article/Article/991434/deputy-secretary-third-offset-strategy-bolsters-americas-military-deterrence/.
[16] *Id.*

concerning the divide that could lead to confrontation between the cultural difference between Islamic countries and western countries, which caused copious critical comment several decades ago.[17]

*Google's Principles.* When it was announced that Google had procured a contract with DARPA, known as Project Maven, to develop AI systems for the procurement of computational power graphic processing units including graphic processing units that allow the training of machine-learning algorithms with the goal of automating analysis of video footage gathered by drone, approximately 3000 employees at the company signed a letter opposing the company's involvement in "the business of war."[18] The protest apparently led to the company's decision not to renew a contract with the military establishment for AI when the current contract expires. Google thereafter set forth a series of suggested recommended practices to be incorporated into its research and development and adapt them over time.

In its *Artificial Intelligence at Google: Our Principles*,[19] Google states that it will not pursue the design or deployments of AI applications with respect to:

- Technologies that cause or likely to cause overall harm unless the benefits substantially outweigh risks;
- Weapons or other technologies whose principal purpose is to cause injury to people;
- Technologies that gather or use information for surveillance that violate internationally accepted norms; or
- Technologies whose purpose contravenes accepted principles of international law and human rights;
- Protections against biases based on gender, race, or sexual orientation.[20]

---

[17] Samuel P. Huntington, *The Clash of Civilizations*, FOREIGN AFFAIRS (Summer 1993).

[18] Jade Leung and Sophie-Charlotte Fischer, *JAIC: Pentagon debuts artificial intelligence hub*, BULLETIN OF THE ATOMIC SCIENTISTS (Aug. 8, 2018), https://thebulletin.org/2018/08/jaic-pentagon-debuts-artificial-intelligence-hub/. For a discussion of Project Maven, see Cheryl Pellerin, *Project Maven to Deploy Computer Algorithms to War Zone by Year's End*, DEPARTMENT OF DEFENSE (July 21, 2017), https://dod.defense.gov/News/Article/Article/1254719/project-maven-to-deploy-computer-algorithms-to-war-zone-by-years-end/.

[19] https://ai.google/primciples/.

[20] *Id.*

Whether the principles will be followed strictly or loosely interpreted have been questioned by some ethicists. The interpretations of the principles within Google are left to its executives which some commentators contend require the need for outside ethicists observers to hold Google to the spirit of its principles.[21] Nevertheless, Google has provided initial adherence to its promise by its withdrawal from the U.S. Pentagon's $10 billion cloud-computing contract known as the Joint Enterprise Defense Infrastructure cloud (JEDI), asserting conflict with its principled corporate values. The purpose of the JEDI program is to transfer its immense amount of data to a commercially operated cloud. Opposition by other major tech companies, such as IBM, Microsoft, and Oracle, was not about the ethics of assisting military progression but rather that the entire sum was to be given to one winner of the contract bid.[22]

Google's competitors, among them Amazon and Microsoft, continue to seek AI-based contracts with the Pentagon.[23] Microsoft also faced scrutiny from its technologists whereby a group of its workers signed a petition requesting executives to terminate its $479 million government contract to develop augmented-reality technology, "Integrated Visual Augmented System" for the military. Microsoft's CEO, Satya Nadella, responded in favor of its military-based research emphasizing that it is in the best interests of the U.S. to maintain a strong defense and that the company will "remain engaged as an active corporate citizen in addressing the important ethical and public policy issues relating to AI and the military."[24] It is questionable whether refusal to engage in military uses of AI technology is helpful given the aggressive nature of China's multi-year plan (see Chap. 8) to catch up and surpass the U.S. in AI superiority.[25]

---

[21] Josh Smith, *Google Sets Limits on Its Use of AI But Allows Defense Work*, WIRED (June 7, 2018), https://www.wired.com/story/google-sets-limits-on-its-use-of-ai-but-allows-defense-work/.

[22] Naomi Nix, *Google Drops Out of Pentagon's $10 Billion Cloud Competition*, BLOOMBERG (Oct. 8, 2018), https://www.bloomberg.com/news/articles/2018-10-08/google-drops-out-of-pentagon-s-10-billion-cloud-competition.

[23] Megan Henney, *Microsoft, Amazon stand by military work, despite employee backlash*, FOX BUSINESS (Nov. 1, 2018), https://www.foxbusiness.com/technology/microsoft-amazon-oracle-defend-us-military-contracts.

[24] Klint Finley, *Microsoft CEO Defends Army Contract for Augmented Reality*, WIRED (Feb. 25, 2019, https://blog.wired.com/story/microsoft-ceo-defends-army-contract-augmented-reality/.

[25] Daisuke Wakabayashi and Scott Shane, *Google Will Not Renew Pentagon Contract That Upset Employees*, NEW YORK TIMES (June 1, 2018), https://www.nytimes.com/2018/06/01/technology/google-pentagon-project-maven.html.

It has been suggested that the conflict between JAIC and technologists, not only at Google, but also at Amazon and Microsoft, could be ameliorated by an understanding among them that ethics and safety are non-negotiable commitments. Strong safety norms that already exist in the U.S. military, such as those found among Navy submariners, aircraft carrier deck operators, and other areas, could lead to a comparable safety-oriented approach that integrates AI as an extension to military conduct. Standards for such approaches spearheaded under JAIC would be welcomed advances, leading to a commitment between the military and developers of AI-enabled systems.[26]

The dilemma posed by the opposition of scientists and technologists is that China faces no internal opposition between civilian and military concerning its very significant AI program which includes military procurement of weapons systems and usages. Among the recent alarms and warnings is the comment by the financier, George Soros, in a speech to the World Economic Forum in January 2019, wherein he expressed his fear that AI-centric tech companies can become enablers of authoritarian regimes like that in China. An example of possible misuse, which could lead to near total control over the populations, is China's "social-credit" system that is being developed by companies, e.g., a subsidiary of Alibaba. The program permits the tracking of citizens' reputations by logging onto their financial activities, online interactions, energy use, and other activities.[27] Although operated piecemeal until intended full implementation by 2020, the ratings will determine in part whether you can travel on trains, obtain visas to study or do business abroad, gain entry in the nation's best schools, and even whether one may use particular high-end hotels.[28]

---

[26] Jade Leung, *supra*, note 227.

[27] Tom Simonite, *The 'Mortal Danger of China's Push into AI'*, CENTRAL TIBETAN ADMINISTRATION (Jan. 24, 2019), https://www.tibet.net/2019/01/the-mortal-danger-of-chinas-push-into-ai/.

[28] Alexandra Ma, *China has started ranking citizens with a creepy 'social credit' system — here's what you can do wrong, and the embarrassing, demeaning ways they can punish you*, BUSINESSINSIDER (Oct. 29, 2018), https://www.businessinsider.com/china-social-credit-system-punishments-and-rewards-explained-2018-4.

# U.S. Presidents' AI Initiatives

Although the political rhetoric has intensified which emphasized the alleged divide between the Republican and Democrat parties, nevertheless, as discussed below, the leaders of both parties, acting in their capacities as chief executives of the nation, have placed great emphasis on AI research; the new technological developments emanating and based on AI; the need for retraining of the workforce to accomplish the goals of AI; the necessity of maintaining leadership for the nation's security including military capabilities; and to counter cyberattacks that could potentially prove highly destructive to the nation's infrastructure.

# President Barack Obama's Initiatives

There were studies conducted by the NSTC and the Office of Science and Technology Policy (OSTP)[29] concerning preparation for the future of AI and its relationship to the economy in conjunction with OSTP, the Council of Economic Advisers, and other agencies. In the Report of October, 2016, *Preparation for the Future of Artificial Intelligence*,[30] there were 23 recommendations that essentially concern the role of the federal government in the application of AI for the common good. While touting the major benefits of AI in diverse areas such as health care, transportation, the environment, criminal justice, and economic inclusion, nevertheless, a major role of government is to examine whether existing regulations are adequately addressing the risks attendant to the new technological developments, and, if not, how government can engage in regulatory responses that minimize the cost of compliance and not retard the

---

[29] The Office of Science and Technology was established by the *National Science and Technology Policy, Organization, and Priorities Act* of 1976, Pub.L. 94-282, May 11, 1976, 90 Stat. 459 (42 U.S.C. 6601 et seq.). A copy of the legislation may be found at the Legal Information Institute, Cornell U., https://www.law.cornell.edu/topn/national_science_and_technology_policy_organization_and_priorities_act_of_1976.

[30] *Preparing for the Future of Artificial Intelligence*, EXECUTIVE OFFICE OF THE PRESIDENT, OFFICE OF NATIONAL SCIENCE AND TECHNOLOGY COUNCIL COMMITTEE ON TECHNOLOGY (Oct. 2016), https://obamawhitehouse.archives.gov/sites/default/files/whitehouse_files/microsites/ostp/NSTC/preparing_for_the_future_of_ai.pdf.

adoption of beneficial innovations. Government has a major role in funding AI R&D, identifying areas of opportunity, and recommending ways to coordinate R&D to maximize benefit and build a highly trained workforce.[31]

As in almost all subsequent reports, a major emphasis is on the importance of training the workforce to be able to understand and apply AI-based initiatives through federal STEM education and training programs as well as computer science. Public policy must address the risks of a segment of the population that will be most impacted by the negative effects of automation on lower-wage jobs which will increase inequality between those currently possessing such jobs and the more educated workers. The Report also raises questions of fairness, safety, and governance as the technologies become more broadly utilized which may lead to unintended consequences. A major challenge is the transition from the "closed world" of the laboratory to the "open world" where unpredictable events can occur. Thus, it is necessary to adapt measures to assure safety in building critical systems and infrastructure such as aircraft, power plants, bridges, and vehicles to teach AI practitioners verification, validation, how to manage risk, and how to communicate with the stakeholders exposed to the risks. There are global considerations that require dialogue and cooperation among countries, multilateral institutions, and other stakeholders particularly in the areas of cybersecurity and military weapons systems.[32]

In conjunction with the Report, a strategic plan was set forth in a companion document *National Artificial Intelligence Research and Development Strategic Plan*,[33] which proposed seven strategies for future adoption. They are: (1) make long-term investments in AI research; (2) develop effective methods for human-AI collaboration; (3) understand and address the ethical, legal, and societal implications of AI; (4) ensure the

---

[31] *Id.* at 1–2. The recommendations are at 40–42.

[32] *Id.* at 2–3.

[33] *National Artificial Intelligence Research and Development Strategic Plan*, EXECUTIVE OFFICE OF THE PRESIDENT, OFFICE OF NATIONAL SCIENCE AND TECHNOLOGY COUNCIL COMMITTEE ON TECHNOLOGY (Oct. 2016), https://obamawhitehouse. archives.gov/sites/default/files/whitehouse_files/microsites/ostp/NSTC/national_ai_rd_strategic_plan.pdf.

safety and security of AI systems; (5) develop shared public datasets and environments for AI training and testing; (6) measure and evaluate AI technologies through standards and benchmarks; and (7) better understand the national AI R&D workforce needs.[34] Accordingly, the Report made two recommendations: (1) develop an AI R&D implementation framework to identify science and technology opportunities and support effective coordination of AI R&D investments consistent with Strategies 1–6 of this plan; and (2) study the national landscape for creating and sustaining a healthy AI R&D workforce, consistent with Strategy 7 of this plan.[35]

As with any technological advances there are winners and losers, with the latter having to scramble for alternate income sources by new learning outcomes which often downgrades their former work status by taking more menial jobs. The administration of Barack Obama was particularly concerned with the economic and social implications of AI on the future workforce. After considerable study, it rendered its report, *Artificial Intelligence, Automation, and the Economy*,[36] which issued a series of recommendations to prepare the economy for the anticipated significant changes brought about by automation, particularly robotic substitutions of workers. It noted the changes to the economy since the 1800s with the transformation of the economy from one of farming to industrial production. It further noted that there has been a decline in productivity among almost all of the major global economies thereby causing a slowdown of economic growth for workers. Thus, it was projected that AI could enhance worker productivity with attendant overall economic benefits to the workforce.

---

[34] *Id.* at 16–36.

[35] *Id.* at 37.

[36] ARTIFICIAL INTELLIGENCE, AUTOMATION, AND THE ECONOMY, EXECUTIVE OFFICE OF THE PRESIDENT (Dec. 2016), https://www.whitehouse.gov/sites/whitehouse.gov/files/images/EMBARGOED%20AI%20Economy%20Report.pd.

*The report* followed an earlier study by the Office of the President, PREPARING FOR THE FUTURE OF ARTIFICIAL INTELLIGENCE, OFFICE OF THE PRESIDENT (Oct. 2016), https://obamawhitehouse.archives.gov/sites/default/files/whitehouse_files/microsites/ostp/NSTC/preparing_for_the_future_of_ai.pdf.

The report further noted that technology is transforming the economy from an unskilled-biased technical outcome to a skilled-based change which results in a deeper negative impact upon unskilled workers. An example of the potential impact is the replacement of drivers of trucks and other vehicles with automated vehicles that will affect some 2.2–3.1 million workers. Future projections of employment, according to the study will encompass:

- *Engagement.* Rather than replacement of workers, it is projected that workers will increase their productivity by "augmented intelligence," i.e., they would complement AI-automation technologies. Examples given are healthcare professionals who will be able to better translate diagnoses by early detection brought about by AI; shipping companies will become more efficient whereby workers would handle the last 100 feet of delivery of goods; and highly-skilled software developers and engineers will augment their skills leading to increased demand for jobs in generating, collecting, and managing relevant data to feed into AI training.[37]
- *Development.* AI will bring demand for jobs in generating, collecting, and managing relevant data to feed into AI training processes. Examples given are recognition of cancer in x-ray machine outcome and extending even to philosophical issues concerning creation of frameworks for ethical evaluations and sociologists' investigations into the impact of technology brought about by AI.
- *Supervision.* There will be necessarily positions related to the monitoring, licensing, and repair of AI. Example given is the need for supervision and updates of automated vehicles including their registration, testing, and repairs. Numerous other skill-based positions will be enhanced by AI leading to greater efficiency and quality control.
- *Response to Paradigm Shifts.* There will be major shifts, e.g., in the design of infrastructure and traffic laws and urban planning.[38]

---

[37] *Id.* at 18.
[38] *Id.* at 19.

The report made the following recommendations stated as strategies:

- *Strategy #1: Invest in and Develop AI for its Many Benefits.* AI will open up new markets and opportunities in numerous major areas such as health, education, energy, economic inclusion, social welfare, transportation, and the environment. There is a need for investment in AI research and development particularly by government especially concerning cyber defense and fraud detection; development of a larger, more diverse workforce necessitating AI training and education in computer science, statistics, mathematical logic, and information theory; use of data sets to determine individuals' fitness for credit, insurance and even employment; and support market competition to encourage startups and lower costs;
- *Strategy #2: Educate and Train Americans for Jobs in the Future.* There will be a need to prepare college and career-ready skills in math, reading, computer science, and critical thinking; better educate the youth in math and the sciences (U.S. ranks 28th of 38 OECD countries) by assuring that all children get off to the right start with access to high-quality education; have all high school students possess skills in computer science; assure that all Americans have access to an affordable post-secondary education that prepares them for good jobs; expand access to training and retraining and expanding availability of job-driven training and lifelong learning to meet future needs; target resources for effective education and training programs; and expand access to apprenticeships.
- *Strategy #3: Aid Workers in the Transition and Empower Workers to Ensure Broadly Shared Growth.* The study calls for the modernization and strengthening of the social safety net such as unemployment insurance, Medicaid, Supplemental Nutrition Assistance Program (SNAP), and Temporary Assistance for Needy Families (TANF), particularly for those persons displaced by automation. The authors suggested giving workers improved guidance to navigate job transitions; increase wages, competition, and worker bargaining power; raise the minimum wage; modernize overtime and spread work; strengthen unions; give workers a voice and bargaining power to

protect wages; identify strategies to address differential geographic impact; reduce geographic barriers to work; pursue place-based solutions; and, finally, modernize tax policy.[39]

# President Donald Trump's Initiatives: 2018 White House Summit

There have been a number of additional initiatives taken by U.S. presidents to assure U.S. dominance in AI. The National Science and Technology Council (NSTC) was created pursuant to NSTC Executive Order No. 12881 on November 23, 1993[40] and is a cabinet level position composed mostly of members of the President's cabinet and other persons concerned with scientific efforts and pursuits. Its function is to coordinate science and technology policies among the various organizations within the Executive Branch. It created the Select Committee on Artificial Intelligence in May 2018 to advise and assist the NSTC in improving the effectiveness and productivity of federal AI research and development. The meeting brought together over 100 senior government officials, technical experts from top academic institutions, heads of industrial research labs, and American business leaders who are adopting AI technologies to benefit their customers, workers, and shareholders.[41]

The principal functions of the Select Committee are:

* Facilitate AI R&D planning, coordination, and communication among Federal departments and agencies;

---

[39] *Id.* at 27–41.

[40] *Charter of the National Science and Technology Council*, WHITE HOUSE OFFICE OF SCIENCE AND TECHNOLOGY (Nov. 23, 2013), https://obamawhitehouse.archives.gov/administration/eop/ostp/nstc/about/executiveorder.

[41] *Summary of the 2018 White House Summit on Artificial Intelligence for American Industry*, WHITE HOUSE OFFICE OF SCIENCE AND TECHNOLOGY POLICY (May 10, 2018), https://www.whitehouse.gov/wp-content/uploads/2018/05/Summary-Report-of-White-House-AI-Summit.pdf.

- Identify, define, and advise the NSTC on interagency priorities and plans related to AI, including priority areas of AI R&D critical to national security, and recommend options for Administration R&D priorities;
- Encourage agency AI-related programs and initiatives, including partnerships with academia and industry, that enhance global, national, regional, state, and local competitiveness and foster long-term economic growth and job creation;
- Identify opportunities to improve the quality of Federal datasets for AI applications, and increase access to Federal data and computational resources for the non-Federal AI R&D community, as appropriate and as permitted by law; and
- Coordinate with other NSTC committees and facilitate NSTC clearance of documents generated by interagency groups that are established under its sponsorship.[42]

The major findings of the 2018 White House Summit are as follows.

*Prioritize Funding.* The federal government has prioritized AI R&D and related technologies to an extent that is both classified within the intelligence and defense communities and unclassified which has grown by over 40 percent between 2015–2018. Agencies are directed to focus their R&D on emerging technologies, including machine learning and autonomous systems. The Administration's budget for fiscal year 2019 for the first time has designated AI and autonomous and unmanned systems as Administration R&D priorities.

*Removal of Regulatory Barriers.* A second finding is the current Administration's efforts to remove regulatory barriers to the deployment of AI-powered technologies. Non-regulatory guidance to automated vehicle developers was given by the U.S. Department of Transportation in September 2018 to enable the safe integration of driverless automobiles. In the following month in a presidential memorandum, states and

---

[42] *Summary of the 2018 White House Summit on Artificial Intelligence for American Industry*, WHITE HOUSE OFFICE OF SCIENCE AND TECHNOLOGY POLICY (May 10, 2018), App. A, Charter, https://www.whitehouse.gov/wp-content/uploads/2018/05/Summary-Report-of-White-House-AI-Summit.pdf.

localities were given permission to conduct innovative commercial and public drone operations that previously were prohibited under Federal Aviation Administration (FAA) regulations. The U.S. Food and Drug Administration approved in November 2018 the first ever AI-based device for medical diagnostics to detect diabetic retinopathy which is a leading cause of blindness.

*Training Future Workforce.* Under the President's Executive Order of June 15, 2017,[43] it was noted that 350,000 jobs are available but unfilled due to lack of training and education. Accordingly, industry-recognized apprenticeships are to be funded and a cabinet-level Task Force on Apprenticeship Expansion was created to establish guidelines, require-ments, and qualifications in cooperation with business concerns and labor organizations especially directed at high school and college students to meet the future needs of AI businesses. In a Presidential Memorandum,[44] directed to the Secretary of Education, the Secretary is directed to expand access to high-quality STEM education, especially in the area of com-puter science and its application. Committing $200 million in grant funds that were matched by a private industry commitment of $300 million.

*Strategic Military Advantage.* AI is given recognition for military pur-poses in accordance with the President's National Security Strategy[45] and the National Defense Strategy.[46] Among the programs to be instituted or continued are the emphasis on AI-based defense systems, autonomous weaponry, and other scientific and technology-based defenses.

---

[43] *Expanding Apprenticeships in America*, Exec. Order No. 3245 (June 15, 2017), https://www.whitehouse.gov/presidential-actions/3245/.

[44] PRESIDENTIAL MEMORANDUM FOR THE SECRETARY OF EDUCATION (Sept. 25, 2017), https://www.whitehouse.gov/presidential-actions/presidential-memorandum-secretary-education/.

[45] *National Security Strategy of the United States of America* (Dec. 2017), OFFICE OF THE PRESIDENT, https://www.whitehouse.gov/wp-content/uploads/2017/12/NSS-Final-12-18-2017-0905.pdf.

[46] *National Defense Strategy of the United States of America*, OFFICE OF THE PRESIDENT, (2018), https://dod.defense.gov/Portals/1/Documents/pubs/2018-National-Defense-Strategy-Summary.pdf.

*Leveraging AI for Government Services.* A call was made for the use of automation software to improve efficiency of government services and maximizing Federal data sharing with the public to support non-Federal AI research applications. In addition, the General Services Administration is conducting pilot programs leveraging AI including a tool to predict regulatory compliance.

*Lead International AI Negotiations.* The Office of Science and Technology Policy (OSTP) delegations to the 2017 and 2018 G7 Innovation and Technology Ministerials negotiated on S&T cooperation agreements, between the U.S. and France, which recognize the importance of AI innovation for economic growth and which supports efforts to promote trust in and adoption of AI technologies. Additional collaboration in international R&D agreements are being pursued, which includes the Science and Technology (S&T) agreement between the U.S. and the U.K.

In an assessment by the Brookings Institution, a major policy think tank in Washington, D.C., a concern was expressed that the U.S. Government is not doing enough to support AI research comparing the expenditure of $1.1 billion with China's $150 billion commitment. Most of the AI impetus is from private industry that has been able to take advantage of the excellent U.S. system of higher education for its entrepreneurs and researchers Nevertheless, although the expressed goals of the President's initiative were welcomed, the worry is that China is leading with massive government funding of AI and that it also leads in the number of academic papers presented, published, and citations thereof (although disputed by some scholars). It also has very successful AI-based companies such as Baidu and others; spearheads advances in 5G networks of high-speed mobile communications technology; has made huge investments in AI, especially in its current use of facial recognition technology, alleged by others as for control of population purposes; and, highly likely, for military-use technological advancements. On a positive note, the Report indicated that the U.S. Department of Defense has announced an implementation plan that is directed toward strengthening the military's defense against potential aggressive actions of other potential enemy-nations. It also emphasized the need for advances in non-military AI research and development, such as vision, funding, and infrastructure that can play a role in the maintenance of national competitiveness and security.[47]

# President Donald Trump's AI Executive Order

The fear of the China syndrome of planned AI superiority in the forthcoming years has caused President Trump's advisers, especially the former defense secretary, Jim Mattis, academics, and industry executives, to urge him to make AI superiority a major priority for the security of the U.S.[48] Accordingly, on February 11, 2019, the President signed an Executive Order setting forth principles, objectives, roles and responsibilities, and R&D respecting AI.[49]

The Order states the following five principles: The U.S. must: (1) drive technological breakthroughs in AI across the Federal Government, industry, and academia in order to promote scientific discovery, economic competitiveness, and national security; (2) drive development of appropriate technical standards and reduce barriers to the safe testing and deployment of AI technologies in order to enable the creation of new AI-related industries and the adoption of AI by today's industries; (3) train current and future generations of American workers with the skills to develop and apply AI technologies to prepare them for today's economy and jobs of the future; (4) foster public trust and confidence in AI technologies and protect civil liberties, privacy, and American values in their application in order to fully realize the potential of AI technologies for the American people; and (5) promote an international environment

---

[47] Darrell M. West, *Assessing Trump's artificial intelligence executive order*, BROOKINGS (Feb. 12, 2019), https://www.brookings.edu/blog/techtank/2019/02/12/assessing-trumps-artificial-intelligence-executive-order/.

[48] Cade Metz, *Trump Signs Executive Order Promoting Artificial Intelligence*, NEW YORK TIMES (Feb. 11, 2019), https://www.nytimes.com/2019/02/11/business/ai-artificial-intelligence-trump.html.

[49] EXECUTIVE ORDER ON MAINTAINING AMERCAN LEADERSHIP IN ARTIFICIAL INTELLIGENCE (Feb. 11, 2019), https://www.whitehouse.gov/presidential-actions/executive-order-maintaining-american-leadership-artificial-intelligence/.

that supports American AI research and innovation and opens markets for American AI industries, while protecting our technological advantage in AI and protecting our critical AI technologies from acquisition by strategic competitors and adversarial nations.

All executive departments and agencies are to meet the following objectives:

- Promote sustained investment in AI R&D in collaboration with industry, academia, international partners and allies, and other non-Federal entities to generate technological breakthroughs in AI and related technologies and to rapidly transition those breakthroughs into capabilities that contribute to our economic and national security.
- Enhance access to high-quality and fully traceable Federal data, models, and computing resources to increase the value of such resources for AI R&D, while maintaining safety, security, privacy, and confidentiality protections consistent with applicable laws and policies.
- Reduce barriers to the use of AI technologies to promote their innovative application while protecting American technology, economic and national security, civil liberties, privacy, and values.
- Ensure that technical standards minimize vulnerability to attacks from malicious actors and reflect Federal priorities for innovation, public trust, and public confidence in systems that use AI technologies; and develop international standards to promote and protect those priorities.
- Train the next generation of American AI researchers and users through apprenticeships; skills programs; and education in STEM, with an emphasis on computer science, to ensure that American workers, including Federal workers, are capable of taking full advantage of the opportunities of AI.
- Develop and implement an action plan, in accordance with the National Security Presidential Memorandum of February 11, 2019 (Protecting the United States Advantage in Artificial Intelligence and Related Critical Technologies) (the NSPM [National Security Presidential Memoranda]) to protect the advantage of the U.S. in AI and technology critical to U.S. economic and national security interests against strategic competitors and foreign adversaries.

The initiative is to be coordinated through the NSTC with funding given a top priority. Each agency is to review and determine which programs are to be given AI priority; review its data and models to enable discovery and usability by the AI-research community without compromising safety, security, privacy, and confidentiality; identify barriers to access; identify new technologies and opportunities and best practices; provide educational grants for the study of AI by students at all levels of education from high school to graduate programs including funding for fellowships, alternative programs, commissioning programs for the U.S. Armed Forces; and other such initiatives. An action plan is to be developed to protect U.S. leadership in AI and AI technology that is critical to the U.S. economic and national security interests against strategic competitors and adversarial nations (China).[50]

## FY 2020 AI Budget Priorities

The President's *FY 2020 Administration Research and Development Budget Priorities Memorandum* for the heads of all executive departments and agencies, places great emphasis on emerging technologies from AI and quantum computing, to biotechnology, advanced wireless communications, and space commercialization. The emphasis placed for the expenditure of federal moneys is to be focused primarily on basic and early-stage applied research, paired with targeted deregulation, and investment in STEM education and workforce development.[51] The R&D Priority Areas stated in the Memorandum are as follows:

- *Security of the American People.* A major goal of the Administration's National Security Strategy is the nation's ability to "be able to fight and win the wars of the future." In order to do so, investments in R&D will be required in AI, autonomous systems, hypersonics (defense

---

[50] *Id.*

[51] Mick Mulvaney and Michael Kratsios, *Memorandum for the Heads of Executive Departments and Agencies*, M-18-22, EXECUTIVE OFFICE OF THE PRESIDENT (July 31, 2018), https://www.whitehouse.gov/wp-content/uploads/2018/07/M-18-22.pdf.

against greatly excessive speed such as by missiles' attacks),[52] a modernized nuclear deterrent, and advanced microelectronics, computing, and cyber capabilities.

- *American Leadership in AI, Quantum Information Sciences, and Strategic Computing.* Agencies are to invest in fundamental and applied AI research, including machine learning, autonomous systems, and applications at the human-technology frontier. Agencies are to prioritize quantum information science (QIS) R&D, which applies the best understanding of the sub-atomic world to generate new knowledge and technologies. Earlier examples of QIS-related technologies include semiconductor microelectronics, photonics, the global positioning system (GPS), and magnetic resonance imaging (MRI) which underpin significant parts of the national economic and defense infrastructure.[53] Additional priorities include strategic computing, devices for high-performance computing that accelerate delivery of low power, high performance devices; and which support a national high-performance computing ecosystem.

- *American Connectivity and Autonomy.* Agencies are to support the development and deployment of 5G wireless networks[54] and beyond including by prioritizing R&D to manage spectrum, secure networks, and increase access to high-speed Internet. These networks underlie autonomous and unmanned systems such as drones and self-driving cars, rely heavily on robust and secure connectivity to provide novel, low-cost capabilities across a broad range of commercial sectors, including transportation. Additional R&D is needed to safely and effi-

---

[52] For a discussion of the threat posed by hypersonics, see Robert Farley, *Understanding the Threat Posed by Hypersonic Weapons*, THE DIPLOMAT (Oct. 6, 2017), https://thediplomat.com/2017/10/understanding-the-threat-posed-by-hypersonic-weapons/.

[53] A discussion and program emanating from the executive branch of the U.S. government concerning QIS is detailed in a report by the Subcommittee on Quantum Information Science under the Committee of Science of the National Science & Technology Council, *National Strategic Overview for Quantum Information Science*, OFFICE OF THE PRESIDENT (Sept. 2018), https://www.whitehouse.gov/wp-content/uploads/2018/09/National-Strategic-Overview-for-Quantum-Information-Science.pdf.

[54] "5G" refers to fifth-generation wireless which is the latest cellular technology that is designed to provide greatly increased speed and responsiveness of wireless networks. It will also allow mobile operators to support certain uses of business cases, and does not require large, high-power cell towers but rather transmits signals through a large number of small cell stations. *5G*, Margaret Rouse, https://searchnetworking.techtarget.com/definition/5G.

ciently integrate autonomous driving systems and unmanned aircraft systems (UAS), including urban air mobility aircraft, and the national airspace.

- *American Manufacturing.* Rather than the pessimism surrounding potential loss of jobs when new technologies come into play, the Report emphasizes that the next generation of manufacturing technologies will create and keep jobs, ensure products are made in the U.S., and strengthen the nation's manufacturing base. Priority is to be given to technological areas which includes smart and digital manufacturing, advanced industrial robotics especially those enabled by the industrial Internet of things, machine learning, and associated materials including high performance materials, critical materials, and additive manufacturing. Government agencies are to cooperate with manufacturers to cause U.S. to maintain leadership in semiconductor design and fabrication with access to advanced microelectronics.
- *American Space and Commercialization.* The Report indicated that the U.S. focus should be on ensuring American leadership in space for long-duration spaceflight, in-space manufacturing, in-situ resource utilization, long-term cryogenic fuel storage and management, and advanced space-related power and propulsion capabilities. Priority is to be given to demonstrations and flight tests to ensure an industrial base for commercial activity in space, on celestial bodies, and microgravity-related research.
- *American Energy Dominance.* The Report stated that agencies should invest in next-generation energy technologies to efficiently convert them into useful energy services such as light, heat, mobility, power, etc. Agencies should invest in early-stage, innovative technologies that show promise in harnessing American energy resources safely and efficiently.
- *American Medical Innovation.* Agencies are to prioritize medical breakthroughs by funding basic medical research especially in areas underserved by industry; ensure health data security, interoperability, accessibility, and portability—including data generated through emerging medical technologies; and R&D efforts that will lead to more efficient and effective healthcare for veterans, with a particular focus on mental health and suicide prevention, and also for the elderly.

- *American Agriculture.* Agencies should prioritize R&D that enables advanced and precision agriculture and aquaculture technologies, including the use of embedded sensors, data analytics, and machine learning techniques to minimize agricultural inputs and maximize the quantity and quality of agricultural products. In addition, they should prioritize investments in pre-competitive research regarding the safety of microorganisms, plants, and animals developed using gene editing, in order to greater leverage biotechnology products for agriculture.
- *R&D Priority Practices* should include educating and training a workforce for the twenty-first century to include adaptability to the increasingly technical nature of work across all employment sectors and ongoing technical training; experiential learning, such as apprenticeships, internships, and employer-educator partnerships; initiatives that reskill Americans for the new types of jobs; and increase education in science, technology, engineering, and mathematics, including computer science.
- *Managing and Modernizing R&D Infrastructure.* Agencies should prioritize infrastructure investments; innovative management approaches; and long-term stewardship of scientific infrastructure.
- *Maximize Interagency Coordination and Cross-Disciplinary Collaboration.* The NSTC is the primary means to coordinate high priority science and technology initiatives across the Federal government, and agencies are to cooperate and support their respective R&D programs.
- *Transferring Technology from Laboratory to Marketplace.* Agencies should focus on the basic and early-stage applied research to build blocks of new technological advances, and expand efforts that empower the private sector to accelerate the transfer of research discoveries from the laboratory to the marketplace.
- *Partnering with Industry and Academia.* Agencies should engage in public-private collaborations to help align basic research with future private sector needs, establish testbeds and datasets reflective of real-world conditions, transfer techniques and technologies across sectors, and submit their basic research results to the private sector. Agencies should consider methods to reduce regulatory and administrative barriers and align incentives for engagement in innovative technologies.

# DARPA

From the President of the U.S. to Congressional leaders, there has been a coordinated effort to meet the challenges of the AI revolution. Although Congress enacts legislation with the consent of the President, much of the effort to meet the challenges posed by AI is funded through DARPA which is primarily responsible for forward-looking, innovative scientific efforts in a broad range of pursuits including that of top-secret military endeavors. Dating back when the former Soviet Union spun ahead of the U.S. in the space effort in 1957, DARPA was given the task to initiate game-changing military capabilities such as precision weapons and stealth technology, but, in addition, has initiated advances that aided civil society in creation of the internet, automated voice recognitions and language translation, and also the Global Positioning System (GPS) embedded in cell phones and automobile smart devices.[55]

Funding some 200 programs in science and engineering, DARPA, in the area of AI, has expressed great interest in the creation and advancement of AI technologies. It is presently funding a third wave of AI technologies with the first wave having focused on handcrafted knowledge or rule-based systems capable of narrowly defined tasks. The second wave created statistical pattern recognizers from large amounts of data that resulted in its funding of natural language understanding, problem solving, navigation and perception technologies leading to autonomous vehicles personal assistants, near-natural prosthetics, and a broad range of military applications.[56]

*DARPA'S Third Wave Initiative.* DARPA's Third Wave of contextual adaptation addresses the limitations of the first and second waves which were dependent on large amounts of high-quality data which did not adapt to changing conditions, offered limited performance guarantees, and were unable to provide users with explanations of results achieved. Accordingly, DARPA is looking for new theories in its billion-dollar

---

[55] *About DARPA*, DARPA, https://www.darpa.mil/about-us/about-darpa.

[56] *DARPA Announces $2 Billion Campaign to Develop Next Wave of AI Technologies*, DARPA (Sept. 7, 2018), https://www.darpa.mil/news-events/2018-09-07. For a detailed PowerPoint presentation, see John Launchbury, *A DARPA Perspective on Artificial Intelligence*, DARPA, https://www.youtube.com/watch?v=-O01G3tSYpU.

investments in new and existing programs called the *"AI Next" campaign* which speaks of making multiple research investments aimed at transforming computers from being specialized tools to partners able to engage in problem-solving. It seeks to attain AI-based computers which can acquire human-like communication and reasoning capabilities with the ability to recognize new situations and environments and make the appropriate adaptation to them. Among the projects are the automation of Department of Defense business processes; improving the robustness and reliability of AI systems; enhancing the security and resiliency of machine learning and AI technologies; reducing power, data, and performance inefficiencies; and pioneering the next generation of AI algorithms and applications.[57]

An example is the DARPA solicitation of Sept. 28, 2018 as follows:

> The Defense Advanced Research Projects Agency (DARPA) Defense Sciences Office (DSO) is announcing a new Artificial Intelligence Exploration (AIE) Opportunity that is focused on elevating Artificial Intelligence (AI) to the role of an insightful and trusted collaborator in scientific discovery and the scientific process. This AIE Opportunity announces the Artificial Intelligence Research Associate (AIRA) program, and invites submissions of innovative basic research proposals to address two main objectives: 1) explore and develop novel new AI algorithms and approaches for discovery of scientific laws and governing equations for complex physical phenomena; 2) explore new approaches to assess where data are too sparse, noisy, or are otherwise inadequate to build predictive models; to generate testable hypotheses; to identify high value experiments that could alleviate the problems of data shortfalls; and to quantify the confidence of predictions outside of the training space.[58]

DARPA is seeking to develop schema-based AI capability (case-based reasoning) to enhance reasoning about complex world events and generate actionable insights. The concept involves the process of uncovering rele-

---

[57] *Id.*

[58] *Artificial Intelligence Research Associate*, FEDBIZOPPS.GOV, Solicitation Number: DARPA-PA-18-02-02, https://www.fbo.gov/index?s=opSafely Ensuring Lives Future Deployment and Research in portunity&mode=form&id=ee78d74decc4851c873de9633967a3da&tab=core&_cview=0.

vant connections across enormous quanta of data and the static elements that underlie it which current tools and systems are not yet capable of deriving.[59] In order to uncover complex events in multimedia information for use by investigators, DARPA created the Knowledge-directed Artificial Intelligence Reasoning Over Schemas (KAIROS) program which seeks to create a schema-based AI capable of enabling contextual and temporal reasoning about complex-real world events to generate knowledge of how they will unfold. The research objectives are to take place in two-stages: (1) a focus on creating schemas from large volumes of data by detecting, classifying, and clustering sub-events based on linguistic inference and common sense reasoning; and (2) a focus on applying the library of schemas during stage one to multimedia, multi-lingual information to uncover and extract complex events.[60] With respect to the controversy discussed above concerning technologists opposed to their work being used for military purposes, DARPA has apparently shifted its emphasis away from an appeal to public service and patriotism to funding with a focus in part on matters affecting ethics, safety, and privacy.[61]

# U.S. Department of Homeland Security

The mission of the U.S. Department of Homeland Security (DHS) "is to ensure a homeland that is safe, secure, and resilient against terrorism and other hazards."[62] Thus, its major concern is the growth of AI-driven technologies and its impact upon the security of the U.S. In July, 2017, it issued a Report, *Artificial Intelligence Risk to Critical Infrastructure*,[63]

---

[59] Quote of Dr. Boyan Onyshkevych, *Generating Actionable Understanding of Real-World Phenomena with AI*, DARPA (Jan. 4, 2019), https://darpa.mil/news-events/2019-01-04.

[60] *Id.*

[61] Drew Harwell, *Defense Department pledges billions toward artificial intelligence research*, WASHINGTON POST (Sept. 7, 2018), https://www.washingtonpost.com/technology/2018/09/07/defense-department-pledges-billions-toward-artificial-intelligence-research/?utm_term=.9ee6688ef8a7.

[62] *Our Mission*, DEPARTMENT OF HOMELAND SECURITY, https://www.dhs.gov/our-mission.

[63] *Artificial Intelligence Risk to the Critical Infrastructure*, July 2017, DEPARTMENT OF HOMELAND SECURITY, https://publicintelligence.net/dhs-aritificial-intelligence/.

whose focus is the major risks to the otherwise positive aspects of the new technology. The four risks that it noted are: (1) mass job displacement; (2) privacy concerns; (3) lack of awareness of technological limitations; and (4) safety and ethical shortcomings. For the first vulnerability, the concern of DHS is that of potential social unrest and security challenges and a decline in tax revenue resulting therefrom. The second concern is the vulnerability of data privacy as AI adoption will bring about the collection of a growing amount of personal data, from web traffic to facial and voice recognition data, all of which may become vulnerable to hacking. In turn, it may lead to a backlash over the government's collection of this data which could inhibit security solutions. Another concern is the overestimation of AI capabilities by companies which might cause companies to overlook building robust security into AI technologies and adopt products that have major limitations as to effectiveness.[64]

A third vulnerability is the susceptibility to manipulation and infliction of harm. The concern is that robots, lacking in human and moral intelligence, may make harmful decisions not controlled by humans. Malicious actors and adversaries could use AI products to launch cyber or physical attacks on infrastructure, leverage open-source releases to develop their own AI capabilities, and/or infiltrate CI [critical infrastructure] systems that also use open-source tools.

The DHS Report advocates certain measures to mitigate risks: expand public-private resiliency planning to mitigate mass unemployment and resulting consequences; encourage companies to improve protections against internal and external security breaches and to address data privacy and vulnerability gaps as part of their innovation and ethical research efforts; formulate and disseminate best practices for safe AI integration across sectors, acknowledging the technological limitations and the need for human oversight; and highlight the role for government regulation to ensure safe adoption of AI technology.[65]

---

[64] *Id.* at iii.
[65] *Id.*, at iv.

# Autonomous Vehicles and U.S. Policy

## Federal Regulation

*The Self Drive Act.* There are both federal and state regulations either in force or proposed. The most important attempt at the federal level is the proposed *Safe Ensuring Lives Future Deployment and Research in Vehicle Evolution Act* (Self Drive Act).[66] The context of the proposed statute is the fact that there are approximately one million vehicles with self-driving features on the road as of 2018 which is expected to rise to ten million within two years. It was further noted that 42,400 people died as a result of traffic accidents and 2.5 million people have had injuries during the past year almost all due to human error. Self-driving vehicles are touted as the means to diminish such fatalities by 90 percent once they are fully and properly automated with appropriate AI features. The Subcommittee on Digital Commerce and Consumer Protection of the Energy and Commerce Committee of the House of Representatives voted 54-0 in favor of the proposed Act to send to the House which promptly passed the proposed Act by voice vote. The Senate has not yet acted on the measure. According to the Committee, the Act would advance safety by prioritizing the protection of consumers; reaffirm the role and responsibilities of federal and state governments; update the federal motor vehicles standards to account for advances in technology and the evolution of highly automated vehicles; and maximize opportunities for research and development in the U.S. to create jobs and grow economic opportunities so that the U.S. can remain as a global leader in the industry.[67] It was referred to the Senate Commerce, Science, and Transportation Committee for consideration.

Additional comments by the Committee alleged that the proposed Act would increase safety on the testing, development, and deployment of self-driving cars by clarifying the role for the National Highway Traffic

[66] *Safely Ensuring Lives Future Deployment and Research in Vehicle Evolution Act*, H.R. 3388, 115th Cong. 1st Sess. (2017–2018), https://www.congress.gov/bill/115th-congress/house/bill/3388.

[67] *The Self-Drive Act: House Passes Bipartisan Legislation Paving the Way for Self-driving Cars on America's Roads*, HOUSE ENERGY AND COMMERCE COMMITTEE, https://energycommerce.house.gov/selfdrive/.

Safety Administration (NHTSA) of the U.S. Department of Transportation for regulating the safety of the design, construction, and performance of self-driving cars; improve NHTSA's access to safety data for future updates and development of safety standards; establish NHTSA safety assessment certifications for manufacturers; and enhance protections for cybersecurity, privacy, and consumer education. The Act would also purportedly support greater mobility for Americans by establishing a Federal Advisory Council to ensure manufacturers and regulators understand the needs of populations traditionally underserved by public transportation as well as senior citizens and individuals with disabilities. It would also be responsible for promoting educational outreach with respect to self-driving technology and its use by senior citizens and individuals with disabilities, and the implementation of this technology within communities traditionally underserved by public transportation. In addition, it would ensure that manufacturers and regulators understand current impediments that may prevent individuals with disabilities from using self-driving cars.[68]

There are possible negative aspects of the proposed Act. Among them is the preemption of state efforts to regulate autonomous vehicles. The Act specifically states that "No State or political subdivision of a State may maintain, enforce, prescribe, or continue in effect any law or regulation regarding the design, construction, or performance of highly automated vehicles, automated driving systems, or components of automated driving systems unless such law or regulation is identical to a standard prescribed under this chapter."[69] States are permitted to impose comparable or higher standards and may continue their normal tasks of licensing, registration, supervision of motor vehicle dealers, and the like.

Another possible negative aspect of the Act is the exemption granted to manufacturers relating to bumper and other safety standards for the first 100,000 vehicles manufactured within a 12-month period for the ostensible reason to "make easier the development or field evaluation of (I) a feature of a highly automated vehicle provided a safety level of at least equal to the safety level of the standards for which the exemption is

---

[68] *Id.* The Act may be found at https://www.congress.gov/bill/115th-congress/house-bill/3388/txt.
[69] §3 of the Act.

sought; or (II) has an overall safety level at least equal to the overall safety level of nonexempt vehicles."[70] Other commentators query whether the Act poses yet another expansion of federal administrative authority to the detriment of states' regulatory measures.[71]

## State Regulations of Autonomous Vehicles

Most older persons have significant doubts concerning the belief that driverless vehicles are not only safe but may be instrumental in saving lives both of drivers and passengers. Such fear was illustrated by reports that an Uber driverless vehicle struck and killed a pedestrian in March, 2018 while crossing the street in Tempe, Arizona and by an alleged incident when one of its vehicles swerved off the road onto a sidewalk and kept driving. After a nine-month period when it ceased providing driverless automobiles, Uber resumed such use after recruiting a former federal safety official to conduct an external review of its program, reverted to using two people in every vehicle, and other safety improvements.[72]

Unless eventually preempted by the federal government, states have already been active in examining possible regulation concerning autonomous vehicles. By 2017, 33 states introduced legislation or were subject to executive orders related to autonomous vehicles and at least 9 other states are considering some form of governance thereof. Twenty-nine states—Alabama, Arkansas, California, Colorado, Connecticut, Florida, Georgia, Illinois, Indiana, Kentucky, Louisiana, Maine, Michigan, Mississippi, Nebraska, New York, Nevada, North Carolina, North Dakota, Oregon, Pennsylvania, South Carolina, Tennessee, Texas, Utah, Virginia, Vermont, Washington, and Wisconsin—and Washington D.C. have enacted legislation related to autonomous vehicles while the

---

[70] §6 of the Act.

[71] Jennifer Huddleston Skees, *The Self Drive Act: 4 Questions left unanswered about federal regulation of autonomous vehicles*, THE TECHNOLOGY LIBERATION FRONT (Sept. 5, 2017), https://techliberation.com/2017/09/05/the-self-drive-act-4-questions-left-unanswered-about-federal-regulation-of-autonomous-vehicles/.

[72] Aarian Marshall, *After a Deadly Crash, Uber Returns Robocars to the Road*, WIRED (Dec. 20, 2018), https://www.wired.com/story/uber-returns-self-driving-after-deadly-crash/.

Governors in Arizona, Delaware, Hawaii, Idaho, Illinois, Maine, Massachusetts, Minnesota, Ohio, Washington, and Wisconsin have issued executive orders related to autonomous vehicles.[73]

*NHTSA Recommendations.* We have discussed NHTSA's five levels of automation beyond the 0 or *no automation* level (level 0) to that of *full automation* whereby the vehicle is capable of performing all driving functions under all conditions.[74] NHTSA has delineated the respective roles for the agency and for the states.

NHTSA's responsibilities are:

- Setting Federal Motor Vehicle Safety Standards (FMVSSs) for new motor vehicles and motor vehicle equipment (with which manufacturers must certify compliance before they sell their vehicles);
- Enforcing compliance with FMVSSs;
- Investigating and managing the recall and remedy of noncompliances and safety-related motor vehicle defects nationwide; and
- Communicating with and educating the public about motor vehicle safety issues.[75]

States' responsibilities are:

- Licensing human drivers and registering motor vehicles in their jurisdictions;
- Enacting and enforcing traffic laws and regulations;
- Conducting safety inspections, where states choose to do so; and
- Regulate motor vehicle insurance and liability[76]

---

[73] *Autonomous Vehicles: Self-Driving Vehicles Enacted Legislation*, NATIONAL CONFERENCE OF STATE LEGISLATURES (Nov. 7, 2018), http://www.ncsl.org/research/transportation/autonomous-vehicles-self-driving-vehicles-enacted-legislation.aspx.

[74] *Automated Driving Systems 2.0: A Vision for Safety*, NATIONAL HIGHWAY TRAFFIC SAFETY ADMINSITRATION at 4, https://www.nhtsa.gov/sites/nhtsa.dot.gov/files/documents/13069a-ads2.0_090617_v9a_tag.pdf.

[75] *Id.* at 20.

[76] *Id.*

Recommendations to states:

- Ensure that the driver understands how to operate a self-driving vehicle safely;
- Ensure that on-road testing of self-driving vehicles minimizes risks to other road users;
- Limit testing operations to roadway, traffic, and environmental conditions suitable for the capabilities of the tested self-driving vehicles;
- Establish reporting requirements to monitor the performance of self-driving technology during testing;
- Ensure that the process for transitioning from self-driving mode to driver control is safe, simple, and timely;
- Self-driving test vehicles should have the capability of detecting, recording, and informing the driver that the system of automated technologies has malfunctioned;
- Ensure that installation and operation of any self-driving vehicle technologies does not disable any federally required safety features or systems; and
- Ensure that self-driving test vehicles record information about the status of the automated control technologies in the event of a crash or loss of vehicle control.[77]

The latest emanation from the U.S. Department of Transportation concerns a comprehensive, multimodal approach toward safely integrating automation. Under the authority of the U.S. Department of Transportation, Federal Motor Carrier Safety Administration (FMCSA), the Department regulates the safety of commercial motor carriers operating in interstate commerce as well as commercial motor vehicle drivers.

*Judicial Determinations.* Courts have begun to injuries to persons and/ or property that have resulted from implementation of AI-based concepts. Autonomous vehicles (without human control) have been in operation for a number of years and are anticipated to be used

---

[77] *Autonomous Vehicle Report*, FLORIDA HIGHWAY SAFETY AND MOTOR VEHICLES (Feb. 10, 2014), https://www.flhsmv.gov/html/HSMVAutonomousVehicleReport2014.pdf.

substantially within the next decade, once the many variables have been dealt with by AI researchers. AI Law will become a standard law school course or be a part of a tort law course in the near future.

Although there is a paucity of cases associated with AI, the following cases are illustrative of litigation that will inevitably occur as AI increasingly becomes a part of our daily lives.[78] In *Cruz v. Talmadge*,[79] a lawsuit, later settled, ensued whereby the plaintiffs sued the owners and operators of a motor coach that was 12 feet in height when it was crushed while proceeding under an underpass whose height was 10 feet causing extensive personal injuries. The claim among others was that the driver was following the directions of Garmin and/or TomTom GPS system. In *Nilsson v. General Motors, LLC.*, which was the first case commenced with respect to an autonomous vehicle (self-driving automobile),[80] it was alleged that the defendant driver, Manuel DeJesus Salazar, while sitting on the driver's seat, kept his hands off the self-driving vehicle manufactured by General Motors and allegedly gave command instructions to the vehicle to change lanes to the left but the vehicle failed to act in accord with the instructions thereby striking a motor cyclist and causing serious injuries.

In Chap. 2, we looked at the many applications and beneficial uses of AI from a mainly positive viewpoint. In Chap. 3, we were mainly concerned with AI policies and initiatives mainly from the U.S. government perspective. We will proceed in the following chapters with an in- depth examination of specific concerns that AI systems have initiated which directly affect individuals and businesses. In Chap. 4, we scrutinize how biases may affect the outcomes of AI programs especially in the criminal law realm. We then proceed to a discussion of ethics and privacy that are interrelated and are deeply intertwined with AI programs, and, finally, we discuss the "bread-and-butter" issue of how AI, particularly robots, are greatly changing the nature of work and job availability because of automation replacing jobs.

---

[78] Cases cited by Huu Nguyen, *Artificial Intelligence Law is Here, Part One*, ABOVE THE LAW, https://abovethelaw.com/legal-innovation-center/2018/07/26/artificial-intelligence-law-is-here-part-one/.

[79] *Cruz v. Talmadge*, 244 F.Supp.3d 231 (1977).

[80] *Nilsson v. General Motors, LLC.* 4:18-cv-00471-KAW (N.D. Ca., Jan. 22, 2018).

# Part II

## Privacy and Ethical Concerns, Bias, Jobs, Intellectual Property Rights and International Initiatives

Part II

# 4

# Ethics and Privacy I: Facial Recognition and Robotics

Although we have discussed some of the regulatory actions taken that address certain AI-based innovations, in this chapter we will examine a number of other major legal issues that inevitably will arise as AI proliferation becomes more invasive in everyday human affairs. Among the concerns discussed are whether regulation of AI is necessary; ethical considerations, right of privacy, particularly as it relates to facial recognition, robotics, and lethal weapons and national and international initiatives relating to them.

## Need for Regulation?

In *Holbrook v. Prodomax Automation Ltd.*,[1] it was alleged that the decedent, who was employed to do maintenance duties at her place of employment, was killed when a robot from a section of the firm entered the deceased's area and struck and crushed her head between a hitch assembly it was attempting to place and another assembly already in the fixture. This representative case and others illustrate some of the issues which will

---

[1] *Holbrook v. Prodomax Automation Ltd.*, 1:17-cv-00219-PLM-PJG (W.D. Mich. March 7, 2017).

© The Author(s) 2020
R. Girasa, *Artificial Intelligence as a Disruptive Technology*,
https://doi.org/10.1007/978-3-030-35975-1_4

arise as robots and related AI creations bring about injuries to persons and properties. Classical tort theories of products liability and negligence would appear to be the bases for litigation albeit the degree of liability and theories upon which to make claims will be left to future determination.

As with virtually all innovative technologies, there are the relatively small handful of persons who greatly benefit from the creations and those many persons who are shunted aside in a lost quandary. The latter initiate outcries that governments should intervene to protect victims of criminal or unfair trade practices that inevitably arise because of greed and other malfeasance of those persons who have mastered the technologies. Movies such as 2001: A Space Odyssey (1968),[2] the Star Wars enterprises, Alien (1979), Blade Runner (1982) and numerous other movies,[3] which have featured creatures with AI attempting to take over the human race or possess other destructive tendencies, elicit intense emotional fears in average audiences. The general public is aware of the occasional highly publicized purported misuse of AI such as the cloning in whole or in part of not only animals but also of human embryos.[4] Major innovators leading AI advances have weighed in concerning both positive and negative opinions concerning the need for regulation. On the one hand, those persons advocating governmental hands-off policies emphasize the positive aspects of AI, in essence stating that any regulation would stifle AI progress that has so greatly benefitted humanity and will continue to do so in an upward spiral; on the other hand, some technologists relate the abuses of persons pursuing AI which may lead to substantial harm to the populace.

Whether regulation should be inaugurated to a greater or lesser degree is a common topic discussed almost daily in various publications. Politically, it appears at times that the U.S. Republican Party leadership

---

[2] ARTHUR C. CLARKE, 2001: A SPACE ODYSSEY, New American Library (1968), and movie of the same title directed by Stanley Kubrick (2018).

[3] *36 of the best movies about AI, ranked*, ZDNET (Jan. 18, 2018), https://www.zdnet.com/pictures/15-of-the-best-movies-about-ai-ranked/.

[4] Thomas Porostocky, *Pro and Con: Should Gene Editing Be Performed on Human Embryos?*, NATIONAL GEOGRAPHIC (Aug. 1968), https://www.nationalgeographic.com/magazine/2016/08/human-gene-editing-pro-con-opinions/.

wants little or no regulation of business activities in order to spur and maintain economic growth while Democrat Party representatives appear to demand excessive regulation. The question then arises whether AI should be regulated, and if so, the degree of regulation and by whom? We previously discussed some issues relating to robotics and suggested regulatory enactments relating thereto. The following chapters examine some of the major issues that AI has brought about and regulatory measures, if any, which have been or should be enacted.

# Facial Recognition Programs, Robotics, and Lethal Weapons

We commence the discussion with basic philosophical questions of ethics and privacy and then proceed to relate how the latest technologies affect how human society applies these principles.

## What Is the Meaning of Ethics?

*Ethics* or moral philosophy is the study of what is right and wrong; the principles of how one should live in order to be happy; one's duty to others exemplified by the biblical and commonly held ideal of almost all religious beliefs: "Do unto others what you would want to be done unto you." The study and elucidation of ethics have their bases from earliest times of the law code of Hammurabi (about 1750 BC), through the Old Testament (Ten Commandments and other references) and New Testament, and philosophical writings commencing popularly from ancient Greek times with Plato's *Protagoras*, and Aristotle's *Nicomachean Ethics* and the *Eudemian Ethics* which discuss the nature of happiness, virtue, and excellence and the character traits that one should possess in order to achieve that state.[5] The study of ethics in recent times has evolved

---

[5] There are innumerable references to the study and nature of ethics. For a general discussion from which this comment is derived, see Aristotle, *Ethics*, STANFORD ENCYCLOPEDIA OF PHILOSOPHY (June 15, 2018), https://plato.stanford.edu/entries/aristotle-ethics/.

to include *metaethics* (study of the kinds of things that exist in the universe—physical and non-physical such as thoughts, spirits, and gods); whether moral values are eternal truths and many other related issues?[6]; *normative ethics* (how one should act) and its numerous subdivisions; *applied ethics* (how ethics relates to actual human behavior); *moral philosophical psychology* (study of moral development—e.g., altruism, egoism, and the like); and *descriptive ethics* (describes how people live, i.e., choices made, aesthetics, and etiquette).[7]

AI has raised the spectrum of ethical issues almost unlike any other technology since the production and use of the atomic bomb. Issues range from the fear of enslavement of human beings to robotic machines run amok, to loss of jobs, military usage, privacy implications, and ethical challenges.

## Privacy

Privacy is variously defined but may be summarized by the expression "the right to be left alone."[8] There are a number of subcategories of privacy including the following: (1) *information privacy*, i.e., rules that concern the gathering and use of personal data, such as credit reports and medical records; (2) *bodily privacy*, i.e., protection extended to persons with respect to drug testing and the like; (3) *communications privacy*, or privacy with respect to communications by the various modes thereof; and (4) *territorial privacy*, which governs invasions of an individual such

---

[6] *Ethics*, INTERNET ENCYCLOPEDIA OF PHILOSOPHY, https://www.iep.utm.edu/ethics/. See, also, Peter Singer, *Ethics Philosophy*, ENCYCLOPAEDIA BRITANNICA, https://www.britannica.com/topic/ethics-philosophy.

[7] *Ethics*, WIKIPEDIA, https://en.wikipedia.org/wiki/Ethics.

[8] Comment by U.S. Justice of the Supreme Court, Louis Brandeis, who co-authored with his partner, Samuel D. Warren, the first major discussion on privacy entitled The Right of Privacy, Harvard Law Review, Dec. 15, 1890. In his dissent in *Olmstead v. United States*, 277 U.S. 438, 478, Brandeis characterized "the right to be let alone" as "the right most valued by civilized men," In *Griswold v. Connecticut*, 381 U.S. 479, 483, the U.S. Supreme Court said: "[T]he First Amendment has a penumbra where privacy is protected from governmental intrusion," Footnote 25, *Whalen v. Roe*, 429 U.S. 589 (1977).

as into one's workplace or public space (dressing rooms and the like).[9] Philosophically, privacy may be viewed as: (1) the degree of *control of information* that individuals have about themselves and to prevent others from unauthorized access; (2) *undocumented personal knowledge* known by others; and (3) *restricted access*, i.e., protection against intrusion, zones of protection.[10] In the realm of journalism communications, another view philosophically is that privacy "is the protection of one's innermost self by determining who and what enters our personal life space." It is not focused on journalists and their desire for a good story but rather should be on the individual's rights to control information about him- or herself.[11]

The *Restatement of Torts* refers to the tort of privacy as the invasion of the right of privacy of another as follows: (1) One who invades the right of privacy of another is subject to liability for the resulting harm to the interests of the other. (2) The right of privacy is invaded by: (a) unreasonable intrusion upon the seclusion of another, or (1) *intrusion upon seclusion* i.e., intentionally intruding upon the solitude or seclusion of another person or such person's private affairs or concerns[12]; (2) *appropriation of the name and likeness* of another person for one's own use or benefit[13]; (3) *publicity given to private life* if it would be offensive to that person (e.g., telling others a person has AIDS or other highly personal conditions or illnesses) or not of legitimate concern to the public.[14] Although similar in nature with a high degree of overlap, invasion of privacy is a type of unethical behavior which is more generic in content.

---

[9] David Banisar and Simon Davies, *Global Trend in Privacy Protection: An International Survey of Privacy, Data Protection, and Surveillance of Laws and Development*, 1 J. MARSHALL J. COMPUTER & INFO. L (Fall, 1999), https://repository.jmls.edu/cgi/viewcontent.cgi?referer=&httpsredir=1&article=1174&context=jitpl.

[10] James H. Moor, *The Ethics of Privacy Protection*, 39 LIBRARY TRENDS (Summer/Fall, 1990), at 69–82.
https://www.ideals.illinois.edu/bitstream/handle/2142/7714/librarytrendsv39i1-2h_opt.pdf?sequence=1.

[11] Christopher Meyers, *Journalism Ethics: A Philosophical Approach*, OXFORD SCHOLARSHIP ONLINE (May, 2010), http://www.oxfordscholarship.com/view/10.1093/acprof:oso/9780195370805.001.0001/acprof-9780195370805-chapter-14.

[12] §652B of *Restatement of the Law, Second, Torts*, https://cyber.harvard.edu/privacy/Privacy_R2d_Torts_Sections.htm.

[13] *Id.* §653C.

[14] *Id.* §652C.

Closely allied with ethics and privacy is that of *confidentiality* which has been defined as "the process of protecting an individual's privacy" whereby information that has been entrusted to another person in a relationship of trust will not be revealed without the consent of such person. There may be legal ramifications for exposure of the information such as in an attorney-client, doctor-patient, accountant-client, and other comparable relationships that are governed by rules of behavior of professional associations to which the licensed individual belongs. There are a number of government regulations specifying the right of individuals to their privacy rights such as the Food and Drug Administration which requires informed consent of participants; Certificates of Confidentiality issued by the National Institutes of Health exempting researchers from being compelled to give testimony or information concerning their research participants; and other governmental and organizational privacy tests.[15] The Health Insurance Portability and Accountability Act of 1996 as amended (HIPAA) is another major statutory privacy law which protects against unauthorized disclosure of protected health information.[16]

The most feared mode of privacy invasion is that by governments. There has been a proliferation of scholarly articles emanating from disclosures such as that by Edward Snowden, who, as an employee of the Central Intelligence Agency (CIA), revealed thousands of documents concerning the secret National Security Agency's (NSA) government global surveillance program in 2013 in conjunction with other European governments and telecommunications companies. It caused many observers to consider the possible futuristic consequences envisioned by George Orwell in his novel, *Nineteen Eighty-Four*, (1984), wherein the inhabitants of the planet are subject to extreme government surveillance and propaganda.[17] There were historical examples of nations engaged in such practice such as the former Soviet Union and presently, North Korea. There are AI databases in China wherein its usage is unknown and can only be surmised. An odd database that raises privacy concerns therein, is

---

[15] *Current Issues in Research Ethics: Privacy and Confidentiality*, http://ccnmtl.columbia.edu/projects/cire/pac/foundation/.

[16] Health Insurance Portability and Accountability Act, Pub.L. 104–191, 110 Stat. 1936, enacted August 21, 1996).

[17] GEORGE ORWELL, NINETEEN EIGHTY-FOUR, Secker and Warburg, U.K. (1949).

one which a security researcher uncovered that lists 1.8 million Chinese women, mainly in Beijing, with their names, addresses, phone numbers, educational backgrounds, and marital status, and a "breed ready" statistic whereby it is speculated its use is to keep track of the shortage.[18]

*Alexa and Privacy Litigation.* With the proliferation of technological devices that enable extreme invasion of one's privacy, the capability of governments and even corporate entities to propagate their views and make those persons in opposition to have raised significant concerns among civil rights groups and other persons and organizations of their loss of liberties guaranteed under law. There are many commentators who caution about the possible misuse of AI and the threat to democracy. For example, Amy Webb, a futurist and New York University Professor, warned in her book about the short-term outlook of the tech giants that may ultimately lead to the support of totalitarian regimes, such as the alleged consolidation and mining of massive amounts of data by Tencent, Alibaba, and Baidu in support of China's authoritarian regime. She worries about AI machines and processes, such as DeepMind, which, ultimately, may construct anonymous decisions that could be terribly detrimental to humans and contrary to democratic ideals. Her way forward is for people to take care of the private information they provide online. She also noted universities' role in educating students in a broad hybrid range of subjects as provided in the liberal arts coupled with the social sciences and computer science. Businesses should take care in hiring to avoid bias and excess risk. She further recommends the creation of a Global Alliance on Intelligence Augmentation (GAIA) that would engage in data collection and sharing and create global norms and standards.[19]

Privacy invasion is also evident in a case involving Amazon's Alexa or Amazon Echo which is a voice command device whereby when one utters

---

[18] Shannon Liao, *An exposed database tracked whether 1.8 million Chinese women were "breed ready,"* THE VERGE (March 11, 2019).

[19] Karen Hao, *Why AI is a threat to democracy – and what we can do to stop it,* MIT TECHNOLOGY REVIEW (Feb. 26, 2019), https://www.technologyreview.com/s/613010/why-ai-is-a-threat-to-democracyand-what-we-can-do-to-stop-it/. The cited book is Amy Webb, *The Big Nine: How the Tech Titans and Their Thinking Machines Could Warp Humanity,* PUBLIC AFFAIRS (March 5, 2019).

the word "Alexa," "Echo," "Computer" or other substituted word, and the device responds to questions asked. In addition, these devices play requested music, stream podcasts, play audiobooks, set alarms, connect to other devices as a hub, and other uses.[20] Questions have arisen whether the device is constantly recording conversations taking place within one's home; whether it is "on" when the command word is uttered; or whether it is "off" at all other times. It appears to be off when not in response to a verbal inquiry but the issue of unintentional recording of what is occurring when supposedly off does arise as evidenced by prosecutors' continual requests for search warrants to investigate its possible recordings in crime scenes. It is conceivable for the device to be accidentally turned on if a "wake" word is uttered even though its usage was not meant to arouse it. There has been at least one instance when the device was unintentionally turned on thereby recording a private conversation.[21]

There are at least two criminal cases wherein the issue of unintentional recording arose. In one, *Arkansas v. Bates*,[22] police sought records of the Amazon Echo device based on a person's alleged hearing of music streaming through the device while an alleged murder was taking place. The search warrant described the requested device as "certain records, namely electronic data in the form of audio recordings, transcribed records, or other text records related to communications and transactions between an Amazon Echo device … that was located at [the defendant's] residence … and Amazon.com's service and other computer hardware maintained at Amazon's.com." The defendant, James Bates, was accused of murder in the death of one Victor Collins after both were drinking and watching football. The body of Collins was found face-down in Bates' hot tub.

Amazon opposed the request for the warrant asserting that it violated the privacy rights of its customers particularly when the data may include expressive content which is protected by the First Amendment of the U.S. Constitution.[23] Amazon cited as precedent, *Zhang v. Baidu.com*

---

[20] *Amazon Echo*, WIKIPEDIA, https://en.wikipedia.org/wiki/Amazon_Echo.

[21] John Kruzel, *Is your Amazon Alexa spying on you?*, POLITIFACT (May 31, 2018), https://www.politifact.com/truth-o-meter/statements/2018/may/31/ro-khanna/your-amazon-alexa-spying-you/.

[22] State of Arkansas v. Bates, Case No. 04CR-16-370 (Ark. Cir., 2016).

[23] Huu Nguyen, *Artificial Intelligence Law is Here, Part Three*, EVOLVE THE LAW (Oct. 4, 2018), https://abovethelaw.com/legal-innovation-center/2018/10/04/artificial-intelligence-law-is-here-part-three/.

which held that "the First Amendment protects as speech the results produced by an Internet search engine."[24] It did later accede to the request when the defendant consented to its search. The case was ultimately dismissed for lack of sufficient evidence to hold the defendant.[25] In a more recent case involving a double homicide in New Hampshire, a judge ordered Amazon to turn over Alexa recordings that allegedly occurred on the date of the homicides. The device was on the kitchen counter when the murders took place. The trial of the defendant, Timothy Verill, for the murders of Christine Sullivan and her friend Jenna Pelligrini, was to take place in May, 2019, later postponed to October, 2019.[26]

# Facial Recognition Programs

We discussed facial recognition as one of the advances in AI technology in Chap. 1. Legal and ethical issues may arise whereby several U.S. states, such as Illinois' *Biometric Information Privacy Act*,[27] Washington's *Biometric Identifiers Act*[28] and Texas' *Personal Identity Information Act*,[29] have enacted legislation forbidding its use without a person's consent.[30] States may have comparable protections under various privacy laws

---

[24] Zhang v. Baidu, 10 F. Sup.3d 433 (S.D.N.Y. 2014). See Sylvia Sui, *State v. Bates: Amazon Argues that the First Amendment Protects Its Alexa Voice Service*, JOLT DIGEST (March 25, 2017), http://jolt.law.harvard.edu/digest/amazon-first-amendment.

[25] Nicole Chavez, *Arkansas judge drops murder charge in Amazon Echo case*, CNN (Dec. 2, 2017), https://www.cnn.com/2017/11/30/us/amazon-echo-arkansas-murder-case-dismissed/index.html.

[26] Patrick Hearn, *New Hampshire judge tells Amazon to turn over Echo recordings in murder case*, DIGITAL TRENDS (Nov. 12, 2018), https://www.digitaltrends.com/news/alexa-court-new-hampshire-judge-requests-echo-recordings/.

[27] Biometric Information Privacy Act, Ill. 740 ILCS 14/1 (2008), http://www.ilga.gov/legislation/ilcs/ilcs3.asp?ActID=3004.

[28] (2017) Wash, HB 1483, Ch. 299, *Biometric Identifiers*, http://lawfilesext.leg.wa.gov/biennium/2017-18/Pdf/Bills/Session%20Laws/House/1493-S.SL.pdf#page=1.

[29] Tex. Personal Identity Information, Title 11, §503, https://statutes.capitol.texas.gov/Docs/BC/htm/BC.503.htm.

[30] Ben Sobel, *facial recognition technology is everywhere. It may not be legal*, WASHINGTON POST (June 11, 2015), http://washingtopost.com/news/the-switch/wp/2015/06/.

including the right of publicity,[31] while in other states visitors to prisons are subjected to face recognition software.[32] Similarly, in the United Kingdom (U.K.), there are facial recognition programs of prison visitors, according to the Ministry of Justice. Although controversial to civil rights advocates, nevertheless, they have been proven successful in thwarting drug smuggling in "low rights environments" such as inmates in prisons. Some 23,000 drug packages were seized in 2018 partly as a result of the software.[33] Facial recognition programs are increasingly becoming widespread because of the fear brought about by the many mass shootings that occur in the U.S. annually which will continue with the proliferation of the gun culture and governmental protections given under the "right to bear arms" stated in the Second Amendment of the U.S. Constitution.[34] Thus, towns and cities, such as Lockport, New York, have installed facial recognition systems which scan faces of students to observe so-called potentially dangerous students and their movements. Similarly, in private settings, facial recognition cameras have been used at the California Rose Bowl to protect entertainers from possible attacks by stalkers and masses of fans in an endeavor to prevent mass shooting or other criminal activities such as the occurrence at Mandalay Bay in Las Vegas wherein a sole shooter killed 59 persons and injured over 500 at an outdoor entertainment event.[35]

*Amazon's Rekognition Program.* There is some evidence that facial recognition programs are prone to error particularly when used for identifi-

---

[31] Richard Brand and Eva Pulliam, *Faces in the crowd: legal considerations for use of facial recognition technology at sports arenas*, LAWINSPORT (Aug. 29, 2018), https://www.lawinsport.com/topics/articles/item/faces-in-the-crowd-legal-considerations-for-use-of-facial-recognition-technology-at-sports-arenas.

[32] *Prisons are using face recognition on visitors to prevent drug smuggling*, MIT TECHNOLOGY REVIEW, https://www.technologyreview.com/the-download/613080/prisons-are-using-face-recognition-on-visitors-to-prevent-drug-smuggling/.

[33] Lizzie Dearden, *Prison visitors to have faces and irises scanned as government targets drug smuggling*, INDEPENDENT (March 6, 2019), https://www.independent.co.uk/news/uk/home-news/facial-recognition-prisons-iris-scanning-drug-smuggling-government-gauke-a8809166.html.

[34] The Second Amendment states: "A well regulated Militia, being necessary to the security of a free State, the right of the people to keep and bear Arms, shall not be infringed." Proponents of unfettered gun rights emphasize the send part of the sentence while ignoring the preamble to the sentence and vice versa for opponents of gun rights.

[35] Rose Eveleth, *In the Face of Danger, We're Turning to Surveillance*, WIRED (March 21, 2019), https://www.wired.com/story/surveillance-safety/.

cation of African Americans, ethnic minorities, women, and young people. Amazon's Rekognition program has been particularly controversial. Amazon claims that its program makes it easy to add image and video analysis to a company's applications which can identify the objects, people, text, scenes, activities, and any inappropriate content. It says it is highly accurate in its facial analysis and facial recognition on images and video that is provided. Based on deep learning technology it is highly scalable and does not require machine learning to use.[36] It is questionable whether its accuracy can match that of individuals' responses to the vision of another person's face. The field of neuroscience is undergoing major studies concerning how cells of the brain operate as face detectors. The process of machine learning operates on a set of 50 numbers which represent the measurement of a face along a set of axes much like that of a set of six nodes in the inferotemporal cortex of both brain hemispheres of a human person.[37]

The American Civil Liberties Union (ACLU), however, alleges that the Amazon software is flawed and that, in a test it conducted, the software incorrectly matched 28 members of Congress as having been arrested for a crime. The false matches were disproportionately of people of color.[38] Some Amazon investors have urged the company to halt sales of its software contending that it may be used to violate the rights of individuals unless a third-party evaluation concludes that it does not cause or contribute to violations of civil and human rights.[39] Nevertheless, Amazon is determined to continue selling the software to both government and companies asserting its value to law enforcement albeit with the understanding that appropriate guidelines would be utilized.[40]

---

[36] *Amazon Rekognition*, AMAZON, https://amazon.com/rekognition.

[37] Doris Y. Tsao, *Face Values*, SCIENTIFIC AMERICAN ((Feb. 2019), pp. 23–29.

[38] Jacob Snow, *Amazon's Face Recognition Falsely Matched 28 Members of Congress with Mugshots*, ACLU of Northern Ca. (July 28, 2018), https://www.aclu.org/blog/privacy-technology/surveillance-technologies/amazons-face-recognition-falsely-matched-28.

[39] Rachel Metz, *Amazon investors want it to quit selling facial recognition tech to the government*, CNN BUSINESS, KMOV4 (Jan. 17, 2019). https://www.kmov.com/news/amazon-investors-want-it-to-quit-selling-facial-recognition-tech/article_2cdff0ec-6baa-536f-ba5c-1b09e7b28e27.html.

[40] Nick Statt, *Amazon told employees it would continue to sell facial recognition software to law enforcement*, THE Verge (Nov. 8, 2018), https://www.kmov.com/news/amazon-investors-want-it-to-quit-selling-facial-recognition-tech/article_2cdff0ec-6baa-536f-ba5c-1b09e7b28e27.html.

Amazon's Rekognition's program is not the only one exhibiting flaws. Google had to issue its apologies to a black software developer who charged that Google's photo service had labeled photos of him with a black friend as "gorillas." Although Google then erased gorillas from its lexicon, WIRED Magazine did some testing and found a number of discrepancies such as using the search term "African American" which showed an image of a grazing antelope. The author of the article noted that image recognition is an illustration of the problems with the then existing machine-learning technology, although Google's CloudVision API fared much better.[41] Similarly, researchers who tested features of Microsoft and IBM's face-analysis services determined that they were both excellent at identifying white males but much less accurate in identifying persons with black skin (error rate for IBM's algorithm of 0.3 percent for white males vs. 35 percent for darker female faces). A possible explanation is that there was much less training data that was used to create the face-analysis algorithms.[42]

It should be noted, however, that AI recognition is based on machine learning and, as such, does constantly improve as more and more data is added. It is exemplified by IBM's plans to add over 1 million images to lessen bias and improve its accuracy with much clearer images gathered from cameras, sensors, smartphones, social media sites, and other sources not only domestically but also globally. It has been predicted that by 2023 there will be an 80 percent reduction in missing persons in advanced nations compared with 2018.[43]

Due to the public outcry concerning civil and human rights, including that from Amazon's shareholders concerning its facial Rekognition

---

[41] Rick Madonik, *When It Comes to Gorillas, google Photos Remains Blind*, WIRED (Jan. 11, 2018), https://www.wired.com/story/when-it-comes-to-gorillas-google-photos-remains-blind/.

[42] Tom Simonite, *Photo Algorithms ID White Men Fine-Black Women, Not So Much*, WIRED (Feb. 6, 2018), https://www.wired.com/story/photo-algorithms-id-white-men-fineblack-women-not-so-much/.

[43] David Rand, *Facial recognition can drive business goals, but where do we draw the line?* HEWLETTPACKARD ENTERPRISE (Feb. 25, 2019), https://www.hpe.com/us/en/insights/articles/facial-recognition-can-drive-business-goals-but-where-do-we-draw-the-line-1902.html, quoting Gartner.

software, Amazon has proposed guidelines for legislative enactment both in the U.S. and abroad as follows:

(1) Facial recognition should always be used in accordance with existing laws, including laws that protect civil rights.
(2) When facial recognition technology is used in law enforcement, human review is a necessary component to ensure that the use of a prediction to make a decision does not violate civil rights.
(3) When facial recognition technology is used by law enforcement for identification, or in a way that could threaten civil liberties, a 99 percent confidence score threshold is recommended.
(4) Law enforcement agencies should be transparent in how they use facial recognition technology.
(5) There should be notice when video surveillance and facial recognition technology are used together in public or commercial settings.[44]

In making the recommendation, Amazon joined with Microsoft, which had appealed earlier for governmental regulation not only federally but also by Microsoft's president, Brad Smith's call for regulation by its home state turf of the State of Washington.[45] In a Microsoft blog referencing complaints about facial recognition software by the ACLU Union, he noted that Microsoft had called for national privacy legislation as early as 2005 and has stated its support for the E.U.'s General Data Protection Regulation (discussed in Chap. 8). He said that regulation is particularly important given facial recognition's "broad social ramifications and potential for abuse." He feared governments may monitor the exercise of political and other traditions that heretofore have been expectations of a free society. He also worried about its misuse in decisions concerning eligibility for jobs, credit, or purchases without human intervention.

---

[44] Tim Hinchliffe, *Amazon proposes ethical guidelines on facial recognition software use*, THE SOCIABLE (Feb. 11, 2019), https://sociable.co/business/amazon-ethical-facial-recognition-software-use/.

[45] Monica Nickelsburg, *Microsoft want Washington State to double down on infrastructure and privacy*, *Microsoft wants Washington state to double down on infrastructure and privacy*, GEEKWIRE (Feb 11, 2019), https://www.geekwire.com/2019/microsoft-wants-washington-state-double-infrastructure-privacy/.

Brad Smith stated that the issues, among others, that needed to be addressed concerning facial recognition are the following:

- Should law enforcement use of facial recognition be subject to human oversight and controls, including restrictions on the use of unaided facial recognition technology as evidence of an individual's guilt or innocence of a crime?
- Similarly, should we ensure there is civilian oversight and accountability for the use of facial recognition as part of governmental national security technology practices?
- What types of legal measures can prevent use of facial recognition for racial profiling and other violations of rights while still permitting the beneficial uses of the technology?
- Should use of facial recognition by public authorities or others be subject to minimum performance levels on accuracy?
- Should the law require that retailers post visible notice of their use of facial recognition technology in public spaces?
- Should the law require that companies obtain prior consent before collecting individuals' images for facial recognition? If so, in what situations and places should this apply? And what is the appropriate way to ask for and obtain such consent?
- Should we ensure that individuals have the right to know what photos have been collected and stored that have been identified with their names and faces?
- Should we create processes that afford legal rights to individuals who believe they have been misidentified by a facial recognition system?[46]

Google's CEO Sundar Pichai also weighed in concerning AI's possibility of ethical, legal, and other challenges. In the company's latest filing of the parent company Alphabet's earnings with the Securities and Exchange Commission, he cautioned that new products and services incorporating or using AI and machine learning can raise new or exacerbate existing

---

[46] Brad Smith, *Facial recognition technology: The need for public regulation and corporate responsibility*, MICROSOFT ON THE ISSUES (July 13, 2018), https://blogs.microsoft.com/on-the-issues/2018/07/13/facial-recognition-technology-the-need-for-public-regulation-and-corporate-responsibility/.

ethical, technological, legal, and other challenges that could affect the company's brand and future demand for its products and services. Microsoft similarly warned about the possible flaws in AI algorithms given that the technology is new and may give rise to deficiencies in decision-making, predictions, and analyses.

There appears to be an upheaval by AI researchers concerned with the possible misidentification and misuse of face recognition programs as evidenced by an open letter signed by at least 62 researchers calling upon Amazon and other companies to cease selling the technology to law enforcement officials.[47] Included among the signatories is Yoshua Bengio, one of the "fathers" of deep learning and one of the recipients of the 2018 A.M. Turing award in 2018.[48] In an attempt to ameliorate both its employees and external criticisms, Google had announced the formation of an Advanced Technology External Advisory Council (ATEAC), in late March, 2019, composed of eight members which included economists, philosophers, policymakers, and technologists to deal with the many AI issues and their ethical implications. The problem arose that sparked immediate criticisms of the initiative was the revelation that one member of the Council, Dyan Gibbens, was associated with the development of autonomous systems for the defense industry, and another, Kay Coles James, is the president of the Heritage Foundation whose policy position opposed the regulation of carbon emissions. A third member, Alessandro Acquisti, stated he did not wish to be associated with the Council.[49] Accordingly, the Council was dissolved only ten days after its formation.[50]

Additional criticisms of ethics boards include the claim that tech companies' boards are just "ethics washing"; that they lack any "institutional

---

[47] Will Knight, *AI researchers ask Amazon to stop selling face recognition to law enforcement*, TECHNOLOGY REVIEW (April 3, 2019), https://www.technologyreview.com/the-download/613263/ai-researchers-ask-amazon-to-stop-selling-face-recognition-to-law-enforcement/.

[48] *Fathers of the Deep Learning Revolution Receive ACM A.M. Turing Award*, ACM, https://www.acm.org/media-center/2019/march/turing-award-2018?linkId=100000005610544.

[49] Will Knight, *Google employees are lining up to trash Google's AI ethics council*, TECHNOLOGY REVIEW (April 1, 2019), https://www.technologyreview.com/s/613253/googles-ai-council-faces-blowback-over-a-conservative-member/.

[50] Manas Mishra and Akshay Balan, *Google dissolves AI ethics council after just 10 days*, REUTERS (April 5, 2019) https://venturebeat.com/2019/04/05/google-dissolves-ai-ethics-council-after-just-10-days/.

framework"; lack transparency concerning whose interests are safe-guarded; lack mechanisms to carry out boards' recommendations; and that Google's commitment to ethics is highly questionable given its alleged cooperation with the Chinese government to censor its search engine and its surveillance programs that assisted the autocratic Philippine government to engage in extrajudicial killings. Ironically, critics of these programs often look to government to legislate privacy protections in private companies.[51]

An extensive discussion of AI facial recognition and other ethical issues may be found in *AI Now Report 2018*.[52] The Report is concerned with the video, audio, images and social media content that identifies and targets individuals and groups. The fear is that automation, scale of analysis, and predictive capacity allow automation of surveillance capabilities which exceed human capabilities to control thereby giving a small number of actors wide-ranging means of population controls. International exam-ples cited in the study were China, which is using the facial recognition technology to monitor activities, especially in the Hong Kong-Shenzhen border. It is also more pervasively utilized in the Xinjiang Autonomous Region including the application of drones, surveillance cameras, spy-ware, and other AI-based technologies. Machine-learning tools have been employed to generate lists of persons for "re-education camps" that num-ber up to one million persons. Venezuela has adopted a new smart card ID which links together social programs with personal finances, voting records, medical history, and other personal data.[53]

As stated previously, a major flaw of facial recognition is the error-prone program that has had difficulty when shown the faces of people of color. It appears that a Chinese startup, Yitu Tech, has overcome most of

---

[51] Critique of ethics boards is discussed in James Vincent, *The Problem with AI Ethics*, THE VERGE (April 3, 2019), https://www.theverge.com/2019/4/3/18293410/ai-artificial-intelligence-ethics-boards-charters-problem-big-tech.

[52] Meredith Whittaker, Kate Crawford, Roel Dobbe, Genevieve Fried, Elizabeth Kaziunas, Varoon Mathur, Sarah Myers West, Rashida Richardson, Jason Schultz, and Oscar Schwartz, *AI Now Report 2018*, AI NOW INSTITUTE (Dec. 2018), https://ainowinstitute.org/AI_Now_2018_Report.pdf. AI NOW INSTITUTE is an interdisciplinary research institute at New York University that is concerned with the social implications of AI technologies. It is cited herein on a number of ethical issues arising from AI-based technologies.

[53] *Id.* at 13–14.

the alleged blunders. Its face identification accuracy algorithms was tested affirmatively by the U.S. Department of Commerce's National Institute of Standards and Technology (NIST) and DARPA and is also currently applied in China by police and at subway stations and ATMs. Among the startup programs tested by NIST, the U.S. startup, Ever AI, ranked seventh with the top five being Russian and Chinese. A French program Idemia, ranked in the top six firms, is being used by the U.S. to screen passport applications managing some 360 million faces on file.

Accuracy has now improved to 99.7 percent in testing as indicated in Microsoft's entry. Of 60 programs tested by NIST, 13 were from the U.S., 12 were Chinese and 7 were from Russia. IBM's and Amazon's facial recognition programs, which are currently being sold to local U.S. law enforcement agencies, have not been submitted for assessment—it was the Amazon program that had the skin color difficulty referred to previously.[54] Another Chinese company, SenseNets, has been used by China to watch the Uyghur Muslim population of China's Xinjiang providence, by requiring Uyghurs to install spyware on their mobile devices thereby enabling researchers to watch 6.7 million GPS recorded coordinates. Purportedly, the company, upon learning of its government's use to spy, had shut down the program.[55]

The AI Report also noted the emergence of a subset of facial recognition, namely *affect recognition* which seeks to identify a person's inner "true feelings" by observations of facial expressions, which the Report alleges is a pseudoscience. The initial purpose, as tested by the Transportation Administration (TSA) in its Screening of Passengers by Observation Techniques (SPOT), was for surveillance of potential terrorists. Although the testing proved to be less than salient, nevertheless, as machine learning technology progressed, coupled with computer vision, there has been greater interest by Amazon, IBM, and Microsoft in its possible usage and has been advertised as "emotion analysis." With a

---

[54] Tom Simonite, *Why Chinese Companies Plug a US Test for Facial Recognition*, WIRED (March 6, 2019), http://peoplenetv.com/why-chinese-companies-plug-a-us-test-for-facial-recognition/.
[55] Emily Dreyfuss, *Security News This Week: Database Leak Details China's Oppressive Tracking of Muslims*, WIRED (Feb. 16, 2019), https://www.wired.com/story/database-leak-details-chinas-oppressive-tracking-of-muslims-security-roundup/.

database of 7.5 million faces from 87 countries, it is being used to train the algorithm at Affectiva Computing's laboratory at MIT.

It would appear that results would be highly questionable inasmuch as individuals' expressed emotions vary greatly, often spontaneously, e.g., from anger to a quiet "poker face" to highly noticeable redness of face, and so on. The debate concerning its validity and danger of misinterpretation that could result in harmful analyses is ongoing but advocates believe that the accumulation of data ultimately may prove beneficial under limited circumstances.[56] The Report equates the technology with Nazi race science, having little basis in practice and open to widespread substantial abuse.

The consequence of facial and affect recognition programs is the greatly increased concerns by civil right organizations especially when exploited by law enforcement agencies as evidenced by its use by the Orlando, Florida police department and the Sheriff's department in Washington County that use the Amazon Rekognition system for observation of hundreds of thousands of mugshots. IBM and the New York City Department have used facial recognition software to analyze "ethnicity searches" while retailers have begun using the software to scan "unhappy customers," monitor crowds, and detect shoplifters. The issues raised are the lack of laws and regulations to govern the alleged invasion of privacy and, more particularly, its use to control citizenry at the behest and control of governmental agencies and countries that have little regard for the civil rights of individuals.[57]

The U.S. Federal Trade Commission, in a staff report, recommends that companies which use the facial recognition technologies:

- Design their services with consumer privacy in mind;
- Develop reasonable security protections for the information they collect, and sound methods for determining when to keep information and when to dispose of it;

---

[56] Oscar Schwartz, *Don't look now: why you should be worried about machines reading your emotions*, THE GUARDIAN (March 6, 2019), https://www.theguardian.com/technology/2019/mar/06/facial-recognition-software-emotional-science.

[57] *Id.* at 15–17.

- Consider the sensitivity of information when developing their facial recognition products and services—for example, digital signs using facial recognition technologies should not be set up in places where children;
- Make sure consumers are aware of facial recognition technologies when they come in contact with them, and that they have a choice as to whether data about them is collected;
- Provide clear notice to consumers that the technology is in use before consumers come into contact with the signs;
- Provide consumers with an easy to use choice not to have their biometric data collected and used for facial recognition, and the ability to turn the feature off at any time and have the biometric data previously collected from their photos permanently deleted.[58]

# Current U.S. Government's Efforts of Facial Recognition

*President Trump's Executive Order.* On March 6, 2017, President Donald Trump signed an Executive Order,[59] in essence, pausing the entry of nationals from certain designated countries mainly in the Middle East. §5 of the Order called upon the Department of Homeland Security and other federal departments to develop a "uniform baseline and vetting standards and procedures" of diverse means for determining eligibility of entry. §8 of the Order provides as follows:

> Expedited Completion of the Biometric Entry-Exit Tracking System. (a) The Secretary of Homeland Security shall expedite the completion and implementation of a biometric entry-exit tracking system for in-scope travelers to the United States, as recommended by the National Commission on Terrorist Attacks Upon the United States.

---

[58] *FTC Recommends Best Practices for Companies That Use Facial Recognition Technologies*, FEDERAL TRADE COMMISSION (Oct. 22, 2012), https://www.ftc.gov/news-events/press-releases/2012/10/ftc-recommends-best-practices-companies-use-facial-recognition.

[59] *Exec. Order Protecting The Nation From Foreign Terrorist Entry Into The United States*, Exec. Order (March 6, 2019), https://www.whitehouse.gov/presidential-actions/executive-order-protecting-nation-foreign-terrorist-entry-united-states-2/.

The Department of Homeland Security (DHS), through its U.S. Customs and Border Protection (CBP), thereafter instituted the implementation of a biometric capability program to track air passenger departures nationally.

The Office of Inspector General (OIG) issued a Report stating its findings of CBP's implementation of the President's Order, specifically the progress of CBP's Biometric Entry-Exit Program.[60] In essence, the program is somewhat flawed when initiated but is expected to substantially improve in 2019. In a pilot program at nine airports in 2017, only 85 percent of all passengers processed with the said system were confirmed due to poor network availability, inadequate quality digital images, and other miscellaneous factors. Nevertheless, CBP processes over one million passengers arriving at the various ports of entry who are screened for a variety of data including biometric information such as fingerprints and photos to confirm identity and document nonimmigrant entry into the U.S. The current U.S. facial recognition program is being expanded to 20 top U.S. airports within two years using the technology on travelers traveling abroad on 16,300 weekly flights (100 million passengers).

Privacy concerns, as might be expected, have been raised by the ACLU and other privacy organizations both from a technical legal aspect as well as issues of inaccuracy and bias. In administrative law, formal rulemaking process requires: advanced notice in the Federal Register of the proposed rule enactment or change with an opportunity for affected persons to make comments; a mandatory hearing; a report from the agency enacting the proposed rule; and finally the publication of the final rule in the Federal Register. None of the stated procedures was adhered to. The fear, in summary, is the extraordinary extension of surveillance techniques and programs that track virtually every person engaged in travel abroad. The CBP dismisses the claims of privacy concerns over its biometric facial recognition program stating that it employs strong technical security

---

[60] *Progress Made, but CBP Faces Challenges Implementing a Biometric Capability to Track Air Passenger Departures, Nationwide,* Office of Insp. Gen. (Sept. 21, 2018), OIG-18-80, https://www.oig.dhs.gov/sites/default/files/assets/2018-09/OIG-18-80-Sep18.pdf.

safeguards and limits the amount of personally identifiable information collected from passengers.[61]

# AI Code of Ethics

A partial result of the alleged possible and actual abuses of AI is the call for a code of ethics whether by governments or by industry. One commentator suggested that the establishment of such a code would be extremely difficult because the questions arise as who gets to define the ethical principles to be followed and who enforces violations of the proposed code?[62] Similarly, inasmuch as AI is a generic underpinning of numerous technologies and processes, a global code, though praiseworthy, would either have to be extraordinarily long and difficult to comprehend or too general to be of any use. Added to the numerous possible emanations of AI-based technologies are the different concepts of the right of privacy and what constitutes ethics, all of which can be altered greatly over time—consider opinions or interpretations of homosexuality, abortion, women's rights, and other issues among European and Middle Eastern nations whose views differ greatly and which have changed radically over the past several decades.[63]

Although a uniform code of ethics may be unachievable, nevertheless, almost every profession within a particular country has a code of ethics which, if violated by members, could lead to loss of right to practice, e.g., medicine, law, etc. wherein professional organizations enforce rules of practice and punish misfeasors. Codes of conduct can be promoted and enforced by nation-states or collective groups thereof. An example is the Partnership on AI, which was founded by AI major players Amazon, Google, DeepMind, Microsoft, IBM, and later included Apple. It is a

---

[61] Davey Alba, *The US Government Will be Scanning Your Face At 20 Top Airports, Documents Show*, BUZZFEED NEWS (March 11, 2019). https://mcviewpoint.com/2019/03/11/the-us-government-will-be-scanning-your-face-at-20-top-airports-documents-show/.

[62] Karen Hao, *Establishing an AI code of ethics will be harder than people think*, MIT TECHNOLOGY REVIEW (Oct. 31, 2018), https://www.ethicalpsychology.com/2018/11/establishing-ai-code-of-ethics-will-be.html.

[63] Laura Cox, *A Universal Code of Ethics for Artificial Intelligence?*, DISRUPTION HUB (Oct. 9, 2018), https://disruptionhub.com/universal-code-of-ethics-artificial-intelligence/.

consortium whose mission is to establish best practices for AI systems and to educate the public.[64]

There may be little choice for AI and other Silicon Valley promoters to employ an enforceable code of ethics particularly with Democrat Representatives in control of the U.S. House of Representatives. They have called for a probe of the privacy policies of the tech giants. Although there is little likelihood of any meaningful legislation emanating from only one House of Congress, nevertheless, committee hearings will take place calling upon the major executives of Facebook, Google, Twitter, and other leaders to respond to privacy practices within their domain. New federal online-privacy protections against abusive content, purported takeover of sites by Russians to influence the presidential election of President Trump, racial hatred and other malfeasance on social media platforms, and other alleged abuses, have led to a demand for consumer protection against the said platforms.[65] Internet service providers have been protected by law which deem such sites as exempt from liability analogizing them to postal deliveries.[66] Notwithstanding all of the controversies attendant to facial recognition programs, the U.S., as in many other countries, has decided to use facial scanning at its 20 top airports and in other environments.

## European Commission's Draft AI Ethics Guidelines

In accordance with Communications of April 25, 2018 and December 7, 2018, the E.C. created a High-Level Expert Group on AI to draft (1) Ethics Guidelines and (2) Policy and Investment Recommendations. It

---

[64] Partnership on AI, https://www.partnershiponai.org/.

[65] Tony Romm, *Democrats vow Congress will 'assert itself' against tech – starting with Silicon Valley's privacy practices*, WASHINGTON POST (Feb 26, 2019), https://www.washingtonpost.com/technology/2019/02/26/democrats-vow-congress-will-assert-itself-against-tech-starting-with-silicon-valleys-privacy-practices/?utm_term=.c5c7bfbfb2dd.

[66] §230 of the *Telecommunications Act of 1996*, Pub.L 104-104, 110 Stat. 56, granted internet service providers (ISPs) a broad exemption from liability as a publisher. It states that "no provider or user of an interactive computer server shall be treated as the publisher or speaker of any information provided by another information content provider."

thereafter issued Draft AI Guidelines on December 18, 2018 for "Trustworthy AI."[67] It states that *trustworthy AI* has two components: (1) its development, deployment and use should respect rights and applicable regulation, as well as core principles and values, ensuring an "ethical purpose," and (2) it should be technically robust and reliable. *Ethics* is defined as responding to the questions of "what is a good action," "what is right," and "what is the good life?"[68] The fundamental rights of human beings set forth in the Guidelines are: (1) respect for human dignity; (2) freedom for the individual; (3) respect for democracy, justice, and the rule of law; (4) equality, non-discrimination, and solidarity including the rights of persons belonging to minorities; (5) citizens' rights.[69]

Based on the stated rights, the document states that the following principles and values are to be respected:

- The Principle of Beneficence: "Do Good"—AI systems should be designed to improve individual and collective well-being by generating prosperity, value creation, and wealth maximization and sustainability.
- The Principle of Autonomy: "Preserve Human Agency"—AI development means freedom from subordination to, or coercion by, AI systems;
- The Principle of Justice: "Be Fair"—The development, use, and regulation of AI systems must be fair, ensuring that individuals and minority groups maintain freedom from bias, stigmatization, and discrimination; and
- The Principle of Explicability: "Operate Transparently"—AI systems must be auditable, comprehensible, and intelligible by human beings, and also accountable.[70]

The "critical concerns" raised by AI, according to the Guidelines, are: identification of individual persons by either public or private entities

---

[67] *Draft Ethics Guidelines for Trustworthy AI*, at 1 (18 Dec. 2018), https://ec.europa.eu/futurium/en/system/files/ged/ai_hleg_draft_ethics_guidelines_18_december.pdf. The Guidelines are a draft subject to possible extensive revision.

[68] *Id.* at 2.

[69] *Id.* at 8.

[70] *Id.* at 8–10.

without their consent; covert AI systems that conceal from human beings that they are interacting with robots; normative and mass citizen scoring without consent in deviation of fundamental rights—general assessment of "moral personality" or "ethical integrity"; lethal autonomous weapon systems in which human control is essentially absent; and futuristic concerns of AI systems whereby AI systems may be developed that are able to possess "artificial consciousness," i.e., have a subjective experience of artificial moral agents, or have unsupervised, self-improving artificial general intelligence.[71]

Thus, the Guidelines propose the following requirements for trustworthy AI: accountability, data governance, design for all, governance of AI autonomy, non-discrimination, respect for and enhancement of human autonomy, respect for privacy, robustness, safety, and transparency. Methods for achieving the ethical goals are technical and non-technical means. *Technical means* would consist of (1) *ethics and rule of law by design*—assure that the ethical impact of an AI system be ethically and legally compliant; (2) *architectures for trustworthy AI*—rules of behavior that cannot be violated that control the behavior of an intelligent agent especially for systems that can learn and adapt its behavior; (3) *testing and validating*—go beyond traditional testing to include data, all inputs to the system, and the behavior of the system as a whole; (4) *traceability and auditability*—document both the decisions AI systems make and the process that formulates the decisions so as to make them traceable; and (5) *explanation*—be able to explain why the AI system had a given behavior and why it has provided a given interpretation.[72]

The *non-traditional methods* for a trustworthy AI are: (1) *regulation*—many forms including compensation, liability for harm, and other remedies for safety violations; (2) *standardization*—agreed standards of design, manufacturing, and business practices; (3) *accountability governance*—internal and external governance framework such as ethics panels or boards; (4) *codes of conduct*—organizations and stakeholders create and adapt ethical guidelines to be followed; (5) *education and awareness to foster an ethical mind-set*—ensure role of education in fostering proper

---

[71] *Id.* at 11–13.
[72] *Id.* at 18–21.

skills and training and also ethical training of workers; (6) *stakeholder and social dialogue*—active participation and partnership with organizations to spread the benefits of AI in healthcare, transportation, and the many other benefits; and (7) *diversity and inclusive design teams*—development of AI systems are to reflect the diversity of users and of society in general.[73] The Guidelines conclude with the methodology of assessment for the stated goals and principles.

# Robotics

## Debate Concerning Fear of Usage of Robots

Respecting the fear of humanoid robotics or other creatures eventually taking over humans and reminiscent of analogous takeovers as featured in the movie *Planet of the Apes* and Mary Shelley's *Frankenstein*, it may be wise to recall the *Three Laws of Robotics* as penned by the late Isaac Asimov:

- First Law—A robot may not injure a human being or, through inaction, allow a human being to come to harm.
- Second Law—A robot must obey the orders given it by human beings except where such orders would conflict with the First Law.
- Third Law—A robot must protect its own existence as long as such protection does not conflict with the First or Second Laws.[74]

A fourth law was later added by Asimov known as *zeroth law*—A robot may not harm humanity, or, by inaction, allow humanity to come to harm. [75]

As with any famous comment, there are negative rebuttals. The ethicist, Peter W. Singer, reminds his readers that the Asimov laws are fiction having been recited in stories for the I, Robot series; that no technology

---

[73] *Id.* at 21–22.

[74] Isaac Asimov, *Runaround*, I ROBOT RUNAROUND (The Isaac Asimov Collection ed.), Doubleday (1942), at 40.

[75] Peter W. Singer, *Isaac Asimov's Laws of Robotics are Wrong*, BROOKINGS (May 18, 2009), https://www.brookings.edu/opinions/isaac-asimovs-laws-of-robotics-are-wrong/.

can replicate the said laws within a machine (albeit this may be questioned given the advances in robotics since 2009 when the op-end was written); and the reality is that robots such as MAARS, (Modular Advanced Armed Robotic System) are designed specifically to cause harm.[76] Other commentators stress that the laws are wholly inadequate given the combination of AI with robotics incorporating the latter with superintelligence making them far more susceptible to wrongful use and thus requiring the development of machine ethics for the robots.[77] The oft-quoted Oren Etzioni suggested that AI practitioners take an oath analogous to the Hippocratic Oath taken by doctors. The essence is that they acknowledge their indebtedness to scientists and engineers for their contributions and agree to share their knowledge as others have before them; that AI is an art as well as a science; that they will apply their services for the benefit of humanity and accept responsibility and tread with care AI's power to save and take lives and not play God; respect privacy; prevent harm; collaborate with other practitioners for the common good knowing that encountering data may affect the lives, freedom, and economic stability of others; and that they have special obligations to their fellow human beings.[78]

Professor Jack M. Balkin of Yale Law School has a different take with respect to Asimov's laws of Robotics. Although, he noted, that Asimov wrote mainly about robots, he was not aware of intelligent computers. Balkin states that we are rapidly moving from the age of the Internet to what he refers to as the "Algorithmic Society," which he defined as "a society organized around social and economic decision making by algorithms, robots, and AI agents…."[79] He suggests that given the proliferation of robotics, laws are needed governing the designers and operators of

---

[76] Id.

[77] George Dvorsky, *Why Asimov's Three Laws of Robotics Can't Protect Us*, GIZMODO.COM (March 28, 2014), https://io9.gizmodo.com/why-asimovs-three-laws-of-robotics-cant-protect-us-1553665410.

[78] Oren Etzioni, *A Hippocratic Oath for artificial intelligence practitioners*, TECHCRUNCH (March 14, 2018), https://techcrunch.com/2018/03/14/a-hippocratic-oath-for-artificial-intelligence-practitioners/.

[79] Jack M. Balkin, *The Three Laws of Robotics in the Age of Big Data*, 78 OHIO STATE L. J. (2017), https://papers.ssrn.com/sol3/papers.cfm?abstract_id=2890965.

data and their collection, use, distribution, and sale. The three Balkin Laws of Robotics are:

- First Law: Algorithmic Operators Are Information Fiduciaries With Respect To Their Clients And End-Users;
  - Balkin treats the algorithmic operators as information fiduciaries and as such owe a duty of care and loyalty to their clients especially concerning their trust and privacy. Laws should be enacted that impose such duties upon their end users and clients. This is particularly true for services pertaining to home robots and smart homes.
- Second Law: Algorithmic Operators Have Duties Toward the General Public;
  - Algorithms may harm persons other than end users, e.g., for high speed trading, or to sway elections.
- Third Law: Algorithmic Operators Have A Public Duty Not To Engage in Algorithmic Nuisance;
  - Balkin speaks of socially unjustified use of data that harms innocent persons such as when police departments use algorithmic-based data that creates discrimination against innocent persons, or when used to discriminate in employment, housing, and access to credit. Ultimately, the author's fear is the danger that with robotics and AI, organizations and people may use these devices to affect, control, and manipulate other human beings.[80]

Numerous scientists and technologists, concerned with the advancement in robotic armed systems, have signed an Open Letter to the U.N. Convention on Certain Conventional Weapons stating:

> As companies building the technologies in Artificial Intelligence and Robotics that may be repurposed to develop autonomous weapons, we feel especially responsible in raising this alarm. We warmly welcome the decision of the UN's Conference of the Convention on Certain Conventional

---

[80] *Id.*

Weapons (CCW) to establish a Group of Governmental Experts (GGE) on Lethal Autonomous Weapon Systems. Many of our researchers and engineers are eager to offer technical advice to your deliberations....

We entreat the High Contracting Parties participating in the GGE to work hard at finding means to prevent an arms race in these weapons, to protect civilians from their misuse, and to avoid the destabilizing effects of these technologies....

Lethal autonomous weapons threaten to become the third revolution in warfare. Once developed, they will permit armed conflict to be fought at a scale greater than ever, and at timescales faster than humans can comprehend. These can be weapons of terror, weapons that despots and terrorists use against innocent populations, and weapons hacked to behave in undesirable ways. We do not have long to act. Once this Pandora's box is opened, it will be hard to close. We therefore implore the High Contracting Parties to find a way to protect us all from these dangers.[81]

## Autonomous Lethal Weapons and National Security

The discussion previously focused on facial recognition software and the dangers inherent in its possible misuse by governments whereby some scientists and technologists either refuse to engage in its development or implore their employers to protect against such occurrences. Their concern is greatly amplified when addressing autonomous lethal weapons for military purposes. Some commentators make a distinction between an "automated system" and "autonomous system" for lethal weapons. An *automated system* is one which is programmed to logically follow a predefined set of rules in order to provide an outcome. An *autonomous system* is capable of understanding higher-level intent and direction. From an understanding and its perception of its environment, it is able to take appropriate action to bring a desired state. It is capable of deciding a course of action from a number of alternatives without depending on human oversight and control, although they may also be present. The

---

[81] *An Open Letter to the United Nations Convention on Certain Conventional Weapons*, FUTURE OF LIFE INSTITUTE, https://futureoflife.org/autonomous-weapons-open-letter-2017.

overall activity may be predicable but the individual actions may not be so.[82] Often, the expressions are used interchangeably. Another author defined *autonomous weapon system* as "a weapon system that, based on conclusions derived from gathered information and preprogrammed constraints, is capable of independently selecting and engaging targets."[83]

Ethical issues raised by such developments are generally not "black-and-white" without nuances but usually are tempered by gray areas that illustrate both positive and negative uses and purposes. "Killer robots" or drones are designed to kill or destroy upon certain set circumstances or conditions that are preprogrammed. An example might be a relatively recent innovated circumstance whereby if a weapons system on a plane detects a forthcoming missile, it automatically destroys both the missile and targets destructively from where it emanated. The problem is the classic U.S. military doctrine of Mutual Assured Destruction (MAD) which presupposes that if each of antagonistic nations, in the past super-powers such as the U.S. and the former USSR, possesses sufficient nuclear weaponry to destroy the other side, then either side, if attacked for any reason by the other, would retaliate without fail with equal or greater force. The outcome for both nations would be catastrophic resulting in immediate irreversible escalation of hostilities resulting in both combatants' mutual, total, and assured destruction.[84]

Thus, the current U.S. Army Robotic and Autonomous Systems Strategy (RAS) is the classic MAD doctrine which it alleges is to improve its capability "to maintain, overmatch and render an enemy unable to respond effectively. The Army must pursue RAS capabilities with urgency because adversaries are developing and employing a broad range of advanced RAS technologies as well as employing new tactics to disrupt

---

[82] SELECT COMMITTEE ON ARTIFICIAL INTELLIGENCE, REPORT, 2017–19, HL Paper 100, at 102, https://publications.parliament.uk/pa/ld201719/ldselect/ldai/100/100.pdf, citing Ministry of Defense, *Unmanned aircraft systems* (12 Sept. 2017), https://www.gov.uk/government/upload/system/uploads/attachment_data/file/673940/doctrine_uk_uas_jdp_0_30_2.pdf.

[83] Rebecca Crootof, *The Killer Robots are Here: Legal and Policy Implications*, 36 Cardozo L.R. 1837-1915, at 1837, https://www.researchgate.net/publication/288825550_The_Killer_Robots_Are_Here_Legal_and_Policy_Implications.

[84] Military, *Mutual assured destruction*, WIKIPEDIA, http://military.wikia.com/wiki/Mutual_assured_destruction.

U.S. military strengths and exploit perceived weaknesses."[85] It is thereby developing and deploying Unmanned Ground Systems and Unmanned Aircraft Systems that meet five capability objectives, namely, (1) increased situational awareness; (2) lighten soldiers' physical and cognitive workloads; (3) sustain the armed force with increased distribution, throughput, and efficiency; (4) facilitate movement and maneuver, and (5) protected the forces.

Russia and China are moving forward with comparable AI-based weaponry and robotics. The Russian Minister of Defense stated its intention to replace human soldiers with robots ostensibly for mine clearing and emergency situations but also as replacements for purposes of combat. Its navy is also using Autonomous Underwater Vehicles to detect and defuse mines and for patrolling purposes.[86] In 2017, the Russian military exhibited its Terminator-like killing machine with deadly accurate shooting skills.[87] China has also indicated its projected AI strategy with its President, Xi Jinping, calling for the substantial increase in military AI research to enable it to prepare for a possible military conflict with the U.S. It was possibly a response to the U.S. Pentagon's *Third Offset Strategy* to experiment with the latest AI-based weaponry.[88] China has posed the first credible military threat to the U.S. since the fall of the Soviet Union some three decades ago. China's future AI plans, as previously discussed, will elevate its AI capabilities to rival that of the U.S. within a decade both for commercial purposes and also for militaristic purposes as evidenced by its increasing confrontational attitude in opposition to U.S. presence in its region.[89]

---

[85] *Robotic and Autonomous Systems Strategy*, U.S. ARMY, http://www.arcic.army.mil/App_Documents/RAS_Strategy.pdf.

[86] Dmitry Litovkin, *Russian army to replace soldiers with robots*, RUSSIA BEYOND (Jan. 18, 2013), https://www.rbth.com/articles/2013/01/08/russian_army_to_replace_soldiers_with_robots_21693.html.

[87] Jon Lockett, *Putin's Terminator Russian military leaders unveil terrifying robot army including battle-ready android gunslinger*, THE SUN (April 20, 2017), https://www.thesun.co.uk/news/3370091/russian-military-robot-army-android-gunslinger/.

[88] James Johnson, *China and the US are racing to develop AI weapons*, PHYS ORG (June 20, 2018), https://phys.org/news/2018-06-china-ai-weapons.html.

[89] Gregory C. Allen, *China's Artificial Intelligence Strategy Poses a Credible Threat to U.S. Tech Leadership*, COUNCIL OF FOREIGN RELATIONS (Dec. 4, 2017), https://www.cfr.org/blog/chinas-artificial-intelligence-strategy-poses-credible-threat-us-tech-leadership.

The U.S. Third Offset Strategy is one that emphasizes AI-based weapons development. It states that its research leads to five common technological-operational components:

- *Deep-Learning Systems.* These machines would be used for indications and warnings in cyber defense, electronic warfare attacks and large-density missile raids when human reactions just aren't fast enough. They would also be used for big-data analytics; for example, a deep-learning system might be able to analyze 90,000 Facebook posts made by ISIL in one day, crunch that data and find patterns from it, pulling out what might be of use.
  - Additional AI-based programs are the DARPA-funded Adaptive Radar Countermeasures and its Behavioral Learning for Adaptive Electronic Warfare programs that enable pilots to detect unknown radar signals and react immediately without the need for analysis at the Air Force base.
- *Human-Machine Collaboration.* This teams up human insight with the tactical acuity of computers by allowing machines to help humans make better, faster decisions. Pairing the two will combine the ability of humans to think on the fly with the quick problem-solving methods of artificial intelligence.
  - Current examples of this are unmanned underwater vehicle systems and the Aegis weapon system that uses computers and radar to track and guide weapons to destroy enemy targets. Its F-35 plane will be a flying sensor that can take in a huge amount of data, analyze it and then display it on the pilot's helmet, allowing him to make better decisions.
- *Human-Machine Combat Teaming.* While the above *collaboration* helps humans make better decisions, human-machine *combat teaming* works with unmanned systems to perform operations.
  - *Examples* are the Army's Apache helicopter and its Gray Eagle Unmanned Aerial Vehicle and the Navy's P-8 aircraft and Triton UAV. Both are designed to operate together. There are also swarming UAV's like the Perdix mini-drone, which has a 3D-printed airframe and electronics made from cellphones.

- *Assisted Human Operations.* They are wearable electronics, combat apps, heads-up displays and even exoskeletons that can help warfighters in all possible contingencies.
  - Currently, The Air Force Research Laboratory is perfecting skin biosensors that look and feel like a Band-Aid except they're equipped to read all sorts of data, like your heart rate, hydration, and other vital signs.
- *Network-Enabled, Cyber-Hardened Weapons.* It is the prioritization of cybersecurity. Every weapon and system will have to be prepared for cyberattacks.[90]

*IARPA and Autonomous Weapons Systems.* The U.S. Intelligence Advanced Research Projects Activity (IARPA), begun on October 1, 2007, arose out of the ashes of the World Trade Center attack on September 11, 2001 when it was revealed that the lack of coordination among the agencies of the federal government interagency was a major cause for lack of preparation for the attack. IARPA, which is under the direction of the Office of the Director of National Intelligence (ODNI), is modeled on DARPA but its mission differs in that it seeks to fill in gaps with its program of integration and coordination among 16 agencies of the federal government, with a focus on national security needs rather DARPA's focus on military requirements. It formulated a "100 Day Plan" by aligning to six integration and transformation focus areas, namely: (1) Create a Culture of Collaboration; (2) Foster Collection and Analytic Transformation; (3) Build Acquisition Excellence and Technology Leadership; (4) Modernize Business Practices; (5) Accelerate Information Sharing; and (6) Clarify and Align DNI's Authorities.[91] It was a consolidation of National Security Agency's Disruptive Technology Office, the National Geospatial-Intelligence Agency's National

---

[90] Katie Lange, *3d Offset Strategy 101: What It Is, What The Tech Focuses Are*, DoD LIVE, http://www.dodlive.mil/2016/03/30/3rd-offset-strategy-101-what-it-is-what-the-tech-focuses-are/.

[91] *United States Intelligence Community (IC) 100 Day Plan for INTEGRATION and COLLABORATION*, OFFICE OF THE DIRECTOR OF NATIONAL INTELLIGENCE, https://fas.org/irp/dni/100-day-plan.pdf.

Technology Alliance, and the Central Intelligence Agency's (CIA's) Technology Innovation Center.[92]

In a major study conducted by the Harvard Belfer Center on behalf of IARPA, with respect to autonomous weapons, it noted initially that autonomous weapons systems have been used since World War II with the German V-1 buzz bomb and the Norden Bombsight. By reason, in part, by the exponential growth of such systems for commercial and military use coupled with major reduction in costs, both nations and non-state actors now have the ability to obtain and utilize such systems. Advances in AI will augment additional robotic support to warfighters and lessen the need for manned combat missions. Over the next several years, there will be increased technological capabilities which will transform military power and warfare. As autonomous systems based on AI and machine learning proliferate, human manpower will decrease in favor of AI-based weaponry. Lethal weapons will be at the mainstream of military use. A major problem is the ability of terrorists to obtain and use improvised explosive devices and other means to cause immense harm to human populations.[93]

The Harvard study then issued a series of recommendations to IARPA, in summary, that the DoD should engage in war games to identify disruptive military innovations; fund analyses of such technology; prioritize AI R&D spending; invest in counter-AI capabilities to meet risks; encourage U.S. entry into treaties to restrict wrongful AI applications; engage in fail-safe AI technologies; and other related programs.[94] In another study, the author bemoans the fact that R&D spending in the automotive sector is triple that of the aerospace and defense industries. She fears that the imbalance in technology access in favor of civilian use will "introduce new unforeseen and disruptive dynamics for military operations." Her concern is that defense companies may lack the capacity to develop and

---

[92] *Intelligence Advanced Research Projects Activity*, WIKIPEDIA, https://en.wikipedia.org/wiki/Intelligence_Advanced_Research_Projects_Activity.

[93] Greg Allen and Taniel Chan, *Artificial Intelligence and National Security*, HARVARD BELFER CENTER (July, 2017) at 13–25, https://statewatch.org/news/2017/jul/usa-belfer-center-national-security-and-ai-report.pdf.

[94] *Id.* at 58–69.

test safe and controllable autonomous systems especially systems that engage in firing weapons.[95]

## Opposition to Enhanced AI-Based Weaponry

Grounded, in part, on the DoD AI-based technological advances, the fear, with justification, is that there may inevitably be a substantial escalation in possible armed conflicts given the greatly increased security risks including terrorism and regional conflicts coupled with autonomous drones and missiles, virtual bots, and malicious software crippling major internal structures.[96] Project Maven (discussed in Chap. 2) integrates AI and machine learning to counteract AI military capabilities of adversaries and competitors increasingly. The work to be accomplished includes triaging and labeling data so that algorithms could be trained, cleaned up, and labeled to prepare it for machine learning.[97] The Project marks the first use by the DoD to deploy deep learning and neural networks for use in combat.[98] The Project, which involves Google, is not without controversy inasmuch as some 3000 Google employees signed a petition to end the company's involvement in military use of the project.[99] As a result, Google announced its plan not to renew its contract with the Pentagon.[100]

[95] M.L. Cummings, *Artificial Intelligence and the Future of Warfare*, CHATHAM HOUSE Research Paper (Jan. 26, 2017), https://www.chathamhouse.org/sites/default/files/publications/research/2017-01-26-artificial-intelligence-future-warfare-cummings-final.pdf.

[96] Javier Andreu Perez, Fani Deligianni, Daniele Ravi, and Guang-Zhong Yang, *Artificial Intelligence and Robotics*, UK-RAS NETWORK (2016), at 39, https://arxiv.org/ftp/arxiv/papers/1803/1803.10813.pdf.

[97] Cheryl Pellerin, *Project Maven to Deploy Computer Algorithms to War Zone by Year's End*, U.S. Dept. of Defense (July 21, 2017), https://dod.defense.gov/News/Article/Article/1254719/project-maven-to-deploy-computer-algorithms-to-war-zone-by-years-end/.

[98] Gregory C. Allen, *Project Maven brings AI to the fight against ISIS*, BULLETIN OF THE ATOMIC SCIENTISTS (Dec. 21, 2017), https://thebulletin.org/2017/12/project-maven-brings-ai-to-the-fight-against-isis/.

[99] Adam Frisk, *What is Project Maven?, The Pentagon AI Project Google employees want out of*, GLOBALNEWS (April 5, 2018), https://globalnews.ca/news/4125382/google-pentagon-ai-project-maven/.

[100] Kate Conger, *Google Plans Not to Renew Its Contract for Project Maven, a Controversial Pentagon Drone AI Imaging Program*, GIZMODI (June 1, 2018), https://gizmodo.com/google-plans-not-to-renew-its-contract-for-project-mave-1826488620.

Approximately 4000 AI/Robotics researchers, joined by nearly 30,000 other signatories, signed an open letter in opposition to autonomous weapons which "engage targets without human intervention" but exclude weapons such as cruise missiles which are directed by humans who make targeting decisions. They call for a ban on such weapons because they are beyond any meaningful human control. AI technology will make them feasible as a third revolution in warfare (gunpowder and nuclear weapons being the first two revolutions). The signatories are aware of the global arms race but wish it not to extend to autonomous weapons which will be very easily available and cheap to manufacture. Among projected uses will be assassinations, destabilization of nations, and selective killing of particular ethnic groups. The ban should be added to current bans on chemical and biological warfare and called-for bans on space-used nuclear weapons and blinding laser weapons.[101]

There are a number of governmental and non-governmental organizations (NGOs) dedicated to the prevention or expansion of military robots and other AI-based lethal weaponry. Examples include the International Committee for Robot Arms Control (ICRAC), an NGO which, according to its website,[102] is an international committee of experts in robotics technology, artificial intelligence, robot ethics, international relations, international security, arms control, international humanitarian law, human rights law, and public campaigns. Its mission is to lower the threshold of armed conflict; prohibit the development, deployment and use of armed autonomous unmanned systems; not permit machines to make the decision to kill people; place limits on the range and weapons carried by "man in the loop" unmanned systems and on their deployment in postures threatening to other states; a ban on arming unmanned systems with nuclear weapons; and prohibit the development, deployment and use of robot space weapons.

---

[101] *Autonomous Weapons: An Open Letter From AI & Robotics Researchers*, Open Pen Letter, FUTURE OF LIFE INSTITUTE (July 28, 2015), https://futureoflife.org/open-letter-autonomous-weapons/.

[102] *About*, International Committee for Robot Arms Control, https://www.icrac.net/about-icrac/.

The Stockholm International Peace Research Institute (SIPRI) is particularly engaged in advocating peaceful initiatives, concentrating mainly on the need for human control of lethal autonomous weapon systems. Its recommendations were made in the context of the *UN Convention on Certain Conventional Weapons*.[103] SIPRI rendered a Report in 2017 wherein it made recommendations for future discussions by the UN organization. The recommendations were as follows:

- Discuss the development of "autonomy in weapon systems" rather than autonomous weapons or Lethal Autonomous Weapon Systems (LAWS) as a general category.
- Shift the focus away from "full" autonomy and explore instead how autonomy transforms human control.
- Open the scope of investigation beyond the issue of targeting to take into consideration the use of autonomy for collaborative operations (e.g., swarming) and intelligence processing.
- Demystify the current advances and possible implications of machine learning on the control of autonomy.
- Use case studies to reconnect the discussion on legality, ethics and meaningful human control with the reality of weapon systems development and weapon use.
- Facilitate an exchange of experience with the civilian sector, especially the aerospace, automotive and civilian robotics industries, on definitions of autonomy, human control, and validation and verification of autonomous systems.
- Investigate options to ensure that future efforts to monitor and potentially control the development of lethal applications of autonomy will not inhibit civilian innovation.

---

[103] U.N. Office for Disarmament Affairs, *U.N. Convention on Prohibitions or Restrictions on the Use of Certain Conventional Weapons Which May Be Deemed to Be Excessively Injurious or to Have Indiscriminate Effects Oct. 10, 1980, as amended on 21 December 2001* (CCW) is usually referred to as the *Convention on Certain Conventional Weapons*, Oct. 10, 1980, https://www.unog.ch/80256EDD006B8954/(httpAssets)/40BDE99D98467348C12571DE0060141E/$file/CCW+text.pdf.

- Investigate the options for preventing the risk of weaponization of civilian technologies by non-state actors.[104]

Some scholars attempt to take a middling approach between the advocacy of continued R&D in autonomous weapons systems and their complete ban. As one author stated, "The right question going is not how to ban autonomous weapon systems, but rather how best to regulate them."[105] Nations such as Israel, Russia, South Korea, and the U.S. having already integrated the systems for military use, assure that "killer robots" are here to stay. The author suggests that "intentional international regulation" is needed whereby nations negotiate and come to an agreement which lawful options are available in accordance with clarified rules and definitions. Governance would be by a comprehensive legal regime comprised of international, transnational, and domestic laws. It could be an additional protocol to the *Convention on Certain Conventional Weapons*[106] or the *Chemical Weapons Convention*[107] or simply piecemeal treaties in the absence thereof. Attempting an outright ban is essentially doomed to failure because nation-states are unwilling to forego their development.[108]

---

[104] Vincent Boulanin and Maaike Verbruggen, *Mapping the Development of Autonomy in Weapon Systems*, STOCKHOLM INTERNATIONAL PEACE RESEARCH INSTITUTE (Nov. 2017), https://www.sipri.org/sites/default/files/2017-11/siprireport_mapping_the_development_of_autonomy_in_weapon_systems_1117_1.pdf.

[105] Crootof, *supra* at note 373 at 1903.

[106] Convention on Prohibitions or Restrictions on the Use of Certain Conventional Weapons Which May Be Deemed to Be Excessively Injurious or to Have Indiscriminate Effects (Convention on Certain Conventional Weapons), Oct. 10, 1980, 1342 U.N.T.S. 137, as amended on 21 December 2001(CCW), https://www.unog.ch/80256EE600585943/(httpPages)/4F0DEF093B4 860B4C1257180004B1B30.

[107] Convention on the Prohibition of the Development, Production, Stockpiling and Use of Chemical Weapons and on their Destruction (Chemical Weapons Convention), April 29, 1997, 1974 U.N.T.S. 45, 32 I.L.M. 800, S. Treaty Doc. No. 103-21 (1993). https://www.opcw.org/chemical-weapons-convention.

[108] Crootof, *supra* at note 373 at 1896–1903.

# Additional AI Peace Initiatives

There are numerous other peace initiatives that reflect the urgency of coming to task with AI advances. A brief summary is as follows.

## Peace Machine

Timo Honkela, a Finish computer science professor at the University of Finland, who is concerned with neural networks and other AI subjects, proposed a Peace Machine before an international group of global peace brokers in 2017. In essence, he stated that the advances in AI and machine learning utilizing neural networks could be used for translations between Indo-European languages which would thereby increase the possibilities of human collaboration and communication over the next ten years. Pekka Haavisto, the president of the European Institute of Peace stated that "…Machines and artificial intelligence can't substitute human beings, but they can provide knowledge, possibilities and support for peace processes," … "Those processes are often about understanding the language, culture and marginalization." Computers would translate the books of the world for humanity and thus have a common understanding of one another which in turn could lessen the misunderstandings among peoples and nations. One of the uses of the Peace Machine would be to improve democracy through AI which would allow greater direct input by the masses to their leaders. Honkela noted: "Misunderstandings and misinterpretations are a very real part of conflict. If the Peace Machine or any other approach can help determine common ground, points of consensus and mutually understood language of agreement, it would be very useful for us in our work to resolve conflict."[109]

---

[109] Niko Nurminen, *Could artificial intelligence lead to world peace?*, ALJEEZERA (May 2017), https://www.aljazeera.com/indepth/features/2017/05/scientist-race-build-peace-machine-170509112307430.html.

## United Nations

The U.N., through its Sustainable Development Goals program, is considering how AI could assist in achieving economic growth and reduce inequalities. At a joint meeting of the U.N. Economic and Social Council (ECOSOC) and the Second Committee, it noted how driverless automobiles, advanced medical diagnosis, and other AI-based advances are profoundly reshaping global and local economies. Accordingly, it met on October 11, 2017, to identify options to harness the potential of rapid technological change and innovation toward achieving Sustainable Development Goals. The U.N. Secretary-General, António Guterres, has called AI "a new frontier" with "advances moving at warp speed." … "Artificial Intelligence has the potential to accelerate progress towards a dignified life, in peace and prosperity, for all people," … "The time has arrived for all of us—governments, industry and civil society—to consider how artificial intelligence will affect our future."

In a study conducted by the U.N. Department of Economic and Social Affairs (DESA) in collaboration with its agencies, it noted the advances of AI, particularly in 3D printing whereby three dimensional solid objects from a digital file in complex shapes can be produced using less materials than traditional manufacturing methods. The development has the potential to change how products are made and address many of the issues of industrialization in developing countries, particularly in least developed countries. The study further noted the effect of AI on the labor market and its near total disruption by the challenge of the substitution of brainpower in revolutionary technological advancement and benefit higher-skilled workers with a high degree of flexibility, creativity, and strong problem-solving and interpersonal skills. Low- and medium-skilled workers, both in manual and cognitive jobs, are expected to face further pressures from ever more capable machines and AI software. This could exacerbate the decline of middle-skilled jobs and rising wage inequality observed in the recent past, particularly in many developed countries. The study further warns that future AI-powered robots could increasingly displace highly educated and skilled professionals, such as doctors, architects, and even programmers. These issues are to be addressed to lessen the threats to global peace.[110]

## International Peace Institute

At an event *Governing Artificial Intelligence* on June 22, 2018, sponsored by the International Peace Institute in conjunction with the U.N. University (UNU),[111] the theme of the conference was whether developers will produce a form of AI that provides ways of ameliorating problems like inequality, climate change, disease, and hunger or one that will serve instead to "entrench" them. Fabrizio Hochschild, Assistant Secretary-General for Strategic Coordination in the Executive Office of the UN Secretary-General, stated that AI could be instrumental in "elevating humankind above the shackles of tedious or menial labor, the opportunity for a new utopia [or] … a potential dystopia, one where killer robots evade human control and where states control our every thought."[112] He added that the options were very consequential and that the only responsible development for AI would be "genuine international consensus, one that brings together governments, the scientists, industry leaders, and civil society representatives, the thinkers, ethicists and others who design, manage, use or are affected by AI." He said his office was focused on four "basic requirements: (1) "being inclusive and people-centered; (2) avoiding harmful, unintended consequences or "malicious use"; (3) making sure that AI "enhances our global collective values, as enshrined in the Charter," and (4) being

---

[110] *The Future of Everything – Sustainable Development in the Age of Rapid Technological Change*, UN SUSTAINABLE GOALS (Oct. 2017), https://www.un.org/sustainabledevelopment/blog/2017/10/looking-to-future-un-to-consider-how-artificial-intelligence-could-help-achieve-economic-growth-and-reduce-inequalities/.

[111] The United Nations University, located in Tokyo, Japan, consists of about 400 researchers engaged in over 180 research projects in conjunction with the 17 UN Sustainable Development Goals including AI-related projects. *UNU Sustainable Development Explorer*, UNITED NATIONS UNIVERSITY, https://unu.edu/explore.

[112] Fabrizio Hochschild, Assistant Secretary-General for Strategic Coordination in the Executive Office of the UN Secretary-General, *Learning to Live with Artificial Intelligence: A Virtuous Circle or a Vicious One?*, INTERNATIONAL PEACE INSTITUTE (June 22, 2018), https://www.ipinst.org/2018/06/governing-artificial-intelligence#15.

prepared to "deal with AI in all of its technological, economic, and ethical dimensions."

Other speakers at the Conference stressed the need for AI to have a voice at the table in addressing: the threat to global economies, their scientific progress, infrastructure, distribution, empowerment, and justice (Sean OhEigeartaigh); the fear of creation of instruments of war (Amandeep Gill); the need for control of lethal war machines while also touting the potential benefits of AI (Izumi Nakamitsu); a reminder that humanity is not artificial and that the risk of AI technology is not from the technology itself but from humans who construct it (Nicolas Economu); the need to understand our values in constructing the machines especially those pertaining to bias and discriminations in many contexts (John C. Havens); the need to combine our many talents to enable machines that do things better than ourselves (Francesca Rossi); another emphasis on collaboration with a focus on AI governance that addresses the digital divide, the appropriate regulatory environment that should be in place that includes all relevant stakeholders and partnerships (Lana Zaki Nusseibeh); the convergence of AI and biology and the potential health benefits arising therefrom, especially in ascertaining how particular diseases develop and related issues (Eleanore Pauwels); a cautionary note that the fear should not be that of superintelligence but rather moderate intelligence with a lot of power and its potential for misuse (Gary Marcus); and the good news of AI contributing to safety in anti-lock braking systems and how to deal with potential biases (Greg Corrado).[113]

As with almost all new innovative technologies, AI's use can be for the benefit of humankind or for destructive purposes. A number of commentators have suggested that we cease looking at AI in a negative way by focusing on loss of jobs and other negative comments. A quote from Avul Pakir Jainulabdeen Abdul Kalam, scientist and former president of India, appears to summarize an alternate method of attaining world peace.

---

[113] *Id.*

Where there is righteousness in the heart, there is beauty in the character. When there is beauty in the character, there is harmony in the home. When there is harmony in the home, there is order in the nation. When there is order in the nation, there is peace in the world.[114]

The author of the article also believes that the key to world peace is better communication coupled with ideas and products that make the world a better place without robbing elements of humanity.

In Chap. 5, we review one of several AI programs, namely, the Internet of Things that poses major technological advances which, if properly managed can be of great benefit to consumers and businesses but they may also present particular risks to the protection of privacy rights.

---

[114] Cited by Arun Kumar Ramasamy, *Can Ai Help Us Humans Achieve World Peace?*, LEADERONOMICS.COM (Feb. 2, 2018), https://leaderonomics.com/functional/ai-communication-and-world-peace.

# 5

# Ethics and Privacy II: The Internet of Things (IoT)

Among the greatest concerns that AI-based systems have raised is the invasion of privacy which has led many to believe either it is seriously threatened or no longer exists. Of particular concern is the Internet of Things (IoT) and the Internet of Things (IoE). We previously discussed how facial recognition and other programs have invaded our individual space and peace of mind. This section of the text will focus on how IoT potentially poses the greatest threat to the right of privacy and how the regulatory actions or lack thereto have dealt with this issue.

## What Is IoT and IOE?

Credit for the name of "Internet of Things" is ascribed to Kevin Ashton, a British pioneer technologist who co-founded the auto-id center at MIT. As he modestly stated: "The only thing for which I can perhaps claim sole credit is the name: three ungrammatical words that now label computing's future."[1] He coined the phrase for a PowerPoint presentation

---

[1] Kevin Ashton, *Beginning the Internet of Things*, MEDIUM.COM (March 18, 2016), https://medium.com/@kevin_ashton/beginning-the-internet-of-things-6d5ab6178801.

© The Author(s) 2020
R. Girasa, *Artificial Intelligence as a Disruptive Technology*,
https://doi.org/10.1007/978-3-030-35975-1_5

at Proctor & Gamble in the Spring 1999. There is no uniform consensus as to the meaning of the expression *Internet of Things*, although there appears to be a commonality of concepts as the following definitions illustrate.

- The Internet of Things, commonly abbreviated as IoT, refers to the connection of devices (other than typical fare such as computers and smartphones) to the Internet. Cars, kitchen appliances, and even heart monitors can all be connected through the IoT. And as the Internet of Things grows in the next few years, more devices will join that list.[2]
- The Internet of Things (IoT) refers to a network comprised of physical objects capable of gathering and sharing electronic information. The Internet of Things includes a wide variety of "smart" devices, from industrial machines that transmit data about the production process to sensors that track information about the human body.[3]
- The Internet of Things connects devices such as everyday consumer objects and industrial equipment onto the network, enabling information gathering and management of these devices via software to increase efficiency, enable new services, or achieve other health, safety, or environmental benefits. Examples are: *connected homes*—smart thermostats, smart appliances, HVAC systems, security, smart lighting, entertainments systems; *connected cars*—safety, vehicle diagnostics, infotainment and navigation, fleet management; *wearables*—fitness banks, smart watches, smart glasses, action cameras; industrial Internet—real-time analytics, factory automation, robotics, supply chain efficiency; *connected cities*—smart meter technology, smart traffic lights, smart parking meters, electric vehicle charging, real-time analysis.[4]

---

[2] Andrew Meola, *What is the Internet of Things (IoT): Meaning & Definition?*, BUSINESS INSIDER (May 10, 2018), https://www.businessinsider.com/internet-of-things-definition.

[3] Will Kenton, *The Internet of Things*, INVESTOPEDIA (Dec. 18, 2018), https://www.investopedia.com/terms/i/internet-things.asp.

[4] *What is the Internet of Things?*, GOLDMAN SACHS (Sept. 4, 2014), https://www.goldmansachs.com/insights/pages/iot-infographic.html.

*Internet of Everything (IoE).* IoT has evolved into a more expansive mode known as the *Internet of Everything* (IoE) which conception was named and developed by Cisco. It is defined as a concept which extends IoT and its emphasis on machine-to-machine communications to one that also encompasses people and processes, i.e., machine-to-people and technology-supported people-to-people.[5] According to Cisco, everything is connected. It gives the example of the massive amount of sailing data that was formally collected and analyzed on a boat from numerous sources with disparate interfaces, formats, and protocols which were cumbersome and time-consuming. Today, the said data is fed through an on-boat network that proceeds to the ship's crew and over Wi-Fi and cellular networks through a main processor, which is then loaded onto a Wi-Fi cloud router to a laptop. The sensor data is analyzed and connected to cloud applications for data analytics, storage, and reporting. The sensors collect, store, and analyze the boat's speed in varying weather and tidal conditions to assist the crew to optimize the boat's speed, sail-trim, and hull efficiency.[6]

Another commentator distinguished IoT and IoE by noting that IoT consists of things as physical objects such as a computer, mobile phone, or smart watch, whereas IoE goes beyond the physical objects and connects to services, data streams, and other non-physical services.[7] Products utilizing IoT can be divided between consumer and enterprise and industrial devices. Included among consumer products are smart speakers, smart lighting, robot vacuums, smart locks, fitness and health wearables, smart thermostats, and indoor security systems. Industrial applications include smart office lighting, drones, automated retail checkout, face recognition cameras, autonomous trucking, and an almost infinite other

---

[5] *Internet of Everything (IoE)*, IoT AGENDA, https://internetofthingsagenda.techtarget.com/definition/Internet-of-Everything-IoE.

[6] *Everything is Connected*, CISCO, https://www.cisco.com/c/r/en/us/internet-of-everything-ioe/sea-change/index.html.

[7] Luke Simmons, *What is the difference between the Internet of Everything and the Internet of Things?*, BLOG, CLOUDRAIL (Oct. 14, 2015), https://blog.cloudrail.com/internet-of-everything-vs-internet-of-things/.

uses.[8] The number of devices connected to IoT is estimated at 7 billion as of the 1st and 2nd quarters of 2018.[9]

# Privacy and the Internet of Things

This author, having gone to restaurants with family and friends on several occasions, was astonished to immediately receive, after leaving the restaurant, a query concerning how I liked the particular named restaurant exited from in order to advise other persons of my and other restaurant patrons' views concerning the food, atmosphere and the like. Similarly, when clicking onto a movie on Netflix or purchasing or even looking at some possible book purchases on Amazon, the services later make suggestions for movies to consider viewing or books to acquire. Although many persons would find the suggestions helpful in choosing other comparable movies or books, nevertheless, one wonders whether there is anywhere to hide from view and not allow anyone to be able to ascertain the movie, books, or other preferences of the viewer. Thus, the problem of privacy and the IoT arises that enables these and innumerable other devices to invade the particular individual's private domain.[10]

# U.S. Government Agencies and IoT[11]

## Federal Trade Commission (FTC)

There are a number of U.S. government agencies that potentially have and may exert jurisdiction over the IoT. A major agency that in the main

---

[8] Gilad Rosner and Erin Kenneally, *Privacy and the Internet of Things*, CENTER FOR LONG-TERM CYBERSECURITY WHITE PAPER (June, 2018), https://cltc.berkeley.edu/wp-content/uploads/2018/06/CLTC_Privacy_of_the_IoT-1.pdf.

[9] Knud Lasse Lueth, *State of the IoT 2018: Number of IoT devices now at 7B Market accelerating*, IOT ANALYTICS (Aug 8 2018), https://iot-analytics.com/state-of-the-iot-update-q1-q2-2018-number-of-iot-devices-now-7b/.

[10] *Internet of Things (IoT)*, ELECTRONIC PRIVACY INFORMATION CENTER, https://www.epic.org/privacy/internet/iot/.

[11] For a detailed analysis from which major headings discussed herein are taken, see, Eric A. Fisher, *The Internet of Things: Frequently Asked Questions*, CONGRESSIONAL RESEARCH SERVICE (Oct. 13, 2015), https://fas.org/sgp/crs/misc/R44227.pdf.

enforces laws in favor of consumer protection is the Federal Trade Commission which was created under the 1914 Federal Trade Commission Act (FTC Act).[12] It has two main functions: (1) to prevent unfair methods of competition, and (2) prevent unfair or deceptive acts or practices in or affecting commerce Congress. It also regulates and enforces violations against privacy and consumer IoT devices.

*FTC 2015 IoT Report.* The FTC has been particularly concerned about the ramification of IoT with respect to privacy. In January, 2015, it issued a Staff Report stating the benefits and risks of IoT and the application of traditional privacy principles to IoT.[13] The Report emanated from a workshop conducted on November 19, 2013, entitled *The Internet of Things: Privacy and Security in a Connected World.* Among the issues investigated was the incursion of privacy rights, particularly by the IoT which enables these and innumerable other devices to invade the particular individual's private domain. Although hacking, installing malware, and other malfeasance have been irritants or possible dangers to one's financial affairs, IoT connectivity has exacerbated the problem by loss of control via computers and smartphones. The enormous amount of data stored conceivably imperils not only the financial well-being of people but also possibly threatens their lives as, e.g., the possibility of hackers to literally assume control over one's vehicle even while driving a vehicle. For example, a smartphone can infer a person's mood, stress levels, personality type, bipolar disorder, demographics such as gender, marital status, job status, age, sleep patterns, and a multitude of other personal information. The concern is that some of the data could be misused without authorization, e.g., by insurance companies, credit and employment decisions, and a variety of other possible misuse.[14]

The Report made reference to the government's prolong reference to its Fair Information Practice Principles (FIPPs) of notice, choice, access, accuracy, data minimization, security, and accountability and whether they should apply to IoT. The Principles, the Report noted, have been adopted by the Organization of Economic Cooperation and Development

---

[12] Federal Trade Commission Act, 15 U.S.C. §§ 41–58, as amended.
[13] *internet of things*, FEDERAL TRADE COMMISSION, STAFF REPORT (Jan. 2015), https://www.ftc.gov/system/files/documents/reports/federal-trade-commission-staff-report-november-2013-workshop-entitled-internet-things-privacy/150127iotrpt.pdf.
[14] *Id.* at 14–16.

(OECD) and the European Union's General Data Protection Directive (discussed in Chap. 8). There was agreement that companies manufacturing IoT devices have to incorporate reasonable security into the devices and that they should engage in data minimization, i.e., limit the data collected and retained and disposed of once the need thereof has been attained. In summary, the Report focused on the several areas of privacy concerns and made the following recommendations.[15]

*Security.* Companies at the commencement of building the IoT devices should (1) conduct a privacy or security risk assessment; (2) minimize the data they collect and retain; and (3) test their security measures before launching their products. Companies should train employees about good security; retain service providers to maintain reasonable security; identify and defend against risks at all levels; implement reasonable access control measures to limit access to a customer's personal identification information; and continue to monitor products and their vulnerabilities.

*Data Minimization.* Companies should limit the data collected and retained, and dispose of it when no longer needed to guard against the risks of data thieves within and outside the company and the risk the data will be used in a way that customers had not intended. Companies would be free to determine their options of no data collection, collect only data for specific intended use, collect non sensitive data, or request customer's consent for the collection of additional sensitive data.

*Notice and Choice.* The FTC opined that customer choice and notice to him or her are important but did not conclude that choice be given by the company in every instance was required due to the costs involved both to the company and to the customer. Choice, when accorded, should be clear and prominent and not buried in lengthy documents. The FTC suggested a use-based approach whereby legislators, regulators, self-regulatory bodies, and individual companies would set permissible and impermissible uses of certain customer data. The Report did note that the FTC does enforce the Fair Credit Reporting Act[16] which restricts the permissible exploitation of customer credit report information but

[15] *Id.* at iii–ix.
[16] 15 U.S.C. §1681.

was hesitant to adopt a pure use-based approach for IoT; rather it suggested giving consumers information and choice about their data.

*Legislation.* The Report was somewhat unclear whether Congress should adopt new legislation to meet the challenges of IoT. It did recommend self-regulatory programs that would adopt privacy- and security-sensitive practices but also did express its concern with respect to threats to data security and that the emerging IoT technologies might exacerbate the threats thereto. It proposed that Congress enact "strong, flexible, and technology-neutral federal legislation to strengthen its existing data security enforcement tools and to provide notification to consumers when there is a security breach."[17] The legislation should not directly target IoT but rather should be broad-based and flexible so as to provide a clear road map for companies about how to provide choices for consumers about data collection and use practices. The FTC would continue its customary enforcement as provided by law with respect to violations of the Federal Trade Commission Act and other relevant statutes within its domain.

*FTC Enforcement Actions.* The FTC has instituted a number of enforcement procedures against IoT-related companies for alleged wrongful conduct. In almost all cases, the conduct consists of deceit particularly with respect to sensitive data affected consumers.

*FTC v. D-Link Systems Corp.* The FTC commenced its first action involving IoT against D-Link Systems Corp.,[18] a Taiwanese corporation, alleging unfair and deceptive practices for failure to take reasonable steps to secure the routers and Internet-protocol cameras they designed for, marketed, and sold to U.S. consumers. In essence, according to the complaint and a summary thereof, hackers are increasingly targeting consumer routers and IP cameras and consumers may be harmed as a result of device compromise and exposure of their sensitive personal information. The essence of the complaint is that D-Link promoted the security of its routers on the company's website, which included materials headlined "EASY TO SECURE" and "ADVANCED NETWORK SECURITY."

---

[17] FTC Report *supra*, note 416 at vii.
[18] FTC v. D-Link Systems, Inc., No. 3:2017cv00039 (N.D. Ca. Jan. 5, 2017).

Despite the claims made by D-Link, the FTC claimed that the company failed to take steps to address well-known and easily preventable security flaws such as: "hard-coded" login credentials integrated into D-Link camera software—also the username "guest" and the password "guest"—that could allow unauthorized access to the cameras' live feed; a software flaw known as "command injection" that could enable remote attackers to take control of consumers' routers by sending them unauthorized commands over the Internet; the mishandling of a private key code used to sign into D-Link software, such that it was openly available on a public website for six months; and leaving users' login credentials for D-Link's mobile app unsecured in clear, readable text on their mobile devices, even though there is free software available to secure the information.

The FTC further alleged that hackers could exploit these vulnerabilities exploiting any of several simple methods. For example, by manipulating a compromised router, an attacker could obtain consumers' tax returns or other files stored on the router's attached storage device. They could redirect a consumer to a fraudulent website, or use the router to attack other devices on the local network, such as computers, smartphones, IP cameras, or connected appliances. The FTC alleges that by using a compromised camera, an attacker could monitor a consumer's whereabouts in order to target them for theft or other crimes, or watch and record their personal activities and conversations.[19] The case resulted in a stipulation of settlement which, among other provisions, called for the D-Link's establishment and implementation of a comprehensive software security program to protect its Covered Devices; evaluate and update changes thereto; obtain initial and biennial assessments; provide annual certifications; discontinue the sale of IP Camera set-up wizard software; and file compliance reports with the SEC. There was no finding of liability or deceptive practices or imposition of a fine.

---

[19] *FTC Charges D-Link Put Consumers' Privacy at Risk Due to the Inadequate Security of Its Computer Routers and Cameras*, FEDERAL TRADE COMMISSION (Jan. 5, 2017), https://www.ftc.gov/news-events/press-releases/2017/01/ftc-charges-d-link-put-consumers-privacy-risk-due-inadequate.

*FTC v. VIZIO, Inc.*[20] VIZIO manufactured televisions sets with tracking devices showing what consumers were watching through its software that collected viewing data from cable or broadband services providers, set-top boxes, external streaming devices, DVD players, and over-the-air broadcasts. It then sold the information to third parties through licensing agreements. Consumers received no notice of the collection of the data or about the devices installed on their television sets. While investigation by the FTC was pending, VIZIO did display a 30-second notice of its practice on its sets but did not provide input or easy access to the settings menu. The FTC's complaint alleged a violation of §5(a) of the FTC Act, 15 U.S.C. § 45(a), which prohibits "unfair or deceptive acts or unfair practices in or affecting commerce" for misrepresentations or deceptive omission of material fact which constitute deceptive acts or unfair practices prohibited by the Act as well as comparable provisions of the State of New Jersey statute. The violations consisted of unfair tracking by the said collection of private data without notice to the consumers or consent by them and deceptive omission and deceptive misrepresentation regarding smart and redress to consumers. The end result was a settlement by the company by the payment of $2.2 million to the FTC and the State of New Jersey and an agreement to secure customers' consent for use of tracking and other comparable devices.[21] It appears that the case created new standards for IoT, namely, "unfair tracking" and "consent and choice" rules.[22]

*In re Nomi Technologies, Inc.*[23] There were prior cases that illustrated the new direction which the FTC was undertaking with respect to privacy rights and IoT given the onslaught of the new technologies on privacy

---

[20] FTC v. VIZIO, Inc. No. 2:17-cv-00758 (D.N.J. Feb. 6, 2017) https://www.ftc.gov/system/files/documents/cases/170206_vizio_2017.02.06_complaint.pdf.

[21] Hayley Tsukayama, *Vizio agrees to pay $2.2 million to settle FTC's television-spying case*, WASHINGTON POST Feb. 6, 2017), https://www.washingtonpost.com/business/economy/vizio-agrees-to-pay-22-million-to-settles-ftcs-television-spying-case/2017/02/06/3d4d4b16-ec8f-11e6-9662-6eedf1627882_story.html?utm_term=.14dbb83db2b9.

[22] Hillary Brill and Scott Jones, *Little Things and Big Challenges: Information Privacy and the Internet of Things*, 66 A. U. L. Rev. 1183 (2017), https://papers.ssrn.com/sol3/papers.cfm?abstract_id=3188958. The said article is an excellent review of privacy and IoT which this author used in part for sources and opinions.

[23] *In re Nomi Technologies, Inc.*, FTC Admin. Proceeding No. C-4538 (2015), https://www.ftc.gov/system/files/documents/cases/150902nomitechcmpt.pdf.

rights, particularly to consumers of devices having IoT devices. In an administrative action, the FTC alleged Nomi represented, directly or indirectly, expressly or by implication, that consumers could opt out of Nomi's "Listen" service at retail locations using this service but did not provide an opt-out mechanism at its clients' retail locations and, therefore, the representation was false or misleading. The said service was used at a retail location since January 2013 without consumers being made aware of its practice. It employed mobile device tracking technology to provide analytics services to brick and mortar retailers through its Listen service by placing sensors in its clients' retail locations that detect the media access control address broadcast by a mobile device when it searches for Wi-Fi networks. Nomi also collected information about each mobile device that comes within range of its sensors or its clients' Wi-Fi access points.

The action resulted in a Consent Agreement whereby, among other provisions, the company shall not misrepresent (A) the options through which, or the extent to which, consumers can exercise control over the collection, use, disclosure, or sharing of information collected from or about them or their computers or devices, or (B) the extent to which consumers will be provided notice about how data from or about a particular consumer, computer, or device is collected, used, disclosed, or shared. In a commentary on the case, the authors noted, as a dissenting member of the FTC stated, that there was no requirement that a privacy notice be given addressing end user data but that the alleged deceit was the company's statement of a privacy policy without the provision of opt-outs.[24]

*USA v. InModi Pte Ltd.*[25] InModi was an action brought by the FTC under the FTC Act and the Children's Online Privacy Protection Act of 1998 (COPPA) and the COPPA Rule (in essence, the Rule requires parental consent to securing private information from a child). InModi is a Singapore company doing business in California

---

[24] Brill, *supra* at note 425, p. 1217.
[25] USA v. InModi Pte Ltd., No. 3:16-cv-3474 (N.D. Ca. June 22, 2016), https://www.ftc.gov/system/files/documents/cases/160622inmobicmpt.pdf.

which provides an advertising platform for mobile application developers and advertisers by integrating its software development kit that Android and iOS application developers can monetize their applications. It does so by allowing third party advertisers to advertise to consumers through various ad formats such as banner ads, interstitial ads (full screen ads), and native ads. Advertisers, in turn, can target consumers across all of the mobile applications that have integrated the InMobi SDK. The company claimed it is the "world's largest independent mobile advertising company" reaching over one billion unique mobile devices.

In a summary of its complaint, the FTC declared that InModi misrepresented that its advertising software would only track consumers' locations when they opted in and in a manner consistent with their device's privacy settings. In fact, the company was actually tracking consumers' locations, whether or not the apps using InMobi's software asked for consumers' permission to do so, and even when consumers had denied permission to access their location information. It further stated that InMobi offers multiple forms of location-based advertising to its customers, including the ability to serve ads to consumers based on their current locations, locations they visit at certain times, and on their location over time. It allegedly also tracked hundreds of millions of consumers including children without their consent and often ignored consumers' expressed privacy preferences.

The end result was a Consent Agreement whereby the company paid $950,000 in civil penalties. It further agreed to the following restrictions: implementation of a comprehensive privacy program including deletion of all information it collected from children; prohibition from further violations of COPPA; prohibition from collecting consumers' location information without their affirmative express consent for it to be amassed; requirement to honor consumers' location privacy settings; deletion of the location information of consumers it collected without their consent; and prohibition from further misrepresenting its privacy practices. The settlement also requires InMobi to institute a comprehensive privacy program that will be independently audited every two years for the next 20 years.[26] Unlike *Nomi*, the alleged deception was to its business partners rather than to consumers.[27]

*In re Turn Inc.*[28] According to the complaint, the FTC commenced an administrative proceeding against Turn Inc., a digital advertising company that enables commercial brands and ad agencies to engage in *targeted advertising* (the practice of using data about a user's interests in order to deliver online advertising targeted to the user's interests). Publicized as the largest independent company in advertising, it uses "cookies" and "web beacons" to track consumers across the Web for marketing and other purposes. The complaint explained that "cookies" are unique, persistent text files stored in a consumer's browser that allow a company to recognize that unique consumer when the consumer's browser makes a connection to the company's servers. Those connections are sometimes enabled by "web beacons," which are invisible embedded codes in web pages that instruct the browser to connect to third party services such as that offered by Turn, Inc. Consumers can delete or otherwise control cookies through settings in their web browsers.

The complaint claimed violation of the Act because it allegedly deceived consumers by tracking them online and through their mobile applications, even after consumers took steps to opt out of such tracking. Its privacy policy represented that consumers could block targeted advertising by using their web browser's settings to block or limit cookies when, in fact, Turn used unique identifiers to track millions of Verizon Wireless customers, even after they blocked or deleted cookies from websites. Its opt-out mechanism only applied to mobile browsers, and did not block tailored ads on mobile applications as the company claimed.

In a Consent Agreement, Turn agreed not to misrepresent the extent of its online tracking or the ability of users to limit or control the

---

[26] *Mobile Advertising Network InMobi Settles FTC Charges It Tracked Hundreds of Millions of Consumers' Locations Without Permission*, FEDERAL TRADE COMMISSION (June 22, 2016), https://www.ftc.gov/news-events/press-releases/2016/06/mobile-advertising-network-inmobi-settles-ftc-charges-it-tracked.

[27] Brill, *supra*, at note 425 at 1219.

[28] *In re Turn*, No. C-4612, April 6, 2016, https://www.ftc.gov/system/files/documents/cases/152_3099_c4612_turn_complaint.pdf.

company's use of their data. It also agreed to provide an effective opt-out for consumers who do not want their information used for targeted advertising and place a prominent hyperlink on its home page that takes consumers to a disclosure explaining what information the company collects and uses for targeted advertising.[29]

*IoT Proposed Legislation.* The U.S. Congress has become aware of the issues attendant to IoT. Accordingly, there were bills proposed for adoption both in the House of Representatives and in the Senate entitled *Internet of Things (IoT) Cybersecurity Improvement Act of 2017*[30] which had not been acted upon, and the 2019 legislation introduced in both houses of Congress entitled *To leverage Federal Government procurement power to encourage increased cybersecurity for Internet of Things devices, and for other purposes.*[31] The proposed bill would require government agencies to insert clauses in government contracts to possess security features for any Internet-connected devices purchased by the government coupled with exceptions thereof. The concern was the emerging cyberthreats to the security of the U.S. and the need for a national standard of IoT security. The standards in the bill applies to IoT companies selling to the U.S. government which require recommendations from the National Institute of Standards and Technology (NIST) for security standards applicable therein reviewable every five years. All IoT vendors would have to comply with the security standards including a vulnerability disclosure policy when transacting with the government.[32]

---

[29] *FTC Approves Final Consent Order with Online Company Charged with Deceptively Tracking Consumers Online and Through Mobile Devices,* FEDERAL TRADE COMMISSION (Dec. 20, 2016), https://www.ftc.gov/news-events/press-releases/2016/12/digital-advertising-company-settles-ftc-charges-it-deceptively.

[30] *Internet of Things (IoT) Cybersecurity Improvement Act of 2017,* S. 1691, 115th Cong. (2017).

[31] S. (unassigned), 116th Cong. (2019), H.R. 1668, 116th Cong., *To leverage Federal Government procurement power to encourage increased cybersecurity for Internet of Things devices,* https://www.govtrack.us/congress/bills/116/hr1668.

[32] Alfred Ng, *Congress introduces bill to improve 'internet of things' security,* CNET (March 11, 2019), https://www.cnet.com/news/congress-introduces-bill-to-improve-internet-of-things-security/.

# Securities and Exchange Commission (SEC)

The SEC is increasingly concerned with AI both from an internal utilization to augment its surveillance of the securities' industry and also to engage in market risk assessment initiatives. Within the agency, the application of machine learning commenced about the time of the 2007 financial crisis with its use of simple word counts to machine-identify structured phrases in text-based documents. The Commission examined corporate issuer filings to determine whether it could have foreseen some of the risks posed by the rise and employment of credit default swaps [CDS] contracts leading up to the financial crisis of 2007 and thereafter. It was accomplished by the application of text analytic methods to machine-measure the frequency with which these contracts were mentioned in filings by corporate issuers. The agency then examined the trends across time and across corporate issuers to learn whether any signal of impending risk emerged that could have been used as an early warning. It then expanded into the analysis of headlines, lead paragraphs, and full texts of articles in trade journals.[33]

Natural language processing was used in the application of modeling methods for unsupervised learning. Analysis was made of tips, complaints, and referrals and examined whether machine learning could digitally identify abnormal disclosures by corporate issuers charged with wrongdoing related to performance discussion. This result is consistent with issuers charged with misconduct playing down real risks and concerns in their financial disclosure. Machine learning methods have now been adopted by the SEC to topic modeling and other cluster analysis techniques to identify latent trends in large amounts of unstructured financial information for further scrutiny if warranted. In addition, machine learning algorithms are being trained by staff as "supervised" machine learning which algorithms incorporate human direction and judgment to help interpret machine learning outputs. The Commission

---

[33] The text is from a speech by the acting director and acting chief economist for the SEC Division of Economic and Risk Analysis, Scott W. Bauguess, *The Role of Big Data, Machine Learning, and AI in Assessing Risks: A Regulatory Perspective*, OPRISK NORTH AMERICA (June 21, 2017), https://www.sec.gov/news/speech/bauguess-big-data-ai#_edn2.

has had a great deal of success from the application of algorithms to new data which is then used to train algorithms to further detect possible fraud in regulatory filings. The agency has been able to process approximately 500 million documents each day which are then reduced to more usable pieces of information, including market quality and pricing statistics. Concerning the future of AI use in the agency, machine learning is a tool that points to possible fraud and other wrongdoings but it will be up to human analyses at all stages of its risk assessment program, coupled with other corroborating factors, to determine whether to refer particular cases for prosecution.[34]

*Robo-Advisers and SEC Guidelines.* Investment advisers, including robo-advisers (automated advisers), are regulated by the SEC under the Investment Advisers Act of 1940 as amended.[35] The Commission has issued a Guidance respecting them which it noted is a robust trend that has the potential to give retail investors more affordable access to investment advisory services. They are generally registered investment advisers which employ innovative technologies to provide discretionary asset management services to their clients through online algorithmic-based programs. A client who wishes to utilize a robo-adviser enters personal information and other data into an interactive, digital platform which the robo-adviser then generates a portfolio for the client and subsequently manages the client's account. There are different models of robo-advisers from offering investment advice directly to the client with limited with limited or no direct human interaction while other robo-advisers render advice in conjunction with investment advisory personnel.[36]

According to the Guidance, robo-advisers, like all registered investment advisers, are subject to the substantive and fiduciary obligations of the Advisers Act.[37] Relying on algorithms, they provide advisory services over the Internet which may cause them to come within the provisions of

---

[34] *Id.*

[35] 15 U.S.C. § 80b-1 through 15 U.S.C. § 80b-21.

[36] *IM Guidance Update*, SECURITIES AND EXCHANGE COMMISSION, No. 2017-02 (Feb. 2017), https://www.sec.gov/investment/im-guidance-2017-02.pdf.

[37] Investment Advisers Act of 1940 as amended, 15 U.S.C. § 80b-1 through 15 U.S.C. § 80b-21.

the Act. The Guidance focused on three areas in order to provide suggestions on how robo-advisers may address them.

1. The substance and presentation of disclosures to clients about the robo-adviser and the investment advisory services it offers;
2. The obligation to obtain information from clients to support the robo-adviser's duty to provide suitable advice; and
3. The adoption and implementation of effective compliance programs reasonably designed to address particular concerns relevant to providing automated advice.[38]

*Substance and presentation of disclosures*, the Guidance noted that the investment adviser has a fiduciary duty to make full and fair disclosure of all material facts in understandable format and to employ reasonable care to avoid misleading clients. The Guidance suggests that a robo-adviser should consider providing: a statement that an algorithm is used to manage individual client accounts; a description of the algorithmic functions used to manage client accounts; a description of the assumptions and limitations of the algorithm used to manage client accounts; a description of the assumptions behind and the limitations of that theory; a description of the particular risks inherent in the use of an algorithm to manage client accounts; a description of any circumstances that might cause the robo-adviser to override the algorithm used to manage client accounts; a description of any involvement by a third party in the development, management, or ownership of the algorithm used to manage client accounts; an explanation of any fees the client will be charged directly by the robo-adviser, and of any other costs that the client may bear either directly or indirectly; an explanation of the degree of human involvement in the oversight and management of individual client; a description of how the robo-adviser uses the information gathered from a client to generate a recommended portfolio and any limitations; and an explanation of how and when a client should update information he or she has provided to the robo-adviser.[39]

---

[38] *Id.* at 2.
[39] *Id.* at 3–4.

*Presentation of Disclosures.* With respect to how disclosures are presented to clients who may not even be able to understand dense disclosures or which are not in plain English, the Guidance suggests as follows: Robo-advisers may wish to consider: whether key disclosures are presented prior to the sign-up process so that information necessary to make an informed investment decision is available to clients before they engage, and make any investment with the robo-adviser; whether key disclosures are specially emphasized; whether some disclosures should be accompanied by interactive or other means to provide additional details to clients who are seeking more information; and whether the presentation and formatting of disclosure made available on a mobile platform have been appropriately adapted for that platform.[40]

*Provision of Suitable Advice.* An investment adviser's fiduciary duty includes an obligation to act in the best interests of its clients and to provide only suitable investment advice. The Guidance noted that robo-advisers may provide investment advice based primarily, if not solely, on client responses to online questionnaires. Factors suggested that a robo-adviser may wish to consider are: whether the questions elicit sufficient information to allow the robo-adviser to conclude that its initial recommendations and ongoing investment advice are suitable and appropriate for that client based on his or her financial situation and investment objectives; whether the questions in the questionnaire are sufficiently clear and/or whether the questionnaire is designed to provide additional clarification or examples to clients when necessary; and whether steps have been taken to address inconsistent client responses. For client-directed changes in investment strategy, the Guidance suggested that a robo-adviser should consider providing commentary as to why it believes particular portfolios may be more appropriate for a given investment objective and risk profile.[41]

*Effective Compliance Programs.* Pursuant to *Rule* 206(4)-7 under the Advisers Act, each registered investment adviser is required to establish an internal compliance program that addresses the adviser's performance of its fiduciary and substantive obligations under that Act. A registered

---

[40] *Id.* at 4.
[41] *Id.* at 6–7.

investment adviser must adopt, implement, and annually review written policies and procedures that are reasonably designed to prevent violations of the Advisers Act and the rules thereunder. A registered investment adviser must also designate a chief compliance officer who is competent and knowledgeable about the Advisers Act to be responsible for administering the written policies and procedures adopted.

The Guidance suggests the following: The robo-adviser should consider whether to adopt and implement written policies and procedures that address areas such as: the development, testing, and backtesting of the algorithmic code and the post implementation monitoring of its performance; the questionnaire eliciting sufficient information to allow the robo-adviser to conclude that its initial recommendations and ongoing investment advice are suitable and appropriate for that client based on his or her financial situation and investment objectives; the disclosure to clients of changes to the algorithmic code that may materially affect their portfolios; the appropriate oversight of any third party that develops, owns, or manages the algorithmic code or software modules utilized by the robo-adviser; the prevention and detection of, and response to, cybersecurity threats; the use of social and other forms of electronic media in connection with the marketing of advisory services; and the protection of client accounts and key advisory systems.[42]

*SEC Enforcement Actions. SEC v. Wealthfront Advisers LLC.*[43] A summary of the case as stated by the SEC is as follows: The SEC instituted a proceeding against Wealthfront which resulted in settlement and consented Order of December 21, 2018. The initial action was against Wealthfront LLC, a robo-adviser in Redwood City, with over $11 billion in client assets under management, made false statements about a tax-loss harvesting strategy it offered to clients. Wealthfront is a registered investment adviser to retail clients that uses a software-based "robo-adviser" platform. It applies a proprietary tax loss harvesting program ("TLH") to clients' taxable accounts. It designed TLH to create tax benefits for clients by selling certain assets at a loss that, if realized, can be used to offset

---

[42] *Id.* at 7–8.
[43] SEC v. Wealthfront Advisers LLC, Ad. Proceeding Order No. 3-18949, Dec. 21, 2018, https://www.sec.gov/litigation/admin/2018/ia-5086.pdf.

income or gains on other transactions, thereby reducing clients' tax liability in a given year. Wealthfront makes available on its website for clients' whitepapers containing client disclosures and outlining TLH, among other topics. From October 2012 through mid-May 2016, the firm falsely stated in its TLH whitepaper that it monitored all client accounts to avoid any transactions that might trigger a wash sale. Generally, a wash sale occurs when an investor sells a security at a loss and, within 30 days of this sale, buys the same or a substantially identical security. The IRS' "wash sale rule" prevents the taxpayers from realizing the tax benefit of having sold the asset to realize a loss.

In fact, until mid-May 2016, Wealthfront did not monitor client accounts to avoid any transaction that might trigger a wash sale. In Wealthfront's TLH program, wash sales could occur, or were permitted, in certain circumstances relating to the management of a client account such as rebalancing a client portfolio or client directed transactions. In addition, the firm retweeted certain tweets from its clients on its Twitter account that constituted testimonials, which investment advisers are not permitted to publish without required disclosure. Wealthfront also paid bloggers for new client referrals, based on the amount of assets the new client initially deposited, without complying with applicable disclosure and documentation requirements. Wealthfront also failed to adopt and implement policies and procedures reasonably designed to prevent violations of the Advisers Act and the rules thereunder. The within proceeding and the proceeding discussed below are the SEC's first enforcement actions against robo-advisers, which provide automated, software-based portfolio management services.

The SEC's order against Wealthfront found that the adviser violated the antifraud, advertising, compliance, and other provisions of the Advisers Act. Without admitting or denying the SEC's findings, Wealthfront consented to the entry of the SEC's order censuring it, requiring it to cease and desist from further violations, and imposed a $250,000 penalty.[44]

---

[44] A summary of the Order is at: *SEC Charges Two Robo-Advisers With False Disclosures*, SECURITIES AND EXCHANGE COMMISSION RELEASE NO. 2018-300 (Dec. 21, 2018), https://www.sec.gov/news/press-release/2018-300.

*SEC v. Hedgeable Inc.* In a separate SEC Order of the same date as Wealthfront, it determined that New York City-based Hedgeable Inc., a robo-adviser, which had approximately $81 million in client assets under management, made a series of misleading statements about its investment performance. According to the Order, from 2016 until April 2017, Hedgeable posted on its website and social media purported comparisons of the investment performance of Hedgable's clients with those of two robo-adviser competitors. The performance comparisons were misleading because Hedgeable included less than 4 percent of its client accounts, which had higher-than-average returns. Hedgeable compared this with rates of return that were not based on competitors' actual trading models. The SEC's order also found that Hedgeable failed to maintain required documentation and failed to maintain a compliance program reasonably designed to prevent violations of the securities laws. The SEC's order against Hedgeable found that the adviser violated the antifraud, advertising, compliance, and books and records provisions of the Investment Advisers Act of 1940. Without admitting or denying the SEC's findings, Hedgeable consented to the entry of the SEC's order which censured it, required it to cease and desist from further violations, and imposed an $80,000 penalty.[45]

## Federal Communications Commission (FCC)

The FCC allocates and assigns spectrum for non-federal entities. It also is concerned with electronic systems that are used in IoT system architecture, i.e., board designs for IoT implementation must comply with FCC guidelines. They include the use of FCC pre-certified IoT RF modules, whenever possible; insure that the design be met for EMC compliance techniques and elements, such as filters and shielding to minimize noise and interference in the design; conduct testing to assure FCC compliance which may also include mandatory testing at an authorized laboratory;

---

[45] *Id.* A copy of the Order is at: SEC v. Hedgeable, Inc., SEC Admin. Proceeding No. 3-18950 (Dec. 21, 2018), https://www.sec.gov/litigation/admin/2018/ia-5087.pdf.

and label the product appropriately and maintain records of test compliance and results.[46]

## Food and Drug Administration (FDA)

The FDA is particularly concerned with cybersecurity of medical devices. As stated in its website, although AI medical devices have significant health benefits, nevertheless, there are risks because medical devices are increasingly connected to the Internet, hospital networks, and other medical devices that provide features that improve health care and increase the ability of health care providers to treat patients. The problem is that these devices also increase the risk of potential cybersecurity threats and are vulnerable to security breaches which may, potentially, impact the safety and effectiveness of the device. Israeli researchers created malware to test systems concerning how to respond to possible cyberattacks that could fake malignant growths to CT or MRI scans and remove them from such scans. The threat was not without basis inasmuch as some 70 real CT lung scans were found to be infected with malware that tricked skilled radiologists to misdiagnose conditions. The fear is that the malware may be used to affect candidates for public office that either demonstrates they are healthy or unhealthy or other misuse.[47] Accordingly, the FDA has issued a series of guidance measures to mitigate against such threats.

On December 18, 2018, it issued a draft guidance, *Content of Premarket Submissions of Management of Cybersecurity in Medical Devices* which provides recommendations to industry regarding cybersecurity device design, labeling, and documentation to be included in premarket submissions for devices with cybersecurity risk. Other guidance recommendations include *Guidance for the Content of Premarket Submissions for Software*

---

[46] *FCC Regulations and Guidelines for Manufacturing IoT Devices*, TEMPO BLOG (Sept. 20, 2018), https://www.tempoautomation.com/blog/fcc-regulations-and-guidelines-for-manufacturing-iot-devices/.

[47] Kim Zetter, *Hospital viruses: Fake cancerous nodes in CT scans, created by malware, trick radiologists*, WASHINGTON POST (April 3, 2019), https://www.washingtonpost.com/technology/2019/04/03/hospital-viruses-fake-cancerous-nodes-ct-scans-created-by-malware-trick-radiologists/?utm_term=.b771a767367a.

*Contained in Medical Devices, Guidance to Industry: Cybersecurity for Networked Medical Devices Containing Off-the-Shelf (OTS) Software* and other suggested best practices.[48]

In its 2018 draft non-binding guidance for managing cybersecurity in medical devices which superseded its 2014 Guidance, the FDA defined two tiers of devices according to their cybersecurity risk: Tier 1—*Higher Cybersecurity Risk* and Tier 2—*Standard Security Risk*, with *risk* defined as "the combination of the probability of occurrence of harm and the severity of that harm." Tier 1 device is one wherein: The device is capable of connecting (e.g., wired, wirelessly) to another medical or 288 non-medical products, or to a network, or to the Internet; and a cybersecurity incident affecting the device could directly result in patient harm to multiple patients. Examples of Tier 1 devices include implantable cardioverter defibrillators, pacemakers, dialysis devices, and infusion and insulin pumps. Tier 2 pertains to a medical device which the said criteria of Tier 1 is not met.

The suggested principles are: (1) *The application of NIST cybersecurity framework in the design of a trustworthy device.* Manufacturers should design devices that prevent unauthorized use; ensure trusted content my maintaining code, data, and execution integrity; and maintain confidentiality of data; (2) *Detect, respond, recover: design expectations.* The principles to be followed are: design the device to detect cybersecurity events in a timely fashion; design the device to respond to and contain the impact of a potential cybersecurity incident; and design the device to recover capabilities or services that were impaired due to a cybersecurity incident. (3) *Labeling recommendations for devices with cybersecurity risks*; the guidance lists 14 recommendations. (4) *Cybersecurity documentation* including design documentation and risk management documentation.

The FDA's provides guidance for medical devices containing off-the-shelf software, i.e., medical devices that use OTS software can connect to networks such as a private intranet or the public Internet, and need updates or patches because their OTS software is found vulnerable to viruses, worms, and other threats. The guidance states that manufactur-

---

[48] *Cybersecurity*, U.S. FOOD AND DRUG ADMINISTRATION, https://www.fda.gov/MedicalDevices/DigitalHealth/ucm373213.htm#guidance.

ers, which chose to use OTS software in their devices and vulnerabilities in OTS software; have to act to keep their devices safe and effective; examine sources of quality data and correct or prevent quality problems; validate their software changes under the Quality System regulation; and they should have a plan for how to make these changes and follow it.

## Department of Homeland Security (DHS)

The DHS oversees the coordination of 16 critical infrastructure sectors, many of which use industrial control systems that are connected to the Internet and to the DHS National Cybersecurity and Communications Integration Center. The Center has an emergency response system in place to address cybersecurity issues.[49] DHS issued a document, *Strategic Principles for Securing the Internet of Things (IoT)*[50] that explains the safety and economic risks attendant to IoT and provides a set of non-binding principles and suggested best practices to build toward a responsible level of security for the devices and systems businesses design, manufacture, own, and operate.

The strategic principles that DHS recommends as summarily stated herein are:

* *Incorporate Security at the Design Phase.* The suggested practices are (1) Enable security by default through unique, hard to crack default user names and passwords; (2) Build the device using the most recent operating system that is technically viable and economically feasible; (3) Use hardware that incorporates security features to strengthen the protection and integrity of the device; and (4) Design with system and operational disruption in mind.
* *Advance Security Updates and Vulnerability Management.* The suggested principles are: (1) Consider ways in which to secure the device over network connections or through automated means; (2) Consider coor-

---

[49] Fisher, *supra* at note 414 at p. 9.

[50] *Strategic Principles for Securing the Internet of Things (IoT)*, U.S. DEPT. of HOMELAND SECURITY (Nov. 15, 2016), https://www.dhs.gov/sites/default/files/publications/Strategic_Principles_for_Securing_the_Internet_of_Things-2016-1115-FINAL....pdf.

dinating software updates among third-party vendors to address vulnerabilities and security improvements to ensure consumer devices have the complete set of current protections; (3) Develop automated mechanisms for addressing vulnerabilities; (4) Develop a policy regarding the coordinated disclosure of vulnerabilities, including associated security practices to address identified vulnerabilities; and (5) Develop an end-of-life strategy for IoT products.

- *Build on Security Practices.* The suggested practices are: (1) Start with basic software security and cybersecurity practices and apply them to the IoT ecosystem in flexible, adaptive, and innovative ways; (2) Refer to relevant Sector-Specific Guidance, where it exists, as a starting point from which to consider security practices; (3) Practice defense in depth; and (4) Participate in information sharing platforms to report vulnerabilities and receive timely and critical information about current cyber threats and vulnerabilities from public and private partners.

- *Prioritize Security Measures According to Potential Impact.* The suggested practices are: (1) Know a device's intended use and environment, where possible; (2) Perform a "red-teaming" exercise, where developers actively try to bypass the security measures needed at the application, network, data, or physical layers; and (3) Identify and authenticate the devices connected to the network, especially for industrial consumers and business networks.

- *Promote Transparency Across IoT.* The suggested practices are: (1) Conduct end-to-end risk assessments that account for both internal and third party vendor risks, where possible; (2) Consider creating a publicly disclosed mechanism for using vulnerability reports; and (3) Consider developing and employing a software bill of materials that can be used as a means of building shared trust among vendors and manufacturers.

- *Connect Carefully and Deliberately.* The suggested practices are: (1) Advise IoT consumers on the intended purpose of any network connections; (2) Make intentional connections; and (3) Build in controls to allow manufacturers, service providers, and consumers to disable network connections or specific ports when needed or desired to enable selective connectivity.

# Department of Transportation (DOT)

The DOT is particularly active in utilizing IoT concepts and advancements in an endeavor to make transportation by automobiles and other vehicles safer and free from cybersecurity threats. Thus, it administers the Mobility-on-Demand (MOD) "Sandbox," an effort to bring non-traditional partners together to promote enhanced, multimodal mobility concepts using advanced technologies and new business models for providing improved transportation service. It supports the design and deployment of connected vehicle technologies, such as vehicle-to-vehicle communications, in a manner that protects consumers from unwarranted privacy risks and prevents unauthorized access to data. As stated by Undersecretary Carlos Monje Jr. before a U.S. Senate Committee, the Department envisions the connected vehicle system will contain multiple technical controls to help mitigate potential privacy risks and prevent tampering with equipment or data. It is also working with privacy experts to develop algorithms to sanitize connected vehicle data sets and develop regulatory strategies and guidance in the area of consumer data privacy.

With respect to cybersecurity, the Department is encouraging the automotive industry to form an Information Sharing and Analysis Center to help the industry proactively and uniformly address cybersecurity threats, while challenging automakers to adopt proactive safety principles and develop best practices that enhance automotive cybersecurity. It collaborated proactively with other government agencies including DARPA, DHS, and the National Science Foundation as well as with vehicle manufacturers, automotive suppliers, and the security research. The Intelligent Transportation Systems (ITS) Joint Program Office (JPO) focuses on managing and providing transportation big data to support new paradigms of data-driven operations. The ITS-JPO is funding multimodal enterprise data management initiatives focusing on enabling effective data capture from ITS-enabled technologies, including connected passenger, transit, and commercial vehicles; mobile devices; and infrastructure, in ways that protect the privacy of users.[51]

---

[51] Carlos Monje, Jr. *How the Internet of Things (IoT) Can Bring U.S. Transportation and Infrastructure into the 21st Century*, Statement before U.S. Senate Comm. On Commerce, Science and Transportation, June 28, 2016, https://www.transportation.gov/government-affairs/testimony/dot-how-internet-things-iot-can-bring-us-transportation-and.

## National Science Foundation (NSF)

The NSF funds research and development in cyberphysical systems research as well as an IoT platform for smart schools. It has awarded multi-million grants to explore STEM education and workforce development with a major emphasis on a cyberphysical engineering platform for designing IoT systems that manage resources, space, and processes of a community on real-time. The idea is to transform a home, school, town and the like into an engineering laboratory for unleashing the potential for learning, research, and exploration.[52]

## Department of Defense (DoD)

The DoD is particularly engaged in the development of IoT. In a major study,[53] it noted the risks and benefits of IoT particularly as they relate to DoD missions. Among the risks are:

- *Expanded Attack Surface*. The numerous types and relative simplicity of IoT devices greatly expands the attack surface exposed to the Internet.
- *Attack Deployment*. The IoT provides many more potential BotNet[54] participants and directions from which attacks can originate and which may use DoD platforms to mount attacks elsewhere, or to directly attack DoD networks and computers.
- *Expanded Aggregation of Information*. The IoT ability to obtain many types of information about the same assets through various IoT capabilities whose information is aggregated for big data analytics greatly

---

[52] *National Science Foundation funds research and development of an IoT platform for smart schools*, ENGINEERING COMPUTATION LABORATORY (May 18, 2017), http://molecularwork-bench.blogspot.com/2017/05/national-science-foundation-funds.html.

[53] *DoD Policy Recommendations for The Internet of Things (IoT)*, U.S. DEPT. OF DEFENSE (Dec. 16, 2016) https://dodcio.defense.gov/Portals/0/Documents/Announcement/DoD%20Policy%20 Recommendations%20for%20Internet%20of%20Things%20-%20White%20Paper.pdf? ver=2017-01-26-152811-440.

[54] A BotNet is a collection of internet-connected devices, e.g., mobile devices, servers, and personal computers that are infected and controlled by a type of malware such as denial-of-service attack, spam, and other harmful malware. *Botnet*, SEARCHSECURITY, https://searchsecurity.techtarget. com/definition/botnet.

increases the potential benefit of the information. The problem is that high quality data may be compromised for those persons or nations seeking to obtain the data.

- *Vulnerability of Manufacturing Supply Base.* The fear is that the great spread of usage of IoT and related industrial control devices may lead to the devices being compromised and thus pose a danger to critical manufacturing capability. IoT presents grave challenges for privacy, confidentiality, security, and information governance.
- *Provenance—Subversion of the Things Themselves.* A major risk also is that IoT devices may also be counterfeited or subverted during their manufacture and distribution with the introduction of "back doors" at various points in the supply chain. The attacker need only open the "back door" to find and exploit a vulnerability.
- *Ownership.* Business models are increasing whereby the use of IoT devices may be strictly limited with respect to the increasing prevalence of software and networking embedded in purchased devices.
- *Miscellaneous Risks and Restrictions.* Uses of IoT devices may not receive needed security patches if their device goes past a certain age or release; there may be licensing restrictions on a user's ability to properly monitor software components installed on their device; devices dependent on a cloud capability provided by the vendor for normal operation may face the cessation thereof if the vendor goes out of business or drops support; and users may be restricted from opening or repairing their owned device when needed.

Benefits as projected by the DoD include the following:

- *Better Management of DoD Assets.* Assets can be tracked and monitored in real-time. Information—both item specific and in aggregate—can be readily available to those who need it anywhere in the DoD.
- *IoT Unique Identification of Things.* The ability to uniquely identify things in the Internet of Things through adoption of the Web and Internet's URI schemes can help DoD achieve long-sought unique identification goals, leveraging a proven approach without re-inventing another UID mechanism.

- *Improved Readiness.* Knowing the real-time status of materiel and weapons systems enables the DoD more rapid and agile response to emergent threats.
- *Ability to do More with Less.* The low cost and pervasive nature of IoT allows tracking, inventory, control, and data gathering activities to be accomplished with significantly less personnel labor, and greatly reduced intermediate processing and handling of information.[55]

## Department of Commerce

The Department of Commerce issued a green paper[56] wherein it stated that the U.S. Government policy approach to emerging technology is to be based on the following principles:

- The Department will lead efforts to ensure the IoT environment is inclusive and widely accessible to consumers, workers, and businesses;
- The Department will recommend policy and take action to support a stable, secure, and trustworthy IoT environment;
- The Department will advocate for and defend a globally connected, open, and interoperable IoT environment built upon industry-driven, consensus-based standards; and
- The Department will support IoT growth and innovation by encouraging expanding markets and reducing barriers to entry, and by convening stakeholders to address public policy challenges.

The Department identified four broad areas of engagement to advance these principles:

- *Enabling Infrastructure Availability and Access.* Fostering the physical and spectrum-related assets needed to support IoT growth and advancement.

---

[55] *Id.* at 3–4.
[56] *Fostering The Advancement of Internet of the Things*, U.S. Department of Commerce (Jan. 2017), https://www.ntia.doc.gov/files/ntia/publications/iot_green_paper_01122017.pdf.

- *Crafting Balanced Policy and Building Coalitions.* Removing barriers and encouraging coordination and collaboration; influencing, analyzing, devising, and promoting norms and practices that will protect IoT users while encouraging growth, advancement, and applicability of IoT technologies.
- *Promoting Standards and Technology Advancement.* Ensuring that the necessary technical standards are developed and in place to support global IoT interoperability and that the technical applications and devices to support IoT continue to advance.
- *Encouraging Markets.* Promoting the advancement of IoT through Department usage, application, iterative enhancement, and novel usage of the technologies; and translating the economic benefits and opportunities of IoT to foreign partners.[57]

## National Institute of Standards and Technology (NIST)

NIST issued a draft report that discussed 17 risk concerns outlined in three risk areas of IoT, to wit.

1. Many IoT devices interact with the physical world in ways conventional IT devices usually do not. The potential impact of some IoT devices making changes to physical systems and thus affecting the physical world needs to be explicitly recognized and addressed from cybersecurity and privacy perspectives. Also, operational requirements for performance, reliability, resilience, and safety may be at odds with common cybersecurity and privacy practices for conventional IT devices.
2. Many IoT devices cannot be accessed, managed, or monitored in the same ways conventional IT devices can. This can necessitate doing tasks manually for large numbers of IoT devices, expanding staff knowledge and tools to include a much wider variety of IoT device software, and addressing risks with manufacturers and other third parties having remote access or control over IoT devices.

---

[57] Quoted from *Id.* at 2–3.

3. The availability, efficiency, and effectiveness of cybersecurity and privacy capabilities are often different for IoT devices than conventional IT devices. This means organizations may have to select, implement, and manage additional controls, as well as determine how to respond to risk when sufficient controls for mitigating risk are not available.[58]

The three risk mitigation goals to meet the challenges are applicable to all IoT devices: (1) *protect device security*—prevent a device from being used to conduct attacks such as participation in denial-of-service attacks; attacks against other organizations, and eavesdropping on network traffic or compromising other devices on the same network segment; (2) *protect data security*—protect the confidentiality, integrity, and/or availability of data such as personally identifiable information collected by, stored on, processed by, or transmitted to or from the IoT device; and (3) *protect individuals' privacy*—protect individuals' privacy beyond risks managed through device and data security protection.[59]

## Miscellaneous U.S. Departments' IoT Engagements

The *State Department* invested up to $25 million in IoT to provide a platform for big data analytics. It awarded a multi-year contract to C3 IoT to analyze data to assist in the reduction of the Department's energy usage and to monitor sensor health.[60] The *U.S. Department of Energy*'s Argonne National Laboratory has invested in a turn-key IoT innovation in remote sensing. It is seeking to develop high-performance and green buildings and smart electrical grids through its Waggle wireless environmental sensing platform which handles the big data difficulty by its

[58] Jeffrey Voas, Richard Kuhn, Phillip Laplante, and Sophia Applebaum, *Internet of Things (IoT) Trust Concerns*, NIST WHITE PAPER (Oct. 17, 2018), https://csrc.nist.gov/publications/detail/white-paper/2018/10/17/iot-trust-concerns/draft. The full draft of the paper can be found at https://nvlpubs.nist.gov/nistpubs/ir/2018/NIST.IR.8228-draft.pdf.

[59] Quoted from *Id.* at v–vi.

[60] Samantha Ehlinger, *State Department invests in IoT*, FEDSCOOP (June 23, 2016), https://www.fedscoop.com/state-department-invests-in-iot/.

transmission of recognized events rather than pure raw data.[61] The *U.S. Federal Aviation Administration* (FAA) regulates aerial vehicles and commercial systems. IoT concepts are being applied to the operation of airspace as an open architecture IoT system and are used to manage and operate individual devices in airspace.[62]

The *National Telecommunications and Information Administration* (NTIA) is an Executive Branch agency within the Department of Commerce, is principally responsible by law for advising the President on telecommunications and information policy issues. NTIA's programs and policymaking focus largely on expanding broadband Internet access and adoption in America, expanding the use of spectrum by all users, and ensuring that the Internet remains an engine for continued innovation and economic growth. With respect to IoT, it is assisting the Department of Commerce in conducting a review of the benefits, challenges, and potential roles for the government in fostering the advancement of the Internet of Things.[63]

# States' Proposals for Privacy Legislation

*California.* California has taken the lead in privacy legislation with the enactment of the *California Consumer Privacy Act of 2018 (CCPA)*[64] The intentions of the statute which goes in effect on January 1, 2020, and as specified in the particulars of the Act are as follows.

(1) The right of Californians to know what personal information is being collected about them.

---

[61] Pablo Valerio, *US Department of Energy claims IoT Breakthrough with Waggle concept*, IoT TIMES (Jan. 26, 2018), https://iot.eetimes.com/us-department-of-energy-claims-iot-breakthrough-with-waggle-concept/.

[62] *The Internet of Things in Commercial Aviation*, WIND, https://www.windriver.com/whitepapers/iot-commercial-aviation/1513-IoT-in-Commercial-Aviation-White-Paper.pdf.

[63] *Internet of Things*, Nat. Telecommunications and Information Adm., https://www.ntia.doc.gov/category/internet-things.

[64] California Consumer Privacy Act of 2018, AB375, Title 1.81.5, https://leginfo.legislature.ca.gov/faces/billTextClient.xhtml?bill_id=201720180SB1121.

(2) The right of Californians to know whether their personal information is sold or disclosed and to whom.
(3) The right of Californians to say no to the sale of personal information.
(4) The right of Californians to access their personal information.
(5) The right of Californians to equal service and price, even if they exercise their privacy rights

*Personal information* is defined as that information that identifies, relates to, describes, is capable of being associated with, or could reasonably be linked, directly or indirectly, with a particular consumer or household. It includes identifiers such as a real name, alias, postal address, unique identifier, online identifier Internet Protocol address, email address, account name, social security number, driver's license number, passport number, or other similar identifiers; commercial information, including records of personal property, products or services purchased, obtained, or considered, or other purchasing or consuming histories or tendencies; biometric information; Internet or other electronic network activity information, professional or employment information; education information; and inferences drawn from any of the information identified in this subdivision to create a profile about a consumer reflecting the consumer's preferences, characteristics, psychological trends, preferences, predispositions, behavior, attitudes, intelligence, abilities, and aptitudes.

Companies that sell the said data to third parties will have to disclose its practice and give consumers the option to opt out of the sale by placing on the company's home page a link to: "Do Not Sell My Personal Information" on its home page. The statute applies to businesses that have gross revenues of over $25 million; alone or in combination, annually buys, receives for the business' commercial purposes, sells, or shares for commercial purposes, alone or in combination, the personal information of 50,000 or more consumers, households, or devices; or derives 50 percent or more of its annual revenues from selling consumers' personal data. Damages include a modest civil penalty of $100–$750 per incident but also actual damages if greater plus injunctive relief. The provisions of the statute cannot be waived by contract or otherwise (Cal Civ. Code §1798.120(d)).

One commentator noted in a comparison with the E.U.'s *General Data Protection Regulation* (discussed in Chap. 8), that the latter is an omnibus law that applies to a much broader area of privacy rights that include not only data subjects but also notification procedures for data breach, data security implementation (right to correct inaccurate or incomplete personal data), cross-border data transfers (California law only applies to resident persons), and additional rights of data subjects such as the right to be forgotten, right of rectification, and a number of other rights.[65] Another commentator stated that the California statute was more comprehensive than the GDPR in certain respects with its broader definition of personal information, broader rights to request data deletion, greater power to access personal information without the numerous exceptions in the GDPR, and greater restrictions on information sharing.[66]

*Vermont.* Vermont became the first state in the U.S. to enact legislation that regulates data brokers who purchase and sell personal information.[67] The statute[68] *An act relating to data brokers and consumer protection*, effective on January 1, 2019, adopts consumer protection provisions relating to data brokers, including creating a new set of definitions, compelling annual registration, requiring a data security program, and necessitating further study of related issues by the Attorney General.

*Data collector* may include the State, State agencies, political subdivisions of the State, public and private universities, privately and publicly held corporations, limited liability companies, financial institutions, retail operators, and any other entity that, for any purpose, whether by automated collection or otherwise, handles, collects, disseminates, or otherwise deals with nonpublic personal information. *Encryption* means use of an algorithmic process to transform data into a form in which the

---

[65] Kristen J. Mathews and Courtney M. Bowman, *The California Consumer Privacy Act of 2018*, PROSKAUER, PRIVACY LAW BLOG (July 13, 2018), https://privacylaw.proskauer.com/2018/07/articles/data-privacy-laws/the-california-consumer-privacy-act-of-2018/.

[66] Stuart D. Levi, *California Privacy Law: What Companies Should Do to Prepare in 2019*, SKADDEN (Jan. 17, 2019), https://www.skadden.com/insights/publications/2019/01/2019-insights/california-privacy-law.

[67] For a discussion, see *Vermont Enacts Nation's First Data Broker Legislation*, HUNTON ANDREWS KURTH (June 13, 2018), https://www.huntonprivacyblog.com/2018/06/13/vermont-enacts-nations-first-data-broker-legislation/.

[68] Vermont Statutes, Act 171 (2018), H. 764, eff.

data is rendered unreadable or unusable without use of a confidential process or key. *Personally identifiable information* means an individual's name, social security number, motor vehicle license number, financial, credit or debit card numbers and, account passwords, personal identification numbers, or other access codes.

A data broker is required annually to register with the Vermont Secretary of State and provide information with respect to whether it permits a consumer to opt out of the data broker's collection of personal information, databases, or of certain sales of data; the method for doing so; which data the consumer is not given the choice to opt out; its collection methodologies; and breaches. There are daily civil penalties up to $10,000 annually and other penalties provided by state law.

## Congressional Proposals for Privacy Legislation

A number of proposals to protect the right of privacy have been introduced by members of the U.S. Congress, albeit passage into law for most of them appears to be questionable absent significant constituents' pressure whose knowledge of the issue is seriously lacking.[69] The *Data Care Act of 2018*,[70] was introduced on December 12, 2018 and awaits passage by the U.S Senate in 2018. It states that an online service provider shall fulfill the following duties of: (1) *care* by reasonably securing individual identifying data from unauthorized access and promptly inform an end user of any breach thereof; (2) *loyalty* by not using any individual identifying data or its derivation that will benefit the online service provider to the detriment of the end users or which will result in reasonably foreseeable harm to the end user or would be unexpected and highly offensive to a reasonable end user; and (3) *confidentiality* whereby the provider shall not disclose or sell individual identifying data to or share the data unless

---

[69] Far an excellent summary from which this discussion emanates in part is Cameron F. Kerry, *Breaking down proposals for privacy legislation: How do they regulate?*, BROOKINGS (March 8, 2019), https://www.brookings/research/breaking-down-proposals-for-privacy-legislation-how-do-they-regulate/.

[70] Dara Care Act of 2018, S. 3744, 115th Cong. (2019).

the person wherein the data is shared also contracts to provide the same degree of care, loyalty and confidentiality contracted with the end user.

*Individual identifying data* means any data that is collected over the Internet or any other digital network and linked to a specific end user or a computing device that is connected to the end user. Enforcement is by the Federal Trade Commission which shall consider privacy risks imposed by the use of the individual identifying data by the online service provider including size of the provider, complexity of its offerings, nature and scope of the provider's activities, and sensitivity and benefits derived therefrom. *Sensitive data* is any data that includes a person's social security number, personal information collected from a child, a driver's license number, passport number, military ID, or similar data, a financial account number, credit or debit card number, unique biometric data, information such as user name, password, email address and password, data showing date of birth, maiden name, past or present health information and any nonpublic communications unique identifying information. The Act applies to commercial and non-profit enterprises and may also be enforced by individual states.[71]

Additional legislation that is being considered for possible enactment are.

The *Consumer Data Protection Act of 2018*,[72] would empower and direct the FTC to: (1) establish minimum privacy and cybersecurity standards; (2) issue steep fines (up to 4% of annual revenue) on the first offense for companies and 10-20-year criminal penalties for senior executives; (3) create a national Do Not Track system that lets consumers stop third-party companies from tracking them on the web by sharing data, selling data, or targeting advertisements based on their personal information. It permits companies to charge consumers who want to use their products and services but don't want their information monetized; (4) give consumers a way to review what personal information a company has about them, learn with whom it has been shared or sold, and to challenge inaccuracies in it; (5) hire additional staff to police the largely

---

[71] *Id.*, https://www.govinfo.gov/content/pkg/BILLS-115s3744is/pdf/BILLS-115s3744is.pdf.

[72] The Consumer Data Protection Act of 2018, Discussion Draft of Sen. Wyden, https://www.wyden.senate.gov/imo/media/doc/Wyden%20Privacy%20Bill%20one%20pager%20Nov%201.pdf.

unregulated market for private data; and (6) require companies to assess the algorithms that process consumer data to examine their impact on accuracy, fairness, bias, discrimination, privacy, and security.

The FTC is to promulgate regulations related to sensitive personal information or behavioral data and for other purposes. Operators providing services to the public, which involves the collection and other uses of personal data, are to afford users with notice through a privacy and data use policy of a specific request to use their data and require that users provide opt in consent to the dissemination of the data. The policy must be (A) is concise and intelligible; (B) is clear and prominent in appearance; (C) uses clear and plain language; (D) uses visualizations where appropriate to make complex information understandable by the ordinary user; and (E) is provided free of charge. In addition, the data use policy shall include the identity and contact information of the entity collecting the sensitive personal information; the purpose for the use; third parties with whom the data is shared; the storage person for retention of the data; how consent to the collection etc. may be withdrawn; how a user can view the sensitive personal information provided; the kind of sensitive personal information is collected; whether the sensitive personal information will be used to create profiles about users; and how sensitive personal information is protected from unauthorized access or acquisition.

*Other Proposals for Legislative Enactment.* A number of businesses and non-profit organizations concerned with privacy rights has weighed in with proposals. Among them are:

*Center for Democracy & Technology* (CDT).[73] The CDT's proposal is comparable to the legislative proposals stated above. It recites the rights given to individuals with respect to personal information of right to access and correction; data portability; deletion with some exceptions; notice of denial of request to access, correct, or deletion within 30 days to permit covered individual to appeal; and free exercise of individual rights (§2). The proposal states the obligations of covered entities with respect

---

[73] *CDT Federal Baseline Privacy Legislation Discussion Draft*, CENTER FOR DEMOCRACY & TECHNOLOGY (Dec. 5, 2018), https://cdt.org/files/2018/12/2018-12-12-CDT-Privacy-Discussion-Draft-Final.pdf.

to personal information which are the easy-to-use right of redress; security of the information; limitations imposed upon third parties and service providers; disclosures of information to covered persons and periodic privacy protection disclosure (§3). Further recitations concern deceptive practices and the roles of states' Attorney Generals.

Intel Corporation's lengthy proposed bill for enactment, summarily entitled *Innovative and Ethical Data Use Act of 2018*,[74] provides: "A Bill To improve the protection of personal privacy by enacting nationwide standards governing for profit and non-profit private sector organizations' collection, use and sharing of personal data consistent with the Fair Information Practice Principles." In a commentary on the various proposals by a scholar at Brookings, it is argued that privacy protection to date had placed too great a burden on individuals who virtually never read the small-print, difficult to understand notices posted by credit card and other companies to manage their privacy protection rather than on the focus of business behavior as provided for in the draft and Intel's proposed business obligations.[75]

## European Union and IoT Regulation

The E.U. is favorably disposed to the benefits of IoT by the E.U. Commission which initiated a series of policies to accelerate its adoption in order to better the lives of E.U. residents. In March 2015, it launched the Alliance for Internet of Things Innovation to encourage its expansion by coordination with all relevant stakeholders to establish a competitive European IoT and the creation of new business models to promote its enhancement and expansion. In May, 2015, the Commission adopted the Digital Single Market Strategy to avoid the fragmentation of IoT in favor of fostering interoperability of IoT and to promote its vision of a thriving IoT ecosystem that is human-centered and operates as a single market. The single market was further emphasized in the proposed

---

[74] *Innovative and Ethical Data Use Act of 2018*, INTEL CORP., https://usprivacybill.intel.com/legislation.

[75] Cameron F. Kerry, *supra* note 473 at 6.

European data economy initiative of January, 2017.[76] In an earlier study,[77] the Commission noted that in combination with cloud computing and Big Data, the IoT is a disruptive technology of the new age of the "hyper-connected society and acting as a powerful driver of business innovation," but is coupled with concerns over security risks, privacy protection, and resistance to organizational change. It had projections of IoT connections within the E.U. of 1.8 billion in 2013 (the base year) to almost 6 billion in 2020. The projected business models to emerge in the E.U. were smart energy, transport, manufacturing, government, and health. It recommended the promotion of communities of stakeholders in the main smart environments, supporting the networking and interaction between stakeholders, the sharing of good practices, and the development of skills and training activities. It further recommended a single market for the technologies within the E.U., funding for innovative research and development by member states, and development of global offerings to serve multinational enterprises.[78]

*Privacy Provisions*. The E.U. is well aware of the privacy and other risks that inevitably arise with new technologies. Accordingly, it noted the applicable regulation concerning privacy is the *European General Data Protection Regulation* (GDPR) that took effect on May 25, 2018.[79] The Regulation applies to the processing of personal data wholly or in part by automated means irrespective whether the controller or processor is within or outside of the E.U. The basic principles provides in part that personal data shall be processed lawfully, fairly and in a transparent manner in relation to the data; collected for specified, explicit and legitimate purposes with some exceptions; be adequate, relevant and limited to what is necessary in relation to the purposes for which they are processed; be accurate and kept up to date; kept for no longer than is necessary for the

---

[76] *The Internet of Things*, EUROPEAN COMMISSION DIGITAL SINGLE MARKET, https://ec.europa.eu/digital-single-market/en/policies/internet-things.

[77] *Definition of a Research and Innovation Policy Leveraging Cloud Computing and IoT Combination*, European Commission (SMART 2013/0037 (2014)), file:///C:/Users/Giras/Downloads/DefinitionofaResearchandInnovationPolicyLeveragingCloudComputingandIoTCombination.pdf. [78] *Id*.

[79] *European General Data Protection Regulation* (GDPR), (EU) 2016/679. Text of GDPR may be found at https://gdpr-info.eu/.

purposes for which the personal data are processed; and processed in a manner that ensures appropriate security of the personal data, including protection against unauthorized or unlawful processing and against accidental loss, destruction or damage, using appropriate technical or organizational measures (Art. 2).

Penalties are potentially very severe, namely, fines up to 4 percent of annual global turnover or €20 million (whichever is greater) for failure to have customer consent to process data or for violating the major provisions of the Regulation or 2 percent for not having records in proper order or not notifying the supervising authority concerning a data breach within 72 hours of first becoming aware of the breach, or not conducting impact assessment. Consent must be received from the data subject stated in plain terms and conditions in an easily accessible form. The data subjects have expanded right of access to the data free of charge, have the right to have the controller erase the personal data, and to cease further dissemination of the data.[80]

In this chapter we noted how the IoT poses significant problems for individuals and their privacy rights. The U.S. government has attempted to take some steps, albeit quite limited, to assist consumers and their desire to be free from interference and eavesdropping on their personal data. In the following chapter, we continue the discussion of issues that have ethical and privacy implications including that of AI bias and possible job losses to automation.

---

[80] *GDPR Key Changes*, EU GDPR.ORG, https://eugdpr.org/the-regulation/.

# 6

# Bias, Jobs, and Fake News

We continue the discussion of issues that have privacy and ethical implications by an examination of what some commentators have alleged as bias in AI devices and programs, which require resolution before they are utilized in a manner that will seriously compromise the rights of individuals. We then proceed to the question of how AI will transform the workplace. Will there be fewer, more, or a balance of jobs lost and gained by the new technologies? We conclude the chapter with a current issue that supposedly affected political gains and losses, namely, that of so-called "fake news."

## Bias

Many observers of the development of AI have expressed their concern about inherent biases that underlie AI-based software programs.[1] Machine learning has been particularly queried concerning its reliability and the

---

[1] A sampling of the numerous examples include the following: Will Knight, *Forget Killer Robots-Bias Is the Real AI Danger*, MIT TECHNOLOGY REVIEW (Oct. 3, 2017), https://www.technologyreview.com/s/608986/forget-killer-robotsbias-is-the-real-ai-danger/ and Joy Buolamwini, *Artificial Intelligence Has a Problem With Gender and Racial Bias. Here's How to Solve It*, TIME (Feb. 9, 2019), http://time.com/5520558/artificial-intelligence-racial-gender-bias/.

© The Author(s) 2020
R. Girasa, *Artificial Intelligence as a Disruptive Technology*,
https://doi.org/10.1007/978-3-030-35975-1_6

alleged crisis in *reproducibility* (ability to reproduce comparable results by other researchers). Very often, results depended on the particular data set which could not be replicated by other data sets or in the "real world."[2] Judges and probation department personnel have been relying on data that is often skewed against persons, particularly of color, which may result in unfair sentencing or other biased treatment. Other commentators found it difficult to comprehend how bias can enter into the equation because results or patterns are based on the particular data sets inserted into the computer that train algorithms in deep learning and other AI-based programs.

One observer suggested that bias can enter into the equation in three preliminary stages: (1) *framing the problem*—what scientists who are framing the problem want to achieve. Thus, a credit card company or loan officer may wish to maximize profit from a given loan but in doing so, may elicit a biased income analysis against otherwise worthy potential borrowers; (2) *collecting the data*—the data entered often reflect (usually unintentionally) biases against darker-skinned persons or women; and (3) *preparing the data*—selecting the attributes the researcher wants the algorithm to consider.[3]

## Meaning and Types of Biases

*Bias* generally refers to a strong inclination of the mind or possession of a preconceived opinion about something or someone. It can be one that is in favor or against a thing or person. *Prejudice* is a stronger preconceived inclination generally used in a negative context, e.g., to be prejudiced against a person of color or religion.[4] *Bias in algorithms* refers to an algorithm that has limited flexibility to learn from the true signal from a dataset. It may cause it to overgeneralize or "underfit" the data. *Variance*

---

[2] Pallab Ghosh, *AAAS: Machine learning 'causing science crisis*, BBC (Feb. 18, 2019), https://www.bbc.com/news/science-environment-47267081.

[3] Karen Hao, *This is how AI bias really happens – and why it's so hard to fix*, MIT TECHNOLOGY REVIEW (Feb. 4, 2019), https://www.technologyreview.com/s/612876/this-is-how-ai-bias-really-happensand-why-its-so-hard-to-fix/.

[4] *Bias*, DICTIONARY.COM, https://www.dictionary.com/browse/bias.

*in algorithms* refers to an algorithm's sensitivity to specific sets of training data; it is sensitivity to noise in the data, which may cause the model to "overfit."[5] A *high bias* is a strong inclination toward a set belief that distorts the outcome of the subject under study irrespective of whatever data is added thereto.[6]

There are numerable biases in AI-based technology that have been suspected mainly based on machine learning programs. They include biases in hiring practices, financial services, health services, judicial administration especially with respect to pretrial bail and posttrial sentencing in criminal cases, and almost all other areas wherein algorithms are at the bases of programs. Basic types are: sample bias, prejudice or stereotype bias, systemic value distortion, and model insensitivity.[7] *Sample bias* occurs when the sample statistic does not accurately represent the true value of the parameter as exemplified when the average of the set being studied inaccurately reflects the true average value of the studied target.[8] *Prejudice* or *stereotype bias* is the belief that certain attributes, characteristics, and behaviors replicate the typical qualities of a particular group of people.[9] *Systemic value distortion* are systems that limit choices to either-or, e.g., good or bad, right or wrong etc. which don't allow for nuances or mid-level choices.[10] *Model sensitivity* is the study of how the uncertainty

---

[5] *Bias versus Variance*, ELITEDATASCIENCE, https://elitedatascience.com/bias-variance-tradeoff, and Travis Addair, *What is bias in machine learning algorithms?* QUORA, https://www.quora.com/What-is-bias-in-machine-learning-alrithms.

[6] Alex Guanga, *Machine Learning: Bias VS. Variance*, MEDIUM, https://becominghuman.ai/machine-learning-bias-vs-variance-641f924e6c57.

[7] Two articles quoting Dr. Cheryl Martin, Chief Data Scientist at Alegion are: John K. Waters, *AI Bias: It's in the Data, Not the Algorithm*, PURE AI (July 26, 2018), https://pureai.com/articles/2018/07/26/ai-bias-rooted-in-data.aspx, and Alex Woodie, *Three Ways Biased Data Can Ruin Your ML Models*, DATANAMI (July 18, 2018), https://www.datanami.com/2018/07/18/three-ways-biased-data-can-ruin-your-ml-models/.

[8] *Sampling bias*, SAGE REASEARCHMETHODS, http://methods.sagepub.com/reference/encyclopedia-of-survey-research-methods/n509.xml.

[9] *Understanding Unconscious Bias: Stereotypes, Prejudice, and Discrimination*, CULTUREPLUSCONSULTING, https://cultureplusconsulting.com/2015/05/24/unconscious-bias-stereotypes-prejudice-discrimination/.

[10] *Systemic value*, BUSINESSDICTIONARY, http://www.businessdictionary.com/definition/systemic-value.html.

in the output of a mathematical mode or system can be apportioned, can be apportioned to different sources of uncertainty in its inputs.[11]

Biases are frequently evident in credit rating analyses which are often based on algorithms or other "opaque" methodologies that persons affected cannot challenge legally because they are "opinions" rather than factual statements. Credit agencies had for decades been immune from liability, irrespective of often highly erroneous data formed the bases for opinions. The *Dodd-Frank Act*[12] did attempt in great measure to impose possible liability consequences on credit agencies to incentivize them to become more attentive to the biases for their ratings.

FICO scores,[13] which almost everyone is aware of when applying for a loan, greatly affect whether a person may secure a loan and the percentage rate to be paid. The algorithm or other basis for the score is the subject of more speculation than actual fact. Often a FICO score differs widely among the three major credit agencies thereby evidencing a less than an agreed-upon objective standard. Suggested reforms for the *scored society*, as two authors examined, include: the right of individuals to inspect, correct, and dispute inaccurate data when used by financial and other institutions, although credit agencies do permit such correction as well as how such scores are calculated; the right of notification when the scores are given to third parties; and the licensing and auditing requirements of firms rendering the scores.[14]

In a commentary on the said scored society, another scholar commented that the analyses thereof and that of big data analytics are discriminatory, defined as treated diverse people differently, i.e., against "protected groups" beyond that solely of race but also to include gender and national origin. The types of discrimination are: *explicit discrimination*, which is intended clearly unacceptable bias aimed specifically at

---

[11] *Sensitivity analysis*, WIKIPEDIA, https://en.wikipedia.org/wiki/Sensitivity_analysis.

[12] *Dodd–Frank Wall Street Reform and Consumer Protection Act*, Pub. L. 111–203, H.R. 4173.

[13] FICO score was originally created in 1989 and was the acronym for Fair, Isaac, and Company. It is currently used extensively by the major credit agencies of Experian, Equifax, and TransUnion. *Credit score in the United States*, WIKIPEDIA, https://en.wikipedia.org/wiki/Credit_score_in_the_United_States.

[14] Danielle Keats Citron and Frank Pasquale, *The Scored Society: Due Process for Automated Predictions*, U. of Md. LEGAL STUDIES RESEARCH PAPER, No. 2014-8, https://papers.ssrn.com/sol3/papers.cfm?abstract_id=2376209, 89 Wash. L. Rev. 1 (2014).

certain protected persons and results in unfair distributions of wealth and resources—often, it does not require bigotry per se, but the use of data mining and grouping persons that fit certain characteristics may result in individual discrimination of persons belonging to the discriminated group; *implicit discrimination*, often unintentional, but includes *masking*, i.e., the use of specific and organizational structures that favor particular groups over others, generally by design; *tainted datasets and tools*, e.g., use of old malfeasance of persons against persons who had genuinely reformed for extended time frame; and *blatant proxies, e.g.*, by utilization of zip codes such as "redlining" areas (neighborhoods within the red or other color line), wherein mortgage loans will not be given; height and weight as proxies for gender; age; religion; and other such proxies.[15]

Even though unintended, the problem with biases is their *disparate impact*.[16] The scoring scenario evidences often unintended discrimination that profoundly affects racial minorities. Investigators are frequently baffled by the adverse treatment because often there appears to be no evident "smoking gun" in the algorithms. There is a spiraling down effect from the harm of social segregation that causes minorities to be detached from the rest of society. For example, not permitting mortgages or home equity loans to be given in redlined areas by their very nature brings about a breakdown of the properties and despair of the inhabitants. Social segregation therein is often coupled with stigmatization which then leads to a lowering of aspirations, desire to improve and develop habitable areas, and other socially undesirable results.[17]

## Biases in Criminal Cases

Among the more difficult challenges that judges must contend with when engaged in assessment, both pretrial and after trial, is whether to

---

[15] Tal Z. Zarsky, *Understanding Discrimination in the Scored Society*, 89 WASH. L. REV. 1375 (2015), http://digital.law.washington.edu/dspace-law/bitstream/handle/1773.1/1418/89wlr1375. pdf?sequence=1.

[16] *Id.* at 1396–1399 and Solon Barocas and Andrew D. Selbst, *Big Data's Disparate Impact*, 104 C. L. REV. 671 (2016), https://papers.ssrn.com/sol3/papers.cfm?abstract_id=2477899.

[17] Zarsky *supra*, note 498 at 1398–1402.

incarcerate an accused in criminal cases and the length thereof if incarceration is mandated. Often, it is a guessing game inasmuch as the jurist has limited information derived often from faulty data prepared by probation officers and other similar means. Thus, they frequently resort to assessment tools including those suggested by AI-based systems which take into account a multitude of factors derived from data that may be skewed in favor or against persons depending on the classic categories of race, creed, and other related factors.

In an article concerning a visit by the Chief Justice of the U.S. Supreme Court, John G Roberts Jr., to Rensselaer Polytechnic Institute (RPI) in Troy New York, a question was raised by RPI's president, Shirley Ann Jackson, whether "smart machines, driven with artificial intelligence, will assist with courtroom fact-finding or, controversially, even judicial decision-making." His unexpected response was that it is presently happening. The article then mentioned the case of a Wisconsin man, Eric L. Loomis, who was given a six-year sentence and five years of extended supervision based in part on the judge's use and consideration of a presentence investigation report (PSI) emanating from the COMPAS software with an algorithm that is a trade secret and one which Loomis' attorney(s) were not able to review and challenge. Loomis had been charged with participation in a drive-by shooting which he denied but acknowledged he owned the vehicle that was involved in the shooting. The report stated that Mr. Loomis exhibited "a high risk of violence, high risk of recidivism, high pretrial risk."

Loomis claimed that he was denied due process by the use of the COMPAS report. The Wisconsin Supreme Court, on appeal, refused to disturb the trial judge's findings based on factors that appeared to support the holdings independently of the Report.[18] Justice Ann Walsh Bradley, writing for the court, spoke at length with respect to the nature of the COMPAS risk assessment system and its use in the within case. She noted there were other independent factors that the court considered in addition to the report that supported the imposition of the sentence and that the trial court stated the same sentence would have been imposed without the COMPAS risk sentence report. Justice Bradley acknowledged

---

[18] *State v. Loomis*, 881 N.W. 2d 749 (Wis. 2017).

that the COMPAS report should not be used to determine the severity of the sentence or whether the accused should be incarcerated.

Justice Bradley further noted that inasmuch as the COMPAS risk assessment scores are based on group statistics and not on a particular individual, the trial court is cautioned to weigh that factor in its determinations. The assertion against such usage is that the assessment discriminates based on gender but may be ill-founded because there is widespread agreement that men do have a higher recidivism rate than women. Although it cannot be determinative, a sentencing court may use a COMPAS risk assessment as a relevant factor for such matters as: (1) diverting low-risk prison-bound offenders to a non-prison alternative; (2) assessing whether an offender can be supervised safely and effectively in the community; and (3) imposing terms and conditions of probation, supervision, and responses to violations. Judges are to proceed with caution in using the risk assessment tools to assure they assist but do not determine the final outcome of a jurist's judgment and sentencing.

Justice Roberts noted at the RPI visit that technology is having an impact on the court system which will have to be addressed.[19] It does appear that due process rights of a defendant under the 5th and 14th Amendments to the U.S. Constitution may be violated if he or she is sentenced primarily or in substantial part based on a secret algorithm that attorneys for the accused are not able to examine or question the validity thereof.

*The COMPAS System.* The COMPAS system was developed by Northpointe, a company that has a number of programs relating to criminal justice and which are being utilized in over 200 federal, state, and local criminal justice systems and policymakers. Among the programs offered are the risk assessment program discussed in the Loomis case and also other programs, such as the program Northpointe designates as COMPAS Core, which it claims "is designed for offenders recently removed from the community or currently in the community e.g. jail, probation, community corrections etc." Northpointe asserts that it examines the risk and need factors over the past 12 months to assess the risk of

---

[19] *Sent to Prison by a Software Program's Secret Algorithms*, NEW YORK TIMES (May 1, 2017), https://www.nytimes.com/2017/10/26/opinion/algorithm-compas-sentencing-bias.html.

the particular offender. Persons using the program are able to easily and quickly select any of 22 risk factors to inform decision-making as to sentencing. It compares the scores of a defendant against all other persons in the norm group and allows a reassessment of the offender over time. Some of the features of COMPAS Core include measures of critical risk and need areas, regression, typology, and narrative reports, supervision recommendation, separate male and female norms, and other features. It gives risk scales that include the risks of violate crime, recidivism, and pretrial risk while looking at qualitative factors such as anger, criminal associates, criminal personality, family criminality, history of noncompliance, substance abuse, and other features.[20]

Northpointe states that it has developed for use a fourth-generation risk-need assessment system—the first generation consisted of clinical and professional judgment in the absence of explicit or scoring rules; the second generation with an empirical approach that relied on simple additive point scales with a few standardized factors; and the third generation contained a more explicit, empirically-based, and theory-guided approach and a broader scale of criminogenic factors. With the latest emanation from Northpointe, the company asserts it integrates risk and need assessment with other domains including sentencing decisions, treatment and case management, and recidivism outcomes. It declares it is theory-guided including key constructs such as low self-control theory, strain theory, and related theories. It further states it is a broadband comprehensive assessment; an integration of the strength or resiliency perceptive; uses more advanced statistical models; is an integration with criminal justice databases; has a treatment-explanatory classification to address specific responsivity; and is a gender-sensitive assessment. Northpointe contends that its program had high predictive accuracy by outcome offense, by gender, by ethnicity, and across diverse criminal justice population.[21]

---

[20] *COMPASS CORE Risk/Needs Assessment and Case Planning*, COMPASS CORE, http://www.northpointeinc.com/files/downloads/FAQ_Document.pdf.

For a detailed discussion of the program see TIM BRENNAN, WILLIAM DIETERICH, and BEATE EHRET, HANDBOOK OF RECIDIVISM RISK/NEEDS ASSESSMENT TOOLS, 1st ed. Ch. 3, WILEY (Nov. 29, 2017), https://onlinelibrary.wiley.com/doi/10.1002/9781119184256.ch3.

[21] *Id*. It should be noted that the authors are from Northpointe Institute for Public Management Inc.

The use of the COMPAS system has engendered numerous commentaries, mainly critical, but also some in support of the program, particularly its emanation in later generations which, like other AI-based systems, "learn" from the additional data received from its use and from other social, economic, and scientific sources. Some scholars alleged that black defendants were discriminated against in the use of COMPAS and COMPAS-type risk assessment scores which stated they were twice as likely to be recidivist offenders than white persons although follow-up investigations showed the statistic to be in error.[22] The said findings and critique have met with much criticism. A statistical analysis of data-driven risk assessment instruments, however, was found by one scholar to be more accurate than professional human judgments.[23]

*Suggested Positive and Negative Aspects of Predictive Algorithms.* Courts, judges, prosecutors, probations departments, and the general population are concerned with the proliferation of crime in particular neighborhoods and the recidivist aspects of turnstile justice. The costs of the criminal justice system are staggeringly high, which pose a significant percentage of budgetary allocations at all levels of government. Thus, the issue almost always on the front burner within a community is how to save lives, property, and taxpayers' expense in the criminal justice system. There appears to be little question that automation, standardization of procedures, and attention to criminal populations when time has been served, are vitally important. Hence, the role of AI, which, through unbiased algorithms, has the potential to accomplish optimal goals of lowering costs and, more importantly, lessens danger to communities especially when former criminal inmates have been freed.

The fear is that of algorithm bias, but practitioners in the criminal justice system will attest also to the bias of judges, probation officers, and other levels of the system that occur daily when representing defendants.

---

[22] *Criminal Law – Sentencing Guidelines – Wisconsin Supreme Court Requires Warning before Use of Algorithmic Risk Assessments Sentencing*, 120 HARV. L. REV. 1530 (2017), https://harvardlawreview.org/2017/03/state-v-loomis/, citing at 1534, Julia Angwin et al, *Machine Bias*, PROPUBLICA (May 23, 2016), https://www.propublica.org/article/machine-bias-risk-assessments-in-criminal-sentencing.

[23] Alexandra Chouldechova, *Fair prediction with disparate impact: A study of bias in recidivism prediction instruments*, CORNELL CONFERENCE PAPER (Feb. 2017), https://arxiv.org/abs/1703.00056.

Everyone is prone to bias, not necessarily intentional or overt, but judges may be more liberal or conservative, more or less offended by particular criminal behavior, prone to give maximum or minimum prison sentences, and other biases. Thus, when we speak of algorithm biases, they do not necessarily render a greater unfairness to the legal system and often, unlike individual behavior or bias, can be adjusted to craft a more just system of justice.

Other concerns of critics of algorithm-based analyses used in exercising discretion in criminal cases are that of control and surveillance; fallibility due to lack of data or data skewed against particular races or gender; individuals may be subject to penalties due to their being of a certain racial or national group; the exaggerated use of statistical data that overlook an individual's personal predilections; and other factors that may lend to unfair outcomes. Among the questions to be addressed are: the determination of the role algorithms are to play in judicial decision-making; how the algorithms can be adjusted to improve a more just outcome; additional variables, if any, to be considered in sentencing procedures; the need to properly train court personnel to properly use algorithm-based systems; the extent to which algorithms are to be used; the rights of attorneys to fully understand and be able to address weaknesses or inapplicability of particular algorithm-based outcomes; the ability to make adjustments so as to not fix in stone results of algorithm-based findings and recommendations; and other related issues.[24]

In a lengthy examination of the said risk assessment analyses, the author acknowledged the alleged benefits of risk-assessment tools, namely: (1) the tools are premised upon statistical analysis, e.g., as used in Sentencing Guidelines which is data-driven in contrast to competing philosophical and sociological approaches to sentencing; (2) actuarial scores based on mathematical models are preferential over "subjective" assessments; (3) they are consistent versus the opinions of human professionals who often differ in their evaluations; (4) judges who receive and act on these risk assessment evaluations promote uniformity of sentenc-

---

[24] Angele Christin, Alex Rosenblat, and Danah Boyd, *Courts and Predictive Algorithms*, DATA&SOCIETY (Oct. 27, 2015), https://datasociety.net/output/data-civil-rights-courts-and-predictive-algorithms/.

ing rather than the haphazard choices made by the judge one is either fortunate to have or not have before him or her as the sentencing jurist; (5) actuarial assessments are alleged to be more effective in forecasting recidivist behavior than clinical assessments; (6) savings of moneys because the assessments divide offenders into different risk categories, thus limiting use of incarceration to high risk offenders; and (7) they assist in preventing excessive punishment in particular cases.

In contrast to the cited positive attributes of risk assessment tools, the said scholarly review noted the limits of risk assessments. The first is that of statutory limits imposed by the Sentencing Reform Act of 1984 (SRA) which requires that a judge not consider a person's race, sex, and the like[25]; secondly, constitutional limitations of the equal protection clause of the 14th Amendment of the U.S. Constitution; and thirdly, that courts should not use group assessments in place of looking solely at the individual and his or her conduct in the determination of sentencing. The author suggests: applying the said limitations to assure bias based on gender, etc. is avoided; that each offender is dealt with individually rather than as a member of a group for recidivist determinations especially inasmuch as an individual has no control over one's race, creed, family background and so on; the need to understand how mental illness or substance abuse may diminish culpability; understanding how an individual may not be able to avoid criminal companionship due to their socio-economic status; lack of education; religious beliefs, or lack thereof; and prior criminal behavior that fails to take into account that a person may grow from his or her prior behavior. In summary, the author, as other naysayers, espouse that determinations should be objective, evidenced-based, rather than relying on risk assessment tools which concern large groupings of individuals instead of the particular individual before the court.[26]

Other suggestions whenever risk assessment tools are used by the court include: the need that such usage always rely on recent, local data; the continuous caparison of predictions versus outcomes; a focus on the risks

---

[25] *Sentencing Reform Act of 1984*, Pub. L. 98–473, 98 Stat. 1987 (1984). For a detailed commentary, see *Federal Sentencing: The Basics*, https://www.ussc.gov/sites/default/files/pdf/research-and-publications/research-projects-and-surveys/miscellaneous/201811_fed-sentencing-basics.pdf.

[26] Dawinder Sidhu, *Moneyball Sentencing*, 56 B.C.L.671 (215), http://lawdigitalcommons.bc.edu/bclr/vol56/iss2/6.

that matter most; risk assessments and frameworks must be public; and that there be community oversight of the tools and frameworks.[27] Data & Society,[28] after summarily reciting the arguments pro and con to risk assessment instruments, suggests that certain critical questions be asked when deciding how such assessments are to be used. Included in the suggestions are: the role of algorithms on judicial decision-making; how judges may override assessments; the types of variables that come into play in the variables; how data can be used to prevent biases; how to prevent unfixable "black boxes" of assessments; the training necessary of defense attorneys to enable challenges of risk assessments; whether third parties also be involved; and how to build trust around the algorithms?[29]

Some observers believe that the elimination of bias from AI-based machine-learning systems will be very difficult to accomplish. One author noted four challenges among others that will impede progress in its removal: (1) *unknown unknowns*—lack of realization of certain words that engender biases; (2) *imperfect processes*—deep-learning models are not designed to detect biases; (3) *lack of social context*—the values of one community may differ substantially from the values of another community even within one country (author compared values in Utah with that of Kentucky); and (4) *the definitions of fairness*—how to define in mathematical terms.[30]

Similarly, other observers intimated that the problems of bias arising from machine learning were evident from the outset, which were compounded by the advances in computer technology. Nevertheless, as more and more data sets arise, algorithms "learn" from the prior sets, which expose biases from prior data sets. Steps to be taken to avoid bias include choosing the right learning model for the problem, which often is a combination of models that address different issues; choosing a representative

---

[27] John Logan Koepke and David G. Robinson, *Danger Ahead: Risk Assessment and the Future of Bail Reform*, 93 WASH. L. Rev. (rev. Dec. 23, 2018), https://papers.ssrn.com/sol3/papers.cfm?abstract_id=3041622.

[28] Data & Society is a research institute located in New York City, which, it alleges, is focused on the social and cultural issues arising from data-centric and automated technologies, https://datasociety.net/about/.

[29] *Courts and Predictive Algorithms*, DATA&SOCIETY, https://datasociety.net/output/data-civil-rights-courts-and-predictive-algorithms/.

[30] Karen Hao, *supra*, note 486.

training data set that encompasses diversity of different groups; and monitoring the performance using real data.[31]

A scholar-researcher at Brookings reflected somewhat similar misgivings noting that biases are built into the data as, e.g., judges making sentencing decisions and evaluations about credit worthiness based on alleged-race-neutral algorithms are, in reality, discriminatory against African Americans; biases already in AI systems perpetuate themselves and become amplified as the algorithms evolve—exemplified as previously stated of mortgage-approval decisions based on the type of neighborhoods where the home-purchase loans are to take place—by denying such loans as by redlining[32] decisions by banks, the neighborhoods inevitably decline; teaching AI human rules—very difficult for AI-based systems to discern between legitimate businesses' decisions that treat men and women differently (e.g., auto insurance rates, age for life insurance rate premiums) and when they unlawfully discriminate; and the difficulty of evaluating cases of suspected AI bias which may or may not exist.[33]

IBM noted that racial, gender, or ideological biases in AI systems and algorithms due mainly to bad data will increase in the next several years for which it proposes a solution. It claims that its Watson AI Lab's efforts on shared prosperity draw on recent advances in AI and computational cognitive modeling such as contractual approaches to ethics. They describe principles that people use in decision-making and determine how human minds apply them. The goal is to build machines that apply certain human values and principles in decision-making. IBM scientists also devised an independent bias rating system that can determine the fairness of an AI system.[34]

In an article by two researchers at McKinsey& Co., they suggested that, before an organization considers using an algorithm to solve par-

---

[31] Vince Lynch, *Three ways to avoid bias in machine learning*, TECHCRUNCH (Nov. 6, 2018), https://techcrunch.com/2018/11/06/3-ways-to-avoid-bias-in-machine-learning/.

[32] *Redlining* refers to the practice of banks or other financial lending institutions denying loans to otherwise credit-worthy applicants with respect to the purchase of homes in certain areas that they have marked off-limits by a red line.

[33] John Villasenor, *Artificial intelligence and bias: Four key challenges*, BROOKINGS (Jan. 3, 2019), https://www.brookings.edu/blog/techtank/2019/01/03/artificial-intelligence-and-bias-four-key-challenges/.

[34] *AI and Bias*, IBM, https://www.research.ibm.com/5-in-5/ai-and-bias/.

ticular business problems, it should weigh three issues: (1) when the solution to a problem is needed; (2) the insights that the business entity possesses; and (3) which problems are worth solving. They then suggested the implementation of recommendations consisting of building blocks of a "mature model development and validation processes" for large organizations consisting of: (1) a template consisting of the business context with business impact, data, and cost-benefit trade-offs; (2) professional validation of machine-learning algorithms; and (3) a culture for continuous knowledge development. The authors acknowledge that AI is subject to biases, but they can be understood and managed.[35]

Another possible mode of managing bias is not to remove variables that are tied to biased outcomes, but rather allow one's model to measure it correctly and then subtract the effect of that bias on the outcome.[36] Other suggestions include the need for transparency and integrity of the data based upon a global standard that define the best practices[37]; *algorithmic affirmative action* which involves a transparency of inputs and outputs in place of transparency in the design of the algorithm and which is a set of proactive practices that recognizes the deficiencies in its output and seeks to correct those deficiencies[38]; and *algorithmic audits* that would adapt the social scientific audit methodology to the problem of algorithms for which the authors suggested five designs, to wit: (1) *code audit*—algorithmic transparency which enables researchers to detect algorithmic misbehavior, but likely not effective due to the complexity of computer codes which cannot be interpreted just by reading them, although the code audit may be effective in limited circumstances; (2) *noninvasive user audit*—noninvasive selection of information about users' normal interactions with a platform; (3) *scraping audit*—researcher's repeated queries to a platform and observe the results; (4) *sock puppet*

[35] Tobias Baer and Vishnu Kamalnath, *Controlling machine-learning algorithms and their biases*, MCKINSEY & COMPANY (Nov. 2017), https://www.mckinsey.com/business-functions/risk/our-insights/controlling-machine-learning-algorithms-and-their-biases.
[36] Stas Sajin, *Preventing Machine Learning Bias*, TOWARDSDATASCIENCE (Oct. 31, 2018), https://towardsdatascience.com/preventing-machine-learning-bias-d01adfe9f1fa.
[37] Jayshree Pandya, *Can Artificial Intelligence Be Biased?*, FORBES (Jan. 20, 2019), https://www.forbes.com/sites/cognitiveworld/2019/01/20/can-artificial-intelligence-be-biased/.
[38] Anupam Chandler, *The Racist Algorithm?*, 115 MICH. L. REV. 1023 (2017) at 1039–1045, http://michiganlawreview.org/wp-content/uploads/2017/04/115MichLRev1023_Chander.pdf.

*audit*—use of a classic audit study but where researchers use computer programs to impersonate hired human actors to represent different positions on a randomized manipulation as testers; and (5) *collaborative or crowdsourced audit*—using hired users as testers instead of computer programs.[39]

*Additional Proposed Legislation.* A proposed bill in the Senate entitled the *Algorithmic Accountability Act of 2019*,[40] directs the Federal Trade Commission to require entities that use, store, or share personal information to conduct automated decision system impact assessments and data protection impact assessments. Summary of provisions include: entities subject to the proposed Act are those which have over $50 million in average gross receipts in a 3-year period, and possess or control personal information on more than 1,000,000 consumers or consumer devices; *automated decision system impact* refers to a study evaluating an automated decision system and the automated decision system's development process, including the design and training data of the automated decision system, for impacts on accuracy, fairness, bias, discrimination, privacy, and security that includes, at a minimum a detailed description of the automated decision system, its design, its training, data, and its purpose; and an assessment of the relative benefits and costs of the automated decision system in light of its purpose. Thus, the Act's essential purpose is to address the issue of bias in algorithms apparently in response to Amazon's internal hiring tool that allegedly discriminated against women candidates; facial recognition programs that had difficulty with respect to darker colored persons; and Facebook's ad recommendation algorithm that appeared to be discriminatory in employment and housing recom-

---

[39] Christian Sandvig, Kevin Hamilton, Karrie Karahalios, and Cedric Langbort, Auditing Algorithms: Research Methods for Detecting Discrimination on Internet Platforms, U. of MICH. CONFERENCE PAPER (May 22, 2014), http://www-personal.umich.edu/~csandvig/research/Auditing%20Algorithms%20%2D%2D%20Sandvig%20%2D%2D%20ICA%202014%20Data%20and%20Discrimination%20Preconference.pdf.

[40] S. (unassigned), 116th Cong. (2019), Algorithmic Accountability Act of 2019, https://www.wyden.senate.gov/imo/media/doc/Algorithmic%20Accountability%20Act%20of%202019%20Bill%20Text.pdf?utm_campaign=the_algorithm.unpaid.engagement&utm_source=hs_email&utm_medium=email&utm_content=71709273&_hsenc=p2ANqtz-9E4AfpVeN6rZlMn-sZ6KfITloTxQWGYinXF-cCrW15Zz5OF12kVVm78ky5hq9uufsx_MJHyjG6bXM4YgOmzukvAJ4q4w&_hsmi=71709273.

mendations.[41] It is not the first measure that addresses bias as evidenced by an analogous passage of legislation by the New York City Council, which assigned a task force to recommend ways of overseeing governmental use of algorithms to ascertain whether and how error and transparency in the design exists there and how to ensure accuracy and fairness.[42]

# AI and Jobs

A not untypical news headline is the news that PepsiCo, which saw revenues rise to $64.6 billion and a net profit which increased from $4.9 billion to $12.6 billion for 2018, nevertheless, is spending $2.5 billion to restructure the company by "relentlessly automating" and laying off a sizeable percentage of its 263,000 workforce.[43] Together with concerns about ethics and privacy, the average individual is fearful of loss of his or her occupation to a robot or other AI-based technology. The fear is not without foundation. McKinsey & Company, a global management consulting firm, in a lengthy study,[44] estimated that 50 percent of current work activities can be automated with today's technologies and 60 percent of current occupations already have 30 percent activities that are technically automatable. The percentage of workers affected globally by the year 2030 is between the slowest scenario of near 0 percent (10 million workers) if little automation is adapted, to a medium point of 15 percent (400 million workers) to as much as 30 percent (800 million

---

[41] *The Algorithm*, MIT TECH REVIEW (April 12, 2019), newsletters@technologyreview.com.

[42] *City Council Passes First Bill in Nation to Address Transparency, Bias in Government Use in Algorithms*, NYCLU (Dec. 11, 2017), https://www.nyclu.org/en/press-releases/city-council-passes-first-bill-nation-address-transparency-bias-government-use.

[43] Brian Merchant, *PepsiCo Is 'Relentlessly Automating' Its Workforce and It's Even More Dystopian Than It Sounds*, GIZMODO (Feb. 27, 2019), https://gizmodo.com/pepsico-is-relentless-automating-its-workforce-and-it-1832804035.

[44] *Jobs Lost, Jobs Gained: Workforce Transitions in a Time of Automation*, MCKINSEY GLOBAL INSTITUTE (Dec. 2017), https://www.mckinsey.com/~/media/McKinsey/Featured%20Insights/Future%20of%20Organizations/What%20the%20future%20of%20work%20will%20mean%20for%20jobs%20skills%20and%20wages/MGI-Jobs-Lost-Jobs-Gained-Report-December-6-2017.ashx.

workers). Approximately, 8–9 percent of the global workforce of 2.66 billion people will be in new occupations.[45]

Whereas low level occupations bore the major brunt of job losses due to past new technologies, it is projected by a number of observers, including the famed British scientist, Stephen Hawking, that job losses will seriously impact middle class jobs.[46] The chief economist of the Bank of England, Andy Haldane, warned that AI could cause unemployment to "large swathes" of people and will be more disruptive than the First Industrial Revolution. A director of AI-security provider, Vectra, Matt Walmsley, however, indicated that the future will be humans and machines not machines in place of humans.[47] Other observers argue that AI and automation will eliminate numerous tedious jobs that workers dislike but are compelled to pursue to support their families. On the flip side is the greatly increased ability to engage in occupations that excite or at least not be dreadful coupled with greatly increased medical advances arising from the technologies. The problem of prediction in part is due to AI's application to almost every industry, not to just one segment of the economy, as well as the projected speed of transition rather than a slower past elimination of positions.[48]

The impact of technology and jobs with accompanying job losses and major transitions has a long history with innumerable winners and losers, but overall led to a beneficial uptick in a nation's economy and significant benefits to its inhabitants. In the early 1700s, almost all persons in the then 13 English colonies, later U.S. states, were farmers which figure has diminished today to some 2–3 percent of the workforce nationwide; automobiles replaced horses which affected many jobs by the transition;

---

[45] *Jobs lost, jobs gained: What the future of work will mean for jobs, skills, and wages*, MCKINSEY GLOBAL INSTITUTE (Nov. 2017), https://www.mckinsey.com/featured-insights/future-of-work/jobs-lost-jobs-gained-what-the-future-of-work-will-mean-for-jobs-skills-and-wages.

[46] Rob Price, *Stephen Hawking: Automation and AI is going to decimate middle class jobs*, BUSINESS INSIDER (Dec. 2, 2016), https://www.businessinsider.com/stephen-hawking-ai-automation-middle-class-jobs-most-dangerous-moment-humanity-2016-12.

[47] Rene Millman, *Bank of England warns of large-scale job losses from AI*, INTERNET OF BUSINESS (Aug. 20, 2018), https://internetofbusiness.com/bank-of-england-joins-chorus-of-disapproval-about-ai-job-losses/.

[48] Calum McClelland, *The Impact of Artificial Intelligence – Widespread Job Losses*, IOT FOR ALL (Aug. 17, 2018), https://www.iotforall.com/impact-of-artificial-intelligence-job-losses/.

and the cotton gin processed cotton by separating cotton fibers from the seeds thus ending manual separation and thereby make cloth more available and cheaper.[49] The railroad industry has seen a decline from 3 percent of the U.S. workforce (1.35 million workers) to 0.1 percent (187,000 workers), while the quanta of freight moved nationally has tripled from 655 billion revenue ton-miles to 1.85 trillion ton-miles by 2014.[50] Other historical transitions date back to ancient China and ancient Egypt and continuing on through the many centuries making its greatest impact in the Industrial Revolution, which took place between the years of 1760 through the middle of the nineteenth century, owing to new created machines, chemicals manufacturing, and water power.[51]

It will be almost impossible to predict job elimination even five years hence with the exponential growth of AI progression. One commentator quoting McKinsey and others noted that 18.5 million jobs were created by the personal computer which also led to some job losses, but the overall effect heretofore has been almost universally positive. Moreover, effects will vary widely from country to country, but developed countries may suffer most due to high wages paid for efforts which will be replaced by AI machines.[52] Another commentator, chief scientist and CTO at KoreConX, suggested that, although there will be an overall significant loss of jobs, prices of commodities would, nevertheless, diminish and the number of hours of employment may drop substantially to accommodate other persons who will work the additional hours.[53]

[49] Martin Kelly, *Historical Significance of the Cotton Gin*, THOUGHTCO (March 5, 2018), https://www.thoughtco.com/the-cotton-gin-in-american-history-104722.
[50] Glenn Luk, *Technology Has Already Taken Over 90% of the Jobs Humans Used to Do.*, FORBES (Jan. 18, 2018), https://www.forbes.com/sites/quora/2018/01/18/technology-has-already-taken-over-90-of-the-jobs-humans-used-to-do/#529511c21bdd.
[51] *Industrial Revolution*, WIKIPEDIA, https://en.wikipedia.org/wiki/Industrial_Revolution. A lengthy history may be found in *Technological unemployment*, WIKIPEDIA, https://en.wikipedia.org/wiki/Technological_unemployment.
[52] James Vincent, *Automation threatens 800 million jobs, but technology could still save us, says report*, THE VERGE (Nov. 30, 2017), https://www.theverge.com/2017/11/30/16719092/automation-robots-jobs-global-800-million-forecast.
[53] Kiran Garimella, *Job Loss From AI? There's More to Fear!*, FORBES (Aug. 7, 2018), https://www.forbes.com/sites/cognitiveworld/2018/08/07/job-loss-from-ai-theres-more-to-fear/#17781bbb23eb.

The debate among scholars about the future of jobs has centered on the conflicting views about the oft-cited work of the University of Oxford Professors Carl Benedikt Frey and Michael A. Osborne.[54] They studied the probability of computerization for 702 detailed occupations in order to project expected impacts of future computerization on the U.S. labor market. After reciting a history of technology and its effect on the labor market, they noted that robots, with improved sensors, are able to produce goods that possess a higher quality and are more reliable than human labor. Coupled with declining costs in robotics and expanding technological capabilities, they estimated that 47 percent of the total U.S. employment is at high risk for replacement by automation. This figure is somewhat comparable to that of the McKinsey study. They characterized occupations from low to medium to high risk categories for replacement. Jobs that mainly feature manual dexterity are at high risk while positions which require novel ideas and artifacts are at low risk. Thus, positions which feature interpretations of emotions, facial expressions, and role playing are at low risk. Also at low risk are engineering and science occupations and legal work due to the requirement of creative intelligence. All of the jobs investigated and their probability of replacement by automation are stated in the appendix to the study.[55]

The jobs listed by the Frey and Osborne study that were most likely to be replaced by automation with a 99 percent chance thereof were data entry keyers; new accounts clerks; photographic process workers and processing machine operators; tax preparers; cargo and freight agents; watch repairers; insurance underwriters; mathematical technicians; hand sewers; title examiners, abstractors, and searchers; and telemarketers. The least likely (0.4 percent chance) to be replaced, according to the study, are recreational therapists, first line supervisors of mechanics, installers, and repairers; emergency management directors; mental health and substance abuse social workers; audiologists; occupational therapists; orthodontists and prosthetics; healthcare social workers; occupational therapists; first-line supervisors of firefighting and prevention workers; oral and maxil-

---

[54] Carl Benedikt Frey and Michael A. Osborne, *The Future of Employment: How Susceptible Are Jobs To Computerization?*, https://www.oxfordmartin.ox.ac.uk/downloads/academic/The_Future_of_Employment.pdf.

[55] *Id.* at 36–42, 57–72.

lofacial surgeons; lodging managers; dieticians and nutritionists; choreographers; sales engineers; instructional coordinators; physicians and surgeons; psychologists; elementary school teachers, except special education; general dentists; and first-line supervisors of police and detectives.[56]

The Frey and Osborne study received critical attention both supportively and critically. In an OECD study concerning jobs and automation in the 21-member states, the authors of the study, using a "task-based approach" (robots compete against human labor in the production of different tasks), arrived at a far more optimistic assessment. They concluded that only 9 percent of workers' tasks within occupations will be affected by automation, mainly those held by low qualified workers. The said approach is grounded on how automation affects the tasks which workers perform for their jobs and how easily these tasks can be automated. They do agree that automation of jobs is lower in those positions which require high educational requirements and vice versa for low education-based jobs. The fact that it is possible for automation to replace workers does not mean the substitution will actually take place. They further noted that experts tend to overestimate the potentialities of automation especially with respect to jobs that require flexibility, judgment, and common sense. There is also a societal preference for human contact rather than machines. With automation creating greater efficiencies and productivity, there will be a greater demand for such products and services which will lead to greater employment opportunities. The authors were much more concerned with rising inequality and the critical need to reeducate and retrain affected workers.[57]

In another well-cited study which used the task-based approach, the authors examined the effects of exposure to robots on employment in different sectors of the economy. The greatest heavily-robotized effects were centered on the manufacturing sector especially automobile manufacturing, electronics, metal products, chemicals, pharmaceuticals, plas-

---

[56] Frey, *supra*, note 537 at 57–72.

[57] Melanie Arntz, Terry Gregory, and Ulrich Zierahn, *The Risk of Automation for Jobs in OECD Countries: A Comparative Analysis*, OECD SOCIAL, EMPLOYMENT AND MIGRATION WORKING PAPERS, No. 189, OECD Publishing, Paris, https://doi.org/10.1787/5jlz9h56dvq7-en.

tic, food, glass, and ceramics and smaller effects on construction, business services, wholesale services, and retail. Three sectors that were substantially less affected were finance, the public sector, and nonrobotized manufacturing such as recycling, basic metals, textiles, paper, furniture, and transportation equipment excluding automobiles.[58] A more pessimistic note by yet another scholar suggested that the current technological shift challenges a basic assumption that machines are tools that increase the productivity of workers; rather, machines themselves are turning into workers blurring the line between labor and capital which has no precedent.[59]

In a Rand Corporation study, the authors suggested that there are two factors which determine an occupation's susceptibility to replacement by automation. They are: (1) the *amount of chaos* that a worker has to contend with, i.e., the number of tasks associated with the particular occupation which a worker has to learn, manage, and need to switch among the varying scenarios (e.g., surgeons, firefighters, politicians); and (2) the *typical response times* required for the worker to perform the tasks effectively within the occupation. The greater the degree of chaos and the shorter response time required to perform the tasks, the less likely that an AI-based system could perform and replace the human worker. Conversely, jobs requiring long response times and low levels of chaos are much more susceptible to automation. Suggested responses by the authors to the effects of automation on the labor market include: the government's role in detecting and addressing vulnerability of AI; development of fail-safe procedures and regulations; possible safety net provisions; and a sound immigration policy inasmuch as many AI-experts are foreign-born but who are educated within the U.S.[60]

A Pew Research study was conducted in 2014 in which 1896 expert participants were asked for their opinions regarding the effect of AI and

---

[58] Daron Acemoglu and Pascual Restrepo, *Robots and Jobs: Evidence From U.S. Labor Markets*, MIT Working Paper 17-04 (March 17, 2014) at 32–33, https://papers.ssrn.com/sol3/papers.cfm?abstract_id=2941263.

[59] Martin Ford, RISE OF THE ROBOTS: TECHNOLOGY AND THE THREAT OF A JOBLESS FUTURE, BASIC BOOKS (2015).

[60] Osonde A. Osoba and William Welser IV, *The Risks of Artificial Intelligence to Security and the Future of Work*, RAND Corporation (2017), https://www.rand.org/pubs/perspectives/PE237.html.

robotics on daily life and on job replacement by the year 2025. The results were almost evenly split with 48 percent who believed that robots and digital agents will have significant replacement effects on blue and white collar workers while 52 percent stated that they envisioned a future in which there will not be a net job loss by the technological innovations. All agree there will be major changes in the types of jobs that will be created and that the current social structures and education are not adequately preparing workers for the transitions that will take place.[61] An additional aspect is the issue of bias as it pertains to job hiring whereby it is estimated that AI screening of job applicants without human intervention results in removal of 70 percent from consideration. While the benefits of AI replacement of human resources management are touted for cost-reduction by the said automatic declination of numerous job applicants whose profiles are not in accord with the key words or concepts in the program, nevertheless, it is likely that many applicants are unfairly removed from consideration due to origin, ethnicity, gender, and religious affiliation. The use of programs may run afoul of state and federal antidiscrimination and privacy laws.[62]

In a Forbes magazine article, the writer stated that among the problems facing job seekers are their lack of digital skills, the need to know how and when to use algorithms, lack of coordination across functions, and how to access data. He added that AI will come in waves, namely, the current wave where AI analyzes structured data and performs simple tasks; then onto the second wave of repeatable tasks, automatic exchange of information and, finally, a major impact on jobs in 1–2 decades which may require learning new skills and reorganization of workforces.[63] Another possible scenario is that, as the need for jobs diminishes coupled with loss of income, the prices for necessary goods will also decline leading thereafter to a gradual lessening of work hours and greater leisure

---

[61] Aaron Smith and Janna Anderson, *AI, Robotics, and the Future of Jobs*, PEW RESEARCH CENTER (Aug. 6, 2014), https://www.pewinternet.org/2014/08/06/future-of-jobs/.

[62] Austin James Marsh, Employment Practices and Future Technologies – Taking the Human Out of Human Resources, LEXOLOGY (March 29, 2019), https://www.lexology.com/library/detail.aspx?g=993edd9f-3142-4e4f-916b-a944b02d4b5e.

[63] Matthew Lieberman, *Why the Real AI Jobs Issue Isn't Unemployment*, FORBES (Feb. 14, 2018), https://www.forbes.com/sites/forbestechcouncil/2018/02/14/why-the-real-ai-jobs-issue-isnt-unemployment/.

time to spend with one's loved ones. Society would transit to where we live to work to one where we work less and enjoy more albeit with much less income.[64]

An engineering publication rendered its estimation of job replacement by 2030 as follows: manufacturing (46%); wholesale and retail trade (44%); administrative and support services (37%); transportation and storage (56%); accommodation and food services (26%); financial and insurance (32%); construction (24%); real estate (28%); public administration and defense (33%); health and social work (17%); agriculture, forestry, and fishing (19%); education (9%); and arts and entertainment (22%). Engineering jobs projected to be safe are computer hardware engineers; mechanical engineers, and architects.[65]

The countries highly likely to be affected by AI machines are the most populous countries of China and India. With their billion plus populations the transition from a labor-intensive economy to a technologically-based one raises possible dire consequences due to the inherent need to find occupations and income for the masses to avoid starvation and political and economic disruptions. A possible scenario that offers hope is the so-called China "Cobot" multi- million-dollar investment by the Swiss-Swedish concern ABB, which is building a "factory of the future" in Shanghai. The factory is one in which robots will be building robots but which will work with human persons rather than causing their replacement. A Denmark company, Universal Robots, is the world's largest cobot producer which is expected to grow within China from a market value of $54 million in 2017 to $190 million by 2020. The global cobot market is expected to reach $9 billion by 2025 with China as the main source. Cobot is designed to assist not replace workers thus possibly solving the conundrum of worker replacement by machines.[66] Solutions,

[64] Kiran Garimella, *Job Loss from AI? There's More to Fear!*, FORBES (Aug. 1, 2018), https://www.forbes.com/sites/cognitiveworld/2018/08/07/job-loss-from-ai-theres-more-to-fear/#49ef7f7723eb.

[65] John Loeffler, *The Rise of AI and Employment: How Jobs Will Change to Adapt*, SQUARE TERMINAL (Nov. 4, 2018), https://interestingengineering.com/the-rise-of-ai-and-employment-how-jobs-will-change-to-adapt. The articles cited statistics of PWC UK Economic Outlook Report, http://pwc.to/1iTbYJZ.

[66] Ben Halder, *How China's 'Cobot' Revolution Could Transform Automation*, OZY (March 24, 2019), https://www.ozy.com/fast-forward/how-chinas-cobot-revolution-could-transform-automation/93044.

in additional to a cobot-type scenario, will be for a partnership of government and industry such as increased assistance for retraining workers, expansion of the income tax credit, college-business partnerships, and other government initiatives.[67]

The old saw about economists is that they are excellent in explaining past economic behavior but are inept in predictions about the future.[68] Given the ostensible competencies of the commentators and their respective organizations, we must leave it to future years to observe the outcome which truly is not predictable because no one can gage the next explosive creative endeavors that are likely taking place in someone's garage just as transpired by Steve Jobs and Steve Wozniak. Although AI has expanded exponentially, yet, unemployment is almost at record lows albeit many in low paying jobs. It is truly unknown and a fools' venture to predict whether AI will create few, the same, or much greater new forms of employment while, at the same time, raising human standard of living as it has in past decades.[69]

The Millennium Project has undertaken the questionable attempt to make future work and other AI-based predictions for the year 2050.[70] The study presented several possible scenarios. In one, the author projected a "mixed bag of employed and self-employed." Employment will continue in government and in certain segments of the private sector including synthetic biology, AI support systems, urban management, and fields that merge humans and AI, such as virtual reality educational tourism. Repetitive work will be almost entirely taken over by robots. STEM education will be fruitful in the maintenance of some jobs but there will

---

[67] Rich Barlow, *Economist predicts job loss to machines, but see long-term hope*, PHYS ORG (March 19, 2018), https://phys.org/news/2018-03-economist-job-loss-machines-long-term.html.

[68] See, e.g., Tamsin McMahon, *Why economists can't predict the future*, MACLEAN'S (Feb. 11, 2014), https://www.macleans.ca/economy/economicanalysis/why-economists-cant-predict-the-future/. Some argue economists cannot explain the past as well as the future, Ben Chu, *Economists do not predict the future and can't explain the past*, INDEPENDENT (Aug. 17, 2014), https://www.independent.co.uk/news/business/comment/economists-do-not-predict-the-future-and-cant-explain-the-past-9673649.html.

[69] See contrasting arguments by Carl Benedikt Frey and Robert D. Atkinson, *Will AI Destroy More Jobs Than It Creates Over the Next Decade?* THE WALL STREET JOURNAL (April 2, 2019) at R4.

[70] *Future Work/Technology 2050 Global Scenarios*, THE MILLENNIUM PROJECT (July 23, 2018), http://www.millennium-project.org/future-work-technology-2050-global-scenarios/.

be widespread broad discrepancies of unemployment percentages from regions to regions. Transportation will almost be entirely autonomous.

A second scenario envisioned political and economic turmoil brought about by the concentration of wealth and unemployment, including in the tech field. AI intelligence will have attained the superintelligence, which has made humans uneasy but also desirous of control over the new type of intelligent species. A third scenario is one in which humanity attains much greater freedom over its lives, providing for basic income guarantees, with AI intelligence having taken over much of the labor formerly required of humans. The Project is spelled out in great detail and does appear to be reasonable in outlook. Again, it cannot be repeated too strongly, we have no idea of what the world will look like in 30 years hence, given the explosive gains taking place almost daily in the technology.

The bottom line appears to be that no one really knows with near total certainty whether job losses, whatever the percentage and types may be, will be fully or far less replaced by newly created industries. All one needs to reflect is to return to the year 1980 and try to project accurately at that time what the world will look like politically, socially, economically, and, in particular, the job market for the year 2019. If one assumes that super-intelligence will evolve sooner rather than much later decades-wise, the event will be a threat unlike any technology of the past that could serve as a precedent. Clearly, jobs will require new skills and education. Human persons will have to respond to threats of AI robotic-like persons dominating their lives which will be the role of governments and major interest groups to address. Global society will have to coexist with the existential threat and make decisions which of the crossroads to take: one dominated by a few human persons using AI as a means of social control, or a more democratic society that takes full advantage of the many benefits that may accrue that can lead humanity beyond its planet to infinite creations and possibilities.[71]

---

[71] See also the discussion by Calum McClelland, *The Impact of Intelligence – Widespread Job Losses*, IOT FOR ALL (Aug. 17, 2018), https://www.iotforall.com/impact-of-artificial-intelligence-job-losses/.

## "Fake News" and the Threat to Democratic Values

*Fake news* refers to news that is verifiably false that is intentionally placed in various forms of written communication using recognized news and social media outlets particularly that of newspapers and Facebook. The events leading up to the presidential election of President Donald J. Trump in 2016, although they continue to be nuanced, explored, and revealed, as well as alleged Russian interference in the elections of major candidates running for office in other countries, raise the specter of whether candidates for office can be elected or defeated according to the wishes of foreign state actors. The use of AI-based technology has enabled foreign states, particularly Russia, to attempt to place in leadership positions those candidates that would have a more temperate view respecting relations with the nation. The claim is that Russian agents, acting on behest of President Vladimir Putin, had determined that the current president would be more favorably disposed to the two nations' bilateral relationship than the candidate, Hillary Clinton.

The alleged means used to accomplish the interference were by the Internet Research Agency "troll farm" in Saint Petersburg, Russia, which created numerous social media accounts funneled through conduits such as Facebook, Twitter, Google, and WikiLeaks, whereby the messages impersonated radical groups, promoted rallies, and other usages for the four-year period between 2013–2017. It should be noted that the current president was not officially a candidate for public office when the alleged interference began. A second alleged means with the Russian military service, GRU, hacked thousands of private emails between the Democratic National Committee and top Clinton aides, which were then revealed through WikiLeaks and were a source of substantial embarrassment to the parties affected.[72]

Interference by foreign sources into elections of another country's candidates is highly offensive and universally disapproved. For example, studies by political scientists of fake news in the 2016 U.S. presidential

---

[72] *Russian interference in the 2016 United States elections*, WIKIPEDIA, https://en.wikipedia.org/wiki/Russian_interference_in_the_2016_United_States_elections.

election discovered that there were 115 pro-Trump fake stories shared on Facebook 30 million times including his alleged endorsement by the Pope while there were 41 pro-Clinton fake stories shared some 7.6 million times. Most persons disapprove of the use of fake news even if the news favored their candidate.[73] A Twitter analysis also illustrated a relatively lopsided favorable result for Trump which was retweeted by humans thereby illustrating the meaningful political discussion over this social media site.[74] Other scholars note how Twitter and Facebook are primary examples of social media and that mainly young people develop their political sensibilities from such sites. The problem to be addressed is the use of *cyber troops* defined as governments, military or political parties, which spend significant resources to generate content in order to manipulate domestic and/or foreign audiences' public opinion at their behest. Their role in generating public opinion is likely to increase as a global phenomenon.[75]

*Digital Gerrymandering.* Digital gerrymandering is defined by one commentator as "the selective presentation of information by an intermediary to meet its agenda rather than to serve its users," is a betrayal to the user and nonuser alike of the media service. The solution, however, such as the creation of a government agency to oversee fake news, would call into question First Amendment freedoms and may lead to adulterations from new sources.[76] Others assert the use of AI bots (AI program to conduct a conversation orally or textually) to engineer an election is a decided

[73] Michael Tomz and Jessica L.P. Weeks, *Public Opinion and Foreign Electoral Intervention*, (Paper, Am. Pol. Sci. Assc. Aug. 2018), https://web.stanford.edu/~tomz/working/TomzWeeks-ElectoralIntervention-2018-08-24.pdf; and Hunt Allcott and Matthew Gentzkow, *Social Media and Fake News in the 2016 Election*, NAT. BUR. OF ECO RESEARCH WORKING PAPER, No. 23089 (rev. April 2017), http://www.nber.org/papers/w23089.

[74] Samuel C. Woolley and Douglas Guilbeault, "*Computational Propaganda in the United States of America: Manufacturing Consensus Online*"; and Samuel Woolley and Philip N. Howard, Eds. WORKING PAPER 2017.5. Oxford, UK: Project on Computational Propaganda, http://comprop.oii.ox.ac.uk/.

[75] Samantha Bradshaw and Philip N. Howard, *Troops, Trolls and Troublemakers: A Global Inventory of Organized Social Media Manipulation*, WORKING PAPER 2017.12. Oxford, UK: Project on Computational Propaganda.

[76] Jonathan Zittrain, *Engineering An Election*, 127 HARV. L.R. FORUM 335 (June, 2014), http://harvardlawreview.org/wp-content/uploads/2014/06/vol127_Symposium_Zittrain.pdf.

threat to democracy if used to mislead, but may also provide the means to support democracy.[77]

Apparently, the U.S. elections were not the only ones that were interfered with by Russian operatives. It was alleged that there was Russian political meddling in 27 European and North American countries since 2004 consisting of cyberattacks, disinformation campaigns, and other means that included the U.S., Canada, and France.[78] It was also suggested that China, Iran, North Korea, as well as Russia, have also initiated some attempts at propagandistic interference with U.S. elections and/or organizations.[79] The indictment and arrest by the U.S. by the special prosecutor, Robert Mueller, of Elena Alekseevna Khusyaynova, a Russian woman, who allegedly defrauded the U.S. in its presidential election of 2016 for, among other charges, financing of the social media connected with the Russian Internet Research Agency, as well as the indictments of 27 other Russians connected with election interference, have become a cause célèbre. She and others were accused of the spread of information to inflame issues, such as gun and LGBT rights, adherence to the national anthem, and other inflammatory issues through social media are illustrative of the Russian efforts.[80] Whether or not the said Russian efforts were enough to change the results of the presidential election is questionable. With respect to the U.S. mid-term elections of 2018, there appears to have been little or no Russian interference.[81]

Interference in foreign elections is not a relatively new occurrence, but has precedents tracing back to past decades. For example, there is sub-

[77]Vyacheslav Polonski, *Artificial Intelligence Has the Power to Destroy or Save Democracy*, blog, COUNCIL OF FOREIGN RELATIONS (Aug. 7, 2017), https://www.cfr.org/blog/artificial-intelligence-has-power-destroy-or-save-democracy.

[78]*Alleged Russian political meddling documented in 27 countries since 2004*, USATODAY (Sept.7,2017),https://www.usatoday.com/story/news/world/2017/09/07/alleged-russian-political-meddling-documented-27-countries-since-2004/619056001/.

[79]Olivia Beavers and Jacqueline Thomsen, *Russia election meddling fears expand to other countries*, THE HILL (Aug. 25, 2017), https://thehill.com/policy/cybersecurity/403559-russia-election-meddling-fears-expand-to-other-countries.

[80]*Read the criminal complaint against Russian charged with election interference*, CNN (Oct. 19, 2018), https://www.cnn.com/2018/10/19/politics/criminal-complaint-elena-alekseevna-khusyaynova-russia/index.html.

[81]*Department of Justice 2018 Election Security Fact Sheet*, DEPT. OF JUSTICE (Nov. 3, 2018), https://www.justice.gov/opa/pr/department-justice-2018-election-security-fact-sheet.

stantial evidence that the U.S. was directly involved in the election of candidates or military takeovers in Chile, Honduras, Guatemala, and other countries in Latin America. The interference was previously based on the Monroe Doctrine, named after President James Monroe, who stated the position of the U.S. that any foreign interference in any country in the America would be treated as a hostile act against the U.S.[82] He iterated the doctrine in, what is now called, the State of the Union address to Congress that "The American continents … are henceforth not to be considered as subjects for future colonization by any European powers."[83] Currently, the U.S. President and his former national security adviser, John Bolton, have called for regime change in Venezuela with expressed or implied threat of possible military action in support of an alternate candidate for office who alleged that he is the true elected president of the country.[84] The Russian alleged interference is noteworthy because of the level of sophistication and the clandestine, AI-based means used to accomplish the act.

There are other privacy and ethical issues that almost daily raise concern, which is beyond the scope of this text. In the following chapter, we will explore another area of law that has been profoundly affected by AI, namely, that of intellectual property rights.

---

[82] *Monroe Doctrine*, WIKIPEDIA, https://en.wikipedia.org/wiki/Monroe_Doctrine.

[83] Daryl Worthington, *The USA and Latin America: A History of Meddling*, NEW HISTORIAN (April 12, 2015), https://www.newhistorian.com/the-usa-and-latin-america-a-history-of-meddling/3476/.

[84] Caitlin Oprysko, *John Bolton threatens to tighten the screws on Venezuela*, POLITICO (March 6, 2019), https://www.politico.com/story/2019/03/06/foreign-bank-sanctions-nicolas-maduro-1207019.

# 7

# Intellectual Property Rights and AI

Among the panoply of issues wrought by AI concerns is the protection of intellectual property rights (IPRs). The current laws and practices that offer protection appear to be wanting given wholly unparalleled questions that have arisen due to the new technologies. Issues which have no precedent that have arisen include: Who owns a patent if a machine creates another machine? Who has the copyright of photographs if a monkey takes a self-fi without intervention of the human person? We begin with a general discussion of IPRs and then relate the discussion to the latest technologies.

## Basics of Intellectual Property Protection in the U.S.

### Patent

A *patent* is a limited duration property right relating to an invention, granted by the United States Patent and Trademark Office (USPTO) in exchange for public disclosure of the invention. Patentable materials

© The Author(s) 2020
R. Girasa, *Artificial Intelligence as a Disruptive Technology*,
https://doi.org/10.1007/978-3-030-35975-1_7

include machines, manufactured articles, industrial processes, and chemical compositions. The duration of patent protection depends on the type of patent granted.

- *Design Patents*—15 years from issuance for applications filed on or after May 13, 2015 (14 years from issuance if filed before May 13, 2015);
- *Utility Patents and Plant Patents*—20 years from the date on which the application for the patent was filed in the United States or, in special cases, from the date an earlier related application was filed.[1]

Remedies for wrongful use include the following: injunction (order to cease violation); damages adequate to compensate for the infringement including lost profits, but in no event less than a reasonable royalty for the use of the invention by the infringer, together with interest and costs as determined by the court; for willful violations, the court may increase the damages up to three times the amount found or assessed by either the jury or the court and may award, in exceptional cases, reasonable attorney fees to the prevailing party.

## Trademark

A *trademark* is a word, phrase, symbol, and/or design that identifies and distinguishes the source of the goods of one party from those of others. A *service mark* is a word, phrase, symbol, and/or design that identifies and distinguishes the source of a service rather than goods. Some examples include: brand names, slogans, and logos. The term *trademark* is often used in a general sense to refer to both trademarks and service marks. Unlike patents and copyrights, trademarks do not expire after a set term of years. They can last forever provided the holder files specific documents with the U.S. Patent and Trademark Office (USPTO); pays the required fees, and engages in its actual "use," i.e., so long as the holder

[1] *Trademark, Patent, or Copyright?* U.S. Patent and Trademark Office, https://www.uspto.gov/trademarks-getting-started/trademark-basics/trademark-patent-or-copyright.

continues to use the mark in commerce to indicate the source of the goods and services.[2]

Dependent on the nature of the violation, remedies include: an injunction barring violation; destruction of the infringing articles; seizure of the goods and counterfeit marks; triple damages of the value of the damages sustained or profit made; reasonable attorneys' fees; and statutory damages at the election of the plaintiff to recover instead of actual damages and profits, in the amount of not less than $1000 or more than $200,000 per counterfeit mark per type of goods or services sold, offered for sale, or distributed, as the court considers just. If the court finds that the use of the counterfeit mark was willful, statutory damages award is up to $2,000,000 per counterfeit mark per type of goods or services sold, offered for sale, or distributed, as the court considers just.

## Copyright

A *copyright* is a form of protection provided by the laws of the United States for "original works of authorship," fixed in a tangible medium including literary, dramatic, musical, architectural, cartographic, choreographic, pantomimic, pictorial, graphic, sculptural, and audiovisual creations. It is that body of exclusive rights granted by law to copyright owners for protection of their work. Copyright protection does not extend to any idea, procedure, process, system, title, principle, or discovery. Similarly, names, titles, short phrases, slogans, familiar symbols, mere variations of typographic ornamentation, lettering, coloring, and listings of contents or ingredients are not subject to copyright. Generally, the duration of a copyright is the life of the author plus 70 years. For an anonymous work, a pseudonymous work, or a work made for hire, the copyright endures for a term of 95 years from the year of its first publication or a term of 120 years from the year of its creation, whichever expires first. For works prior to 1978, other rules may apply.[3]

---

[2] *Copyright Definitions*, U.S. Copyright Office, https://www.copyright.gov/help/faq/definitions.html.

[3] *How Long does Copyright Last?*, U.S. Copyright Office, https://www.copyright.gov/help/faq/faq-duration.html.

The exclusive rights of the copyright owner given to the copyright holder under U.S. law are: (1) to reproduce the work; (2) to prepare derivative works; (3) to distribute copies or phonorecords (material object that embodies sound—e.g., cassettes, CDs) of the work to the public by sale, rental, lease, or lending; (4) in the case of literary, musical, dramatic, and choreographic works, and motion pictures and other audiovisual works, to perform the work publicly; (5) In the case of literary, musical, dramatic, and choreographic works, pantomimes, and pictorial, graphic, or sculptural works, including the individual images of a motion picture or other audiovisual work, to display the copyrighted work publicly; (6) in the case of sound recordings, to perform the copyrighted work publicly by means of a digital audio transmission.[4] Typographic ornamentation, lettering, coloring, and listings of contents or ingredients are not subject to copyright.

Remedies available to a party whose copyright protections have been violated include: injunctions; impounding, destruction, or other reasonable disposition of all copies, plates, records, and the like; actual damages suffered by the copyright owner due to the infringement, and any profits of the infringer attributable to the infringement; statutory damages at the copyright owner's election to recover in lieu of actual damages and profits, in the amount of not less than $750 or more than $30,000 as the court deems just; and for willful infringement, a court may, in its discretion, increase the statutory damages award to a sum of not more than $150,000 plus costs and attorney's fees.

## Trade Secret

A *trade secret* consists of information and can include a formula, pattern, compilation, program, device, method, technique, or process. To meet the most common definition of a trade secret, it must be used in business, and give an opportunity to obtain an economic advantage over competitors who do not know or use it. This protection is very limited because a trade secret holder is only protected from unauthorized disclosure and

---

[4] 17 U.S. Code, §106.4.

use which is referred to as *misappropriation*. If a trade secret holder fails to maintain secrecy or if the information is independently discovered, becomes released, or otherwise becomes generally known, protection as a trade secret is lost. Trade secrets do not expire and thus protection continues until discovery or loss. The classic example is the formula for Coca Cola which apparently cannot be reverse engineered. As long as it remains a secret formula known only to a very select few persons, it can remain a trade secret literally forever.

Persons who engage in theft or other misuse of a trade secret may be prosecuted criminally in federal court under the federal *Economic Espionage Act of 1996*[5] (EEA) or sued civilly in either federal courts under the *Defend Trade Secrets Act of 2016*[6] or in almost all state courts under the *Uniform Trade Secrets Act*. The EEA §1832(a) states: Whoever, intending or knowing that the offense will benefit any foreign government, foreign instrumentality, or foreign agent, knowingly—(1) steals, or without authorization appropriates, takes, carries away, or conceals, or by fraud, artifice, or deception obtains a trade secret; (2) without authorization copies, duplicates, sketches, draws, photographs, downloads, uploads, alters, destroys, photocopies, replicates, transmits, delivers, sends, mails, communicates, or conveys a trade secret; (3) receives, buys, or possesses a trade secret, knowing the same to have been stolen or appropriated, obtained, or converted without authorization; or attempts or conspires to commit any of the said offenses are subject to a fine of up to $5 million and/or imprisonment of up to 15 years (business entities— a fine up to $10 million or three times the value of the theft whichever is higher).

Civil lawsuits under the said federal *Defend Trade Secrets Act of 2016* or the states' *Uniform Trade Secrets Act*. Courts generally will examine the six factors to be considered in determining whether information constitutes a trade secret:

- The extent to which the information is known outside the claimant's business

---

[5] Pub. L. §§104–294, U.S.C. §§1831 et. seq.
[6] Pub. L. §§114–153, May 11, 2016.

- The extent to which it is known by employees and others involved in the business
- The extent of measures taken by the claimant to guard the secrecy of the information
- The value of the information to the business and its competitors
- The amount of effort or money expended by the business in developing the information
- The ease or difficulty with which the information could be properly acquired or duplicated by others.[7]

In addition to private litigation and criminal enforcement of intellectual property rights (IPR), the U.S. State Department's Office of Intellectual Property Enforcement (IPE) is responsible for assuring protection of IPRs globally by deterring access to counterfeit and pirated goods, ensuring that holders of U.S. IPRs are protected abroad, and by promoting protection and enforcement against violations thereof. It is estimated that misuse of IPRs cost the U.S. economy $180 billion in theft of trade secrets, $18 billion in pirated software, and $29 billion in the displacement of goods by pirated and counterfeit goods.[8]

# International Regulation of Intellectual Property Rights

## Patents and Trademarks

*The Paris Convention for the Protection of Industrial Property* of March 20, 1883 (as amended through 1979),[9] states it applies to the wide range of industrial property including patents, trademarks, industrial designs,

---

[7] *Trade secret*, LEGAL INFORMATION INSTITUTE, Cornell L.S., https://www.law.cornell.edu/wex/trade_secret.

[8] *Intellectual Property Enforcement*, U.S. DEP'T OF STATE, https://www.state.gov/e/eb/cba/ipe/index.htm.

[9] Paris Convention for the Protection of Industrial Property (March 20, 1883; effective July 7, 1884, and amended June 2, 1934 and July 14, 1967) (the Paris Convention). The Convention may be found at https://www.wipo.int/treaties/en/ip/paris/.

utility models, service marks, trade names, geographical indications, and the repression of unfair competition. It also includes agriculture and mining.

Among the protections given are: (1) *national treatment*—the requirement that all contracting states (states which signed onto the Convention—a "state" in international law is a country) are to grant the same protection to nationals of other contracting states and also to nationals of noncontracting states if domiciled or have a real and effective industrial or commercial establishment in a contracting state; (2) *right of priority*—any person from a contracting state which duly files an application in one of the contracting states may apply for protection in any of the other contracting states which will be deemed having been filed on the same day as the initial application. The period of priority are 12 months for patents and utility models and 6 months for industrial designs and trademarks; (3) *exceptions to registrations*—patents granted in different contracting states for the same invention are independent of each other: the granting of a patent in one contracting state does not oblige other contracting states to grant a patent; a patent cannot be refused, annulled, or terminated in any contracting state on the ground that it has been refused or annulled or has terminated in any other contracting state; and a contracting state may enact legislative measures providing for the grant of compulsory licenses to prevent the abuses which might result from the exclusive rights conferred by a patent may do so only under certain conditions.[10]

*Service and Collective Marks.* The Paris Convention does not require the filing and registration of marks but leaves it to the contracting states to make that determination. Therefore, no application for the registration of a mark filed by a national of a contracting state may be refused, nor may a registration be invalidated on the ground that filing, registration, or renewal has not been effected in the country of origin. The registration of a mark obtained in one contracting state is independent of its possible registration in any other country, including the country of origin.

---

[10] World International Property Organization WIPO), *Summary of the Paris Convention for the Protection of Industrial Property*, www.wipo.int/treaties/en/ip/paris/summary_paris.html. WIPO is one of 15 specialized organizations in the United Nations. www.wipo.int/portal/en/index.html.

Consequently, the lapse or annulment of the registration of a mark in one contracting state will not affect the validity of the registration in other contracting states.

Where a mark has been duly registered in the country of origin, it must, on request, be accepted for filing and protected in its original form in the other contracting states. Nevertheless, registration may be refused in well-defined cases such as: where the mark would infringe the acquired rights of third parties; where it is devoid of distinctive character; where it is contrary to morality or public order; or where it is of such a nature as to be liable to deceive the public. Prohibited from registration are state emblems, official signs, and hallmarks of contracting states. Protection is also given to collective marks, industrial designs, trade names, and unfair competition.[11]

## Copyrights

The *Berne Convention for the Protection of Literary and Artistic Works*[12] was originally adopted in 1886. It was amended a number of times having been adopted in Paris in July, 1971 and amended with minor changes anew on September 28, 1979. It is administered by the World Intellectual Property Organization (WIPO) wherein 191 countries are member states.[13] The aim of the Convention is to protect the rights of authors in their literary and artistic works which include the following:

Every production in the literary, scientific and artistic domain, whatever may be the mode or form of its expression, such as books, pamphlets and other writings; lectures, addresses, sermons and other works of the same nature; dramatic or dramatico-musical works; choreographic works and entertainments in dumb show; musical compositions with or without

---

[11] *Id.*

[12] Berne Convention for the Protection of Literary and Artistic Works (1971), https://www.wipo.int/treaties/en/text.jsp?file_id=283698.

[13] The World Intellectual Property Organization (WIPO), established in 1967, is an agency of the United Nations (UN) with 191 member states that administers the several international conventions acting as the global forum for intellectual property services, policy, information, and cooperation, https://www.wipo.int/about-wipo/en/.

words; cinematographic works to which are assimilated works expressed by a process analogous to cinematography; works of drawing, painting, architecture, sculpture, engraving and lithography; photographic works to which are assimilated works expressed by a process analogous to photography; works of applied art; illustrations, maps, plans, sketches and three-dimensional works relative to geography, topography, architecture or science.[14]

The Convention sets forth a minimum number of rights that are to be accorded to authors, though allowing states considerable freedom to decide the general and specific categories of works that are not protected unless fixed in some material form. Rights include translations, adaptations, reproduction, broadcasting of the works, public recitation, adaptations, arrangements, cinematographic adaptation and reproductions, arrangements of music and other forms of a literary or artistic work, and collections of such works, such as encyclopedias and anthologies.[15]

It is up to the individual states to determine the protection to be given to official texts of a legislative, administrative, and legal nature and to their official translations. Also, it is left to the states to determine the extent of the application of their laws to works of applied art and industrial designs and models, as well as the conditions under which such works, designs, and models shall be protected. Works protected in the country of origin solely as designs and models shall be entitled in another member country of the Convention only to such special protection as is granted in that country to designs and models; however, if no such special protection is granted in that country, such works shall be protected as artistic works. Protection does not extend to news of the day or to miscellaneous facts having the character of mere items of press information.[16]

The duration of the copyright is life of the author plus 50 years of the new year after the author's death, but U.S. law and that of the E.U. is life plus 70 years or 95 years if author is anonymous or corporately owned. If jointly owned, the term begins after the death of the last surviving

---

[14] Berne Convention, Art. 2(1).
[15] Berne Convention, Art. 2 (2)–(5).
[16] Berne Convention Art. 2 (4)(7).

author.[17] Protection is given to the author whether the work is published or not published (U.S. law is in accordance, but requires a filing in order to sue in federal court). Such protection is available without any formalities and is independent of the rights accorded to authors in the country of origin. Thus, if the author's own country does not afford protection of the covered works, the author would still have protection in the countries belonging to the Convention although the member states can invoke the principle of reciprocity to limit such protection.[18] An author, irrespective of any economic right he or she may have, has the right to claim authorship of a work and to object to the distortion or other mutilation of the work that would be prejudicial to the author. Such rights are extended to the copyright holder after the author's death, at least until the cessation of economic rights.[19]

The Convention does not provide an enforcement mechanism for breach of the rights of authors. It merely provides that member states are to enact "domestic law to give effect to the provisions of this Convention." There is no stated penalty for countries not abiding by the provisions of the Convention. Seizures of infringing copies of works are authorized but left to domestic law for enforcement. Developing countries are given much flexibility in enacting protective laws in accordance with their social, economic, and cultural situations. Enforcement is thus left to countries such as the U.S. or those in the E.U. to determine what, if any, penalties are to be imposed for violations of the Convention.

## Trade Secrets

Internationally, the U.S. and most countries of the world are members of the World Trade Organization (WTO) and a party to the *Agreement on Trade-Related Aspects of Intellectual-Property Rights* (TRIPS). Thus, the U.S. is obligated to afford trade secret protection. Article 39 provides that member states are to protect against unfair competition as provided in the *Paris Convention* (1967), §2 states: "Natural and legal persons shall

---

[17] Berne Convention Art. 7.
[18] Berne Convention Art. 5.
[19] Berne Convention, Art. 6.

have the possibility of preventing information lawfully within their control from being disclosed to, acquired by, or used by others without their consent in a manner contrary to honest commercial practices so long as such information: (a) is secret in the sense that it is not, as a body or in the precise configuration and assembly of its components, generally known among or readily accessible to persons within the circles that normally deal with the kind of information in question; (b) has commercial value because it is secret; and (c) has been subject to reasonable steps under the circumstances, by the person lawfully in control of the information, to keep it secret."[20]

## AI and Intellectual Property Protection

A significant issue is whether AI rights are protected by IPR Conventions? In Wales, one commentator suggested that under §16(2) of the Copyrights Designs and Patents Act of 1988, AI systems cannot violate copyright regulations inasmuch as copyright can only be infringed by a person and thus, the person in control of the system would be held liable. Additional issues concern the creation of content by AI systems and whether they can be considered as authors if no human person participates in the creation? For patent protection, the challenge will be who owns the patent rights and whether an AI system or machine that creates the invention can be allowed ownership of the patent?[21]

The Director General of WIPO, Francis Gurry, characterized AI as the new digital frontier that will have enormous impact on the world. For example, commercial AI-generated music and other AI-created inventions will inevitably raise issues concerning the identity of the author and inventor and who is to be awarded for their creations. The debate concerns those advocates of the "open" movements for science, data, and publication who state data should have no protective pro-

---

[20] World Trade Organization, *Standards concerning the availability, scope, and use of intellectual property rights*, §7, Art. 39, https://www.wto.org/english/docs_e/legal_e/27-trips_04d_e.htm.

[21] Greenaway Scott, *Artificial Intelligence: Challenges for Intellectual Property*, BUSINESSNEWSWALES (Aug. 7, 2018), quoting Lorna Bolton, https://businessnewswales.com/artificial-intelligence-challenges-for-intellectual-property/.

prietary boundaries, while others allege the age-old view that IPR protections provide incentives for investment in the creation of new knowledge. Regarding ownership of an AI-created work, Gurry cites three factors that have made AI a priority for AI and for the global IP community: (1) *quality*; (2) *cost*; and, most importantly, (3) *volume*, as evidenced by the filing of 3.1 million patent applications, 7 million trademark applications, and 963,000 industrial applications covering 1.2 million designs worldwide in 2016. Ironically, the AI-empowered image search tool for trademarks has permitted prompt, accurate results in seconds for trademarks, which also achieves better quality and lower administrative costs.[22]

WIPO developed an AI-powered neural machine translate tool known as "WIPO Translate" that is shared with 14 intergovernmental organizations and global patent offices. It has launched an automatic patent classification for the International Patent Classification system, using neural network technology that enables patent classification and search more easily of "prior art" (evidence that the invention was previously known). WIPO is deploying intelligent machine answering services for WIPO customer service activities. Gurry does not see blockchain as altering the basic function of the grant of a property right by a state. Barriers to AI-use include lack of expertise of professionals needed and the data and algorithms that AI depends on. Multilateral cooperation will be required to achieve functional interoperability of IP systems and ensure fair competition.[23]

In WIPO's most recent Report of January 2019, prepared by numerous researchers based on data through the end of 2016,[24] it noted the following.

---

[22] World Intellectual Property Organization, *Artificial Intelligence and Intellectual property: an interview with Francis Gurry*, WIPO MAGAZINE (Sept. 2018), https://wipo.int/wipo_magazine//en/2018/05/article_0001.html.

[23] *Id.*

[24] World Intellectual Property Organization, *WIPO's First "Technology Trends" Study Probes Artificial Intelligence: IBM and Microsoft are Leaders Amid Recent Global Upsurge in AI Inventive Activity*, Jan. 31, 2019, https://www.wipo.int/pressroom/en/articles/2019/article_0001.html. The executive summary from which the text material is derived from can be found at https://www.wipo.int/edocs/pubdocs/en/wipo_pub_1055-exe_summary1.pdf.

## Patent Filings

- With the emergence of AI in the 1950s, innovators and researchers have filed almost 340,000 AI-related inventions and published over 1.6 million scientific publications.
- The boom in scientific publications has occurred since 2001 with the ratio of scientific papers to inventions having decreased from 8.1 in 2010 to 3:1 in 2016 thus illustrating the translation of theory to actual practice.
- Machine learning is the dominant AI technique in patent filings and is included in one-third of the 134,777 patent filings, having an average annual growth of 28 percent with 20,195 patent applications in 2016 as compared with filings of 9567 in 2013.
- Companies represent 26 out of the top 30 AI patent applicants, with universities or public research organizations accounting for the remaining four.
- The leading companies that filed AI-based patent applications were U.S.-based International Business Machines (IBM) with 8290 inventions at the end of 2016; Microsoft Corp. with 5930 filings; Japan-based Toshiba Corp. with 5930 filings; Republic of Korea-based Samsung Group with 5102 filings; and Japan-based NEC Group with 4406 filings.
- Chinese organizations ranked as one of the leaders of the top 30 academic patent players with the Chinese Academy of Sciences ranking 17th of the top 20 academic players with over 2500 patent filings and accounted for 10 of the top 20 in AI-related publications.

## AI Techniques

- Machine learning, especially neural networks underlying machine translation, is the dominant AI technique in over one-third of all identified inventions. Machine learning including ride-sharing services increased from 9567 patent applications in 2013 to 20,195 in 2016.
- Deep learning, a machine-learning technique revolutionizing AI that includes speech recognition systems, is the fastest growing AI technique with a nearly 20-fold increase in patent applications, from 118 in 2013 to 2399 in 2016.

## AI Applications

- Computer vision including image recognition used especially for autonomous vehicles accounted for 49 percent of all AI-related patents.
- AI for robotics grew from 622 patent applications in 2013 to 2272 in 2016.
- Patent applications for control methods, which manage the behavior of devices such as robotic arms, rose from 193 in 2013 to 698 in 2016.

## AI in Industrial Sectors

- The transportation sector, including autonomous vehicles, had one of the fastest AI-related growths with 8764 filings in 2016 up from 3738 filings in 2013.
- AI used for improving networks in the telecommunications field yielded 6684 filings in 2016, up 84 percent from 3625 in 2013.
- Life and medical sciences whereby AI was applied to robotic surgery and drug personalization, grew to 4112 filings in 2016, up 40 percent from 2942 in 2013.
- Personal devices, computing, and human-computer interaction grew to 3977 filings in 2016, up 36 percent from 2915 in 2013, for an 11 percent average annual growth rate.[25]

# U.S. Protection of AI-Based IPRs

## Copyrights

U.S. protection follows closely the various IPRs conventions administered by WIPO. Software is included in the protection given by copyright law as "an original work now known or later developed.... (1) literary works."[26] It protects the expression contained in the software but not any

---

[25] *Id.*

[26] U.S. Copyright Law, §102(a), https://www.copyright.gov/title17/92chap1.html. See also, U.S. Copyright Office, *What Does Copyright Protect?*, https://www.copyright.gov/help/faq/faq-protect.html.

mathematical formals, algorithms, logic, or system design.[27] An issue that the new technology raises is whether creations by nonhumans, either nonhuman animals or AI machine-created works such as by computers, are covered by the said IPR conventions. The following case appears to be dispositive of whether IPR protection may be granted to a nonhuman animal and/or has the right to sue for infringement.[28] Whether or not the same reasoning applies to AI-creations may ultimately be determined by Congressional or states' legislative enactments.

### NARUTO v. SLATER

#### No. 16-15469 (9th Cir. April 23, 2017)

Opinion by Carlos T. Bea, J.

*Facts:* Naruto was a seven-year-old crested macaque [genus of Old World Monkeys] that lived—and may still live—in a reserve on the island of Sulawesi, Indonesia. In 2011, a wildlife photographer, David Slater, left his camera unattended in the reserve. Naruto allegedly took several photographs of himself (the "Monkey Selfies") with Slater's camera. Slater and Wildlife Personalities, Ltd., ("Wildlife") published the Monkey Selfies in a book that Slater created through Blurb, Inc.'s ("Blurb") website in December 2014. The book identifies Slater and Wildlife as the copyright owners of the Monkey Selfies. However, Slater admits throughout the book that Naruto took the photographs at issue. For example, the book describes one of the Monkey Selfies as follows: "Sulawesi crested black macaque smiles at itself while pressing the shutter button on a camera." Another excerpt from the book describes Naruto as "[p]osing to take its own photograph, unworried by its own reflection, smiling. Surely a sign of self-awareness?"
In 2015 People for the Ethical Treatment of Animals ("PETA") and Dr. Antje Engelhardt filed a complaint for copyright infringement against Slater, Wildlife, and Blurb, as Next Friends on behalf of Naruto. The complaint alleges that Dr. Engelhardt has studied the crested macaques in Sulawesi, Indonesia for over a decade and has known, monitored, and studied Naruto since his birth. The complaint does not allege any history or relationship

---

[27] An excellent summary of AI issues is *Protecting Artificial Intelligence IP: Patents, Trade Secrets, or Copyrights?* JONES DAY (Jan. 2018), https://www.jonesday.com/files/Publication/c2577689-4a50-409a-98f6-a9bc7c9620a9/Presentation/PublicationAttachment/04cf20ba-60eb-4620-93cc-e90380f84c85/Protecting%20Artificial%20Intelligence%20IP.pdf.

[28] For a detailed description of the occurrence of selfies by the monkey discussed in the following case, see, *Monkey selfie copyright dispute*, WIKIPEDIA, https://en.wikipedia.org/wiki/Monkey_selfie_copyright_dispute.

between PETA and Naruto. Instead, the complaint alleges that PETA is "the largest animal rights organization in the world" and "has championed establishing the rights and legal protections available to animals beyond their utility to human beings ...." Slater, Wildlife, and Blurb filed motions to dismiss under Fed. R. Civ. P. 12(b)(1) and 12(b)(6) on the grounds that the complaint did not state facts sufficient to establish standing under Article III or statutory standing under the Copyright Act. The district court granted the motions to dismiss.

*Issue:* Whether a monkey may sue humans, corporations, and companies for damages and injunctive relief arising from claims of copyright infringement?

*Decision:* The Court of Appeals unanimously upheld the lower court's dismissal of the case (J. N.R. Smith concurring)

*Reasoning:*
Next Friend Standing. We gravely doubt that PETA can validly assert "next friend" status to represent claims made for the monkey both (1) because PETA has failed to allege any facts to establish the required significant relationship between a next friend and a real party in interest and (2) because an animal cannot be represented, under our laws, by a "next friend." First, "[i]n order to establish next-friend standing, the putative next friend must show: (1) that the petitioner is unable to litigate his own cause due to mental incapacity, lack of access to court, or other similar disability; and (2) the next friend has some significant relationship with, and is truly dedicated to the best interests of, the petitioner." .... Here, we are concerned with the second requirement. PETA does not claim to have a relationship with Naruto that is any more significant than its relationship with any other animal. Thus, PETA fails to meet the "significant relationship" requirement and cannot sue as Naruto's next friend....
\*\*\*\*\*\*\*\*\*\*\*\*\*\*\*\*\*\*\*\*\*\*\*\*\*\*\*\*\*\*\*\*\*\*\*\*
Here, we follow the Supreme Court's lead in holding that "the scope of any federal doctrine of 'next friend' standing is no broader than what is permitted by the ... statute." .... Although Congress has authorized "next friend" lawsuits on behalf of habeas petitioners,... and on behalf of a "minor or incompetent person,"..., there is no such authorization for "next friend" lawsuits brought on behalf of animals.
\*\*\*\*\*\*\*\*\*\*\*\*\*\*\*\*\*\*\*\*\*\*\*\*\*\*\*\*\*\*\*\*\*\*\*\*
Several provisions of the Copyright Act...persuade us against the conclusion that animals have statutory standing to sue under the Copyright Act.... ("It is a fundamental canon of statutory construction that the words of a statute must be read in their context and with a view to their place in the overall statutory scheme."). For example, the "children" of an "author," "whether legitimate or not," can inherit certain rights under the Copyright

Act.... Also, an author's "widow or widower owns the author's entire termination interest unless there are any surviving children or grandchildren of the author, in which case the widow or widower owns one-half of the author's interest."....The terms "children," "grandchildren," "legitimate," "widow," and "widower" all imply humanity and necessarily exclude animals that do not marry and do not have heirs entitled to property by law... Based on this court's [prior precedent] and the text of the Copyright Act as a whole, the district court did not err in concluding that Naruto—and, more broadly, animals other than humans—lack statutory standing to sue under the Copyright Act.

The U.S. Copyright Office in its *Compendium of U.S. Copyright Office Practices*, §306 "The Human Authorship Requirement" states that "The U.S. Copyright Office will register an original work of authorship, provided that the work was created by a human being. The Copyright law only protects 'the fruits of intellectual labor' that 'are founded in the creative powers of the mind'.... Because copyright law is limited to 'original intellectual conceptions of the author,' the Office will refuse to register a claim if it determines that a human being did not create the work....[29] It further provided that [t]o qualify as a work of 'authorship' a work must be created by a human being.... Works that do not satisfy this requirement are not copyrightable."

"The Office will not register works produced by nature, animals, or plants. Likewise, the Office cannot register a work purportedly created by divine or supernatural beings, although the Office may register a work where the application or the deposit copy(ies) state that the work was inspired by a divine spirit." The Copyright Office specifically gives as examples, a photograph taken by a monkey, a mural painted by an elephant, driftwood shaped and smoothed by the ocean, and also works produced by a machine or mere mechanical process, which operate randomly or automatically without any creative input or intervention from a human author.[30]

---

[29] U.S. Copyright Office, *Compendium of U.S. Copyright Office Practices*, 3d Ed. Sept. 2017, https://www.copyright.gov/comp3/.

[30] *Id.*, §313.2, *Works That Lack Human Authorship*.

Are art works or musical compositions created by AI machines protected by copyright? An example is the remarkable ability of machine learning and deep learning to create individual men and women faces that are composites of human faces, which are indistinguishable from the latter.[31] It would appear that the Copyright Office would reject any claim of ownership with respect to AI-based machines that operate without human intervention. The E.U. is in agreement that copyright protection in the E.U. is given to works such as computer programs, databases, or photographs only if they are original in the sense that they are of the author's own intellectual creation as provided for under Articles 1(3) of Directive 91/250, 3(1) of Directive 96/9, and 6 of Directive 2006/116.[32]

Inasmuch as the machines were initially created, programmed, data inserted etc. by humans, why can one not claim that she/he/it should receive protection from the emanations of the AI-based machine? Where is the dividing line between works created by AI-based programs but under the direct or indirect supervision of human persons? As one commentator noted, AI-generated works may be divided under two categories: one in which the AI programs were directly guided by human persons in essence as a tool of the individual, while the second scenario is where the AI-program acts with little or no direct human intervention, but rather acts by analyzing the features and qualities of the subject matter to create new versions which the human actor is seeking.

The oft-cited case that very early discussed the use of a tool to create a work is that of *Burrow-Giles Lithographic Co. v. Sarony*[33] wherein the U.S. Supreme Court gave a photograph copyright protection as an original work of art although it was a machine (camera) which took the photograph. The photo was made of Oscar Wilde by the photographer Napoleon Sarony who selected and arranged the costume, draperies, and other accessories as a backdrop to the photo in addition to arranging the light, shading, and other aspects of the photo. Its relevance is that it is analogous to the cited case, whereby the inventors and creators of the

---

[31] Karen Hao, *Inside the world of AI that forges beautiful art and terrifying deepfakes*, MIT TECHNOLOGY REVIEW (Dec. 1, 2018), https://www.technologyreview.com/g/deepfakes/.

[32] *Infopaq Intn'l v. Danske Dagblades*, ECJ (17 July 2009), Swarb.co.uk, https://swarb.co.uk/infopaq-international-v-danske-dagblades-forening-ecj-17-jul-2009/.

[33] *Burrow-Giles Lithographic Co. v. Sarony*, 111 U.S. 53 (1884). Text of the case can be found at https://www.law.cornell.edu/supremecourt/text/111/53.

machine learning AI programs should be entitled to copyright protection inasmuch as they have expended the considerable time, moneys, and ingenuity to fashion the tool that generates the work of art. The ostensible purpose of copyright protection as stated under Article 1, §8, clause 8, of the U.S. Constitution is "To promote the Progress of Science and useful Arts, by securing for limited Times to Authors and Inventors the exclusive Right to their respective Writings and Discoveries." Given the underlying purpose of the constitutional mandate, some commentators strongly advocate that protection be given to AI generated works of artistic creation inasmuch as the AI-programs and machine learning programs are themselves the conception of human persons.[34]

Another commentator writing in WIPO Magazine noted that protection is given to the author of the program that generates the work of artistic creation as evidenced in the statutes and interpretations in Hong Kong, India, Ireland, New Zealand, and the U.K.[35] §9(3) of the *Copyright, Designs and Patents Act* (CDPA) of the U.K. specifically states with respect to AI-generated works:

> (3) In the case of a literary, dramatic, musical or artistic work which is computer-generated, the author shall be taken to be the person by whom the arrangements necessary for the creation of the work are undertaken.[36] CDPA §178 provides: "[c]omputer-generated" is defined as "generated by computer in circumstances such that there is no human author of the work."

Thus, by analogy, using photography as in the U.S. Supreme Court case previously cited wherein a photographer is given copyright protection who utilizes automatic settings and timers to take photographs on a camera, it is a small step forward to permit protection to AI-generated works.[37]

---

[34] Kalin Hristov, *Artificial Intelligence and the Copyright Dilemma*, 57 IDEA 431, No. 3, at 438, https://papers.ssrn.com/sol3/papers.cfm?abstract_id=2976428.

[35] Andres Guadamuz, *Artificial intelligence and copyright*, WIPO MAGAZINE (Oct. 2017), https://www.wipo.int/export/sites/www/wipo_magazine/en/pdf/2017/wipo_pub_121_2017_05.pdf.

[36] *Copyright, Designs and Patents Act*, U.K., http://www.legislation.gov.uk/ukpga/1988/48/section/9.

[37] *AI and IP: copyright in AI-generated works (UK law) Can copyright subsist in AI-generated work*, CLIFFORD CHANCE (Dec. 18, 2018), https://talkingtech.cliffordchance.com/en/ip/copyright/ai-and-ip%2D%2Dcopyright-in-ai-generated-works%2D%2Duk-law-.html.

A number of commentators are beginning to weigh in in favor of extending copyright protection to artistic works created by robots, computers, and other works derived from AI-based programs. Some scholars note that not permitting owners of the AI programs would place them in the public domain to the detriment of those human persons who created the initial programs. Examples are the AI painting *Le Comte de Belamy* which was sold to a collector by the collective Obvious[38] and the creation of new folk songs by the AI machine "Bot Dylan" which generated new folk songs using 23,000 pieces of Irish folk music to create the compositions.[39] One commentator referred to the artistic creation titled "The Next Rembrandt," which appeared to be a work by the famed seventeenth century painter Rembrandt Harmenszoon van Rijn, but was created by a computer that used machine learning to almost perfectly reproduce a comparable work. It did so by analyzing the artist's use of color, brush-strokes, and geometric patterns so as to make the new creation virtually indistinguishable from that of the famed artist. Similarly, other nonhuman creations include a Japanese computer program which generated a short novel which almost won a national literary contest and a Google-owned DeepMind program that emulated music styles of famed classical composers.[40]

Adding to the confusion and need for regulatory reexamination is the latest emanation from McCormick & Company, famed for dissemination of spices nationally and internationally, which, in coordination with IBM, is marketing newly AI-based spice creations based on data points called "One."[41] Should the company not have IPR protection? The elements of copyright law are mainly complied with, namely (1) original work of authorship; (2) fixed in a tangible medium, and (3) has some degree of creativity. The only hindrance is that of creativity or product of

---

[38] Ryan E. Long, *Artificial Intelligence Art – Who Owns the Copyright*, CIS (May 9, 2018), http://cyberlaw.stanford.edu/blog/2018/05/artificial-intelligence-art-who-owns-copyright-0.

[39] Nicole Martinez, *Can an AI Machine Hold Copyright Protection Over Its Work?*, ART LAW JOURNAL (June 1, 2017), https://alj.artrepreneur.com/ai-machine-copyright/.

[40] Yasser M. El-Gamal and Ehab Samuel, *Copyright Protection for AI Machine Created Works?*, MANETT PHELPS & PHILLIPS LLP (Sept. 28, 2017), https://www.manatt.com/Insights/Articles/2017/Copyright-Protection-for-AI-Machine-Created-Works.

[41] Molly Price, *AI gets spicy with new McCormick flavors*, CNET (Feb. 6, 2019), https://www.cnet.com/news/ai-gets-spicy-with-new-mccormick-flavors/.

the mind which runs into the roadblock of the U.S. Supreme Court case of *Goldstein v. California*[42] wherein the court, citing *Burrow* discussed above, stated "… although the word 'writings' might be limited to script or printed material, it may be interpreted to include any physical rendering of the fruits of creative intellectual or aesthetic labor."[43] The issue is whether an AI-created work meets the said criteria?[44]

An additional issue that eventually will have to be addressed, even if copyright protection is permitted for AI-creations, is who is to receive the ownership of the copyright. In England and New Zealand, ownership is given to the programmer who initiated the AI mechanism. A second issue is who is criminally responsible for any violations of penal law resulting from AI-directed behavior?[45] A query made by another scholar is the application of the First Amendment to AI or algorithmic authorship, particularly as evidenced in search engines. Inasmuch as liability, especially criminal liability, is premised on intent, how does this element apply to AI programs? One author noted that copyright and the First Amendment concern different questions: for copyright, it is whether a work is minimally creative under Copyright law while the First Amendment examines a work as speech or action that needs to be protected. The emergent technological output by machine authors will be disruptive requiring determination of authorship and a balancing of rights between protection of original works of authorship and the right of freedom of speech.[46] Further issues to be addressed in the future are the application of moral rights, licensing, and work made for hire, to AI created artistic works.[47]

---

[42] Goldstein v. California, 412 U.S. 546 (1973). Text of the case may be found at https://www.law.cornell.edu/copyright/cases/412_US_546.htm.

[43] *Id.*, at 561.

[44] For a discussion, see Martinez, *supra* at note 606.

[45] Swapnil Tripathi and Chandi Ghatak, *Artificial Intelligence and Intellectual Property Law*, 7 Christ U. L. J. 83–97 (2017) at 89, RESEARCH GATE, https://www.researchgate.net/publication/323557478.

[46] For a discussion of the implications of AI authorship and freedom of speech, see Margot E. Kaminski, *Authorship, Disrupted: AI Authors in Copyright and First Amendment Law*, 51 UC Davis Law Review 589 (2017), https://papers.ssrn.com/sol3/cf_dev/AbsByAuth.cfm?per_id=1735610.

[47] Article 6bis of The Berne Convention recites the "moral rights" as "(1) Independently of the author's economic rights, and even after the transfer of the said rights, the author shall have the right to claim authorship of the work and to object to any distortion, mutilation or other

With respect to AI patent protection, there is some degree of confusion respecting the extent and degree of protection to be afforded. Among the issues that will be subject to litigation are: Who is the inventor if it is the existing AI machine that discovers or creates the new innovation? Who is liable for injury or other harm if the AI system is the culprit in bringing about financial or other harm to others? Are only the initial inventors of the AI-based machine liable vis-à-vis suppliers, distributors, sellers of its products or services? Who owns the data, information, or results of production?[48] These and other issues will have to be addressed by the U.S. Congress and by international bodies that concern IPRs.

## Patents

As stated previously, AI inventions and processes have emerged as trailblazers in patent filings. Robotics, machine learning, and other filings have created much uncertainty whether and to what extent they should receive patent protection under the Patent Act.[49] Numerous questions have arisen whether they comply with the fundamental provisions of §101 of the Act, which states:

> Whoever invents or discovers any new and useful process, machine, manufacture, or composition of matter, or any new and useful improvements thereof, may obtain a patent therefor, subject to the conditions and requirements of this title.

Only an individual, or individuals if a joint invention, not a company or a machine, may be an inventor.[50] The primary question that needs to be

---

modification of, or other derogatory action in relation to, the said work, which would be prejudicial to his honor or reputation." For a discussion of some of the issues from a European perspective, see Begona Gonzalez Otero, *Before the Singularity: Copyright and the Challenges of Artificial Intelligence*, KLUWER COPYRIGHT BLOG, http://copyrightblog.kluweriplaw.com/2018/09/25/singularity-copyright-challenges-artificial-intelligence/.

[48] For a discussion, see Hogan Lovells, *Litigating intellectual property issues: The impact of AI and machine learning*, LEXOLOGY (Jan. 19, 2019), https://www.lexology.com/library/detail.aspx?g=1176050a-f4ee-4919-891e-366d06c46f45.

[49] Patent Act, 35 U.S.C. §§1–376.

[50] 35 U.S.C. §100(f). There are similar restrictions in the U.K., Ireland, India, Hong Kong, and New Zealand. *Artificial Intelligence: Why AI Inventions Will Disrupt Patent*, CILGLOBAL IP LTD,

addressed when filing an AI-based patent is whether it complies with the elements recited in §101.

*Earlier Precedents.* The U.S. Supreme Court and lower federal courts have addressed the issue in a number of cases concerning software patent eligibility and whether they are mathematical formulas such as found in algorithms and laws of nature which per se are not patentable. Earlier, the court in *Gottschalk v. Benson*,[51] which held that an invention that related to the processing of data to the programmed conversion of numerical information, i.e., by a method for converting ordinary-coded decimal numerals into pure binary numbers, was not patentable inasmuch as they were no more than abstract mathematics. In *Bilski. V. Kappos*[52] the court agreed with the patent examiner's conclusion that a claimed invention, which explains how commodities buyers and sellers in the energy market can protect, or hedge, against the risk of price changes, describes a series of steps instructing how to hedge risk constituted a mathematical formal and thus was not patentable. The invention is not implemented on a specific apparatus, merely manipulates an abstract idea, and solves a purely mathematical problem.

In another oft-cited case that denied eligibility because it merely was a correlation of nature was *Mayo Collaborative Services v. Prometheus Laboratories*,[53] wherein the court found the patents issued to Prometheus were not patentable. The litigation concerned the use of thiopurine drugs to treat autoimmune diseases whereby physicians are enabled to determine whether a particular patient's dose was too high and, thus, risked harmful side effects. The methodology used to assist the physicians was, according to the court, well-known in the prior art and added nothing to the laws of nature.

http://www.cilglobalip.com/blog/2018/09/07/artificial-intelligence-why-ai-inventions-will-disrupt-patent-law/.

[51] *Gottschalk v. Benson*, 409 U.S. 63 (1972). Text of case can be found in FindLaw, https://caselaw.findlaw.com/us-supreme-court/409/63.html.

[52] *Bilski v. Kappos*, 561 U.S. 593 (2010). Text of case can be found in JUSTIA, https://supreme.justia.com/cases/federal/us/561/593/.

[53] *Mayo Collaborative Services v. Prometheus Laboratories*, U.S. Supreme Court *slip opinion*, No. 10-1150 (2012), https://www.supremecourt.gov/opinions/11pdf/10-1150.pdf.

A seminal case oft-cited as possibly determinative of future AI-cases is *Alice Corp. v. CLS Bank Intern.*[54] The court again held ineligible the bases for patent eligibility because they fell under the exception of the laws of nature, natural phenomena, and abstract ideas. Alice Corp. was the assignees of several patents which claimed to facilitate the exchange of financial obligations between two parties by using a computer system as a third-party intermediary. The patents in suit claimed (1) a method for exchanging financial obligations, (2) a computer system configured to carry out the method for exchanging obligations, and (3) a computer-readable medium containing program code for performing the method of exchanging obligations. CLS Bank and others, which operate a global network that facilitates currency transactions, filed suit against petitioner arguing that the patent claims at issue are invalid, unenforceable, or not infringed.

The Supreme Court, in a unanimous opinion authored by Justice Clarence Thomas, recited that the representative method claim does no more than simply instruct the practitioner to implement the abstract idea of intermediated settlement on a generic computer. Taking the claim elements separately, the function performed by the computer at each step— creating and maintaining "shadow" accounts, obtaining data, adjusting account balances, and issuing automated instructions—is "[p]urely 'conventional.'" considered "as an ordered combination," these computer components "ad[d] nothing ... that is not already present when the steps are considered separately." Viewed as a whole, these method claims simply recite the concept of intermediated settlement as performed by a generic computer. They do not, e.g., purport to improve the functioning of the computer itself or effect an improvement in any other technology or technical field. An instruction to apply the abstract idea of intermediated settlement using some unspecified, generic computer is not "enough" to transform the abstract idea into a patent-eligible invention.[55]

The decision in *Alice* has been severely criticized by many commentators and by the Director of the USPTO, Andrei Iancu, who indicated

---

[54] *Alice Corp. v. CLS Bank Intern.*, 573 U.S. 208 (2014). Text of case can be found at https://www.supremecourt.gov/opinions/13pdf/13-298_7lh8.pdf.
[55] *Id.*

that his office is presently working with Congress to amend the Patent Act to clarify issues raised by the court decision.[56] Both he and other commentators were mystified by the Alice line of cases which established a two-part test for the requirements of patentability under §101 of the Patent Act, namely, (1) whether an invention is directed as an "abstract idea" or "law of nature?" and (2) if so, whether the invention includes an "inventive concept?" It is the second test that has caused great confusion as to AI-based inventions that has allegedly muddied the waters concerning eligibility.[57] Draft language suggested by the Intellectual Property Owners Association, would nullify eligibility of an invention or process "(a) if and only if the claimed invention as a whole (i) exists in nature independently of and prior to any human activity or (ii) is performed solely in the human mind;" and adds that eligibility of a claimed invention "shall be determined without regard to … [c] (ii) the manner in which the claimed invention was made or discovered; or (iii) whether the claimed invention includes and inventive concept."[58]

The USPTO has attempted to adjust to AI filings and determinations for eligibility by assigning applications to particular technological classes so that examiners can develop expertise in analyzing whether an application meets the statutory standards. Thus, one of the technological classes is Class 706, "Artificial Intelligence." Because of the *Alice* decision, a later Federal Circuit decision also denied eligibility in *Electric Power Group, LLC v. Alstrom SA*[59] to the patents that describe and claim systems and methods for performing real-time performance monitoring of an electric power grid by collecting data from multiple data sources, analyzing the data, and displaying the results. The court stated that the claims do not

---

[56] *Remarks Delivered by Director Iancu at the Intellectual Property Owners Association 46th Annual Meeting*, United States Patent and Trademark Office (Sept. 24, 2018), https://www.uspto.gov/about-us/news-updates/remarks-director-iancu-intellectual-property-owners-46th-annual-meeting.

[57] Herbert C. Wamsley, *American Innovation at Risk: The New Congress Must Clarify Which Inventions Are Eligible for Patents*, IP WATCHDOG (Dec. 19, 2018), http://www.ipwatchdog.com/2018/12/19/new-congress-must-clarify-which-inventions-eligible-patents/id=104383/.

[58] *Joint IPO-AIPLA Proposal Concerning Legislative Amendment of 35 U.S.C. § 101*, Letter to Hon. Andrei Iancu (May 3, 2018), https://www.ipo.org/wp-content/uploads/2018/06/IPO-AIPLA-Ltr-to-Iancu-re-Joint-101-Proposal.pdf.

[59] *Electric Power Group LLC. V. Alstrom S.A.*, 830 F.3d 1350 (Fed. Cir. 2016).

go beyond requiring the collection, analysis, and display of available information in a particular field, specifying those functions in general terms, without limiting them to technical means for performing the functions that are arguably an advance over conventional computer and network technology. The claims, defining a desirable information-based result and not limited to inventive means of achieving the result, fail under §101.[60] As a result of the stated cases, the USPTO has lowered substantially the number of eligible applications. The decision was criticized because it is often impossible for persons to perform calculations of AI systems due to their dynamic nature and that the AI systems employ repeated or continuous learning rather than being static. They are "more than just a set of algorithms but are designed in terms of variables, hyper-parameters, optimization variables, training data sets, validation data sets etc."[61]

In a recent severely criticized case, *Athena Diagnostics v. Mayo Collaborative*,[62] Athena Diagnostics is the exclusive licensee of the '820 patent, which was used to diagnose neurological disorders by detecting antibodies to a protein called muscle-specific tyrosine kinase. The company marketed a test called FMUSK that evaluates those antibodies. Thereafter, Mayo developed two competing tests, which caused Athena to file for infringement of its patent. A majority of the Federal Appeals court agreed with Mayo dismissing the patent as directed to a natural law and thus is exempt from patent protection. It cited the earlier *Mayo v. Prometheus* discussed above as binding precedent and "reaffirm[ed] that use of a man-made molecule in a method claim employing standard techniques to detect or observe a natural law may still leave the claim directed to a natural law." The critique by most observers is that the court is simply wrong in not granting protection to discoveries of the type in this and the other *Mayo* case. The concern is that the purpose of patent law, i.e.,

---

[60] *Id.* A text of the decision may be found at http://www.cafc.uscourts.gov/sites/default/files/opinions-orders/15-1778.Opinion.7-28-2016.1.PDF. A discussion of the impact of the *Alice* and *Electric Power* decision is that of Kate Gaudry and Samuel Hayim, *Artificial Intelligence Technologies Facing Heavy Scrutiny at the USPTO*, IPWATCHDOG (Nov. 28, 2018), http://www.ipwatchdog.com/2018/11/28/artificial-intelligence-technologies-facing-heavy-scrutiny-uspto/id=103762/.

[61] Gaudry, *Id.*

[62] *Athena Diagnostics v. Mayo Collaborative*, No. 17-2508 (Fed. Cir. 2019), discussed by Donald Zuhn, PATENT DOCS, https://www.jdsupra.com/legalnews/athena-diagnostics-inc-v-mayo-71769/.

to encourage the creation of new and innovative discoveries via inventions or processes will be undermined by the court's interpretations of §101 of the Patent Act.[63]

The apprehension that progress in inventions may be stymied is reflective in commentaries regarding the results in another AI medical inventions case: *Ariosa Diagnostics, Inc. v. Sequenom, Inc.*[64] In 1996, Drs. Dennis Lo and James Wainscoat discovered cell-free fetal DNA ("cffDNA") in maternal plasma and serum, the portion of maternal blood samples that other researchers had previously discarded as medical waste. cffDNA is noncellular fetal DNA that circulates freely in the blood stream of a pregnant woman. Applying a combination of known laboratory techniques to their discovery, Drs. Lo and Wainscoat implemented a method for detecting the small fraction of paternally inherited cffDNA in maternal plasma or serum to determine fetal characteristics, such as gender. The invention, commercialized by Sequenom as its MaterniT21 test, created an alternative for prenatal diagnosis of fetal DNA that avoids the risks of widely used techniques that took samples from the fetus or placenta. In 2001, Drs. Lo and Wainscoat obtained the '540 patent which relates to this discovery.

The court determined that the discovery did not qualify for eligibility. Among other findings, it stated that the dependent claims are broad examples of how to detect cffDNA in maternal plasma. They are focused on the use of the natural phenomenon in combination with well-understood, routine, and conventional activity. The court agreed that the method reflects a significant human contribution in that Drs. Lo and Wainscoat combined and utilized man-made tools of biotechnology in a new way that revolutionized prenatal care. It was a discovery regarding cffDNA that may have been a significant contribution to the medical field that alone does not make it patentable. In light of this and other

---

[63] Gene Quinn, *The Federal Circuit is Shirking Its Constitutional Duty to Provide Certainty for Critical Innovation*, IPWATCHDOG (Feb. 12, 2019), https://www.ipwatchdog.com/2019/02/12/federal-circuit-shirking-constitutional-duty-provide-certainty-critical-innovation/id=106234/.

[64] *Ariosa Diagnostics, Inc. v. Sequenom, Inc.*, 788 F.3d 1371 (Fed. Cir. 2015). A commentary on the case and concerning several applications for medical patents that were denied is by Susan Y. Tull, *Patenting the Future of Medicine*: FINNEGAN (Jan/Feb. 2018), https://www.finnegan.com/en/insights/patenting-the-future-of-medicine-the-intersection-of-patent-law-and-artificial-intelligence-in-medicine.html.

cases cited, the commentator of the case stated that it will be up to Congress, the USPTO, and the courts to resolve the issue of subject matter eligibility so that innovation is not stymied.[65]

*Current AI Patent Issues.* A pertinent comment followed by a series of questions and issues made by one intellectual property firm is *Artificial Intelligence: Why AI Inventions Will Disrupt Patent.*[66] Issues raised include whether the advances in AI technology are eligible for patent protection under laws passed which could not have envisioned the escalation of inventions and processes that are daily occurring. Patent laws globally applied to humans performing the creativity in new inventive processes and machines. Are inventions created by machines themselves rather than directly by humans eligible for patent protection? Who is responsible in the event that these nonhuman-created machines cause harm to other persons? At what juncture do the claimed inventions go beyond ineligibility as laws of nature, natural phenomena, and abstract ideas?

Major companies like Apple, Google, Tesla, Microsoft, and other innovative companies are spending extraordinary sums for machine learning algorithms, neural networks, analytics, and other processes and techniques. Images of people, musical compositions, art works, voice-created responses, and the like are almost daily being created by machines initially made by humans, but now virtually or themselves based on the extraordinary data and experiences imputed into the machines. There has been an uptick in the number of machine learning patent applications of many software and business methods patents, escalating over 20 percent from 2016 to 2017 and some 38 percent the following year largely in response to the court's invalidation in *Alice*.[67] As Justice Breyer stated in his conclusion in *Mayo Collaborative* above, "We must hesitate before departing from established general legal rules lest a new protective rule that seems to suit the needs of one field produce unforeseen results in

---

[65] Tull, *id.*

[66] *Artificial Intelligence: Why AI Inventions Will Disrupt Patent*, CILGLOBAL IP LTD. (July 9, 2018), http://www.cilglobalip.com/blog/2018/09/07/artificial-intelligence-why-ai-inventions-will-disrupt-patent-law/.

[67] Brian Higgins, *Patenting Artificial Intelligence: Innovation Spike Follows Broader Market Trend*, ARTIFICIAL INTELLIGENCE TECHNOLOGY AND THE LAW (Dec. 17, 2017), http://aitechnologylaw.com/2017/12/patenting-artificial-intelligence-invention-market-trend/.

another. And we must recognize the role of Congress in crafting more finely tailored rules where necessary…. We need not determine here whether, from a policy perspective, increased protection for discoveries of diagnostic laws of nature is desirable."

A second issue is posed by the requirements of §112(a) of the Patent Act[68] states:

> The specification shall contain a written description of the invention, and of the manner and process of making and using it, in such full, clear, concise, and exact terms as to enable any person skilled in the art to which it pertains, or with which it is most nearly connected, to make and use the same, and shall set forth the best mode contemplated by the inventor or joint inventor of carrying out the invention.

The problem, as noted by two commentators, is that AI inventions may face an almost insurmountable barrier inasmuch as systems are not static remaining as they are but grow and learn as their operations occur. Cited are Google, Tesla, Apple's Siri, Microsoft's Cortana, and other digital assistants that daily inculcate new capabilities by learning from past behavior. With the AI industry spending a projected sum of over $57 billion by 2021 and as further evidenced by the filing of some 9000 new patents over the prior three years, filers of patents have an immense hurdle to overcome. The *Alice* case requirements above cited necessitates that it be shown how the invention or process is a "new and useful application" under the Patent Act. They suggest applicants be able to respond to the type of data that is used, their source how the data is processed; the training algorithm used, and how often they are trained or retrained.[69]

Another commentator suggested that there are three basic challenges that patent applicants are encountering: (1) the sheer volume of information; (2) the language of that information that is non-English and in non-Latin character sets; and (3) the increasing complexity and obscurity

---

[68] 35 U.S. Code §112, Specification.
[69] Christopher White and Hamid R. Piroozi, Protecting Artificial-Intelligence Systems Using Patent Applications, AMERICAN BAR ASSOCIATION (April 25, 2018), https://www.americanbar.org/groups/young_lawyers/publications/tyl/topics/resources-technology/protecting-artificial-intelligence-systems-using-patent-applications/.

of that information.[70] In June, 2018, the 10th million patent was published by the USPTO that is accompanied by over 100 million other patent documents, and over 70 million journal articles. The key statistic cited by the author is that one million took place in just the past three years. Moreover, 62 percent of the 5.6 million patent documents published globally in 2017 are in Chinese, Japanese, or Korean languages. Obviously, the quanta of data are beyond ordinary capabilities of anyone to decipher but AI, through machine learning algorithms and natural language progressing, is able to digest, translate, analyze, and aid in the understanding of the massive volume of documentation. There are varying approaches to effectuate their understanding, ranging from deep learning, artificial neural networks, Bayesian networks,[71] and semantic analysis and indexing.[72]

In *Blue Spike, LLC v. Google Inc.*,[73] the plaintiff asserted its patents' rights were violated by Google, which were "Method and Device for Monitoring and Analyzing Signals." They addressed the creation of "abstracts" (essentially digital fingerprints, hashes, or the like) from various "signals" (electronic versions of human-perceptible works in formats such as audio, visual, audiovisual, or text) based on perceptible qualities inherent to those signals. The abstracts of "reference signals" are added to a reference database. After describing the patents in greater detail, the court determined, after discussing *Alice* and other U.S. Supreme Court precedents, that they were abstract ideas and were not protected under §101 of the Patent Act.

Interestingly, AI is has become a form of intellectual toolbox by empowering interested persons in making patent searches to assess what

---

[70] Bob Stembridge, *Artificial intelligence: Hype vs. reality and the impact on the patent industry*, CLARIVATE ANALYTICS (Aug. 8, 2018), https://clarivate.com/blog/ip-standards/artificial-intelligence-hype-vs-reality-impact-patent-industry/.

[71] A Bayesian network is a type of statistical model that represents a set of variables and their conditional dependencies by use of a directed acyclic graph. Example cited is a graph showing probabilistic relationships between diseases and symptoms. *Bayesian network*, Wikipedia, https://en.wikipedia.org/wiki/Bayesian_network.

[72] Joff Wild, *Artificial intelligence and the future of the patent system*, IAM (July 11, 2018), https://www.iam-media.com/law-policy/artificial-intelligence-and-future-patent-system.

[73] No. 16-1054 (Fed. Cir. 2016). Text of case may be found at https://www.leagle.com/decision/infdco20150909993.

invention or process has been made available to the public and whether it meets the requirements that it be new, an inventive step, and is disclosed clearly and completely. Suggestions are made that avoidance of reduction to nonpatentable mathematical methods may consist of including in the patent application a quantifiable technical parameter and a corresponding test to illustrate that the claimed subject matter provide for a measurable effect. The patent prosecutor should avoid "buzzwords" in favor of terms from a network structure from a functional perspective and precisely define the inputs and outputs of the AI and the training database.[74]

A third issue troubling commentators due to the emergence of AI in its relationship with patent law is "Who is the infringer?" The scenario as envisioned by a patent law firm is the common life cycle of AI-based technology whereby the AI program is developed by one entity, sold to another, operated by a third entity, and trained by a fourth entity which is then used to develop a product which allegedly infringes on a party holding an issued patent. Is the maker of the AI program a direct infringer? The owner thereof? What if the AI program required extensive training to make the product alleged to have infringed on the patent? There are numerous other indirect issues such as: contributory infringement by the creator of the AI program; whether the infringement was knowingly made; where the alleged infringer is located; how to offer proof of infringement; how one pleads infringement; and other related issues.[75]

Given the decisions which appear to narrow the eligibility of subject matter for patent protection, particularly as they relate to the meaning of "abstract idea," the USPTO has attempted to clarify what heretofore has yet to be defined statutorily. In its 2019 Revised Patent Subject Matter Eligibility Guidance and based on federal court decisions,[76] the USPTO

---

[74] Joel Nagerl, Frank Steinbach, and Benedikt Neuberger, *Artificial Intelligence: a game changer for the patent system*, IAM (Sept. 25, 2018), https://www.iam-media.com/artificial-intelligence-game-changer-patent-system.

[75] *Catch Me If You Can: Litigating Artificial Intelligence Patents*, JONESDAY (Dec. 2017), https://www.jonesday.com/catch-me-if-you-can-litigating-artificial-intelligence-patents-12-19-2017/.

[76] United States Patent and Trademark Office, *2019 Revised Patent Subject Matter Eligibility Guidance*, https://www.federalregister.gov/documents/2019/01/07/2018-28282/2019-revised-patent-subject-matter-eligibility-guidance. The PDF version of the Guidance may be found at https://www.govinfo.gov/content/pkg/FR-2019-01-07/pdf/2018-28282.pdf.

defined *abstract idea* exception includes the following groupings of subject matter: "(a) Mathematical concepts—mathematical relationships, mathematical formulas or equations, mathematical calculations; (b) certain methods of organizing human activity—fundamental economic principles or practices including hedging, insurance, mitigating risk; commercial or legal interactions, including agreements in the form of contracts; legal obligations; advertising, marketing or sales activities or behaviors; business relations; managing personal behavior or relationships or interactions between people, including social activities, teaching, and following rules or instructions); and (c) mental processes—concepts performed in the human mind including an observation, evaluation, judgment, opinion."[77]

It does also state: "Claims that do not recite matter that falls within these enumerated groupings of abstract ideas should not be treated as reciting abstract ideas, except as follows: In the rare circumstance in which a USPTO employee believes a claim limitation that does not fall within the enumerated groupings of abstract ideas should nonetheless be treated as reciting an abstract idea, the procedure described in Section III. C for analyzing the claim should be followed." According to one commentator, the definition and guidance when the definition of abstract idea does apply does appear to be less onerous in meeting eligibility.[78]

In a further clarification the revised guidance includes a two-prong inquiry for whether a claim is "directed to" a judicial exception. "In the first prong, examiners will evaluate whether the claim recites a judicial exception and if so, proceed to the second prong. In the second prong, examiners evaluate whether the claim recites additional elements that integrate the identified judicial exception into a practical application." If a claim both recites a judicial exception and fails to integrate that exception into a practical application, then the claim is "directed to" a judicial

---

[77] *Id.* at 52.

[78] Sean P. Ritchie and Terry L. Wright, *New Guidance from the USPTO To Clarify Patent-Eligible Subject Matter Determination*, MONDAQ (Feb. 20, 2019), http://www.mondaq.com/unitedstates/x/782540/Patent/New+Guidance+From+The+USPTO+Aims+To+Clarify+PatentEligible+Subject+Matter+Determination.

exception. In such a case, further analysis pursuant to the second step of the *Alice/Mayo* test is required.[79]

## International Application of Patent Laws and Regulations

We previously addressed China's aggressive AI advancement by the number of patents, particularly in deep learning, that it has published in China, especially since 2017. One estimate is that Chinese entities filed 99 patents (32 percent of 314 filed with WIPO in 2017) largely financed by the Bank of China that concerned blockchain technology, while the U.S. filed 92, and 473 pertaining to AI technology (31 percent) while the U.S. filed 65 patents. The Chinese firm, Baidu, is a leader in the said filings.[80] The problem with evaluating the relative progress in AI technology advancement is the lack of agreement on the analysis of comparative data. Although everyone acknowledges that China is making enormous advances, some commentators question whether it is a matter of quantity versus quality. Although with respect to scholarly papers that were published for the period of 1998–2017 showed that 28 percent were by European authors, China was second with 25 percent and the U.S. with 17 percent, nevertheless, U.S. AI-authors were cited 83 percent more than the global average.[81] Similarly, another study alleges that a report by China's own Tsinghua University stated that China had only one of the top ten global AI patents. It has 18,232 talents compared with 28,526 in the U.S., but only 5.4 percent of the Chinese talents were deemed to be outstanding as compared with 18.1 percent in the U.S.[82]

---

[79] *U.S. Patent and Trademark Office announces revised guidance for determining subject matter eligibility*, U.S. PATENT AND TRADEMARK OFFICE PRESS RELEASE 19-01 (Jan. 4, 2019), https://www.uspto.gov/about-us/news-updates/us-patent-and-trademark-office-announces-revised-guidance-determining-subject.

[80] Antony Peyton, *China bosses blockchain and AI patents*, FINTECH (Jan. 21, 2019), citing UHY, an accounting and consultancy network. https://www.bankingtech.com/2019/01/china-bosses-blockchain-and-ai-patents/.

[81] *The Global AI Race – Which Country is Winning?* NANALYZE (Dec. 31, 2018), citing a Scopus database, https://www.nanalyze.com/2018/12/global-ai-race-country-winning/.

[82] Lance Ng, *U.S. vs China in AI – A Realistic, No B.S. Assessment*, MEDIUM (Nov. 23, 2018), https://medium.com/behind-the-great-wall/us-vs-china-in-ai-a-realistic-no-b-s-assessment-a9cef7909eb6.

Another study was less concerned about the global competition in AI technology than with the fear of the concentration of AI research and ownership of AI products which account for up to 15 percent of the total production of goods. Citing the Release of the UNESCO Science Report of November 2015 and the July 2018 issue of the UNESCO Courier, the fear raised is that the concentration of the technology and the increase in AI customer base to companies will give them a level of power that can have a negative effect on both democracy and the economy. Among the firms cited were Tata of India, the government-owned China National Chemical Corp., the U.S. pharmaceutical Actavis, Qualcomm, and Google.[83]

In a White Paper of the World Economic Forum,[84] the authors arrived at four conclusions: (1) the current legal standard for patent eligibility of AI needs to be carefully evaluated to determine whether the standard has a negative impact on AI and AI-driven technologies; (2) whether AI inventions created entirely by AI should be protected with patents; (3) current laws and regulations failure to adequately determine who should be liable for any harm caused by AI-created inventions; and (4) whether the definition of the patent standard for obviousness, i.e., "person of ordinary skill in the art" with respect to the differences between the subject matter of the proposed invention and the prior art should be reevaluated.

*The New European Patent Office Guidelines.* The European Patent Office (EPO) in its latest clarification of November 1, 2018,[85] stated:

Artificial intelligence and machine learning are based on computational models and algorithms for classification, clustering, regression and dimensionality reduction, such as neural networks, genetic algorithms, support

---

[83] Susan Schneegans [cited as source for the article], *Towards a monopolization of research in artificial intelligence?* UNESCO (July 20, 2018), http://www.unesco.org/new/en/media-services/single-view/news/towards_a_monopolization_of_research_in_artificial_intellige/.

[84] Kay Firth-Butterfield and Yoon Chae, *Artificial Intelligence Collides with Patent Law*, White Paper, WORLD ECONOMIC FORUM (April 2018), http://www3.weforum.org/docs/WEF_48540_WP_End_of_Innovation_Protecting_Patent_Law.pdf.

[85] European Patent Office, *Guidelines for Examination in the European Patent Office*, https://www.epo.org/law-practice/legal-texts/guidelines.html. For a summary of the major changes in the Guidelines, see *Top 9 changes to the 2018 EPO Guidelines for Examination*, KLUWER PATENT BLOG, http://patentblog.kluweriplaw.com/2018/10/01/top-9-changes-2018-epo-guidelines-examination/.

vector machines, k-means, kernel regression and discriminant analysis. Such computational models and algorithms are per se of an abstract mathematical nature, irrespective of whether they can be "trained" based on training data....[86]

Mathematical models are excluded from patentability if directed to a purely mathematical method and the claim does not require any technical means. However, if a claim is targeted either to a method involving the use of technical means (e.g., a computer) or to a device, its subject matter has a technical character as a whole and is thus not excluded from patentability although merely specifying the technical nature of the data or parameters of the mathematical method may not be sufficient for eligibility. If the claimed subject matter as a whole is not excluded from patentability, it is examined in respect of the other requirements of patentability, in particular novelty and inventive step. When the claimed invention is based on a mathematical method, it is assessed whether the mathematical method contributes to the technical character of the invention. A mathematical method may contribute to the technical character of an invention, i.e., contribute to producing a technical effect that serves a technical purpose, by its application to a field of technology and/or by being adapted to a specific technical implementation.[87]

Examples of AI and machine learning that find applications in various fields of technology are the use of a neural network in a heart-monitoring apparatus for the purpose of identifying irregular heartbeats makes a technical contribution and the classification of digital images, videos, audio, or speech signals based on low-level features (e.g., edges or pixel attributes for images). However, classifying text documents solely in respect of their textual content is not regarded to be per se a technical purpose but a linguistic one. Classifying abstract data records or even "telecommunication network data records" without any indication of a technical use being made of the resulting classification is also not per se a

---

[86] G-II 3.3.1 of the *Guidelines*, https://www.epo.org/law-practice/legal-texts/html/guidelines2018/e/g_ii_3_3_1.htm.

[87] G-II 3.3 of the *Guidelines*, https://www.epo.org/law-practice/legal-texts/html/guidelines2018/e/g_ii_3_3.htm.

technical purpose, even if the classification algorithm may be considered to have valuable mathematical properties such as robustness.[88]

A new subcategory of patents that is developing as a result of AI is intellectual property analytics, which is defined by one set of authors "as the data science of analyzing large amounts of intellectual property information to discover relationships, trends, and patterns for decision making."[89] They discussed the use of AI machine learning and deep learning to examine intellectual property articles to find the most relevant published or in press articles to provide a bibliographic analysis, including cumulative citations per article per year, the top journals in which the relevant articles were published, and their various subcategories of knowledge management, technology management, economic value, and extraction and management of information.

There are numerous commentaries regarding the new AI EPO [European Patent Office] Guidelines that appear substantially to be in conformity to current U.S. interpretations. A cautionary note and strategies to be adopted include an evaluation and determination by counsel as to which forum to use in filing for patents, consideration of the Alice restrictions and EPO Guidelines in crafting their filings, and the importance of illustrating a "further technical effect" beyond that of the "normal" physical interactions between the software program and the computer hardware on which it is run.[90]

## Trademarks and AI

Although the effect of AI on trademarks is not as dramatic and all-encompassing as its implications for copyright and patent laws and regu-

[88] G-II 3.3.1 of the *Guidelines*.

[89] Leonidas Aristodemou and Frank Tietze, *The state-of-the-art on Intellectual Property Analytics (IPA): A literature review on artificial intelligence and deep learning methods for analyzing intellectual property (IP) data*, 55 WORLD PATENT INFORMATION, Dec. 2018, 37–51, https://www.researchgate.net/publication/328462093_The_state-of-the-art_on_Intellectual_Property_Analytics_IPA_A_literature_review_on_artificial_intelligence_machine_learning_and_deep_learning_methods_for_analysing_intellectual_property_IP_data.

[90] Michael T. Renaud and Marguerite McConihe, *Key Strategies for Obtaining Patents Under the EPO's New Guidelines*, NATIONAL LAW REVIEW (Jan. 23, 2019), https://www.natlawreview.com/article/key-strategies-obtaining-patents-under-epo-s-new-ai-guidelines.

lations, nevertheless, there are significant implications for this area of intellectual property rights. Two commentators have addressed the four revolutions the way products are purchased from the earlier transition to self-service stores to online retailing via the world wide web, to social media (Facebook, Twitter, Instagram), and the 4th revolution of AI, each of which has had profound effects on how purchases are marketed and branded. Initially, the issue affecting trademarks concerned brand confusion which then expanded to keyword advertising on Google, and currently the effect of AI on consumer preferences. Examples of how AI is influencing consumer brand choices include Amazon's suggested recommendations for purchases such as when a user looks for or orders a novel or a book on any given subject, other suggested titles are immediately made available to the viewer to consider purchasing. Additional examples are Amazon Echo and Google home devices that utilize Alexa's voice recognition software which analyzes the market and has all of relevant branding information.[91]

Trademark law issues that may arise include: Whether the outsourcing to AI-based machines to make product selections for the consumer has any IPRs implications; whether there are liability implications if the AI program recommends the purchase of a product that violates the IPRs of trademark holder; and whether Amazon could be held liable for failure to exhibit the trademarks of particular companies mentioned in its Adword advertisements.

The positive benefits to attorneys and others engaged in trademark searches, as well as their clients, is the reduction in time to conduct searches—estimated at least 50 percent. An added AI feature is the use of algorithms to predict likely outcomes of possible litigation or the best methodology to maximize litigation success. Another area for trademark attorneys is the protection of their clients' brands which are subject to multiple outlets including some 1000 top level domains wherein it may be necessary to register their clients' brand names to be assured they are not improperly asserted by other persons. Individuals using Facebook and other social media often, likely innocently, exhibit products and

---

[91] Lee Curtis and Rachel Platts, *AI is coming and it will change trade mark law*, HGF (Jan. 2018), http://www.hgf.com/updates/news/2018/01/ai-is-coming-and-it-will-change-trade-mark-law/.

services that may violate the IPRs of the particular companies.[92] Attorneys in the U.S. have also to consider the implications the First Amendment freedom of speech, which often have protected individuals who post "sucks" comments about particular companies and their brands. It appears that a revisiting of trademark law is necessary to meet the challenges posed by AI to protected brands and marks.

In our final chapter, the focus is on international efforts with respect to AI. We have already discussed international concerns and responses to specific topics in other chapters. We continue the conversation with a more in depth review of the advances taking place in the E.U., China, the Middle East, Latin America, and Africa. We conclude the chapter and text with a discussion of possible future trends and a brief overview of consciousness and its application to machine technology.

[92] Jayne Durden, *The changing role of the trademark lawyer, managing complexity and generating insight to drive business advantage*, IPWATCHDOG (Jan. 12, 2017), http://www.hgf.com/updates/news/2018/01/ai-is-coming-and-it-will-change-trade-mark-law/.

# 8

# International Initiatives in AI

The U.S. and China are not alone in their efforts to attain AI supremacy, which has major implications that flow from mastering the technologies associated with it. Other countries and political and economic unions globally, particularly the European Union, are profoundly aware of how AI will impact their nationals. We discuss some of the global developments that are occurring in these nation-states and union to maintain their competitive status.

## European Union (E.U.) and AI

### Declaration of 2018

The E.U. is cognizant of the need for the growth of AI but also the importance of regulation to curb inevitable abuses that may arise from its exponential growth. Accordingly, E.U. Member States signed a Declaration of Cooperation on Artificial Intelligence on April 25, 2018 whereby they agreed to coordinate forces and efforts to compete effectively, mainly with the U.S. and China, in research and development (R&D) of AI but

© The Author(s) 2020
R. Girasa, *Artificial Intelligence as a Disruptive Technology*,
https://doi.org/10.1007/978-3-030-35975-1_8

also to deal with social, economic, ethical, and legal issues in relation thereto.[1] Its coordinated plan on AI between the EU Commission, E.U. member states, Norway, and Switzerland, aims to cover collaborative cross-border activity to increase investment in AI, encourage talent and progress in R&D, widen availability of data, and increase trust among the parties to the plan.[2] The plan is not binding on member states, although the E.U. Commission is exploring national and safety and liability frameworks brought about by the new challenges.

The Commission intends to form public and private partnerships with companies and research organizations to develop a common strategic research agenda on AI which defines priorities and needs of the market and participants. Particular emphasis will be on robotics and big data, while assuring that AI "made in Europe" is ethically sound. The Commission is also proposing the establishment of an enhanced European Innovation Council as part of its program for Research and Innovation, Horizon Europe (2021–2027).[3] The Commission appointed a new 52-member High Level Expert Group on Artificial Intelligence to support the implementation of the European strategy on AI, whose roles include advice on long-term challenges and opportunities, suggested ethical guidelines, and further engagement and outreach mechanisms to interact with stakeholders in the context of AI.[4]

## Communication of 2018

The E.U. Commission issued a *Communication*[5] relating to AI in April 2018 wherein it provided information concerning the embrace of AI

---

[1] European Union, *EU Member States sign up to cooperate on Artificial Intelligence* (April 10, 2018), https://ec.europa.eu/digital-single-market/en/news/eu-member-states-sign-cooperate-artificial-intelligence.

[2] European Union, *Coordinated plan on AI to boost development in Europe* (Dec. 10, 2018), https://www.governmenteuropa.eu/coordinated-plan-on-ai-development/91451/.

[3] European Union, *Questions and Answers: coordinated plan for Artificial Intelligence made in Europe* (Dec. 7, 2018), http://europa.eu/rapid/press-release_MEMO-18-6690_en.htm.

[4] European Union, *High-Level Expert Group on Artificial Intelligence*, https://ec.europa.eu/digital-single-market/en/high-level-expert-group-artificial-intelligence.

[5] An E.U. Communication is one issued by the Commission's Directorate-General for Communication, whose duties include making the public aware of E.U.'s political priorities and

changes, the E.U.'s position in a competitive international landscape, and its initiative for the way forward. While noting that the U.S. has expended large resources both governmentally and privately and China's "Next Generation Artificial Intelligence Development Plan," it stated that Europe has lagged behind to date. In the way forward, it is seeking substantial increases in funding by 2020 from €4.5 billion in 2017 to €20 billion by the end of 2020 and the said sum continuing annually thereafter for the decade. Research and development programs are to be conducted in part through the E.U.'s program Horizon 2020, the European Innovation Council, the more than 400 Digital Innovation Hubs and additions thereto, by upgrading AI excellence centers and other programs aimed at AI enhancement.[6]

Respecting socioeconomic changes, the Commission is cognizant of the effect on work by the emergence of new technologies, particularly, after being presented with the development of automation and robotics. While making life easier for workers by ending repetitive tasks, nevertheless, there are major issues wrought by the technological occurrences. Three main challenges that the Commission has identified are: (1) to prepare society as a whole, i.e., to aid Europeans to develop basic digital skills, that are complementary to and lacking in the innovations such as critical thinking, creativity, and management; (2) the need to focus efforts to help workers in jobs that will be transformed or disappear by means of ensuring access for all citizens to social protection in line with the European Pillar of Social Rights; and (3) the need to train more AI specialists through education, creation of the right environment for specialists to work, and attract more foreign talent.[7]

---

developments, act as spokesperson for the Commission, interact with other E.U. institutions, and inform the Commission of public opinion. European Commission, *Communication*, https://ec.europa.eu/info/departments/communication_en.

[6] European Commission, *Communication from the Commission to the European Parliament, the European Council, the Council, the European Economic and Social committee and the Committee of the Regions: Artificial Intelligence*, https://ec.europa.eu/commission/news/artificial-intelligence-2018-dec-07_en.

[7] *Id.*

Initiatives commenced by the E.U. Commission to enhance job skills for the new labor market include a "New Skills Agenda for Europe,"[8] which includes a Recommendation for Member States on "Upskilling Pathways: New Opportunities for Adults"[9] to improve basic literacy, mathematic, and digital skills; a Recommendation for lifelong learning, particularly in the sciences, technology, engineering, and mathematics; and "Digital Opportunity Traineeships"[10] that support internships for individuals to acquire digital skills in conjunction with the Digital Skills and Jobs Coalition. The efforts are to continue through 2020 with continuing updates, reports on the impact of AI in education, pilot programs for predictions on future competency profiles, and publication of export report addressing the job market.[11]

## General Data Protection

Ethical concerns are also addressed, particularly with respect to privacy and data protection. The European Union, due to the dire historical past emanating from World War II, has been particularly sensitive to privacy concerns. Accordingly, the European Union promulgated Directive 95/46 on October 24, 1995, which gave extensive protection to the privacy right of individuals that far exceeded comparable protections in other parts of the world, including the U.S.[12] The 2016 General Data Protection Regulation (GDPR)[13] superseded the 1995 Directive

---

[8] European Commission, *New Skills Agenda for Europe*, http://ec.europa.eu/legal-content/EN/TXT/?uri=CELEX:5201DC0381.

[9] European Commission, *Digital Education Action Plan*, https://ec.europa.eu/education/sites/education/files/digital-education-action-action-plan.pdf.

[10] European Commission, *Digital Opportunity Traineeships*, https://ec.europa.eu/digital-single-market/en/digital-opportunity-traineeships-boosting-digital-skills-job.

[11] *Id.*

[12] European Union, Directive 95/46/EC of the European Parliament and of the Council of 24 October 1995 on the protection of individuals with regard to the processing of personal data and on the free movement of such data. https://eur-lex.europa.en/legal-content/en/TXT/?uri=CELEX%3A31995L0046.

[13] European Union, *General Data Protection Plan*, Regulation (EU) 2016/679 protection of natural persons with regard to the processing of personal data and the free movement of such data, https://eur-lex.europa.en/eli/reg/2016/679/oj.

governing comparable areas by updating the data protection and privacy not only within the E.U. but also the European Economic Area. The European Data Protection Regulation is applicable as of May 25th, 2018 to all member states requiring them to harmonize data privacy laws across Europe.

A summary of the GDPR encompasses the rights of citizens and rules for businesses. With respect to citizens' rights, the 2016 Regulation adds to the rights of citizens of the E.U. by giving them greater control over their personal data by making it easier to access their data; grants a new right of data portability by enhancing the transmittal of personal data between service providers; enables individuals a clearer right to be forgotten by removing data such persons want deleted; and gives a right to know when the person's personal data has been hacked. Concerning businesses, there is a single set of E.U.-wide rules for data protection; the establishment of a data protection officer responsible for the data protection; a one-stop-shop for businesses wishing to communicate with a supervisory authority; rules governing non-E.U. companies; innovation-friendly rules; privacy-friendly techniques and encryption; removal of notifications, making it easier for businesses to the free flow of personal data within the E.U.; impact assessments; and an easing of record-keeping where data processing is unlikely to result in misuse of personal data.[14]

The problem for companies doing business in or with the E.U. lies at the essence of AI, namely, data collection. China is considered a major threat to the U.S. and its allies by its ability to gather huge troves of data that can used for both social and military AI purposes. Because of the restrictive nature of E.U. data collection, the Regulation thus strikes at the heart of data collection, making big data ostensibly less vital due to its limited capabilities. Machine learning algorithms, gathering of speech and visual patterns, and other modes of marshaling data appear to directly run afoul of the Regulation which requires explicit consent from persons whose data is being collected. Companies affected have to explain the purposes for the data collection; impose limitations to need for doing so; erase the data when no longer required; and obey other restrictions which

---

[14] EUR-Lex, *Summaries of EU Legislation*, https://eur-lex.europa.en/legal-content/EN/TXT/?uri=LEGISUM:310401_2.

would limit accessibility and thus usage while, at the same time, facing competitors like China which are not subject to the limitations.[15] Thus, the conundrum which the E.U. must confront, namely, whether the protection of privacy rights impedes E.U. AI advancement.

## Robotics

The Committee of Legal Affairs issued a Report on January 27, 2017 with recommendations to the Commission on Civil Law Rules on Robotics.[16] The Committee was cognizant of the fact that humankind is on the threshold of a new era whereby sophisticated robots, bots, androids, and other manifestations of AI will bring about a new industrial revolution affecting all of society and having legal and ethical implications. While acknowledging the many benefits from the use of robots in enhancing human life span, and economic and innovative benefits, nevertheless, there are major disruptions that will occur particularly in the workforce among low-skilled employees. Accordingly, the Committee called upon the Commission to address general principles concerning the development of robotics and AI for civil use.[17]

Additional recommendations include the need for enhanced cooperation among the Member States with cross-border rules that encourages cooperation; the designation of a European Agency for robotics and AI; protection of intellectual property rights and the flow of data by providing that existing legal regimes and doctrines be applied to robotics; and that the regulation of robotics be consistent with the General Data Protection Regulation especially regarding privacy rights and security.

Among the general principles are the need for common definitions of cyber physical systems, autonomous systems, smart autonomous robots, and their subcategories. A comprehensive E.U. system of registration of advanced robots should be implemented coupled with the need to aid

---

[15] David Meyer, *AI Has a Big Privacy Problem and Europe's New Data Protection Law Is About to Expose It*, Fortune (May 25, 2018), http://fortune.com/2018/05/25/ai-machine-learning-privacy-gdpr/.

[16] European Union, *AI Policy – European Union*, https://futureoflife.org/ai-policy-european-union/.

[17] The Recommendations may be found at http://www.europarl.europa.eu/sides/getDoc.do?pubRef=-//EP//TEXT+REPORT+A8-2017-0005+0+DOC+XML+V0//EN.

small and medium size businesses to create or make use of robots. Emphasis should be on robots complementing human capabilities rather than their replacement to assure human control over intelligent machines at all times. Specific recommendations were made with respect to robotics concerning research and innovation, ethical principles, and intellectual property rights. Also addressed are autonomous means of transport which includes autonomous vehicles and drones. The Committee called upon the Commission to strengthen financial instruments for research projects in robotics; foster research programs such as long-term risks and opportunities; set up of a framework to meet the connectivity requirements for the E.U. digital future; promote an open environment with open standards; and initiate innovative licensing models, open platforms, and transparency.[18]

The Report addressed autonomous means of transport covering the wide range of transportation that may be remotely monitored, automated, connected, and autonomous ways of road, waterborne and air, trains, aircrafts, and related means. Particular attention was devoted to autonomous vehicles and emphasized the critical importance of reliable positioning and timing information provided by E.U. satellites. Drone technology was also covered with stress on the need for the E.U. to protect the safety, security, and privacy of citizens. The Report emphasized the need for the Commission to provide for obligatory tracking and identification system. It also discussed the need for robot research and development of care robots for the elderly, while recognizing that robots should not replace the important social interaction with other humans. Medical robots are discussed with emphasis on how they may make inroads into high accuracy surgery and perform repetitive procedures to improve patients' outcomes. It calls upon the Commission to ensure the procedures for testing new robotic devices are safe especially those implanted within the human body. Robots will have a major place in repairing and compensating for damaged organs and human functions but the Report warns of hacking consequences and the need for equal access to all such innovative tools.[19]

---

[18] *Id.* at 5.
[19] *Id.* at 7–8.

Additional concerns addressed by the Report were the need to provide education whereby it is projected that, by 2020, Europe may be facing a shortage of up to 825,000 professionals, which will be required for 90 percent of jobs that necessitate knowledge of at least basic digital skills. Thus, the Report calls upon the Commission to provide a roadmap for use and revision of a Digital Competence framework and descriptors of Digital Competencies for all levels of learners. Particular attention is to be paid to training of young women in digital jobs; the analysis of medium- and long-term job trends; the consequences to the social security systems of the Member States; and the improvement of safety in the workplace by the use of robots. The environmental impact was also given emphasis in that robotics and AI can foster effective energy consumption and efficiency. Legal issues to be addressed are liability for damage caused by robots and the establishment of a compulsory insurance scheme to address harms caused by robots.[20]

Research in robotics will continue to be a major priority for the E.U. Since 2010, it has sponsored the European Robotics Forum (ERF) that meets annually, with the latest being held in Bucharest, capital of Romania, on March 20–22, 2019. ERF2019 featured exhibits of companies, universities, and research institutes of their latest robotics' outputs. Ethical issues were also discussed among its 50 plus workshops at the meetings.[21] ERF2018, held in Tampere, Finland, included some 900 scientists, companies, and policymakers who deliberated current societal and technical themes including human-robot collaboration and how robotics can enhance industrial production and service sector operations.[22] Funding, in coordination with SPARC (the Scholarly Publishing and Academic Resources Coalition) and the Partnership for Robotics in Europe, has been allocated sums of €700 million from the E.U. and €2.1 billion from industry. It is anticipated that robotics in Europe will be the major technological-driving technology underlying autonomous

---

[20] *Id.* at 9–11.

[21] European Commission, *European Robotics Forum 2019*, Horizon 2020, https://www.h2020.md/en/european-robotics-forum-2019.

[22] Robohub, European Robotics Forum 2018: Over 900 roboticists meet in Tampere, Finland, https://robohub.org/european-robotics-forum-2018-over-900-roboticists-meet-in-tampere-finland/.

devices and cognitive artifacts and currently is the key driver in large scale manufacturing and will have disruptive effects in the service industry.[23]

## E.U. Commission's Draft AI Guidelines

The E.U. Commission's High-Level Expert Group on Artificial Intelligence released a first draft of its proposed ethics guidelines for the development and use of AI in June, 2018.[24] It sought feedback from stakeholders respecting AI and data protection, such as the future of work, fairness, safety, security, social inclusion, and algorithmic transparency. Accordingly, after receipt of comments over a period of several months, it issued a draft Ethics Guidelines for Trustworthy AI on December 18, 2018.[25] The Commission's vision for Europe concerning AI, as set forth in its Communications of April 25, 2018 and December 7, 2018, was three-fold, namely, (1) increasing public and private investments in AI to boost its uptake, (2) preparing for socioeconomic changes, and (3) ensuring an appropriate ethical and legal framework to strengthen European values.

The Commission's Framework for Trustworthy AI, as set forth in three chapters, commences with (1) *ethical purpose*, i.e., ensure respect of fundamental rights, principles, and values when developing, deploying, and using AI to a (2) *realization of trustworthy AI*, i.e., ensure implementation of ethical purpose as well as technical robustness when developing, deploying, and using AI. The requirements for a trustworthy AI are that it is to be continuously evaluated, addressed, and assessed in the design

---

[23] SPARC, *Robotics in Europe – Why is Robotics Important?*, https://www.eu-robotics.net/sparc/about/robotics-in-europe/index.html.

[24] European Commission Digital Single Market, *Have your say: European expert group seeks feedback on draft ethics guidelines for trustworthy artificial intelligence*, DIGIBYTE (Dec. 18, 2018), https://ec.europa.eu/digital-single-market/en/news/have-your-say-european-expert-group-seeks-feedback-draft-ethics-guidelines-trustworthy.

[25] Eur. Comm'n High-Level Group on Artificial Intelligence, *Draft Ethics Guidelines for Trustworthy AI* (Dec. 18, 2018), https://ec.europa.eu/futurium/en/system/files/ged/ai_hleg_draft_ethics_guidelines_18_december.pdf.

and use phase through technical methods and nontechnical methods. Added thereto is (3) *assessment list for trustworthy AI* based on use cases.[26]

The ethical principals in the context of AI as set forth in the guidelines are: (1) the *Principal of Beneficence*—i.e., to do good by generating prosperity, value creation, and improve well-being for all including protection of democratic values and the rule of law together with protection of the environment, social equity, and economic development; (2) the *Principal of Non Maleficence*, i.e., to do no harm by avoidance of discrimination in data collection including manipulation or negative profiling; (3) the *Principal of Autonomy*, i.e., preserve human agency by freedom from subordination to AI systems by human control accompanied by responsibility and accountability; and (4) the *Principal of Explicability*, i.e., operate transparently, whereby AI systems are auditable, comprehensible, and intelligible coupled with informed consent of individuals interacting with the systems.[27]

The major concerns of the Guidelines are (1) identification without consent of individuals and entities under surveillance; (2) covert AI systems that conceal their applications and connections with individuals including use of robots that appear to be humans; (3) normative and mass citizen scoring without consent in deviation of fundamental rights; (4) lethal autonomous weapons systems that may lead to operations without human control; and (5) potential long-term concerns such as the development of AI artificial consciousness (AI superintelligence).

By *trustworthy*, the Commission noted that the term has two components, (1) its development, deployment, and use should respect fundamental rights and applicable regulation, as well as core principles and values, ensuring an "ethical purpose," and (2) it should be technically robust and reliable. The goal of *ethics*, according to the document, is to identify how AI can advance or raise concerns to the good life of individuals; whether this be in terms of quality of life, mental autonomy, or freedom to live in a democratic society; and issues of diversity, inclusion, and distributive justice.[28]

---

[26] *Id.* at 4.
[27] *Id.* at 8–10.
[28] *Id.* at 1–2.

The Guidelines set forth the requirements of trustworthy AI, which are: (1) *accountability* from monetary compensation to fault finding; (2) *data governance* by assurance of bias elimination and integrity of datasets; (3) *design for all*, i.e., all citizens to use the products or services regardless of age, disability, or status; (4) *governance of AI autonomy by human oversight* to assure proper behavior of the systems and human intervention depending on social impact of the systems; (5) *non-discrimination* either directly or indirectly due to biases, incompleteness, or bad governance models; (6) *respect for and enhancement of human autonomy* by upholding rights, values, principles, and protection of individuals from governmental and private abuses; (7) *respect for privacy* and data protection at all stages of the AI life cycle system; (8) *robustness* by reliability and reproducibility, accuracy, resilience to attack, and a fall back plan; (9) *safety* by prevention of harm to human users, resources, or the environment; and (10) *transparency* by explainability, i.e., being explicit and open about choices and decisions concerning data sources, development processes, and stakeholders.[29]

The third prong in the Guidelines is that of technical and nontechnical methods to achieve a trustworthy AI. For guidance on technical methods, they provide: (1) *ethics and the rule of law by design* to provide linkage between abstract principles and specific implementation decisions that are accessible and justified by legal rules or societal norms such as by *privacy-by-design* or *security-by-design*; (2) *architecture for trustworthy AI*, i.e., be translated into procedures or constraints on procedures anchored into the AI system's architecture; (3) *testing and validating* by careful monitoring regarding stability, robustness, and operation in well-understood and predictable bounds; (4) *traceability and auditability*, i.e., laypersons should be able to understand the causality of algorithmic decision-making processes that affect them and there should be auditors who can conduct evaluations of the systems; and (5) *explanation*, i.e., ability to giver clear reasons for the interpretation and decisions of the systems.[30]

---

[29] *Id.* at 14–18.
[30] *Id.* at 19–21.

The nontechnical methods are: (1) *regulation* by applicable laws; (2) *standardization* for design. Manufacturing, and business practices; (3) *accountability governance* both internally and externally; (4) *codes of conduct* by the organizations using AI systems; (5) *education and awareness to foster an ethical mind-set*; (6) *stakeholder and social* dialogue by availability to all Europeans and involvement of social partners, stakeholders, and the general public; and (7) *diversity and inclusive design teams* in AI systems to reflect the diversity of users and society in general.[31]

The said guidelines are to be promulgated in coordination with the European Group on Ethics in Science and New Technologies. AI will be examined in relation to its suitability of established rules on safety and civil law questions of liability. Examples given include how advanced robots and Internet of Things products empowered by AI may behave in ways not previously anticipated. There are safety concerns which will require the development of and imposition of standards to address intended use and foreseeable misuse of AI generated products. There are currently revaluations of the Product Liability Directive[32] and the Machinery Directive[33] and AI impact thereon. It is projected that a guidance will be issued in the near future concerning these Directives and a report rendered on the broader implications of AI concerning liability and safety. The European Parliament has proposed research on Algorithmic Awareness Building[34] to gather evidence and support the design of policy responses brought about by automated decision-making.

The E.U. has indicated that the most common ethical issues addressed among member states are the involvement of children, patients, and vulnerable populations; the use of human embryonic stem cells; privacy and data protection issues; and research on animals and nonhuman primates. Increasingly, E.U. companies appear to evade data restrictions by a pro-

---

[31] *Id.* at 21–23.

[32] Council Directive 85/374/EEC of 25 July 1985 on the approximation of the laws, regulations, and administrative provisions of the Member States concerning liability for defective products, https://eur-lex.europa.eu/legal-content/EN/TXT/?uri=celex:31985L0374.

[33] The Machinery Directive, Directive 2006/42/EC of the European Parliament and of the Council of 17 May 2006 I, https://eur-lex.europa.eu/legal-content/EN/TXT/?uri=CELEX:32006L0042.

[34] European Parliament, Algorithmic Awareness Building, https://ec.europa.eu/digital-single-market/en/algorithmic-awareness-building.

cess called "ethics dumping," whereby they perform or outsource otherwise unethical activities such as fabrication, plagiarism, falsification, or other research misconduct in countries having less restrictive measures forbidding them. The new guidelines being drafted in the E.U. calls upon member states to have a uniform methodology to investigate and prevent the misconduct.[35] Also troubling to the E.U. is the problem of bias as to gender and race, when AI is used to hire workers, grant loans, and other practices. E.C. guidelines are being drafted to address this additional concern of the E.U. Some companies like Google have drafted their own ethics guidelines on hiring, promotion, and other work-related endeavors.[36]

## Safety Measures and Liability

The E.U. has a number of Directives that hinder unrestrictive use of AI technologies. They are the *Machinery Directive*, the *Medical Devices Directive*, the *Framework Directive on Health and Safety at Work*, the *Directive on the Use of Work Equipment*, and the *Products Liability Directive*.[37] The Directives that most apply to AI-based technologies are: The Machinery Directive, which is binding on all member states, concerns health and safety requirements for products including robots and 3D printers. There is freedom of movement for all machinery within the E.U., which is applicable to manufacturers, distributors, and users thereof. The Directive has left open additional requirements that may be instituted as new technologies emerge.[38] The Product Liability Directive provides for the compensation of persons who may become injured in the

---

[35] European Commission, *Ethics Horizon 2020*, https://ec.europa.eu/programmes/horizon2020/en/h2020-section/ethics.

[36] Yuichiro Kanematsu and Manabu Morimoto, *EU ethical guidelines to tackle AI's racial and gender bias*, Nikkei Asian Review (Nov. 6, 2018), https://asia.nikkei.com/Politics/EU-ethical-guidelines-to-tackle-AI-s-racial-and-gender-bias.

[37] Cecile Huet, *European Commission's Initiatives in Artificial Intelligence*, https://www.eu-robotics.net/sparc/about/robotics-in-europe/index.html.

[38] The Machinery Directive, Directive 2006/42/EC of the European Parliament and of the Council of May 17, 2006, http://ec.europa.eu/growth/single-market/european-standards/harmonised-standards/machinery_en.

event of a manufactured product deficiency. An interpretive guidance will be issued which will cover products arising from new technologies. Like that of product liability legislation in individual states within the U.S., it includes liability without fault of the manufacturer, i.e., there is liability if a product is manufactured defectively, even without fault of the company manufacturing the product, which causes injury to the consumer of the product without possible exception for misuse or knowingly using a defective product.[39]

## Member States Initiatives

Individual Member States of the E.U. have made significant contributions to AI. A sampling of efforts made are as follows.

*United Kingdom.* The Alan Turing Institute, a national institute for data science, is composed of 11 universities and one research council whose mission is to change the world for the benefit of inhabitants through data science research. The U.K. government has increased support for future industries such as AI, Internet of Things, and electric vehicles. The U.K. Science & Innovation Network and the Department of International Trade are attempting to increase understanding, awareness, and knowledge of foreign AI ecosystems, the U.K.'s AI strategies and capabilities, and strengthen partnerships between the U.K. and foreign organizations. The U.K. government on Growing the Artificial Intelligence Industry in the U.K. has made extensive efforts to prepare individuals to seek advanced degrees in AI, create greater diversity in the AI workforce, and support and promote the public sector use of AI.[40]

*Germany.* Germany has made extensive efforts for the promotion of AI funded by both governmental and corporate entities, particularly, Siemens, BMW, Bosch, SAP, and Telecom. The German Informatics Society and the Section for AI (FBKI) and ten special interest groups

---

[39] Product Liability Directive 85/374/EEC, of July, 1985, https://osha.europa.eu/en/legislation/directives/council-directive-85-374-eec.

[40] European Commission, *The European Artificial Intelligence Landscape: Workshop Report*, p. 27, https://ec.europa.eu/digital-single-market/en/news/european-artificial-intelligence-landscape.

have hosted conferences on AI. There are some 90 chairs for AI at universities and a number of research centers including the German Research Centre for AI, the Max-Planck-Institutes for Intelligent Systems, and other institutes. The government has invested extensive funding under the auspices of the Federal Ministry of Education and Research with current annual funding of €40–50 million.[41]

*France.* The France IA Strategy was published in 2017 in which the Prime Minister requested the mathematician and member of Parliament, Cedric Villani, to produce an in-depth report termed the *Villani Report,* in 2018, which outlines the development of an aggressive data policy; boosts the potential of French research; targets four strategic areas; plans for the impact of AI on labor; makes IA more environmentally friendly; opens up the black boxes of AI; and ensures that AI supports inclusivity and diversity. Priority was given to health care, the environment, transport, and defense.[42]

*Finland.* It has been asserted that Finland has made the most extensive progress in Europe with respect to AI and that it purportedly would rank second only to the U.S. to benefit from AI. Its Ministry of Economic Affairs and Employment of Finland is actively engaged in the promotion of AI to spur its usage particularly for defense, economic growth, and especially its use in health care. Its Cognitive Healthcare Vision will transform health care through use of AI for extensive data supporting decision-making; visualization complements traditional ways of working; emphasis of shifts from routine to demanding cases; better access to health services; and other initiatives.[43]

Other E.U. national initiatives include: E.U.'s controversial AI lie detectors being installed at border control checkpoints especially in Hungary, Latvia, and Greece whereby travelers are asked certain questions digitally. The AI-based system then analyzes 38 micro-gestures in scoring points that may give rise to detection of persons possibly lying about their status at which point human officials then intervene. Airports

---

[41] *Id.* at 11.
[42] *Id.* at 10–11.
[43] *Id.* at 8–9.

in Europe and elsewhere appear likely to impose comparable virtual lie detector tests but not without controversy from privacy organizations.[44] Other initiatives include: Denmark's Odense robotics cluster and Startup Hub; Ireland's Insight and UTRC, which is one of 80 funding partners of Insight Research Centre that explores research in AI, data analytics, machine learning, and human-machine interaction; Italy's Italian Association for AI composed of over 900 members with emphasis on machine learning, deep learning, robotics, and other related areas; Norway's strong emphasis on digitalization and commitment to responsible business and ethical AI; Sweden's AI Society, which promotes research and applications of AI; and other national initiatives.[45] Whether or not Europe can compete with the U.S. and China remains in doubt. It has been suggested that Europe pool its resources from national efforts and lead AI initiatives that protect privacy and set ethical stands for all nationals to follow.[46]

# China and AI

## New Generation of Artificial Development Plan

The E.U. acknowledged that its two greatest competitors in AI are the U.S. and China.[47] China is projected to invest some $1.6 trillion in AI and AI-related industries by the year 2030. It accounts for over half of all AI global expenditures for the past five years and expects to increase its AI

---

[44] Melanie Ehrenkranz, *An AI Lie Detector Is Going to Start Questioning Travelers in the EU*, GIZMODO (Oct. 31, 2018), https://gizmodo.com/an-ai-lie-detector-is-going-to-start-questioning-travel-1830126881. Airport adoption and controversy is discussed briefly by Tyler Durden, *Controversial AI 'Lie Detectors' Coming to EU Airports, Border Crossings*, ZEROHEDGE (Nov. 5, 2018), https://www.zerohedge.com/news/2018-11-01/ai-lie-detectors-tests-coming-eu-airports.

[45] *Id.*

[46] *How Europe can improve the development of AI*, THE ECONOMIST (Sept. 22, 2018), https://www.economist.com/leaders/2018/09/22/how-europe-can-improve-the-development-of-ai.

[47] European Union, *supra*, note 660 at 5.

investment tenfold in the next three years.[48] China's State Council announced and released its *New Generation of Artificial Development Plan AI* which was completed and released in July, 2017.[49] The Plan is divided into several sections. It begins with a comment that AI will profoundly change human society and life and change the world. Thus, the mission of the Plan is "to seize the major strategic opportunity for the development of AI, to build China's first-mover advantage in the development of AI, to accelerate the construction of an innovative nation and global power in science and technology."

## I. The Strategic Situation

The Plan began with an analysis of *I. The Strategic Situation* in which it noted that the development of AI has reached a new stage, especially mobile Internet, big data, supercomputing, sensor networks, brain science, and other new theories and technologies. It has accelerated deep learning, cross-domain integration, man-machine collaboration, the opening of swarm intelligence,[50] and autonomous control.

AI, as the focus of international competition, requires China to seize the initiative in AI in order to enhance national security and attain social and economic benefits for its citizens. As a disruptive technology, AI may cause the transformation of employment structures, impact legal and social theories, violate privacy rights, and other areas in China. It already leads globally in the publication of scientific papers on AI, in the number of inventions that have been patented, in voice recognition and in visual

---

[48] Ian Burrows, *Made in China 2025: XI Jinping's plan to turn China into the AI world leader*, ABC (Oct. 5, 2018) https://www.abc.net.au/news/2018-10-06/china-plans-to-become-ai-world-leader/10332614.

[49] Peoples Republic of China, *State Council Notice on the Issuance of the Next Generation Artificial Intelligence Development Plan*, completed July 8, 29017, released on July 20, 2017. The translation of the plan was by Graham Webster, Paul Triolo, Elsa Kania, and Rogier Creemer, *Full Translation: China's 'New Generation Artificial Intelligence Development Plan'* (2017), https://www.newamerica.org/cybersecurity-initiative/digichina/blog/full-translation-chinas-new-generation-artificial-intelligence-development-plan-2017/.

[50] "Swarm intelligence" is the collective behavior of decentralized, self-organized systems, natural or artificial, WIKIPEDIA, https://en.wikipedia.org/wiki/Swarm_intelligence.

recognition technologies, in adaptive autonomous learning, intuitive sensing, and other related areas. Nevertheless, China recognizes its short-comings in basic theory, core algorithms, key equipment, high-end chips, and several other areas.

## II. The Overall Requirements

The Plan then stated *The Overall Requirements*, which is divided in a discussion of the guiding ideology, basic principles, strategic objectives, and overall deployment. Its guiding ideology is the implementation of the policies set forth at the 18th Party Congress, its Plenary Sessions, and the leadership of General Secretary Xi Jinping that stresses the implementation of innovation-driven development strategy to accelerate the deep integration of AI with economy, society, and national defense. The Basic Principles stresses technology-led global development trend of AI, the ability of its communist ideology to concentrate forces to do major undertakings, promote planning and layout of projects, and a talent pool able to carry out the principals. It seeks to be market-dominant, be open-source, and open to industry, academia, research, and production units. For Strategic Objectives, AI development is to take place in three steps.

- By 2020, China will be in step with other major global players whereby AI will become an important engine for economic growth by making extensive progress in big data- cross-medium-, swarm-, hybrid enhanced-, and autonomous-intelligence. It also will have achieved important progress in other foundational theories and core technologies as well as advances in AI models and methods, core devices, high-end equipment, and foundational software. It will have achieved first echelon status, nurtured industries to invest 1 trillion RMB (approximately $144.7 billion, €113 billion).
- By 2025, China expects breakthroughs in AI theory and technology systems, whereby AI industries will enter into a global high-value chain and widely used in intelligent manufacturing, medicine, city, and agriculture, national defense construction, and establish laws and

regulations addressing ethical norms and policy systems, and formation of AI security assessment and control capabilities.

- By 2030, AI applications will have made China into the world's leading AI innovation center with significant results in an intelligent economy and intelligent society applications. Major breakthroughs in each of the areas discussed in 2020 will have taken place and allowing AI to be deeply expansive in the economy and an expensive core technology for key systems, support platforms, and intelligent application of a complete industrial chain and high-end clusters. The scale of AI industries will exceed 10 trillion RMB ($1.44 trillion). China will possess world leading AI technology innovation and personnel training centers and will have comprehensive laws and regulations coupled with ethical norms and policy systems.

Its Overall Deployment will be accomplished by construction of an open and cooperative AI technology innovation system; grasp AI's characteristic high degree of integration of technological attributes and social attributes; adherence to the promotion of the trinity of breakthroughs in AI research and development, product applications, and fostering industry development; and full support science and technology, the economy, social development, and national security.[51]

## III. Focus Tasks

In order to accomplish the goals stated above, the following tasks have been identified to be accomplished.

- Build open and coordinated AI science and technology innovation centers by increasing the supply of available AI sources; strengthen deployment of teams to stimulate enhanced capabilities; establish basic theory systems for a new generation; make breakthroughs in basic application theory bottlenecks; arrange advanced basic theoretical research; and launch cross-disciplinary exploratory research.

---

[51] *Id.*

- Build a next generation AI key general technology system with focus on knowledge computing engine and knowledge service technology; cross-medium analytical reasoning technology; key swarm intelligence theory; new architecture and new technology for hybrid and enhanced intelligence; intelligent technologies of autonomous unmanned systems; intelligent virtual reality modeling technology; intelligent computing chips and systems; and natural language processing technology.
- Coordinate the layout of AI innovation platforms by strengthening the foundational support for AI research and development and applications.
- Accelerate the training and gathering of high-end AI talent; cultivate high-level of AI innovative talents and teams; increase the introduction of high-end AI talent; and construct an AI academic discipline; foster a high-end, highly efficient smart economy; forcefully develop new AI industries for smart software and hardware; smart robots; smart delivery tools; virtual reality and augmented reality; smart terminals; and basic Internet of Things devices; accelerate and promote the upgrade of industrial intelligentization in smart contracts, smart agriculture, smart logistics, smart finance, smart commerce, and smart household goods.
- Forcefully develop smart enterprises by promoting the upgrade of enterprises' smartness levels on a large scale; popularizing the use of smart factories; and accelerating the fostering of AI industry-leading by developing convenient and efficient intelligent services; intelligent education.
- Create AI innovation heights by the launch of AI innovation application pilot demonstrations; construct national AI industrial parks; and construct national AI mass innovation bases.
- Construct a safe and convenient intelligent society through the application of innovative AI throughout intelligent education, health care, pension, and other urgent needs.
- Promote the intelligentization of social governance though intelligent government, smart courts, smart cities, smart transportation, and intelligent environmental protection.
- Use AI to enhance public safety and security capabilities.
- Promote social interaction and mutual trust.

- Strengthen military-civilian integration in the AI domain.
- Build a safe and efficient intelligent infrastructure system, and
- Plan a new generation of AI major science and technology projects.

## IV. Resource Allocation

The Plan is to establish financial support mechanisms guided by the administration and dominated by tMe market; optimize arrangements to build AI innovation bases; and comprehensively plan international and domestic innovation resources.

## V. Guarantee Measures

The Plan also calls for the development of laws, regulation, and ethical norms that promote the development of AI; improve key policies for the support of AI development; establish the AI technology standards and intellectual property system; establish an AI security supervision and evaluation system; vigorously strengthen the training of an AI labor force; and carry out a wide range of AI scientific activities.

## VI. Organization and Implementation

The development plan seeks to strengthen organizational leadership, complete mechanisms, take aim at objectives, and realistically implement the plan with "great spirit." The focus will be on organizational leadership; guarantee implementation; conduct trials and demonstrations; and give public opinion guidance.

The scope of the development plan is quite remarkable with the above recitation being only a glimpse of the almost overwhelming goals recited that are to be accomplished. The Plan has led to numerous commentaries. In an article in the New York Times, the authors noted that China's ambition smacks of far-out sci-fi ideas as an authoritarian state with plans to use AI to predict crimes, track people on all encompassing closed-circuit cameras, censor the Internet, create self-guided missiles, and also to alleviate traffic jams. At the present time, Chinese companies, such as Baidu, Tencent, and Didi Chuxing, are investing heavily in U.S. AI companies ostensibly for peaceful purposes. While China is financing comprehensively in AI research, the budget for the U.S. National Science Foundation is being reduced by the current administration.[52]

At a Governance of AI Program at Oxford University, a detailed assessment of China's ambition was given somewhat mixed results. While noting the 2020 benchmark calls for a tenfold increase of the AI industry over the next three years, it is still playing catch-up with the U.S. having achieved to date only half of U.S. capabilities. China's central government, through its party committees and "special management shares," is seeking to exert greater influence over large tech companies. Other cautionary remarks include the transformation of China's military and the level of civil-military integration, the possibility of large speculative boom-bust cycles, and major concerns about privacy and the willingness of private companies to participate in various social credit systems.[53]

In a thoughtful study by the Eurasia Group, it predicted that a new wave of scientific talent fostered by a government-sponsored large army of young scientists is emerging, which will give great impetus for China to become the leading competitor to the U.S. in the forthcoming years. One of the advantages is the huge data set which underlies AI is more available because of its population size, thereby giving China a large advantage in this regard. For example, China has some 1.4 billion mobile phone users, compared to U.S.' 427 million.[54] The study stated there are four waves of AI development: Internet AI; Business AI; Perception AI;

---

[52] Paul Mozur and John Markoff, *Is China Outsmarting America in A.I.?*, NEW YORK TIMES (May 27, 2017), https://www.bing.com/search?q=paul+mozur+and+john+markoff%2C+is+china+outsmarting+america+in+a.i.%3F%2C+new+york+times+%28may+27%2C+2017%29%2C&form=EDGHPT&qs=PF&cvid=a54d72a889fa456e9d13cabd5b8efe73&cc=US&setlang=en-US&elv=AY3%21uAY7tbNNZGZ2yiGNjfOZNnufoVYZj0krIK2Pedbl4xPe4rz17vQRFMyhQehWUIpw*RBgTKZ73xZfOpyWYogV*DWqPAO8hrUJNjMIH*dA&PC=LCTS.

[53] Jeffrey Ding, *Deciphering China's AI Dream: The context, components, capabilities, and consequences of China's strategy to lead the world in AI*, UNIVERSITY OF OXFORD (March, 2018), https://www.fhi.ox.ac.uk/wp-content/uploads/Deciphering_Chinas_AI-Dream.pdf.

[54] Paul Triolo, *AI in China: cutting through the hype*, EURASIA GROUP (Dec. 6, 2017), https://www.eurasiagroup.net/live-post/ai-in-china-cutting-through-the-hype.

and Autonomous AI. For the Internet AI, it is predicted that China will take the lead because of the massive data set and strong venture capital ecosystem it enjoys, drawing major funding for its startups. Alibaba will be a major rival to Amazon; Tencent to Facebook; and Baidu to Google. China will also lead in both Perception AI and Autonomous AI, with the former involving digitizing the physical world through sensors and smart devices. China will lead due to again its large data set and its less concern about privacy rights. For Autonomous AI, although currently 2 years behind the U.S., it will move ahead due to its very large self-contained manufacturing capabilities. It is only for Business AI that the U.S. is predicted to remain dominant because of Chinese businesses' slow adaptation to adopt data warehousing and enterprise applications.[55]

McKinsey Global Institute reflected on AI's implications for China noting the disruptive impact of AI on China's workforce whereby half of all of its work activities could be automated, which would affect many millions of its workers. It concluded that China has the capability and opportunity to lead in AI globally. The Report acknowledged China's vast troves of data but lags behind the U.S. in creating a data-friendly ecosystem with unified standards and cross-platform sharing. China is on par and may be leading in algorithm development, especially in voice recognition and targeted advertising. China initially lacked microprocessors owing to U.S. prohibitions of export to China but, ironically, due to the prohibition, it now is set to create its own high-end supercomputer chips. Unintended consequences often follow with U.S. trade constraints of sensitive data to China. Restrictions dissuade major companies to scale back their AI development and smaller companies from engaging in AI research due to high compliance costs.[56] Economic implications may be dire for some segments of China's population, especially women. Social implications for China include ethical considerations with respect to the collection of personal data, unintentional discrimination in

---

[55] Eurasia Group, *China embraces AI: A Close Look and A Long View*, SINOVATION VENTURES (Dec. 2017), https://www.eurasiagroup.net/files/upload/China_Embraces_AI.pdf.
[56] Karen Hao, *A US attempt to keep AI out of China's hands could actually help China*, MIT TECHNOLOGY REVIEW (Nov. 21, 2018), https://www.technologyreview.com/s/612453/a-us-attempt-to-keep-ai-out-of-chinas-hands-could-actually-help-china/.

decision-making, and legal implications concerning liability and intellectual property rights.[57]

In another Report of the McKinsey Global Institute, it listed what it terms "10 imperatives" in this new era of AI and automation.[58] They are (1) the opportunity today that digitization presents, i.e., the digitalization of everything beyond big data and the Internet of Things—how it affects a broad range of products and services from smart phones to cloud-based services; (2) that digitalization is progressing unevenly; (3) digitalization is a significant opportunity for Europe; (4) the new wave of automation and AI technologies that are driven by machine-learning algorithms, exponential increases in computing capacity, and massive quanta of data underlying the training of machine leaning models are benefits to business that go beyond labor substitution; (5) AI and automation will boost productivity; (6) the impact on work inasmuch as one-half of all jobs in Europe can be automated; (7) brief lessons from history—how technology does result in the decline of certain jobs but also results in job creation; (8) worker transitions will be significant challenges; (9) technology offers some solutions to the future of work; and (10) imperatives for Europe consisting of leading by example, accelerative efforts to complete a Digital Single Market; embracing and enabling the creation and growth of large-scale digital platforms and digital innovators; and investment to lead in digital ecosystem, digital destination, AI, and other technologies.[59]

A Staff Research Report for the U.S.-China Economic and Security Review Commission contained similar questions pertaining to China's overall 5-year plan including scientific research. It concluded that the Chinese government has imposed major obstacles to the overall success of the plan. They include a top-down governance with the Communist

---

[57] Dominic Barton, Jonathan Woetzel, Jeongmin Seong, and Qinzheng Tian, *Artificial Intelligence: Implications for China*, Discussion Paper, MCKINSEY GLOBAL INSTITUTE (April 2017), https://www.mckinsey.com/~/media/McKinsey/Featured%20Insights/China/Artificial%20intelligence%20Implications%20for%20China/MGI-Artificial-intelligence-implications-for-China.ashx.

[58] James Manyika, *10 imperatives for Europe in the age of AI and automation*, MCKINSEY GLOBAL INSTITUTE (Oct. 2017), https://www.mckinsey.com/featured-insights/europe/ten-imperatives-for-europe-in-the-age-of-ai-and-automation.

[59] *Id.*

Party's reluctance to reduce its involvement in all aspects of society and the economy. The Plan is a step back from its prior 5-year plan which stressed the role of market forces in determining China's long-term economic and social development. The Chinese government has increasingly intervened in all aspects of society including its legal system. By giving preferential treatment to domestic firms as well as imposing high market access barriers, foreign investment firms have become more reluctant to play a role in China's development. It did lower barriers for products and services it strongly desires particularly advanced technology and foreign investments in select industries. Overall, the Report alleges that there are difficult policy trade-offs that will take place that may hamper growth. Examples include China's continued support for its steel industry causing a global glut. China's need for significant private capital will require a major loosening of capital controls.[60]

Other naysayers allege that the Chinese AI sector suffers from a dearth of allocation of resources, especially to funding and subsidies. Some major companies therein depend on government funding for 30–68 percent of their profits, which illustrates their need for subsidies and also the need to have the right government connections. There is also the fear that AI will be used to amass private data that raises the scepter of governmental control and intervention rather than allowing markets to carry on without major intervention.[61] Other commentators fret that bias incorporated into AI algorithms in favor of China will affect its AI through its acquisitions of companies engaged therein. Bias may take place because humans create the algorithms which interpret data. Bias has strained Western creation of algorithms by the values and beliefs of programmers, such as allegedly affected Google's AI software.[62]

---

[60] Katherine Koleski, *The 13th Five-Year Plan*, U.S.-China Economic and Security Review Commission (Feb. 14, 2017), https://www.uscc.gov/sites/default/files/Research/The%2013th%20 Five-Year%20Plan_Final_2.14.17_Updated%20%28002%29.pdf.

[61] *Artificial Intelligence: The Race is on: The Global Policy Response to AI* (Feb. 2018), FTI CONSULTING, http://brussels.ftistratcomm.com/wp-content/uploads/sites/5/2018/02/The-global-policy-response-to-AI-snapshot.pdf.

[62] Ralf, *China's plan for dominance in Artificial Intelligence*, RUDE BAGUETTE (Oct. 4, 2018), http://www.rudebaguette.com/2018/10/04/chinas-plan-for-domination-in-artificial-intelligence/.

# Middle East

Although having been subject to wars and other conflict especially in Iraq, Yemen, and Syria, nevertheless countries of the Middle East have noted the need to update their economies to reflect the changes taking place as a result of AI. With estimates as high as $15.7 trillion being added to the global economy by 2030 as a result of AI, $6.6 trillion due to increased productivity and $9.1 trillion as direct benefits to consumers, the Middle East is expected to partake in its growth to the extent of some $320 billion. The countries expected to contribute greatest to the growth are Saudi Arabia ($135.2 billion—12.4% of GDP), United Arab Emirates (UAE), ($96 billion—13.6% of GDP), Egypt ($42.7 billion—7.7% of GDP), and the combined four nations of Bahrain, Kuwait, Oman, and Qatar ($45.9 billion—8.2% of GDP).[63]

Saudi Arabia, cognizant of the need to transform its oil-based economy which accounts for 43 percent of its GDP, is less reliant on oil due to alternate energy sources and environmental concerns. It has inaugurated Saudi Vision 2030 and National Transformation Programme 2020. The purposes are, among other concerns, the significant rise of youth unemployment and, thus, the need to create new business/government models based on cooperation to generate major changes, and to provide a greater diversification to improve its efficiency and effectiveness for the betterment of its citizens. To illustrate its commitment, it inaugurated NEOM, a planned $500 billion megacity which is part technology, part R&D, part international trade center, and part business and advance manufacturing zone. In a milestone, it granted citizenship rights to Sophia, a humanoid robot created by Hanson Robotics of Hong Kong.[64]

It appears that the United Arab Emirates (UAE) is the leader in the region in digitalizing the many aspects of its economy. Dubai is planning for autonomous transport and services to be 25 percent driverless by the year 2030 including the RTA and Careem Joint Driverless Electric

---

[63] PWC [Pricewaterhousecoopers], *US $320 billion by 2030? The potential impact of AI in the Middle East*, https://www.pwc.com/m1/en/publications/potential-impact-artificial-intelligence-middle-east.html.

[64] Amr Elsaadani, Mark Purdy, and Elizabeth Hakuangwi, *Pivoting with AI*, ACCENTURE CONSULTING, at 5, https://www.accenture.com/t20180509T033323Z__w__/us-en/_acnmedia/PDF-77/Accenture-Impact-AI-GDP-Middle-East.pdf.

Modular Pods[65] project which is electrically powered and door-to-door enabling residents to be picked up and brought to their destination. Consider how this will affect disabled persons. Dubai's Police Driverless Mini Police Cars, powered by robotics, can patrol areas of the city for the multitude of purposes including criminal activity. It also is the first city globally to successfully field-test a new flying taxi service.[66]

## Latin America

Latin America, particularly Central America, has fared poorly in economic, social, and governmental reforms when compared to its northern neighbors. Nevertheless, AI is beginning to influence business and governmental decision-making therein in an endeavor to improve growth and social welfare of its citizens. In a study by the Inter-American Development Bank, it was predicted that AI could raise regional GDP growth in Latin America and the Caribbean from the current 3 percent annual growth by an additional one percent. The report states that AI is the driving force for such growth by improvement in productivity of supply chains and simplification of trade negotiations. The vast amount of data can aid in the analysis of trade flows, tariffs, rules of origin, and sanitary regulations. Algorithms in AI can greatly improve in the prediction of risk profiles. The problem, as stated throughout this text, is the challenge posed by resulting job losses, which can upend the fragile democracies in the region.[67]

The World Wide Web Foundation and Accenture, among other organizations, have conducted extensive investigations and research concerning individual countries in Latin America and how AI will transform their economies to make them more globally competitive. The

---

[65] Noorhan Barakat, *RTA and Careem working on driverless electric modular pods*, GULF NEWS UAE (Oct. 18, 2016), https://gulfnews.com/uae/transport/rta-and-careem-working-on-driverless-electric-modular-pods-1.1914797.

[66] Emmanuel Durou, Deloitte, *National Transformation in the Middle East*, DELOITTE, at 41–43, https://www2.deloitte.com/xe/en/pages/technology-media-and-telecommunications/articles/dtme_tmt_national-transformation-in-the-middleeast-a-digital-journey.html.

[67] *Artificial intelligence to boost Latin American and Caribbean economies: IDB study*, IDB (Aug. 29, 2018), https://www.iadb.org/en/news/artificial-intelligence-boost-latin-american-and-caribbean-economies-idb-study.

Foundation focused on four components of AI and applied them in four case studies to Argentina and Uruguay. The four components are: (1) the process of data collection/creation; (2) the design of the tools; (3) the administrative protocols that surround the tool's output; and (4) the legal and social norms that define the broader context in which the policy is executed. Among the findings are the following: Argentina has shown great interest in AI as evidenced by the number of publications about AI on ministries' websites and exchanges between academic and governmental officials. AI was used by its government to identify the prediction of school dropouts, prediction about teenage pregnancies, and a map to identify business opportunities. For the city of Buenos Aires, Argentina, an algorithm intelligibility (high—basic decision tree) was used to facilitate the identification of business opportunities. Uruguay has become a leading Latin American country in the adoption of information and communications technology (ICT). Among the AI-based studies was one which identified 150 square meters in which there are high probabilities of crimes being committed.[68]

The core recommendations for government officials by the Foundation are to: (1) develop infrastructure and government expertise for the use of AI techniques; (2) ensure transparency, public participation, and accountability in the development and implementation of AI techniques; and (3) establish criteria for the development of impact assessment to be considered before implementing automated systems in public decision-making.[69] According to another report, Mexico is the leading Latin American country in AI intelligence strategy. It has launched a national AI strategy regarding its government's role in shaping its development within the country. It has created an Intergovernmental Commission for Electronic Governance to promote AI usage, particularly with startups.[70]

---

[68] *Algorithms and Artificial Intelligence in Latin America*, WORLD WIDE WEB FOUNDATION (Sept. 2018), http://webfoundation.org/docs/2018/09/WF_AI-in-LA_Report_Screen_AW.pdf.
[69] *Id.*
[70] Emma Martinho-Truswell and Constanza Gomez Mont, *Mexico leads Latin America as one of the first ten countries in the world to launch an official intelligence strategy*, OXFORD INSIGHTS (May 24, 2018), https://www.oxfordinsights.com/insights/2018/5/24/mexico-leads-latin-america-as-one-of-the-first-ten-countries-in-the-world-to-launch-an-artificial-intelligence-strategy.

The Accenture Report emphasizes that AI has the capability of overcoming the limitations of capital investment slowdown and declining labor force so as to expand opportunities of value and growth. It analyzed five countries in South America wherein AI could expand GDP by a percent by the year 2035. Among the developments of significant AI autonomous machines usages are mining companies in Peru, job recruiters in Chile, and a multitude of customers of banks, airlines, and retailers using chatbots to engage in their respective requests and operations. AI factors spurring growth in its usage are the unlimited access to computing power, public cloud computing, and data storage.[71]

The Report sets forth three channels of AI-led growth, namely, *intelligent automation* (e.g., Peru University development of a 4-wheeled robot; chatbots, and self-learning leading to new creations); *labor and capital augmentation* (recruitment websites, robot collection of customer information); and *innovation diffusion* (e.g., driverless vehicles, accurate insurance risks, public health initiatives). Among the countries examined by Accenture and AI's effect upon their economies, it noted that Brazil has the potential to boost its gross value added (GVA) in 2035 by $432 billion (0.9%); Columbia by $78 billion; Chile by $63 billion; Argentina by $59 billion; and Peru by $43 billion.

# Africa

Africa is composed of at least two cultural and racial divisions: northern Africa with the Maghreb countries of Tunisia, Morocco, and Algeria comprising mainly Caucasian and Muslim populations, and sub-Saharan Africa, which, historically, with exceptions, has fared poorly economically compared to the remaining nations globally. AI appears to offer a major lifeline for economic, social, and political development. Tunisia, owing in great part to the efforts of its first president, Habib Bourguiba, who embraced gender and other forms of equality for its population, and

---

[71] Armen Ovanessoff and Eduardo Plastino, *How Artificial Intelligence Can Drive South America's Growth*, ACCENTURE (2017), https://www.accenture.com/t20170919T060656Z__w__/us-en/_acnmedia/PDF-49/Accenture-How-Artificial-Intelligence-Can-Drive-South-Americas-Growth.pdf.

its current representative government, has led advancements in technology on the continent. Thus, it enacted a new Start-Up Act on April 2, 2018 as part of its "Digital Tunisia 2020," which embraced its trend toward political and economic modernization.[72]

It is anticipated that the Act will encourage entrepreneurs to embrace the new technologies, especially that of blockchain and AI, to make Tunisia competitive both nationally and internationally. It has already about seventeen tech hubs and a number of other programs encouraging the development of the economy. The capital of Tunisia, Tunis, was selected in November, 2017 as the central location of the African Union's planned Digital African Excellence Center which will train Africa's exceptionally youthful population in governmental and private sector governance. The Act provides for tax exemptions for startups for up to eight years; state-funded salaries for up to three founders per company during the first year of its operations; expansion of households' and schools' digital infrastructure; promotion of outside funding by permitting entrepreneurs to set up foreign currency accounts to procure materials and set up branches abroad; and other measures.[73]

There are a number of hopeful developments whereby governments and private businesses and think tanks seek to bring the continent into the mainstream. A major concern reflected globally is the fear of loss of jobs especially given the extent of poverty in African countries. Nevertheless, there is a realization that failure to innovate would continue to leave the continent in an underdeveloped quagmire. Research organizations, such as Accenture, have promulgated the need for the adoption of blockchain and AI. Thus, for South Africa, its research opines that real gross value added by AI in South Africa would be 3.5 percent by 2035. The three main channels, as stated above for Latin America, through which the said value would be added are: (1) intelligent automation; (2) augmentation of existing labor and capital; and (3) innovation diffusion. It posits the need for South Africa to create a vibrant ecosystem grounded on contributions by universities, startups, large companies,

[72] Wafa Ben-Hassine, *New Technologies for a New Tunisia*, ATLANTIC COUNCIL (Jan. 28, 2019), https://www.atlanticcouncil.org/blogs/menasource/new-technologies-for-a-new-tunisia.
[73] Katrin Sold, *The Tunisian Startup Act*, CARNEGIE ENDOWMENT FOR INTERNATIONAL PEACE (June 26, 2018), https://carnegieendowment.org/sada/76685.

policymakers, and multi-stakeholder partnerships; turn AI investments into AI-driven growth; and practice responsible AI. Policymakers should take the lead in the design, execution, and monitoring of AI.[74]

Additional helpful developments taking place in sub-Saharan Africa are: Google's new AI research lab in Ghana headed by Moustapha Cisse, who initiated an African Masters in Machine Learning program; Ubemwa, which is building deeper neural networks to power cheaper health diagnostic tools for disease diagnoses[75]; AI Expo Africa, which is to take place in early September, 2019 will bring together numerous community members, speakers, sponsors, and many others for the largest business-focused AI and Data Science community event in Africa[76]; workshops[77]; and research by Accenture and the World Economic Forum (WEF) as part of WEF's multi-year Digital Transformation Initiative.[78] In Nigeria, Data Science Nigeria launched the country's first AI-focused hub at the University of Lagos and banks, such as Diamond Bank and United Bank for Africa have adopted AI-powered digital assistants.[79]

On a cautionary note, although AI has had many positive applications such as health care, where there is a great shortage of doctors and medical access, agricultural planning, reduction of financial costs, and improvement of public transportation, nevertheless, there is also a fear that AI

---

[74] *Artificial Intelligence: Is South Africa Ready?*, ACCENTURE, http://www.ee.co.za/article/artificial-intelligence-south-africa-ready.html.

[75] Kwasi Gyamfi Asiedu & Commentary, *Google is throwing its weight behind artificial intelligence in Africa*, QUARTZ AFRICA (June 14, 2018), https://qz.com/africa/1305211/google-is-making-a-big-bet-on-artificial-intelligence-in-africa-with-its-first-research-center/; and Alexander Udu Tsado, *A Recipe for AI in Africa*, THE JOURNAL BLOG (Aug. 27, 2018), https://blog.usejournal.com/a-recipe-for-ai-in-africa-225abac137b3.

[76] AI Expo Africa, http://aiexpoafrica.com.

[77] *Workshop to launch AI Network of Excellence in sub-Saharan Africa*, IDRC (April 3, 2019), https://www.idrc.ca/en/search/gss/canaux%20de%20communication%20more%3Aproject.

[78] *Here's what a digitally transformed South Africa could look like in 2026*, BUSINESSTECH (Jan. 25, 2019), https://businesstech.co.za/news/technology/295282/heres-what-a-digitally-transformed-south-africa-could-look-like-in-2026/.

[79] Akindare Okunola, *Artificial Intelligence in Nigeria is An Infant Space With Huge Potential* (Aug. 8, 2018), TECHCABAL, https://techcabal.com/2018/08/08/artificial-intelligence-in-nigeria-is-an-infant-space-with-huge-potential/.

could be used by unscrupulous government officials to emphasize ethnic and religious divisions and to attack nascent democratic institutions.[80]

# International Conventions and Declarations

## Asilomar AI Principles

The Future of Life Institute (FLI) began as a non-profit organization in 2014 by Max Tegmark, his wife, and several other persons in order to build assure that technology, particularly AI, is used to benefit humankind and avoid its possible self-destruct tendencies. It was soon joined or in consultation with many of the major players in AI including Elon Musk, SpaceX and Tesla pioneer, the physicist, Stephen Hawking, Bill Gates of Microsoft, and others.[81] At the 2017 conference at the Asilomar Conference Grounds, Puerto Rico, attended by several hundred persons with diverse backgrounds including the said Elon Musk, Larry Page, cofounder of Google, AI research leaders from companies such as DeepMind, Google, Facebook, Apple, IBM, Microsoft, and Baidu, a set of principles known as The Asilomar Principles were formulated which received 97 percent support from the attendees (see Appendix B).

The Principles set forth its research goal, which is to create beneficial intelligence with investments funded to ensure its goal covering three main areas: (1) research issues, (2) ethics and values, and (3) longer-term issues. Among the research areas to be addressed are computer science, economic, law, ethics, and social studies. Ethics and values are highly emphasized that focused on the lack of transparency, personal privacy, shared benefit and prosperity, human control, and AI arms race. Longer-term issues to be addressed are the need to be cautious when making assumptions about future AI capabilities; the importance of AI as a fundamental change in humankind; the risks posed by AI; the need for strict safety and control measures governing AI systems to self-improve or

---

[80] Clayton Besaw and John Filitz, *Artificial Intelligence in Africa is a Double-edged Sword*, OUR WORLD (Jan. 16, 2016), https://ourworld.unu.edu/en/ai-in-africa-is-a-double-edged-sword.
[81] Max Tegmark, LIFE 3.0: BEING HUMAN IN THE AGE OF ARTIFICIAL INTELLIGENCE, Vintage Books (2017) at 34–35.

self-replicate; and that superintelligence must only be developed in the service of widely shared ethical norms and for the benefit of all human-kind.[82] Issues that have to be attended to will continually arise that bring into question who and what we are and whether we should tinker with the outer limits of experimentation (given our current mode of thinking). A current controversial occurrence and question is whether human brain genes should be implanted in monkeys as Chinese scientists have carried out.[83] Does such research and many other questionable investigations, such as cloning of humans, implementation of human uterus in cows, and other comparable bizarre works not violate current ethical norms, such as Asilomar Principles 9–11 (responsibility, value alignment, and human values)?

The State of California adopted the Asilomar Principles by Assembly Resolution filed with the Secretary of State on September 7, 2018. It stated that AI development and related public policy are to be guided by the principles.[84]

## Toronto Declaration

Access Now is an international non-profit organization whose mission is to defend and extend the digital rights of users at risk globally. It has developed policies in the critical areas concerned with business and human rights, digital security, freedom of expression, net discrimination, and privacy. Founded in 2009, it has taken an active lead in the promulgation of guidelines and regulatory enactments that oppose online

---

[82] *Id.* at 329–331. An additional source is Future of Life Institute, *Asilomar Principles*, https://futureoflife.org/ai-principles/.

[83] Antonio Regalado, *Chinese scientists have put human brain genes in monkeys – and yes, they may be smarter*, MIT TECHNOLOGY REVIEW (April 10, 2019), https://www.technologyreview.com/s/613277/chinese-scientists-have-put-human-brain-genes-in-monkeysand-yes-they-may-be-smarter/.

[84] Assembly Concurrent Resolution No. 215, Chapter 206, ACR 215, Kiley. 23 Asilomar AI Principles, filed with the Secretary of State (Sept. 7, 2018), http://leginfo.legislature.ca.gov/faces/billTextClient.xhtml?bill_id=201720180ACR215. For a brief discussion, see Future of Life, *State of California Endorses Asilomar Principles* (Aug. 31, 2018), https://futureoflife.org/2018/08/31/state-of-california-endorses-asilomar-ai-principles/.

censorship, Internet shutdowns, and other governmental initiatives that limit freedom of expression. It acts in coordination with numerous international organizations, is a signatory to principles subscribed by comparable organizations, and advises the European Parliament, and participates in UN organizations, and other affiliations.[85] On May 16, 2018, it and a coalition of human rights and technology groups issued a Declaration open for signature by organizations and governments entitled *The Toronto Declaration: Protecting the rights to equality and non-discrimination in machine learning systems* (Declaration) (see Appendix C for a copy of the Declaration).

The focus of the Declaration, according to the Preamble, is to examine the positive and negative implications of the machine learning systems, assure that human rights are protected, protect against discrimination, promote inclusion, diversity, and equity, and provide remedies for those persons wrongfully/adversely affected. It noted that the systems often are opaque, and can lead almost effortlessly to discriminatory and repressive practices unless safeguards are established to mitigate against such occurrences. While observing the many benefits that arise and may arise from machine learning systems, problems may surface that affect privacy, data protection, freedom of expression, participation in cultural life, equality before the law, and meaningful access to remedy. Especially impacted are services and opportunities applicable to health care, education, labor, and employment.[86]

Accordingly, the following principles were set forth with explanatory comments as a framework of international human rights law:

- States have obligations to promote, protect and respect human rights; private sector actors, including companies, have a responsibility to respect human rights at all times. We put forward this Declaration to affirm these obligations and responsibilities.

---

[85] *About Us*, ACCESS NOW, https://www.accessnow.org/about-us/.

[86] Preamble, *The Toronto Declaration: Protecting the rights to equality and non-discrimination in machine learning systems*, Access Now (May 16, 2018), https://www.accessnow.org/cms/assets/uploads/2018/08/The-Toronto-Declaration_ENG_08-2018.pdf.

This Declaration focuses on the right to equality and nondiscrimination, a critical principle that underpins all human rights.

- Governments have obligations and private sector actors have responsibilities to proactively prevent discrimination in order to comply with existing human rights law and standards. When prevention is not sufficient or satisfactory, and discrimination arises, a system should be interrogated and harms addressed immediately.
- This Declaration underlines that inclusion, diversity and equity are key components of protecting and upholding the right to equality and non-discrimination. All must be considered in the development and deployment of machine learning systems in order to prevent discrimination, particularly against marginalized groups.
- States bear the primary duty to promote, protect, respect and fulfill human rights. Under international law, states must not engage in, or support discriminatory or otherwise rights-violating actions or practices when designing or implementing machine learning systems in a public context or through public-private partnerships.
- States must ensure that existing measures to prevent against discrimination and other rights harms are updated to take into account and address the risks posed by machine learning technologies.
- States must take the following steps to mitigate and reduce the harms of discrimination from machine learning in public sector systems:

  - Identify risks
  - Ensure transparency and accountability
  - Enforce oversight

- States have a duty to take proactive measures to eliminate discrimination.
- International law clearly sets out the duty of states to protect human rights; this includes ensuring the right to non-discrimination by private sector actors.
- Private sector actors have a responsibility to respect human rights; this responsibility exists independently of state obligations. As part of fulfilling this responsibility, private sector actors need to take ongoing proactive and reactive steps to ensure that they do not cause or

contribute to human rights abuses—a process called 'human rights due diligence.' There are three core steps to the process of human rights due diligence:

– Identify potential discriminatory outcomes
– Take effective action to prevent and mitigate discrimination and track responses
– Be transparent about efforts to identify, prevent and mitigate against discrimination in machine learning systems

• The right to justice is a vital element of international human rights law. Under international law, victims of human rights violations or abuses must have access to prompt and effective remedies, and those responsible for the violations must be held to account.

The Declaration has been subscribed to date by Amnesty International, Human Rights Watch, and the Wikipedia Foundation. Although not legally enforceable, it provides a guidelines for nation-states to adopt laws and regulations.[87]

# Future Trends and Super Intelligence

Every generation looks back at the prior generation longingly as simpler times which often recalls only the advantages but none of the then deficits. It fails to note the remarkable new innovations, including medical care that are occurring today and which make life far more interesting, healthier, as well as other advantages that surpass prior experiences. At the beginning of each new decade, books are written that offer predictions for the new decade whose accuracy, like weather predictions, may

---

[87] Russell Brandom, *New Toronto Declaration calls on algorithms to respect human rights*, THE VERGE (May 16, 2018), https://www.theverge.com/The Toronto Declaration: Protecting the rights to equ2018/5/16/17361356/toronto-declaration-machine-learning-algorithmic-discrimination-rightscon, and Human Rights Watch, *The Toronto Declaration: Protecting the rights to equality and non-discrimination in machine learning systems*, https://www.hrw.org/news/2018/07/03/toronto-declaration-protecting-rights-equality-and-non-discrimination-machine.

be accurate for the immediate future but increasingly lack validity as each year passes on. Trying to predict today what will occur in the next decade is a fool's errand with technology changing at an exponential rate. Nevertheless, some attempts have been made including the cited effort[88] that are a bewildering mixed bag of positive and negative prognostications by clairvoyant types. We mentioned briefly the fears expressed by Stephen Hawking who worried about a technology we cannot control and Elon Musk who cautioned the need for regulatory oversight to control the possible extremes to which AI technology could lead humanity.

Other AI commentators are as follows: dire workforce consequences were predicted by Steve Wozniak, cofounder of Apple, who feared the replacement of less able persons by robots; Kai-Fu Lee who envisioned serious replacements by automation not just of blue collar workers but also the more educated white collar workers; the rise of superintelligent machines which will not only be comparable to human intelligence but surpass the intelligence of all living creatures[89]; similarly, Ray Kurzweil who is more positive by believing that although AI will surpass the capabilities of the human brain, nevertheless, it may also cause people to live forever; AI as ruler of the world[90]; Heather M. Roff, who fears AI could be used to manipulate how people shop, think, and live their lives[91]; elimination or promotion of bias were proposed by Satya Nadella of Microsoft, who is concerned how machine learning will transform all of our lives; and others who worry understandably about AI and weaponry that can threaten all of humankind.[92]

The latest entry into the discussion is that of Richard Baldwin, whose study entitled *The Globotics Upheaval*[93] speculates that the diffusion of

---

[88] *Many of the cited comments can be found at the following sites: How AI Will Go Out Of Control According To 52 Experts*, CBINSIGHTS (Feb. 19, 2019), https://www.cbinsights.com/research/ai-threatens-humanity-expert-quotes/.

[89] Louis DelMonte, THE ARTIFICIAL INTELLIGENCE REVOLUTION, 2014.

[90] James Barrat, OUR FINAL INVENTION, ARTIFICIAL INTELLIGENCE AND THE END OF THE HUMAN ERA, 2013.

[91] *Heather M. Roff*, BROOKINGS, https://www.brookings.edu/experts/heather-m-roff/.

[92] CBInsights, *supra*, note 748.

[93] Richard Baldwin, THE GLOBOTICS UPHEAVAL: Globalization, Robotics, and the Future of Work, Oxford U. Press (2019). For a review of the book, see Marc Levinson, *When the Robot Gets an Office*, WALL STREET JOURNAL (March 4, 2019), at A15.

robotics and AI worldwide, considered by the author to be Siamese twins, will cause considerable distortion of not only blue collar employment but also profoundly affect the more educated segment of society which heretofore had been mainly exempt from job losses attributable to the advancing technologies. Robotics and instant messaging will enter boardrooms and offices worldwide leading to greater use of freelance employment. Language difficulties of the large segment of the global population that cannot speak English are now overcome by AI advances in instant translations. These "globots" will create disorientation of the workforce at all levels of employments but, whether it is just another phase of job replacements that lead to further employment in newly created industries, will be determined in the near future.

Among those who did have a clear vision of the future when predicted are William Gibson, who wrote the famed novel *Neuromancer*. He envisaged the Internet in 1984, having popularized the concept of a cyberspace, described it as "a consensual hallucination experienced daily by billions of legitimate operators, in every nation, by children being taught mathematical concepts…. A graphic representation of data abstracted from banks of every computer in the human system. Unthinkable complexity. Lines of light ranged in the nonspace of the mind, clusters and constellations of data. Like city lights, receding…."[94]

The conceptual development of superintelligence raises profound philosophical questions including that of whether superintelligence will ever occur particularly in robots, and, if so, whether the robots will possess "consciousness" or some derivative thereof. Is it possible for human persons to create other forms of life which will compete with or even surpass them in terms of what it means to be human and/or in terms of consciousness? A pioneer University of Oxford physicist and a father of quantum computing, David Deutsch, casts serious doubts that superintelligence is achievable. He noted that AGI has experienced little progress in six decades. Assuming the acquisition of what is generally understood as consciousness, can such beings have emotions, self-awareness, be able

---

[94] Ross Dawson, *Best futurists ever: How William Gibson's Neuromancer shaped our vision of technology*, https://rossdawson.com/futurist/best-futurists-ever/william-gibson-neuromancer/.

to engage in creative activity, be benevolent or hostile, or even whether it can have a soul?[95]

The meaning of *consciousness* is variously defined. The dictionary definition is "the quality or state of being aware especially of something within oneself"; and "the state of being characterized by sensation, emotion, volition, and thought."[96] Descartes defined it in terms of the meaning of "thought," which he said includes everything that is within us in such a way that we are immediately aware of it.[97] He said:

> If there were machines which bore a resemblance to our body and imitated our actions as far as it was morally possible to do so, we should always have two very certain tests by which to recognize that, for all that, they were not real men. The first is, that they could never use speech or other signs as we do when placing our thoughts on record for the benefit of others….And the second difference is, that although machines can perform certain things as well or perhaps better than any of us can do, they infallibly fall short in others, by which means we may discover that they did not act from knowledge, but only for the disposition of their organs….[I]t is morally impossible that there should be sufficient diversity in any machine to allow it to act in all the events of life in the same way as our reason causes us to act.[98]

Religious belief varies but most often equates consciousness with the soul. Examples are: Baha'i teachings that the seat of human consciousness is the soul and not the brain, the spiritual and not the physical[99]; the Catholic Catechism states: "The soul is the subject of human consciousness and freedom; soul and body together form one unique human nature. Each human soul is individual and immortal, immediately created

---

[95] The categories are taken from *Philosophy of artificial intelligence*, WIKIPEDIA, https://en.wikipedia.org/wiki/Philosophy_of_artificial_intelligence.

[96] *Consciousness*, MERRIAM WEBSTER DICTIONARY, https://www.merriam-webster.com/dictionary/consciousness.

[97] *Seventeenth-Century Theories of Consciousness*, STANFORD ENCLOPEDIA OF PHILOSOPHY, https://plato.stanford.edu/entries/consciousness-17th/.

[98] *Artificial Intelligence: The History of AI*, STANFORD ENCYCLOPEDIA OF PHILOSOPHY, https://plato.stanford.edu/entries/artificial-intelligence/.

[99] John Hatcher, *Does Consciousness Exist in the Brain or the Soul?*, BAHAITEACHINGS.ORG (May 15, 2017), https://bahaiteachings.org/consciousness-exist-brain-soul.

by God...."[100] Muslim belief of consciousness, according to one observer, is a step between spirit and body. It is one of the properties that distinguishes man from the other living beings and is the most important and distinct property that distinguishes human persons from the other species.[101] It is difficult to describe Jewish belief of consciousness inasmuch as there are many variations of Jewish thought. One manner of thought is expressed by Rabbi Tzvi Freeman, who stated that it is not the same as intelligence or perception but rather "It's absurdly lonely"—you cannot see, touch, replicate, or tell another what it is but we believe we experience it. It is a sense of being me which deals with the "stuff" out there. It is everywhere but some things are more conscious than others.... "The master core of consciousness is sharing the very core of being through the unfolding drama of this world in general, and your life in particular."

*The Turing Test.*[102] A.M. Turing, the famed British scientist, who was responsible for the Enigma machine that aided in the defeat of Germany in World War II, devised a test or "imitation game" to determine whether machines can think.

> It is played with three people, a man (A), a woman (B), and an interrogator (C) who may be of either sex. The interrogator stays in a room apart from the other two. The object of the game for the interrogator is to determine which of the other two is the man and which is the woman. He knows them by labels X and Y, and at the end of the game he says either 'X is A and Y is B' or 'X is B and Y is A'. The interrogator is allowed to put questions to A and B.... In order that tones of voice may not help the interrogator the answers should be written, or better still, typewritten. The ideal arrangement is to have a teleprinter communicating between the two rooms. Alternatively the question and answers can be repeated by an intermediary. The object of the game for the third player (B) is to help the interrogator. The best strategy for her is probably to give truthful answers. She can add such things as 'I am the woman, don't listen to him t' to her answers, but it will avail nothing as the man can make similar remarks. We

---

[100] Jim Blackburm, *What exactly is a soul?*, CATHOLIC ANSWERS (Aug. 4, 2011), https://www.catholic.com/qa/what-exactly-is-a-soul.

[101] Nevzat Tarhan, *Consciousness*, QUESTIONS ON ISLAM, https://questionsonislam.com/article/consciousness#baslik1.

[102] A.M. Turing, *Computing Machinery and Intelligence*, LIX MIND 236 (Oct. 1950), 433–460.

now ask the question, 'What will happen when a machine takes the part of A in this game?' Will the interrogator decide wrongly as often when the game is played like this as he does when the game is played between a man and a woman? These questions replace our original, 'Can machines think'?

Turing predicted that "in about fifty years' time it will be possible to programme computers…to make them play the imitation game so well that an average interrogator will not have more than 70 per cent chance of mating the right identification after five minutes of questioning. The original question/ 'Can machines think!' I believe to be too meaningless to deserve discussion. Nevertheless I believe that at the end of the century the use of words and general educated opinion will have altered so much that one will be able to speak of machines thinking without expecting to be contradicted."

Turing discussed nine common objections that continue to be raised against AI. Among them are: the religious argument that machines do not have a soul—Turing cautions naysayers not to limit God's power or intent in creating other types of souls. With respect to those commentators who fear the possible consequences of machines dominating human persons, he hopes such is not the case. It is fallacious to use possible consequences to argue that machines cannot overtake humans but the reality is that machines may have superior qualities of speed, memory capacities, and other dominant traits. Concerning whether machines can write poetry or a sonnet, he posits that there is no way of knowing whether machines can possess emotions or other conscious experiences. Another argument he presents is the "Lady Lovelace Objection" that machines cannot originate anything. He argues that machines can take us by surprise and that the human brain's storage of data is similar to that of a computer. All of the objections raised continue to be stated in some form by philosophers, scientists, and other intellectuals, which may continue indefinitely.[103] It appears that Turing's timing was off the mark concerning when machines will ascend to dominance but his predictions may come true in the not-too-distant future.

---

[103] *Computing Machinery and Intelligence*, WIKIPEDIA, https://en.wikipedia.org/wiki/Computing_Machinery_and_Intelligence.

Virtually all commentators begin with the Turing test either positively or disputing the basic premises of the test. One should recall the state of AI when he wrote the article and the enormous advances made thereafter in game playing, development of robots and robotics, machine learning, neural networks, and natural language processing. Among the naysayers is the Tufts University philosopher, Daniel C. Dennett, who presented a series of objections that he and other thoughtful commentators have raised that are somewhat comparable to the Turing recitation. Rather than advocating the counter-AI argument that the human person's complexity of consciousness, possession of organs, reproduction, self-repair, and other processes can never be transferred to a conscious machine, Dennett takes a more fundamental approach, namely, that "conscious robots probably will always simply cost too much to make."[104]

Although a naysayer of AI superintelligence, Dennett disposes of several theoretical anti-AI consciousness positions, namely: (1) Robots are purely material things, and consciousness requires immaterial mind-stuff—he finds no reason to believe that the brain is the only complex physical object in the universe; (2) Robots are inorganic and consciousness can exist only in an organic brain—the powers of organic compounds of biochemistry are mechanistically reproducible; (3) Robots are artifacts, and consciousness abhors an artifact; only something natural, born not manufactured, could exhibit genuine consciousness—he posits that it is conceivable to make a full conscious person, but it would be just too much effort to duplicate; and (4) Robots will always just be much too simple to be conscious—Dennett notes how we have been able to make artificial hearts, and other organ replacements. There is no reason why the brain is not replaceable. He notes with approval and was a participant in the "Cog Project" at MIT which is a humanoid robot that has eyes through video cameras, software for visual face recognition, and other features that are independent of the philosophical disputation of whether it is conscious.

Scientists, technologists, social scientists, futurists, and other thinkers have weighed in concerning the concept of consciousness which is beyond

---

[104] Daniel C. Dennett, *Consciousness in Human and Robot Minds*, TUFTS U. (1994), https://ase.tufts.edu/cogstud/dennett/papers/concrobt.htm.

the scope of this text. We relate some of the views that, hopefully, will inspire the reader to explore in much greater depth. A good starting point would be the thought-provoking discussion by Ray Kurzweil, whose book, *How to Create a Mind*[105] and his other volumes on Singularity, Thinking Machines, and other works, assume and explore what it means to be human, the meaning of consciousness, its application to machines, and other related concepts. He speaks of consciousness as "an emergent property of a complex physical system." Different forms of life have consciousness albeit in lesser degrees, such as that possessed by an animal, e.g., a dog, and ascending to a human person. He doesn't believe that science can answer the question but rather all theories require a leap of faith. He predicts that "machines in the future will appear to be conscious and they will be convincing to biological people when they speak of their *qualia* (conscious experience). They will exhibit the full range of subtle, familiar emotional cues; make us laugh and cry; and they will get mad at us if we say that we don't believe that they are conscious."[106] He theorizes that these nonbiological entities will be fully convincing as conscious persons and that society will accept them as such.

John McCarthy, who coined the term "artificial intelligence," noted that AI and philosophy are deeply intertwined because AI shares many of the concepts of philosophy which includes consciousness. In reference to the AI research aided at human-level AI, he emphasizes the ability of AI to learn from experience without being further programmed. AI has ascended from starting small versions of concepts and their relations in limited contexts; to theories of action, i.e., finding consequences of actions that achieve goals; to nonmonotonic reasoning, which is analogous to philosophical "defeasible reasoning"[107]; to robotic unique interpretation of the part of the world with which it interacts; and beyond.[108]

---

[105] Ray Kurzweil, HOW TO CREATE A MIND: THE SECRET OF HUMAN THOUGHT REVEALED, Viking, 2012.

[106] *Id.* at 209.

[107] *Defeasible reasoning* is a type of nondemonstrative reasoning which is rationally compelling but does not assure a full, complete, or final demonstration of a claim, but which also acknowledges it may be fallible. *Defeasible reasoning*, WIKIPEDIA, https://en.wikipedia.org/wiki/Defeasible_reasoning.

[108] John McCarthy, *The Philosophy of AI and the AI of Philosophy*, STANFORD U. (June 26, 2006), http://jmc.stanford.edu/articles/aiphil2.html.

The widely quoted University of California at Berkeley philosophy professor, John Rogers Searle, gave a "common sense" definition of *consciousness* as consisting "of all those states of feelings, or sensations, or awareness; it begins in the morning when you wake up from a dreamless sleep, and it goes on all day, until you fall asleep, or die, or otherwise become unconscious. Dreams are a form of consciousness on this definition. Now that's the common sense definition, that's our target; if you are not talking about that, you are not talking about consciousness."[109] It is a real subjective experience brought about by the processes of the brain. He opposes the idea of a "Strong AI," whereby software could create a conscious being and uses a "Chinese room" argument to, in essence, demonstrate that consciousness is a physical property, like digestion or fire, and that no simulation can ever be comparable.[110]

The debate may continue indefinitely with repeated allegations that consciousness is "resolutely computational" and therefore reproducible in machines, to "technological singularity," whereby AI replaces humans as dominant force in the universe to the Musk and other arguments that any type of conscious robot must be under human control, and so on.[111] In the opinion of this author, it is impossible to predict the effect of AI upon the human race beyond the next five years. We can only hope that, inasmuch as there were comparable fears and optimistic assessments with new technologies of the past that in fact ultimately benefitted human kind, albeit with painful disruptions, AI will in the end greatly enrich our lives which will extend beyond the dimensions of our planet to new horizons now unfeasible. Who knows?

---

[109] *John Searle on Consciousness and the Brain at TEDxCERN (Transcript)*, THE SINGJU POST (March 20, 2017), https://singjupost.com/john-searle-on-consciousness-and-the-brain-at-tedxcern-transcript/2/.

[110] *John Searle*, WIKIPEDIA, https://en.wikipedia.org/wiki/John_Searle. For a discussion of the Chinese room test, see John Searle, *Minds, Brains, and Programs*, BEHAVIORAL AND BRAIN SCIENCES 3(3) (March 20, 2017), 417–457, http://cogprints.org/7150/1/10.1.1.83.5248.pdf.

[111] Anthony Cuthbertson, *Can Machines Be Conscious? Scientists Say Robots Can be Self-Aware, Just Like Human*, NEWSWEEK (Nov. 4, 2017), https://www.newsweek.com/can-machines-be-conscious-robots-consciousness-humans-ai-singularity-699436.

# Appendix A: Recommendations of National Science and Technology Council[1]

Recommendation 1: Private and public institutions are encouraged to examine whether and how they can responsibly leverage AI and machine learning in ways that will benefit society. Social justice and public policy institutions that do not typically engage with advanced technologies and data science in their work should consider partnerships with AI researchers and practitioners that can help apply AI tactics to the broad social problems these institutions already address in other ways.

Recommendation 2: Federal agencies should prioritize open training data and open data standards in AI. The government should emphasize the release of datasets that enable the use of AI to address social challenges. Potential steps may include developing an "Open Data for AI" initiative with the objective of releasing a significant number of government data sets to accelerate AI research and galvanize the use of open data standards and best practices across government, academia, and the private sector.

---

[1] *Preparing for the Future of Artificial Intelligence*, National Science and Technology Council (Oct. 2016), https://obamawhitehouse.archives.gov/sites/default/files/whitehouse_files/microsites/ostp/NSTC/preparing_for_the_future_of_ai.pdf.

© The Author(s) 2020
R. Girasa, *Artificial Intelligence as a Disruptive Technology*,
https://doi.org/10.1007/978-3-030-35975-1

Recommendation 3: The Federal Government should explore ways to improve the capacity of key agencies to apply AI to their missions. For example, Federal agencies should explore the potential to create DARPA-like organizations to support high-risk, high-reward AI research and its application, much as the Department of Education has done through its proposal to create an "ARPA-ED," to support R&D to determine whether AI and other technologies could significantly improve student learning outcomes.

Recommendation 4: The NSTC MLAI subcommittee should develop a community of practice for AI practitioners across government. Agencies should work together to develop and share standards and best practices around the use of AI in government operations. Agencies should ensure that Federal employee training programs include relevant AI opportunities.

Recommendation 5: Agencies should draw on appropriate technical expertise at the senior level when setting regulatory policy for AI-enabled products. Effective regulation of AI-enabled products requires collaboration between agency leadership, staff knowledgeable about the existing regulatory framework and regulatory practices generally, and technical experts with knowledge of AI. Agency leadership should take steps to recruit the necessary technical talent, or identify it in existing agency staff, and should ensure that there are sufficient technical "seats at the table" in regulatory policy discussions.

Recommendation 6: Agencies should use the full range of personnel assignment and exchange models (e.g., hiring authorities) to foster a Federal workforce with more diverse perspectives on the current state of technology.

Recommendation 7: The Department of Transportation should work with industry and researchers on ways to increase sharing of data for safety, research, and other purposes. The future roles of AI in surface and air transportation are undeniable. Accordingly, Federal actors should focus in the near-term on developing increasingly rich sets of data, consistent with consumer privacy that can better inform policy-making as these technologies mature.

# Preparing for the Future of Artificial Intelligence

Recommendation 8: The U.S. Government should invest in developing and implementing an advanced and automated air traffic management system that is highly scalable, and can fully accommodate autonomous and piloted aircraft alike.

Recommendation 9: The Department of Transportation should continue to develop an evolving framework for regulation to enable the safe integration of fully automated vehicles and UAS, including novel vehicle designs, into the transportation system.

Recommendation 10: The NSTC Subcommittee on Machine Learning and Artificial Intelligence should monitor developments in AI, and report regularly to senior Administration leadership about the status of AI, especially with regard to milestones. The Subcommittee should update the list of milestones as knowledge advances and the consensus of experts changes over time. The Subcommittee should consider reporting to the public on AI developments, when appropriate.

Recommendation 11: The Government should monitor the state of AI in other countries, especially with respect to milestones.

Recommendation 12: Industry should work with government to keep government updated on the general progress of AI in industry, including the likelihood of milestones being reached soon.

Recommendation 13: The Federal government should prioritize basic and long-term AI research. The Nation as a whole would benefit from a steady increase in Federal and private-sector AI R&D, with a particular emphasis on basic research and long-term, high-risk research initiatives. Because basic and long-term research especially are areas where the private sector is not likely to invest, Federal investments will be important for R&D in these areas.

Recommendation 14: The NSTC Subcommittees on MLAI and NITRD, in conjunction with the NSTC Committee on Science, Technology, Engineering, and Education (CoSTEM), should initiate a study on the AI workforce pipeline in order to develop actions that ensure an appropriate increase in the size, quality, and diversity of the workforce, including AI researchers, specialists, and users.

Recommendation 15: The Executive Office of the President should publish a follow-on report by the end of this year, to further investigate the effects of AI and automation on the U.S. job market, and outline recommended policy responses.

Recommendation 16: Federal agencies that use AI-based systems to make or provide decision support for consequential decisions about individuals should take extra care to ensure the efficacy and fairness of those systems, based on evidence-based verification and validation.

Recommendation 17: Federal agencies that make grants to state and local governments in support of the use of AI-based systems to make consequential decisions about individuals should review the terms of grants to ensure that AI-based products or services purchased with Federal grant funds produce results in a sufficiently transparent fashion and are supported by evidence of efficacy and fairness.

# Preparing for the Future of Artificial Intelligence

Recommendation 18: Schools and universities should include ethics, and related topics in security, privacy, and safety, as an integral part of curricula on AI, machine learning, computer science, and data science.

Recommendation 19: AI professionals, safety professionals, and their professional societies should work together to continue progress toward a mature field of AI safety engineering.

Recommendation 20: The U.S. Government should develop a government-wide strategy on international engagement related to AI, and develop a list of AI topical areas that need international engagement and monitoring.

Recommendation 21: The U.S. Government should deepen its engagement with key international stakeholders, including foreign governments, international organizations, industry, academia, and others, to exchange information and facilitate collaboration on AI R&D.

Recommendation 22: Agencies' plans and strategies should account for the influence of AI on cybersecurity, and of cybersecurity on AI. Agencies involved in AI issues should engage their U.S. Government and private-sector cybersecurity colleagues for input on how to ensure that AI systems and ecosystems are secure and resilient to intelligent adversaries. Agencies involved in cybersecurity issues should engage their U.S. Government and private sector AI colleagues for innovative ways to apply AI for effective and efficient cybersecurity.

Recommendation 23: The U.S. Government should complete the development of a single, governmentwide policy, consistent with international humanitarian law, on autonomous and semi-autonomous weapons.

# Appendix B: The Toronto Declaration

## Protecting the Right to Equality and Non-Discrimination in Machine Learning Systems

### Index of Contents

© The Author(s) 2020
R. Girasa, *Artificial Intelligence as a Disruptive Technology*,
https://doi.org/10.1007/978-3-030-35975-1

# Preamble

1. As machine learning systems advance in capability and increase in use, we must examine the impact of this technology on human rights. We acknowledge the potential for machine learning and related systems to be used to promote human rights, but are increasingly concerned about the capability of such systems to facilitate intentional or inadvertent discrimination against certain individuals or groups of people. We must urgently address how these technologies will affect people and their rights. In a world of machine learning systems, who will bear accountability for harming human rights?

2. As discourse around ethics and artificial intelligence continues, this Declaration aims to draw attention to the relevant and well-established framework of international human rights law and standards. These universal, binding and actionable laws and standards provide tangible means to protect individuals from discrimination, to promote inclusion, diversity and equity, and to safeguard equality. Human rights are "universal, indivisible and interdependent and interrelated."[1]

3. This Declaration aims to build on existing discussions, principles and papers exploring the harms arising from this technology. The significant work done in this area by many experts has helped raise awareness of and inform discussions about the discriminatory risks of machine learning systems.[2] We wish to complement this existing work by reaffirming the role of human rights law and standards in protecting individuals and groups from discrimination in any context. The human rights law and standards referenced in this Declaration provide solid foundations for developing ethical frameworks for machine learning, including provisions for accountability and means for remedy.

---

[1] UN Human Rights Committee, *Vienna Declaration and Programme of Action*, 1993, http://www.ohchr.org/EN/ProfessionalInterest/Pages/Vienna.aspx.

[2] For example, see the FAT/ML *Principles for Accountable Algorithms and a Social Impact Statement for Algorithms*; IEEE Global Initiative on Ethics of Autonomous and Intelligent Systems, *Ethically Aligned Design*; *The Montreal Declaration for a Responsible Development of Artificial Intelligence*; The Asilomar AI Principles, developed by the Future of Life Institute.

4. From policing, to welfare systems, to healthcare provision, to platforms for online discourse—to name a few examples—systems employing machine learning technologies can vastly and rapidly reinforce or change power structures on an unprecedented scale and with significant harm to human rights, notably the right to equality. There is a substantive and growing body of evidence to show that machine learning systems, which can be opaque and include unexplainable processes, can contribute to discriminatory or otherwise repressive practices if adopted and implemented without necessary safeguards.

5. States and private sector actors should promote the development and use of machine learning and related technologies where they help people exercise and enjoy their human rights. For example, in healthcare, machine learning systems could bring advances in diagnostics and treatments, while potentially making healthcare services more widely available and accessible. In relation to machine learning and artificial intelligence systems more broadly, states should promote the positive right to the enjoyment of developments in science and technology as an affirmation of economic, social and cultural rights.[3]

6. We focus in this Declaration on the right to equality and non-discrimination. There are numerous other human rights that may be adversely affected through the use and misuse of machine learning systems, including the right to privacy and data protection, the right to freedom of expression and association, to participation in cultural life, equality before the law, and access to effective remedy. Systems that make decisions and process data can also undermine economic, social, and cultural rights; for example, they can impact the provision of vital services, such as healthcare and education, and limit access to opportunities like employment.

7. While this Declaration is focused on machine learning technologies, many of the norms and principles included here are equally applicable to technologies housed under the broader term of artificial intelligence, as well as to related data systems.

---

[3] The International Covenant on Economic, Social and Cultural Rights (ICESCR), Article 15 https://www.ohchr.org/EN/ProfessionalInterest/Pages/CESCR.aspx.

## Using the Framework of International Human Rights Law

8. States have obligations to promote, protect and respect human rights; private sector actors, including companies, have a responsibility to respect human rights at all times. We put forward this Declaration to affirm these obligations and responsibilities.

9. There are many discussions taking place now at supranational, state and regional level, in technology companies, at academic institutions, in civil society and beyond, focusing on the ethics of artificial intelligence and how to make technology in this field human-centric. These issues must be analyzed through a human rights lens to assess current and future potential human rights harms created or facilitated by this technology, and to take concrete steps to address any risk of harm.

10. Human rights law is a universally ascribed system of values based on the rule of law. It provides established means to ensure that rights are upheld, including the rights to equality and non-discrimination. Its nature as a universally binding, actionable set of standards is particularly well-suited for borderless technologies. Human rights law sets standards and provides mechanisms to hold public and private sector actors accountable where they fail to fulfil their respective obligations and responsibilities to protect and respect rights. It also requires that everyone must be able to obtain effective remedy and redress where their rights have been denied or violated.

11. The risks that machine learning systems pose must be urgently examined and addressed at governmental level and by private sector actors who are conceiving, developing and deploying these systems. It is critical that potential harms are identified and addressed and that mechanisms are put in place to hold those responsible for harms to account. Government measures should be binding and adequate to protect and promote rights. Academic, legal and civil society experts should be able to meaningfully participate in these discussions, and critique and advise on the use of these technologies.

## *The Right to Equality and Non-Discrimination*

12. This Declaration focuses on the right to equality and non-discrimination, a critical principle that underpins all human rights.
13. Discrimination is defined under international law as "any distinction, exclusion, restriction or preference which is based on any ground such as race, colour, sex, language, religion, political or other opinion, national or social origin, property, birth or other status, and which has the purpose or effect of nullifying or impairing the recognition, enjoyment or exercise by all persons, on an equal footing, of all rights and freedoms."[4] This list is non-exhaustive as the United Nations High Commissioner for Human Rights has recognized the necessity of preventing discrimination against additional classes.[5]

## *Preventing Discrimination*

14. Governments have obligations and private sector actors have responsibilities to proactively prevent discrimination in order to comply with existing human rights law and standards. When prevention is not sufficient or satisfactory, and discrimination arises, a system should be interrogated and harms addressed immediately.
15. In employing new technologies, both state and private sector actors will likely need to find new ways to protect human rights, as new challenges to equality and representation of and impact on diverse individuals and groups arise.
16. Existing patterns of structural discrimination may be reproduced and aggravated in situations that are particular to these technologies— for example, machine learning system goals that create self-fulfilling markers of success and reinforce patterns of inequality, or issues arising from using non-representative or biased datasets.

---

[4] United Nations Human Rights Committee, General comment No. 18, UN Doc. RI/GEN/1/ Rev.9 Vol. I (1989), para. 7.

[5] UN OHCHR, *Tackling Discrimination against Lesbian, Gay, Bi, Trans, & Intersex People Standards of Conduct for Business*, https://www.unfe.org/standards/.

17. All actors, public and private, must prevent and mitigate against discrimination risks in the design, development and application of machine learning technologies. They must also ensure that there are mechanisms allowing for access to effective remedy in place before deployment and throughout a system's lifecycle.

## Protecting the Rights of All Individuals and Groups: Promoting Diversity and Inclusion

18. This Declaration underlines that inclusion, diversity and equity are key components of protecting and upholding the right to equality and non-discrimination. All must be considered in the development and deployment of machine learning systems in order to prevent discrimination, particularly against marginalised groups.
19. While the collection of data can help mitigate discrimination, there are some groups for whom collecting data on discrimination poses particular difficulty. Additional protections must extend to those groups, including protections for sensitive data.
20. Implicit and inadvertent bias through design creates another means for discrimination, where the conception, development and end use of machine learning systems is largely overseen by a particular sector of society. This technology is at present largely developed, applied and reviewed by companies based in certain countries and regions; the people behind the technology bring their own biases, and are likely to have limited input from diverse groups in terms of race, culture, gender, and socio-economic backgrounds.
21. Inclusion, diversity and equity entails the active participation of, and meaningful consultation with, a diverse community, including end users, during the design and application of machine learning systems, to help ensure that systems are created and used in ways that respect rights—particularly the rights of marginalised groups who are vulnerable to discrimination.

## Duties of States: Human Rights Obligations

22. States bear the primary duty to promote, protect, respect and fulfil human rights. Under international law, states must not engage in, or support discriminatory or otherwise rights-violating actions or practices when designing or implementing machine learning systems in a public context or through public-private partnerships.
23. States must adhere to relevant national and international laws and regulations that codify and implement human rights obligations protecting against discrimination and other related rights harms, for example data protection and privacy laws.
24. States have positive obligations to protect against discrimination by private sector actors and promote equality and other rights, including through binding laws.
25. The state obligations outlined in this section also apply to public use of machine learning in partnerships with private sector actors.

### State Use of Machine Learning Systems

26. States must ensure that existing measures to prevent against discrimination and other rights harms are updated to take into account and address the risks posed by machine learning technologies.
27. Machine learning systems are increasingly being deployed or implemented by public authorities in areas that are fundamental to the exercise and enjoyment of human rights, rule of law, due process, freedom of expression, criminal justice, healthcare, access to social welfare benefits, and housing. While this technology may offer benefits in such contexts, there may also be a high risk of discriminatory or other rights-harming outcomes. It is critical that states provide meaningful opportunities for effective remediation and redress of harms where they do occur.
28. As confirmed by the Human Rights Committee, Article 26 of the International Covenant on Civil and Political Rights "prohibits discrimination in law or in fact in any field regulated and protected

by public authorities."[6] This is further set out in treaties dealing with specific forms of discrimination, in which states have committed to refrain from engaging in discrimination, and to ensure that public authorities and institutions "act in conformity with this obligation."[7]

29. States must refrain altogether from using or requiring the private sector to use tools that discriminate, lead to discriminatory outcomes, or otherwise harm human rights.

30. States must take the following steps to mitigate and reduce the harms of discrimination from machine learning in public sector systems.

## Identify Risks

31. Any state deploying machine learning technologies must thoroughly investigate systems for discrimination and other rights risks prior to development or acquisition, where possible, prior to use, and on an ongoing basis throughout the lifecycle of the technologies, in the contexts in which they are deployed. This may include:

   (a) Conducting regular impact assessments prior to public procurement, during development, at regular milestones and throughout the deployment and use of machine learning systems to identify potential sources of discriminatory or other rights-harming outcomes—for example, in algorithmic model design, in oversight processes, or in data processing.[8]

   (b) Taking appropriate measures to mitigate risks identified through impact assessments—for example, mitigating inadvertent discrimination or underrepresentation in data or systems; conducting dynamic testing methods and pre-release trials;

---

[6] United Nations Human Rights Committee, General comment No. 18 (1989), para. 12.

[7] For example, Convention on the Elimination of All Forms of Racial Discrimination, Article 2(a), and Convention on the Elimination of All Forms of Discrimination against Women, Article 2(d).

[8] The AI Now Institute has outlined a practical framework for algorithmic impact assessments by public agencies, https://ainowinstitute.org/aiareport2018.pdf. Article 35 of the EU's General Data Protection Regulation (GDPR) sets out a requirement to carry out a Data Protection Impact Assessment (DPIA); in addition, Article 25 of the GDPR requires data protection principles to be applied by design and by default from the conception phase of a product, service, or service and through its lifecycle.

ensuring that potentially affected groups and field experts are included as actors with decision-making power in the design, testing and review phases; submitting systems for independent expert review where appropriate.

(c) Subjecting systems to live, regular tests and audits; interrogating markers of success for bias and self-fulfilling feedback loops; and ensuring holistic independent reviews of systems in the context of human rights harms in a live environment.

(d) Disclosing known limitations of the system in question—for example, noting measures of confidence, known failure scenarios and appropriate limitations of use.

## Ensure Transparency and Accountability

32. States must ensure and require accountability and maximum possible transparency around public sector use of machine learning systems. This must include explainability and intelligibility in the use of these technologies so that the impact on affected individuals and groups can be effectively scrutinised by independent entities, responsibilities established, and actors held to account. States should:

(a) Publicly disclose where machine learning systems are used in the public sphere, provide information that explains in clear and accessible terms how automated and machine learning decision-making processes are reached, and document actions taken to identify, document and mitigate against discriminatory or other rights-harming impacts.

(b) Enable independent analysis and oversight by using systems that are auditable.

(c) Avoid using 'black box systems' that cannot be subjected to meaningful standards of accountability and transparency, and refrain from using these systems at all in high-risk contexts.[9]

---

[9] The AI Now Institute at New York University, *AI Now 2017 Report*, 2017, https://ainowinstitute. org/AI_Now_2017_Report.pdf.

Enforce Oversight

33. States must take steps to ensure public officials are aware of and sensitive to the risks of discrimination and other rights harms in machine learning systems. States should:

   (a) Proactively adopt diverse hiring practices and engage in consultations to assure diverse perspectives so that those involved in the design, implementation, and review of machine learning represent a range of backgrounds and identities.
   (b) Ensure that public bodies carry out training in human rights and data analysis for officials involved in the procurement, development, use and review of machine learning tools.
   (c) Create mechanisms for independent oversight, including by judicial authorities when necessary.
   (d) Ensure that machine learning-supported decisions meet international accepted standards for due process.

34. As research and development of machine learning systems is largely driven by the private sector, in practice states often rely on private contractors to design and implement these technologies in a public context. In such cases, states must not relinquish their own obligations around preventing discrimination and ensuring accountability and redress for human rights harms in the delivery of services.

35. Any state authority procuring machine learning technologies from the private sector should maintain relevant oversight and control over the use of the system, and require the third party to carry out human rights due diligence to identify, prevent and mitigate against discrimination and other human rights harms, and publicly account for their efforts in this regard.

*Promoting Equality*

36. States have a duty to take proactive measures to eliminate discrimination.[10]

37. In the context of machine learning and wider technology developments, one of the most important priorities for states is to promote programs that increase diversity, inclusion and equity in the science, technology, engineering and mathematics sectors (commonly referred to as STEM fields). Such efforts do not serve as ends in themselves, though they may help mitigate against discriminatory outcomes. States should also invest in research into ways to mitigate human rights harms in machine learning systems.

*Holding Private Sector Actors to Account*

38. International law clearly sets out the duty of states to protect human rights; this includes ensuring the right to non-discrimination by private sector actors.

39. According to the UN Committee on Economic, Social and Cultural Rights, "States parties must therefore adopt measures, which should include legislation, to ensure that individuals and entities in the private sphere do not discriminate on prohibited grounds."[11]

40. States should put in place regulation compliant with human rights law for oversight of the use of machine learning by the private sector in contexts that present risk of discriminatory or other rights-harming outcomes, recognising technical standards may be complementary to regulation. In addition, non-discrimination, data protection, privacy and other areas of law at national and regional levels may expand upon and reinforce international human rights obligations applicable to machine learning.

41. States must guarantee access to effective remedy for all individuals whose rights are violated or abused through use of these technologies.

---

[10] The UN Committee on Economic, Social and Cultural Rights affirms that in addition to refraining from discriminatory actions, "State parties should take concrete, deliberate and targeted measures to ensure that discrimination in the exercise of Covenant rights is eliminated."—UN.

## Responsibilities of Private Sector Actors: Human Rights Due Diligence

42. Private sector actors have a responsibility to respect human rights; this responsibility exists independently of state obligations.[11] As part of fulfilling this responsibility, private sector actors need to take ongoing proactive and reactive steps to ensure that they do not cause or contribute to human rights abuses—a process called 'human rights due diligence'.[12]

43. Private sector actors that develop and deploy machine learning systems should follow a human rights due diligence framework to avoid fostering or entrenching discrimination and to respect human rights more broadly through the use of their systems.

44. There are three core steps to the process of human rights due diligence.

    (i) Identify potential discriminatory outcomes
    (ii) Take effective action to prevent and mitigate discrimination and track responses
    (iii) Be transparent about efforts to identify, prevent and mitigate against discrimination in machine learning systems.

### (i) Identify potential discriminatory outcomes

45. During the development and deployment of any new machine learning technologies, non-state and private sector actors should assess the risk that the system will result in discrimination. The risk of discrimination and the harms will not be equal in all applications, and the actions required to address discrimination will depend on the context. Actors must be careful to identify not only direct

---

[11] See UN Guiding Principles on Business and Human Rights and additional supporting documents.

[12] See Council of Europe's Recommendation CM/Rec(2018)2 of the Committee of Ministers to member States on the roles and responsibilities of internet intermediaries, https://search.coe.int/cm/Pages/result_details.aspx?ObjectID=0900001680790e14.

discrimination, but also indirect forms of differential treatment which may appear neutral at face value, but lead to discrimination.

46. When mapping risks, private sector actors should take into account risks commonly associated with machine learning systems—for example, training systems on incomplete or unrepresentative data, or datasets representing historic or systemic bias. Private actors should consult with relevant stakeholders in an inclusive manner, including affected groups, organizations that work on human rights, equality and discrimination, as well as independent human rights and machine learning experts.

(ii) Take effective action to prevent and mitigate discrimination and track responses

47. After identifying human rights risks, the second step is to prevent those risks. For developers of machine learning systems, this requires.

   (a) Correcting for discrimination, both in the design of the model and the impact of the system and in deciding which training data to use.
   (b) Pursuing diversity, equity and other means of inclusion in machine learning development teams, with the aim of identifying bias by design and preventing inadvertent discrimination.
   (c) Submitting systems that have a significant risk of resulting in human rights abuses to independent third-party audits.

48. Where the risk of discrimination or other rights violations has been assessed to be too high or impossible to mitigate, private sector actors should not deploy a machine learning system in that context.

49. Another vital element of this step is for private sector actors to track their response to issues that emerge during implementation and over time, including evaluation of the effectiveness of responses. This requires regular, ongoing quality assurances checks and real-time auditing through design, testing and deployment stages to monitor a system for discriminatory impacts in context and situ, and to correct errors and harms as appropriate. This is particularly important given the risk of feedback loops that can exacerbate and entrench discriminatory outcomes.

(iii) Be transparent about efforts to identify, prevent and mitigate against discrimination in machine learning systems

50. Transparency is a key component of human rights due diligence, and involves "communication, providing a measure of transparency and accountability to individuals or groups who may be impacted and to other relevant stakeholders."[13]

51. Private sector actors that develop and implement machine learning systems should disclose the process of identifying risks, the risks that have been identified, and the concrete steps taken to prevent and mitigate identified human rights risks. This may include:

   (a) Disclosing information about the risks and specific instances of discrimination the company has identified, for example risks associated with the way a particular machine learning system is designed, or with the use of machine learning systems in particular contexts.

   (b) In instances where there is a risk of discrimination, publishing technical specification with details of the machine learning and its functions, including samples of the training data used and details of the source of data.

   (c) Establishing mechanisms to ensure that where discrimination has occurred through the use of a machine learning system, relevant parties, including affected individuals, are informed of the harms and how they can challenge a decision or outcome.

## The Right to an Effective Remedy

52. The right to justice is a vital element of international human rights law.[14] Under international law, victims of human rights violations or abuses must have access to prompt and effective remedies, and those responsible for the violations must be held to account.

---

[13] UN Guiding Principles on Business and Human Rights, Principle 21.

[14] For example, see: Universal Declaration of Human Rights, Article 8; International Covenant on Civil and Political Rights, Article 2 (3); International Covenant on Economic, Social and Cultural Rights, Article 2; Committee on Economic, Social and Cultural Rights, General Comment No. 3.

53. Companies and private sector actors designing and implementing machine learning systems should take action to ensure individuals and groups have access to meaningful, effective remedy and redress. This may include, for example, creating clear, independent, visible processes for redress following adverse individual or societal effects, and designating roles in the entity responsible for the timely remedy of such issues subject to accessible and effective appeal and judicial review.

54. The use of machine learning systems where people's rights are at stake may pose challenges for ensuring the right to remedy. The opacity of some systems means individuals may be unaware how decisions which affect their rights were made, and whether the process was discriminatory. In some cases, the public body or private sector actors involved may itself be unable to explain the decision-making process.

55. The challenges are particularly acute when machine learning systems that recommend, make or enforce decisions are used within the justice system, the very institutions which are responsible for guaranteeing rights, including the right to access to effective remedy.

56. The measures already outlined around identifying, documenting, and responding to discrimination, and being transparent and accountable about these efforts, will help states to ensure that individuals have access to effective remedies. In addition, states should:

    (a) Ensure that if machine learning systems are to be deployed in the public sector, use is carried out in line with standards of due process.

    (b) Act cautiously on the use of machine learning systems in justice sector given the risks to fair trial and litigants' rights.[15]

    (c) Outline clear lines of accountability for the development and implementation of machine learning systems and clarify which bodies or individuals are legally responsible for decisions made through the use of such systems.

---

[15] For example, see: Julia Angwin, Jeff Larson, Surya Mattu and Lauren Kirchner for ProPublica, *Machine Bias*, 2016, https://www.propublica.org/article/machine-bias-risk-assessments-incriminal-sentencing.

(d) Provide effective remedies to victims of discriminatory harms linked to machine learning systems used by public or private bodies, including reparation that, where appropriate, can involve compensation, sanctions against those responsible, and guarantees of non-repetition. This may be possible using existing laws and regulations or may require developing new ones.

## Conclusion

57. The signatories of this Declaration call for public and private sector actors to uphold their obligations and responsibilities under human rights laws and standards to avoid discrimination in the use of machine learning systems where possible. Where discrimination arises, measures to deliver the right to effective remedy must be in place.

58. We call on states and private sector actors to work together and play an active and committed role in protecting individuals and groups from discrimination. When creating and deploying machine learning systems, they must take meaningful measures to promote accountability and human rights, including, but not limited to, the right to equality and non-discrimination, as per their obligations and responsibilities under international human rights law and standards.

59. Technological advances must not undermine our human rights. We are at a crossroads where those with the power must act now to protect human rights, and help safeguard the rights. This Declaration was published on 16 May 2018 by Amnesty International and Access Now, and launched at RightsCon 2018 in Toronto, Canada.

# Appendix C: The Asilomar AI Principles

Artificial intelligence has already provided beneficial tools that are used every day by people around the world. Its continued development, guided by the following principles, will offer amazing opportunities to help and empower people in the decades and centuries ahead.

## Research Issues

1. **Research Goal:** The goal of AI research should be to create not undirected intelligence, but beneficial intelligence.
2. **Research Funding:** Investments in AI should be accompanied by funding for research on ensuring its beneficial use, including thorny questions in computer science, economics, law, ethics, and social studies, such as:

    - How can we make future AI systems highly robust, so that they do what we want without malfunctioning or getting hacked?
    - How can we grow our prosperity through automation while maintaining people's resources and purpose?

© The Author(s) 2020
R. Girasa, *Artificial Intelligence as a Disruptive Technology*,
https://doi.org/10.1007/978-3-030-35975-1

- How can we update our legal systems to be fairer and more efficient, to keep pace with AI, and to manage the risks associated with AI?
- What set of values should AI be aligned with, and what legal and ethical status should it have?

3. **Science-Policy Link:** There should be constructive and healthy exchange between AI researchers and policy-makers.
4. **Research Culture:** A culture of cooperation, trust, and transparency should be fostered among researchers and developers of AI.
5. **Race Avoidance:** Teams developing AI systems should actively cooperate to avoid corner-cutting on safety standards.

## Ethics and Values

6. **Safety:** AI systems should be safe and secure throughout their operational lifetime, and verifiably so where applicable and feasible.
7. **Failure Transparency:** If an AI system causes harm, it should be possible to ascertain why.
8. **Judicial Transparency:** Any involvement by an autonomous system in judicial decision-making should provide a satisfactory explanation auditable by a competent human authority.
9. **Responsibility:** Designers and builders of advanced AI systems are stakeholders in the moral implications of their use, misuse, and actions, with a responsibility and opportunity to shape those implications.
10. **Value Alignment:** Highly autonomous AI systems should be designed so that their goals and behaviors can be assured to align with human values throughout their operation.
11. **Human Values:** AI systems should be designed and operated so as to be compatible with ideals of human dignity, rights, freedoms, and cultural diversity.
12. **Personal Privacy:** People should have the right to access, manage and control the data they generate, given AI systems' power to analyze and utilize that data.

13. **Liberty and Privacy:** The application of AI to personal data must not unreasonably curtail people's real or perceived liberty.
14. **Shared Benefit:** AI technologies should benefit and empower as many people as possible.
15. **Shared Prosperity:** The economic prosperity created by AI should be shared broadly, to benefit all of humanity.
16. **Human Control:** Humans should choose how and whether to delegate decisions to AI systems, to accomplish human-chosen objectives.
17. **Non-subversion:** The power conferred by control of highly advanced AI systems should respect and improve, rather than subvert, the social and civic processes on which the health of society depends.
18. **AI Arms Race:** An arms race in lethal autonomous weapons should be avoided.

## Longer-Term Issues

19. **Capability Caution:** There being no consensus, we should avoid strong assumptions regarding upper limits on future AI capabilities.
20. **Importance:** Advanced AI could represent a profound change in the history of life on Earth, and should be planned for and managed with commensurate care and resources.
21. **Risks:** Risks posed by AI systems, especially catastrophic or existential risks, must be subject to planning and mitigation efforts commensurate with their expected impact.
22. **Recursive Self-Improvement:** AI systems designed to recursively self-improve or self-replicate in a manner that could lead to rapidly increasing quality or quantity must be subject to strict safety and control measures.
23. **Common Good:** Superintelligence should only be developed in the service of widely shared ethical ideals, and for the benefit of all humanity rather than one state or organization.

# Index

© The Author(s) 2020
R. Girasa, *Artificial Intelligence as a Disruptive Technology*,
https://doi.org/10.1007/978-3-030-35975-1

Made in the USA
Middletown, DE
03 September 2023